Antique Electric Waffle Irons 1900-1960

A History of the Appliance Industry in 20th Century America

William F. George

Order this book online at www.trafford.com
or email orders@trafford.com

Most Trafford titles are also available at major online book retailers.

Print information available on the last page.

ISBN: 978-1-5539-5632-7 (hc)
ISBN: 978-1-4122-5267-6 (e)

Trafford rev. 10/09/2019

 www.trafford.com

North America & international
toll-free: 1 888 232 4444 (USA & Canada)
fax: 812 355 4082

Dedication

This book is dedicated to my parents who taught their children that reading was one of the most valuable and enjoyable skills they could acquire. They were right. I wish they were here to read this.

About The Author

Bill was born in Philadelphia in 1943 but grew up in what was then rural southeast Pennsylvania. He attended Penn State University, acquiring a Bachelor of Science degree in secondary education before pursuing a career teaching science and math. A five year stint of junior high school classrooms in suburban Pennsylvania and rural Ohio, convinced him that a hands-on profession would be far less frustrating and much more mentally rewarding. Two years of specialized training led to a new career as a photo equipment service technician. Bill operated his own wholesale camera repair service in Maryland and Colorado for over 15 years before selling the business and working in industry as a precision scientific instrument-maker. Bill's hobbies reflect his love of tinkering with things old and mechanical. In his spare time, when not gardening or practicing photography, he restores antique pocket watches, vintage Ford cars (five so far dating from 1929 to 1950), antique cameras, and vintage appliances.

Maggie
(The author's advisor on rabbits & squirrels)

A poor quality modern-type waffle iron that failed miserably one Sunday morning led the author on a quest for an old-style, no-nonsense waffle iron just like he remembered his mother using back in the pre-Teflon "Good old days." One vintage waffle iron led to another and another until he had gathered and restored to like-new condition over three hundred of them. Bill's curiosity to know more about these little jewels and the companies that made them led to a four year research project. This book is the culmination of that research, the author's long-time writing avocation, and his love of teaching.

The author, with his wife Pat, lives in Colorado with "Maggie" a wonderfully loving and gentle dog recently acquired through the Springer Spaniel Rescue League. Bill welcomes any inquiries through the publisher or through his waffle iron web site www.WaffleIronCentral.com.

Contents

Acknowledgments

Without the generosity, support and kindness of the following individuals and organizations, this book would not have been possible. If I've forgotten anyone, it was unintensional. Please accept my apology. With great appreciation I wish to thank the following...

> The Reference Librarians of the Longmont, Colorado Public Library for their cooperation and great patience in processing all of my many requests for information and materials;

> Wayne E. Morris, Director of the Portable Appliance Division of the Association of Home Appliance Manufacturers (AHAM), for industry-wide production records and other information about the history of the appliance industry;

> Vicki Matranga of the International Housewares Manufacturers Association and author of a wonderful book, *America at Home* (see Bibliography) for several helpful research leads, particularly concerning Dominion Electric;

> Flat iron collector Jay Raymond of Jenkintown, PA. for supplying information and advertising materials about several appliance firms;

> Bill Blakeslee a collector of early electrical appliances in Ambler, PA. for providing insights into several early manufacturers including Simplex, Detroit Electric, and Edison Electric;

> Dan Ruge of Wichita, Kansas for giving me a number of nice waffle irons and introducing me to Herb Ebendorfer, Curator of The Coleman Museum in Wichita (Mr. Ebendorfer supplied a treasure trove of materials and information from The Coleman Museum concerning that company's electric appliance manufacturing in the 1930's);

> David G. Smith, THE expert on The Griswold and Wagner Companies and co-author of two comprehensive books on their products (See Bibliography), generously supplied from his archives information about Griswold's electric appliances;

> Susanne Felman Jacob, of Chalfont, Pennsylvania, author of *The History of Joanna Furnace*, (See Bibliography), for giving me her insights into colonial era iron furnaces, their methods, products, and especially information about their cast iron waffle irons;

> Nancy Conway, an expert on industrial design and designers, for supplying the numerous patent drawings that appear throughout this book;

> Millie Wilson and Bob Delps of the York Wire and Cable Company, York, Pa. who have for years provided excellent service and supplied me with the high quality special wire needed to restore many of the waffle irons that appear in this book;

> Jerry Lusk, owner of The Camera Broker, Longmont, Colorado, for his always dependable photographic services, supplies, and technicl advice (A camera store of the caliber of the Camera Broker is unmatched even in most large cities);

> Elizabeth Furlow, Curator of Collections for The Museum of History and Industry, Seattle, Washington, for sources of information on industrial history;

> Marion and Roy Phillips, my friends who reside in Aberarth Wales, for information about waffles and waffle irons in England and Wales. (Marian & Roy produce beautifully carved Welsh folk craft items-Crefftau Aberarth Crafts on the Internet;

> Darrell Leonard and her colleagues in the school district at Rotorua, New Zealand, for checking on waffle irons and their usage on the other side of the planet;

Acknowledgments continued:

> Mr. John G. Nelson for a wealth of information about the Nelson Machine and Manufacturing Company and about the Nelson family members who worked there;

> Mrs. Barbara Gent and her daughter Kimberly for the Kolhase family history and photographs of the National Stamping and Electric Works factory operations;

> Jeff Larson who was kind enough to brave February weather, drive to Elgin, Illinois and take pictures for me of the old Toastmaster factory situated there;

> Charlotte Samuels, photographic officer, and the staff of the Department of Prints and Drawings of The British Museum for their excellent print services;

> Louis Campeau of the Canadian Museum of Civilization, Hull, Quebec, for equally fine print services;

> The University of Arkansas Library staff for forwarding materials to me about Hibbard, Spencer, Bartlett & Company;

> Kelly Singer who generously provided me with photos of several Porcelier items in his collection. (When not busy running his Sign-Crafter business in Louisville, Kentucky, Kelly avidly collects Porcelier artifacts);

> Jeff Gordon, (another avid Porcelier collector/expert) for proofreading and making valuable additions and corrections to the Porcelier segment;

> George Waters for sharing with me his insights and special knowledge and materials about his father Glen Waters, his family, other personalities connected with the Waters-Genter Company and the political history of 1930's Minnesota (What fascinating stories and valuable information!);

> To Dan LaBelle and Dan's photographer/wife Vi of Minneapolis, I owe an extra debt of gratitude for supplying me with numerous photos of and information about rare artifacts in their extensive appliance collection. (Dan went way above and beyond the call of duty leading me in the right direction many times with my research and introducing me to several other collectors);

> Michael Sheafe of New York City, a leading authority on classic toasters, for supplying me with vintage advertisementing and valuable information about toasters and their makers (Michael maintains a most interesting toaster web site at www.toasterCentral.com.);

> Georgia and Steve Johnson for giving me hours of computer instructions and programming support, making it possible for me to format this book digitally (My personal appliance collection has also been enlarged considerably with artifacts rescued by Georgia from flea markets and junk shops during her travels through America's heartland.);

> To Ruth and Bob Cullison for a lifetime of friendship and for the many waffle recipes from their cookbook collection;

> To my brother Bob and his wife Sue, a special thanks for the many neat old waffle irons you've added to my collection (You may recognize a few herein.);

> To my sister Dorothy, for her moral support and artistic talents-It's always nice to know you're there;

> To Victor Vale who, from the very beginning of this project, gave a great deal of much-appreciated moral support and more than a few very nice waffle irons (Victor is an avid appliance collector and part time actor/movie producer who resides outside of the Nation's capitol in suburban Maryland.);

> Finally, without the constant support, patience and perseverance of my wife Pat, this book would still be just a dream. This most patient lady has endured many hours of being a computer widow, has devoted a great deal of her own time gathering research information and materials and holds the Guinness Record for test driving the greatest number of antique waffle irons. In addition, I have relied heavily on her magical ability to edit my writing, turning it from gibberish into something resembling Standard English. Pat, as with most things I've accomplished in the last thirty plus years, this wouldn't have happened without you. Thanks so much.

Preface

The history of the electric appliance industry began about a hundred years ago and mirrored that of a growing and confident America during the first half of the twentieth century. Appliance manufacturing in the United States, until the 1960s, was done by a few very large corporations and dozens of small family-owned businesses employing fewer than a hundred employees. Most of these small firms were founded by men who born in the Victorian age, who were instilled with a strong, sometimes all-consuming, work ethic. Most of them, even after years of financial success, were the first into their factory in the morning and last to leave at night. A surprising number were first generation Americans of German or Scandinavian ancestry.

The story of the appliance industry, it turns out, is mostly one of ordinary people from average backgrounds who had modest ambitions and obtained moderate success. Although the electric appliance industry was THE growth industry of the 1920s, much like the computer industry of the 1990s, it produced no titans, no Fords, Rockefellers, or Morgans. Even Edison and Westinghouse only dabbled in electric appliances, each making their fortunes elsewhere. Although the industry created no grand successes, it did support numerous families in middle class comfort and it funded college educations for second and third generation family members who interesting enough almost without fail chose career paths unrelated to appliances or manufacturing.

All of the early appliance pioneers have been gone for well over a quarter of a century. Many of the second-generation descendents have also passed on. With few exceptions, due to the extreme competitive nature of the housewares industry, of which appliances is a small part, the early manufacturers have been bought and sold numerous times or have disappeared entirely. In a 1970's interview, Al Bersted, one of the industry pioneers and one its great success stories, made the observation that over two hundred and fifty electric goods manufacturers, large and small had come and gone by that time.

The men who founded these companies did so not for some noble goal. None was determined to better civilization by creating new wondrous inventions. Each of them was in business simply to make a living. Some loved what they were doing and thrived on fourteen-hour days. Others grew to consider the whole matter a huge unrelenting burden. None had either the luxury of time or the inclination to archive their achievements for posterity. That was unfortunate since these men and their companies created many products that today we take for granted, but which make life for all of us easier, healthier, and just plain nicer to live.

Because so many appliance firms were small and family owned, the company itself became an important part of the family's history. Some were also the economic backbone of smaller communities. Through interviews with relatives of company founders, searches of museum archives, libraries and local historical societies, and by consulting with several very knowledgeable authors and appliance collectors, I've tried to piece together as much of the electrical appliance story as still exists. Some of the stories I found are quite fascinating. I hope you enjoy them.

Introduction

My interest in the history of the electric appliance industry began some years ago when I became disillusioned with the performance of a Teflon coated waffle iron given to my wife and me as a wedding gift by a well meaning friend. The cantankerous little beast ended up in the trash one Sunday morning after one too many waffles stuck to it. I proceeded to go on a flea market search for a solid old-fashioned waffle iron like I remember my mom using so successfully in my youth. What struck me immediately on my quest was the abundance and diversity of nice inexpensive old waffle irons available nearly everywhere I looked.

I brought one home, cleaned it up and used it for awhile. Then I saw a fancier model, bought it, rebuilt it, and tried it out. After about half a dozen such adventures I became curious to know more about old waffle irons in general and eventually the companies that made them. Unlike my other hobbies of gardening, antique watch and vintage automobile restoration, where information abounds, I was unable to find much information published about any vintage appliances except toasters. I wasn't much interested in toasters (they just dry out bread don't they?) and in any case the toaster books on the market had precious little about the companies that manufactured them. So, I decided that it was about time someone should do some serious research on appliance makers and their waffle irons. This book is the result.

The information presented herein comes from a combination of sources including interviews with individuals directly involved in the appliance industry, family members of company founders, numerous historical societies, libraries, archives, and state government record repositories. In many cases the records are scattered and incomplete and sometimes missing entirely. In the latter situation, I have had to rely on knowledgeable collectors and my own intuition to piece together company information from circumstantial evidence gleaned from old literature, vintage advertising, and actual artifacts.

Certain information gathered from interviews cannot always be considered completely accurate since many events have been recalled from decades ago or are from a generation of family members sometimes twice removed from the events in question. Wherever possible in such situations I've tried to corroborate the information with actual documentation. Even then, the documents have sometimes been found to be in error.

This book is being printed using a new technology called On Demand Publishing. Although compromises in photo quality must be accepted at the present time with this process, one great advantage to this method of publishing is that changes and updates to the book can be made on a timely basis. Unlike conventionally published books which may have price guides and other materials as much as several years old, new information, revisions, and corrections can be made and incorporated into this book almost as soon as it's received. Each new copy is as fresh as the first day of publication. Becuase of my ability to revise this book easily, I welcome corrections, clarifcations or any additional information the reader may have concerning vintage waffle irons or the companies that made them. The author can be reached through the publisher.

Using This Book

Nomenclature

Waffle iron construction changed over the years as technology and styling trends evolved. Terms such as "**Leg-mounted**" or "**Tray-mounted**" type refers to type of construction or style, and the connotation is obvious. Other less obvious designations are "**Twin**" models which are those that have two baking units attached to a common base. "**Stacked**" models are those with two cooking units placed one above the other. "**Pedestal**" and "**Low Profile**" types are the most common. The anatomy of these are labeled below.

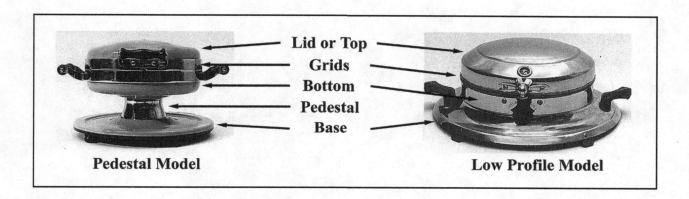

Lid or Top
Grids
Bottom
Pedestal
Base

Pedestal Model   **Low Profile Model**

Model Designations

Although a few companies didn't assign model numbers to their products, most devised a system of letters and/or numbers for differentiating products. These designations may appear on the product or in advertising as a "series number," "catalog number," "serial number," or "article number." In this book for the sake of simplicity, all product designations are referred to as "model numbers." **Model numbers appearing in bold type in the text indicates that this particular model is pictured**.

Dates of Manufacture

Except for Manning Bowman products, which for years were stamped with a date of manufacture, determining the exact date of manufacture for most appliances is impossible. Dates mentioned are approximate based on observations of style, materials, technology, sales receipts, copyrights on directions, sequence of model numbers, advertising literature, and in a few worst cases, pure conjecture. Dates may be listed as "Early," "Mid," or "Late" something. "Early" would be the first third of a decade, "Mid" would be the middle third and "late" would be the last third.

Price Designations

Throughout the book the reader will find connotations such as "advertised price," "list price," or "price new." These are derived from vintage advertisements, original price tags, vintage magazine articles, trade publications, and department store or manufacturers' catalogs, or similar sources. Each is footnoted as to the specific source. If you would like to convert the old prices into today's dollars, see the piece which follows entitled "*What Did It Really Cost In The Good Ole' Days?*".

Using This Book

Nomenclature

With small components fashioned over the years as technology and styling trends evolved, certain shapes of "Drop-mounted" speakers or types of construction... style and the components above. Other boxes by the design... tion are "Tabletop" models in which are those that have two baking units attached to a common base... "Shelf" models are those with two speaking units placed one above the other. "Pedestal" and "Low Profile" types are the most common. The anatomy of these are labeled below.

Pedestal Model   Low Profile Model

Lid or Top
Grille
Bottom
Pedestal
Base

Model Designations

Although most companies identify design model numbers for their products "most devised a system of letter / number numbers for their unique products." These designations vary in use... the product deals advertising as a "paper number," "catalog number," "serial number," or "stock number." In this book the serial number of a product, designation where is preferred to its model number. Model numbers appearing in bold type in the text indicate that this particular model is preferred.

Dates of Manufacture

Except for Manufactory Bowtons products, which for years were stamped with a date of manufacturing, determining the exact date of manufacture for most appliances is impossible. Dates herein are approximate, based on observations of style, materials, technology, sales receipts, copyright declarations, sequence of model numbers, advertisements in trade, and in a few cases, pure conjecture. Unfortunately to be dated "early-Mid" period, something originally would refer to the beginning of a decade, "mid" would be the middle third and "late" would be the last third.

Price Designations

Throughout the book, the reader will find the annotations like "very scarce, price" "very rare" "price new." These are drawn from original advertisements, original purchase, or retail prices. Where rare, price, publications and department store catalog figures, and are, in some cases, based as to the specific source. If you would like to convert the old prices into today's, see the prices which follow which tell you so much of "What Did It Really Cost" in The Good Old Days."

xiv

"What Did It Really Cost In The "Good Ole' Days?"

or

"A nickel ain't worth a dime any more!"... Yogi Berra

Throughout this book are the connotations "advertised price," "list price," or "price new." These were derived from vintage advertisements, magazine articles, trade publications, and department store or manufacturers' catalogs. These "old dollar" prices seem like real bargains until one considers what effect long-term inflation has had on the dollar. To convert old price listings into today's inflated dollars, the reader must first find the **Consumer Price Index (CPI)** for the year in question from the table below. Using the appropriate CPI and the old price in the following formula, the reader can arrive at an approximately equivalent price in modern dollars. In the example below, a waffle iron costing $5.00 in 1930 turns out to cost nearly $49.00 in modern dollars.

Conversion Formula

$$163 \div \textbf{CPI} \times \text{Price} = \text{Cost in 1998 Dollars}$$

Example: What would a 1930 waffle iron priced at $ 5.00 cost in today's dollars?
$$163 \div \textbf{16.7} \times 5.00 = \$ 49.00$$

Consumer Price Index (CPI) by Year [1]

Year	CPI	Year	CPI	Year	CPI	Year	CPI	Year	CPI
1913	9.9	1923	17.1	1933	13.0	1943	17.3	1953	26.6
1914	10.0	1924	17.1	1934	13.4	1944	17.6	1954	26.9
1915	10.1	1925	17.5	1935	13.7	1945	18.0	1955	26.8
1916	10.9	1926	17.7	1936	13.9	1946	19.5	1956	27.2
1917	12.8	1927	17.4	1937	14.4	1947	22.3	1957	28.1
1918	15.1	1928	17.1	1938	14.1	1948	24.1	1958	28.9
1919	17.3	1929	17.1	1939	13.9	1949	23.8	1959	29.1
1920	20.0	1930	16.7	1940	14.0	1950	24.1	1960	29.6
1921	17.9	1931	15.2	1941	14.7	1951	26.0	1961	29.9
1922	16.8	1932	13.7	1942	16.3	1952	26.5	1962	30.2

[1] U.S. Department of Labor Statistics. U.S. City average CPI. (1982-84=100, 1998=163)

Determining the true cost of appliances or other goods from the "Good Old days" isn't quite as simple as the above formula might suggest. One must also consider how much disposable income was available to families for consumer goods. Before World War II most families rented shelter rather than owning a home. Rent was relatively fixed and was a smaller share of total income than what families spend today on rent or a mortgage. Taxes, as a part of total income, was significantly lower than today. Prior to the 1940s many families didn't own an automobile. The lucky minority who did own a car usually owned just one. Even accounting for inflation, vehicles then cost considerably less to own and operate than our modern ones. Most families were not financing college educations for children back then, or taking major vacations, or paying large medical insurance premiums. The number of items available and deemed essential to families in the "good old days" were fewer than today. Families weren't buying microwaves, big screen televisions, DVD players, computers, cell phones, skis, CD players, and the myriad other gadgets and toys that flood the consumer market today. The greater disposable income prior to World War II was divided among fewer items, making each item intrinsically more afforable. In addition, even though toasters, waffle irons, mixers and the like were more costly to purchase initially, many were built in such a way as to be serviced and with modest upkeep were intended to last many years.

So exactly how expensive was the $25.00 Toastmaster toaster that my grandfather purchased for my grandmother in 1937? I'm not sure. My mother inherited it in the 1950s and used it for years. I inherited in the mid-1970s and have used it nearly every morning since. With only one annual oiling, it's produced a great deal of delicous toast in over 60 years, I think it was a real bargain.

"What Did It Really Cost In The "Good Ole" Days?"

"A nickel ain't worth a dime anymore." - Yogi Berra

Throughout this book are numerous "advertised prices" or "price new". These were derived from vintage advertisements, magazine articles, trade publications, and department store or manufacturer catalogs. These "old dollar" prices seem like real bargains, but the further back in time the price new, the more inflation has had on the dollar. To convert old prices (bargain) to "inflated dollars," that is, to find the Consumer Price Index (CPI) for the year in question from the table below, using the appropriate CPI and the applicable price in the following formula, the reader can derive an approximately equivalent price in modern dollars. In our example below, if an item costing $5.00 in 1930 times out to cost about $69.00 in modern dollars.

Conversion Formula

$$163 / CPI \times Price\ of\ Item = 2011\ Dollar$$

Example: That would a 1930 widget, comprised at $5.00 cost in today's dollars?
163 / 16.7 × $5.00 = $48.80.

Consumer Price Index (CPI) by Year

Year	CPI	Year	CPI	Year	CPI	Year	CPI	Year	CPI
1913	9.9	1923	17.1	1933	13.0	1943	17.3	1953	26.6
1914	10.0	1924	17.1	1934	13.4	1944	17.6	1954	26.9
1915	10.1	1925	17.5	1935	13.7	1945	18.0	1955	26.8
1916	10.9	1926	17.7	1936	13.9	1946	19.5	1956	27.2
1917	12.8	1927	17.4	1937	14.4	1947	22.3	1957	28.1
1918	15.1	1928	17.1	1938	14.1	1948	24.1	1958	28.9
1919	17.3	1929	17.1	1939	13.9	1949	23.8	1959	29.1
1920	20.0	1930	16.7	1940	14.0	1950	24.1	1960	29.6
1921	17.9	1931	15.2	1941	14.7	1951	26.0	1961	29.9
1922	16.8	1932	13.7	1942	16.3	1952	26.5	1962	30.2

Determining the true cost, or happiness of other goods from the "Good Ole" days, quite as simple as the above formula might suggest. One interrelated consideration is how much disposable income was available to families for everyday goods...

The History Of The Electric Appliance Industry

or

What happened after Edison invented his light bulb

A turn of the century Commonwealth Edison Electric Company ad touts electric lighting as clean and safe. "The Pure Air Light." Before electric illumination, homes often reeked of oil or gas fumes and everything usually was covered with a thin film of sooty residue.

Until the 1880s activity slowed down considerably after sunset. The feeble lighting resources available to households made it difficult to do anything at night except perhaps trip over things in the dark. Edison and Westinghouse designed competing electrical systems in the 1880s for the sole purpose of better illuminating the world after dark. When electric illumination was introduced it was as though these inventors had lifted a dark curtain from life and extended the day.

This bright, flameless, smoke-free illumination was such a miraculous improvement over the way things had been for so long that no one thought to use electricity for anything other than lighting. In fact, until about 1900, there were few electrically operated gadgets since, if you wanted to use them during the day, there simply wasn't any electricity. For about twenty years, power companies generated electricity only for a few hours in the evenings to make light.

In 1903 electric household appliances were given an initial boost with the invention of a small electric laundry iron by Earl Richardson (see the Edison Electric story for the details about Richardson and his iron). Richardson, a plant supervisor for a small southern California power company, convinced his bosses that if they would generate electricity around the clock on Tuesdays, the traditional laundry ironing day, he could sell a great number of his irons to housewives. These women he thought would be only too eager to be rid of their heavy, cast iron, coal stove heated models. He also reasoned that if he could build electric demand and if the utilities could justify generating around-the-clock power, both he and they would make money and everyone would be better off including his housewife customers. As it turned out, he was right on all counts.

By 1910 most electric companies had abandoned Edison's direct current power system for the more practical and efficient Westinghouse/Tesla 60 cycle alternating system we use today. By the teens, utilities in most major urban areas were providing twenty-four hour electrical service at voltages ranging from 95 to 130. However, it would take until the 1930s before a standard voltage was agreed upon and until the 1940s before direct current service disappeared entirely. With the availability of twenty-four hour electric service, urban hotels, restaurants, and clubs began to invest in laborsaving cooking and housekeeping equipment. Increased availability of electricity in homes prompted several commercial equipment manufacturers to modify some of their heavy-duty items for domestic use.

In the teens, electric vacuum cleaners came on the domestic market. Clumsy at first, they were still a major improvement over the old manually operated suction sweepers of the day. These motor powered cleaners all but eliminated the onerous spring ritual of hanging the carpets outdoors and hand beating the dirt from them. The electric cooking range became available for the home kitchen, liberating women from the heat, smoke, dirt, and drudgery of the coal or wood stove. For the first time in history women could cook meals without first lighting a fire. For those who couldn't afford an electric range, appliance makers offered a variety of at-the-table cooking devices such as electric percolators, hot plates, table stoves, toasters, electric grills, waffle irons, electric frying pans, chaffing dishes, and early slow cookers or crock pots called thermos cookers.

With the outbreak of World War I in 1914, demand for power skyrocketed. Electric motors, which had evolved to become strong, reliable, and relatively compact, were rapidly replacing steam engines and overhead belt and pulley systems as a safe and efficient power source for factory machines. Electric utilities increased their generating capacity and expanded their power grids to meet this new industrial demand. The availability of better paying factory jobs attracted women who had formely worked as low paid housekeepers and maids. The resultant shortage of domestic help suddenly created a significant market for electrically operated household laborsaving or timesaving devices such as electric ranges, washing machines, sewing machines, food mixers, curling irons, and hairdryers.

With the end of hostilities in 1918 came a dramatic reduction in industrial demand for electricity. Suddenly power companies were saddled with excess generating capacity. Since electricity cannot be stored, the only way these utilities could protect their profits was to encourage electric consumption. To that end, many offered home wiring services, encouraged the major housewares manufacturers to develop and build more electrically operated gadgets, offered to underwrite advertising campaigns, and began to sell appliances from utility-owned show rooms.

To boost daytime demand, certain electric companies tried charging variable rates depending on how the electricity was used. For a time, some metered electric ranges separately from lighting circuits and charged reduced rates for power used for cooking. This prompted some appliance makers to modify their ranges by adding extra power sockets and advertising that the housewife could now connect her iron, fan, vacuum cleaner or any other electrically operated device and power it with cheaper cooking rate electricity.

- The Trade Mark Known In Every Home -

UNIVERSAL HOME NEEDS

PACK up your housework troubles and turn them over to UNIVERSAL Home Needs. Instead of worrying about work, the UNIVERSAL housewife plans for her pleasures. Her able UNIVERSAL assistants are always ready to lighten heavy burdens—shorten long tasks.

NO woman can afford to be a weary housekeeper when she can be a happy homemaker. UNIVERSAL helps do more than perform daily tasks quickly and well. They bring order out of chaos and create in the home an atmosphere of cheer and refinement.

THE woman who uses UNIVERSAL Home Needs lives long and keeps young. She does the necessary work without unnecessary toil and thereby keeps in radiant health and spirits.

WHAT you get out of your home depends upon what you put into it. The making of a better home will be in your own hands when you use UNIVERSAL Aluminum Cooking Utensils, Bread Makers, Food Choppers, Cutlery and UNIVERSAL Electric Appliances. The time they save is the time you'll have for rest and pleasure. The hard work you have done in the past is the work they will do in the future.

Write for Booklet No. 105 "The Universalized Home"

Landers, Frary & Clark
New Britain, Ct.

This 1921 Landers ad claims that owning "Universal assistants" will keep one "in radiant health and spirits". Many of the new electric appliances were created as a result of shortages of domestic help during WWI. and did in fact free housewives of much drudgery. **Model E-930** waffle iron is illustrated.

During the immediate postwar period, numerous manufacturers dependent on military contracts scrambled to find peacetime income sources. Some converted to making appliances, encouraged by the fact that by 1920 over 7 million homes had been wired for electricity and seven hundred thousand houses were being electrified yearly. A survey commissioned in 1921 by appliance maker Rutenber Electric, found that a mere 10% of households had an electric toaster, one of the first and least expensive electric appliances a family normally purchased. This same survey found that the average price of a toaster in 1921 was $7.00. Rutenber, in advertising to potential dealers, stated that if the appliance industry sold a toaster to only half the families in America with wired homes, industry income just from toasters would be over $24,500,000.00. (Allowing for inflation that's roughly $220 billion in today's dollars!) Add to that the potential income from selling fans, irons, coffee pots, tea kettles, hot plates, grills, mixers, space heaters, stoves, and waffle irons and one

It is estimated that, by cooking with electricity instead of with coal, the average family of five will save to the country over three tons of coal annually.

Moreover, since the average kitchen range cannot burn every kind of coal, an undue demand is created by the coal-burning homes for certain kinds of fuel, which in many cases must be transported great distances. The central station, on the other hand, can successfully use nearly every kind of coal, and therefore is often enabled to tap great supplies of industrial fuel lying close by.

In localities where water-power furnishes electric current for cooking purposes, the family of five that changes from coal to electric cooking thereby saves to the country nearly five tons of coal annually.

Not only coal but transportation is saved by electric cooking. There are

fewer coal wagons to block the streets, fewer coal cars waiting at the numerous retail coal yards. Fewer locomotives are required to handle local traffic, therefore freight yard congestion can be appreciably relieved.

Electricity saves food, as it produces less shrinkage from cooking than does any other cooking process.

The use of electric cooking ranges and of other electric household devices saves housecleaning labor and time, because it means *no ashes, no smoke, no dust.*

Electric cooking results in better food, more cleanliness, more comfort, less work, less coal, and a relief of winter's traffic troubles.

EDISON ELECTRIC APPLIANCE CO., Inc., *Chicago*

In 1918, Edison Electric calculated that if a family of five cooked with electricity it would save 3 to 5 tons of coal per family per year. That might not have pleased the coal companies but for the housewife it meant no ashes, dust, smoke or stoking a fire to cook breakfast.

(March 2, 1918, *Literary Digest*)

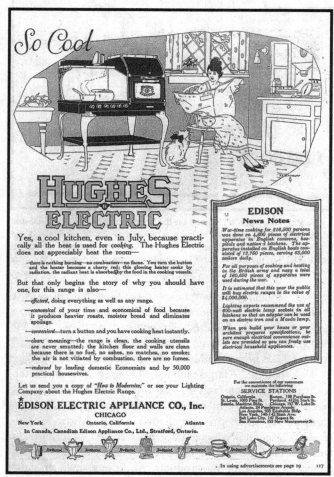

In 1920 Edison Electric pushed electricity as the cool, healthy, convenient alternative to cooking with coal. The ad mentioned that the British army and navy used 160,650 pieces of electric cooking and heating apparatus during WWI and that the public was expected to purchase 4 million dollars worth of electric ranges that year. (July-August, 1920, *Good Housekeeping Magazine*)

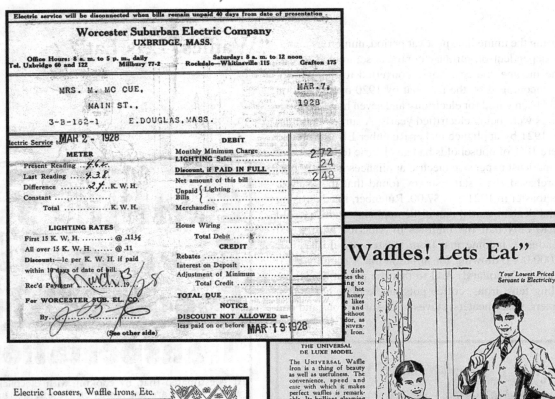

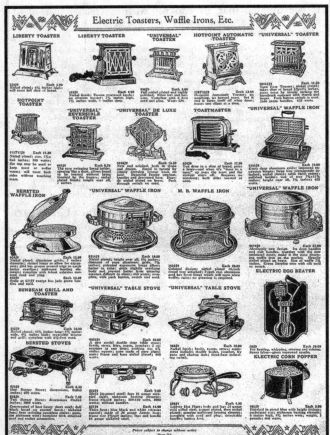

A Landers waffle iron ad printed on the reverse of a March, 1928 Boston Edison electric bill. Joint advertising was initiated by utilities after World War I, to increase electricity usage. The 11 cents per kilowatt-hour rate shown (about $1.25 in modern dollars) is considerably more expensive than rates today.

A 1928 department store catalog page shows the wide selection of "lamp socket" appliances available to consumers by the end of the "roaring twenties". The following waffle irons are illustrated, beginning second row far right; **Landers Model E-9305** ($12.00); **Bersted Unknown Model** ($13.50); Landers **Model E-9314** (18.00); **Manning-Bowman Model 1605** ($20.00); **Landers "Marie Antoinette" Model E-9574** ($ 22.00).

can see why many entrepreneurs of the time thought electric appliances could be the next gold rush. Scores of speculators and entrepreneurs gathered as much cash as they could lay their hands on to get in on the action, and soon "Appliances" became THE growth industry of the "Roaring Twenties."

Although the large established houseware manufacturers were located in New England, the mid-Atlantic States, and the Ohio valley, many of the of the new appliance entrepreneurs set up shop in small towns in the Midwest. This region was centrally located and crisscrossed with railroads, which at the time was the most economical way of obtaining materials and shipping products. Additionally, farm states like Minnesota, Wisconsin, Iowa, Kansas, and Missouri were suffering through a major postwar agricultural recession and had an abundance of inexpensive labor looking for fulltime work. Many of the farm towns already had small agricul-

By Christmas 1930 when this ad appeared, over a year had passed since the stock market crash. G E was still trying to sell a $20.00 **"Ambassador"** waffle iron (roughly $194.00 in modern dollars). Prices like that required a slick looking ad. Sex appeal or not, sales of this iron like many luxury goods was still weak.

tural implement and hardware factories that were easily converted from pounding out shovels, hog troughs, or chicken feeders to making things like toasters, stoves, or popcorn cookers.

Some new enterprises failed almost immediately, usually from inept management, poor quality of goods, inexperience in the consumer goods market, or insufficient capitalization. Nearly all that survived carried large debt loads acquired while rapidly expanding their operations during the boom. In the aftermath of the stock market crash of 1929, demand for consumer goods plummeted. By 1933 sales levels nation-wide were well below pre-World War I levels. Many firms unable to meet their loan payments were forced to close their doors.

A slow economic recovery began in 1934 with the help of various social and economic programs initiated by the newly elected Roosevelt administration, and continued until 1937 when the nation experienced a reversal or recession within a depression. The economy made a second and more significant recovery beginning in 1938 when industry began gearing up to once again supply military goods to European countries about to enter a new world war.

America officially went to war on December 8, 1941. In February 1942 the federal War Production Board issued Order L-41 forbidding the purchase of materials for, or the fabrication of eighty different appliances. On the list of restricted materials were copper, steel, nickel, and chromium,

During the depression, manufacturers struggled to keep costs and prices down to encourage sales. Tooling for new designs was often too expensive. Except for the **Model E-7704** waffle iron, everything here looks dated when this ad appeared in 1935. $7.95 for this waffle iron reflects the deflation that occurred in the early 1930s. A comparable model cost twice as much five years earlier. (1935, *Saturday Evening Post*)

When this ad appeared in 1944 America had been at war for three years. Manufacturers unable to produce consumer goods often ran "patriotic" ads like this encouraging the purchase of war bonds. Though a bit self-serving, (the ads maintained product name recognition during the war while bond sale revenues they generated helped the government pay these same companies for their war production work) bonds redeemed after the war helped fuel a strong post war boom.

all essential in manufacturing nearly every household appliance. The order also forbade manufacturers from selling existing inventories in case the goods had to be commandeered for military use. About the only kitchen appliance that escaped these restrictions was the Silex coffee maker, made primarily of UN-rationed glass.

Small manufacturers of appliances were particularly hard hit by Order L-41. Most were left with little or nothing to make or sell. Many of these firms had just begun to recover from a decade of severely depressed economic activity in the consumer sector. Their bank accounts were thin and much of their machinery was old or worn out from years of neglect. To qualify for potentially lucrative military contracts meant investing in new plants and equipment, something many smaller firms could ill afford. Some tried to keep their doors open by initiating refurbishing and rebuilding services for older products while others simply closed for the duration. Many never reopened. (A detailed account of the wartime trials and tribulations of a typical small family-owned company can be found in the history of Superior Electric Products Company.)

It Grills-Cooks-Fries- Even Makes Waffles!

TOP OPENS OUT FLAT FOR FRYING BACON, EGGS, PANCAKES — CLOSES TO GRILL 2 FULL-SIZE SANDWICHES, CHOPS OR A STEAK!

BRIGHT CHROMIUM, IVORY PLASTIC TRIM

ON-OR-OFF SIGNAL LIGHT-DIAL HEAT CONTROL

COMPLETE WITH QUICK-CHANGE GRILL PLATES, WAFFLE GRIDS, FRYING PAN — EVEN A DRAIN PAN!

HANDY FRYING PAN FOR DEEP FRYING OR COOKING!

LARGE WAFFLE GRIDS FOR CRISP OR FLUFFY WAFFLES!

We're moving at top speed to ship more M-B quality appliances. Order from your favorite store.

Manning Bowman Means Best

Manning, Bowman & Co., Meriden, Connecticut
In Canada: Manning, Bowman & Co. (Canada) Ltd., Oakville, Ont.

Apparently there was either a severe shortage of clothes irons by 1944 or enough cries for help came from the appliance industry to motivate the War Production Board in June of that year to allow selected small companies of 100 employees or less to produce a total of 1,759,338 new irons. The WPB decreed that in order not to jeopardize war production, those companies in regions classified as " Number 1 Labor Areas" with severe labor shortages were only allowed to use unskilled female labor to manufacture them. The federal office of price administration further stipulated that the price charged for the irons was not to exceed the price a standard iron at the time of the attack on Pearl Harbor.

Production of some consumer goods resumed after the war in late 1945, but a major steel strike, other materials shortages, and retooling problems delayed full-scale production of certain items for up to two years. The unavailability of new appliances during the war plus high wartime wages, and equally high personal savings rates created an unprecedented demand for new products which lasted well into the 1950s. Waffle iron production reached record levels in 1946 with 3½ million units, up from a pre-war average of half a million units annually. Since then yearly production has dropped to below 250,000 divided among about ten manufacturers.

The period following World War II and continuing to the present has seen a major shakeout in the housewares industry. Mergers and consolidations have become an almost yearly occurrence. Old firms like Manning-Bowman, and Landers Frary and Clark are long gone. Giants like McGraw-Edison, Westinghouse, and General Electric no longer make small appliances and for better or worse, the firms that still do, manufacture nearly all of their products outside the United States. In 1998, due to poor management decisions, venerable old Sunbeam Corporation had to declare bankrupcy. Today (2002) its stock once valued as high as $52.00 sells for pennies and its former CEO is being investigated for fraudulant business practices similar to those that created the recent Enron debacle.

Although World War II had ended over a year before this 1946 ad appeared, the copy says, "We're moving at top speed to ship more M.B. quality appliances." With post-war materials shortages and tooling delays, manufacturers were hard pressed to meet the tremendous pent-up demand for new consumer goods. Most items like the **Model 412** grill/waffle iron featured here were warmed-over pre-war designs. (October 1946, *Better Homes and Gardens*)

The History of Waffles

A careful search of the basket in the foreground of this early 17th century engraving reveals several large and surprisingly modern looking waffles. They were considered a simple peasant food at that time. (Print courtesy The British Museum, Copyright 2003, The British Museum. All rights reserved.)

When, how, and by whom waffles were first created are facts lost to history. The most fanciful origin for them is related in the story of a medieval knight who, upon returning home from a hard day of storming castles or rescuing damsels in distress, and still wearing his chain mail armor, carelessly sat on an oat cake his wife had set aside. The armor, so the tale goes, left attractive dimples in the cake that the wife ever after duplicated on all of her cakes. Having examined English medieval armor first hand, I can assure you that any oat cake sat upon with chain mail would end up stuck to the bottom of the knight, at least until his horse got a whiff of it.

Waffles actually go back considerably farther than the medieval period. The ancient Greeks made *Obelios,* a type of simple cake, which were baked between flat heated metal plates. This type of cake spread into many parts of Europe and continued essentially unchanged into the 13th century.

Then European blacksmiths began forging honeycomb patterns into the cooking plates. The English term *waffle* for the resulting dimpled cakes didn't appear in the language until the mid-1700s. It came from the Old English word *wefan*, to weave, which in turn came from the Dutch word *wafel* for a wafer that looked woven.

Originally European waffles were simple peasant fare made with flour, water or milk and eggs to which oil was sometimes added. Evidence that these were sold by street vendors can be found in the 1603 engraving, entitled *Greengrocer & Young Peasant* by I. Maetham, in the collection of The British Museum. Three waffle cakes are clearly illustrated in the foreground with garden produce in the basket. The waffles somewhat irregular shape suggests that they may have been made by pouring batter onto large dimpled plates rather than being molded in an iron.

9

Dutch colonists who settled in New York, New Jersey and Pennsylvania in the late 17th century introduced waffles to America. Although they were usually served plain or with jellies in the Old World, maple syrup, readily available in colonial New England, became a standard topping on waffles in the New World. By the mid-18th century, local iron furnaces from Maine to Maryland were turning out various versions of Dutch-inspired waffle and wafer irons. It is recorded that Thomas Jefferson, as Ambassador to France, liked European waffles so much, he brought a French waffle iron with him on his return to Virginia in 1789. Being a southerner, he was apparently unaware of domestic-made irons available in the north.

Colonial era American waffle irons were usually made with small rectangular cast iron bodies incorporating conventional square dimple designs within them. Handles of two feet or more in length, either cast integral to the body or riveted to it, were used to hold the iron over an open fire. The more elaborate irons had ornate dimple designs and a forged hasp attached to the end of the handles to assist in keeping the iron closed. Occasionally a foundry would cast their irons in brass with wrought iron handles. Most opened in a scissors-like fashion, weighed a hefty ten to twelve pounds and produced a thick but small 4 by 5 inch waffle. A surprising number of these irons have survived and are relatively common in New England and along the east coast.

With the introduction of cook stoves into American households during the 19th century, fireplace waffle irons became obsolete, replaced by cast iron models designed to be heated on a stovetop. These were cast by scores of foundries in the east, mid-west, and south well into the first third of the 20th century. Most were 5 to 8 inches in diameter and

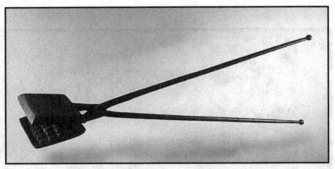

Weighing 10 ½ pounds, this 18th century cast iron fireplace waffle iron gave the cook a real workout. The 30-inch handles helped prevent the cook from being baked along with the waffle.

mounted on a cast supporting ring. Some were hinged like a door but many had ball socket swivel connections allowing the cook to flip the heavy body over without lifting it totally from the support ring. By 1900 the cost of Aluminum had dropped significantly. Along with pots and pans, some waffle irons were being cast with it. As homes became electrified in the first half of the twentieth century, stovetop irons were gradually replaced by electrically heated models.

Waffles have risen and waned in popularity over the years. In Europe they continue to be a popular treat. In Belgium and Portugal they're sold by street venders or in shops everywhere. The French, Dutch, and Germans all serve them as do the Swedes, who celebrate Annunciation Day on March 25th by eating waffles. But don't try to find waffles in England. Although Australians and New Zealanders are quite familiar with, and eat waffles regularly, many Brits are unfamiliar with them. In America, waffles hit their peak of popularity in the 1930s, as an inexpensive treat for the depression era populous. Today they're considered by many to be too time consuming to prepare and too much of a bother to cook. Both ideas are unfortunate misconceptions often held by the same individuals who believe that factory made frozen waffles are an edible food product.

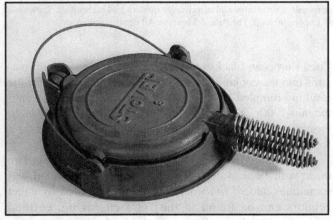

This Stover 8 waffle iron is a typical early 20th century cast iron model. Equipped with a low base, this example was intended for use on a wood or coal stove. High-necked bases were for kerosene or gas ranges.

This large Australian made iron came from the island of Tasmania, proving that waffles are known literally around the world.

Dawson City Yukon Territory-Circa 1898

"There are strange things done 'neath the midnight sun by the men who moil for gold."
Robert Service -The Cremation of Sam McGee.

All night waffles and coffee? I thought those Klondike gold prospectors spent their spare time in saloons, dances halls, and houses of ill repute. In 1898-99, selling waffles in Dawson City, where this photo was taken, was a lot easier and probably more profitable than mucking around in the cold Yukon streams looking for gold (notice the hip boots for sale). Waffle making was a good business choice in this case. Simple equipment and ingredients was all that was necessary. But what did they put on them? One possibility is Birch Syrup, a specialty the author saw being sold in Haines, Alaska recently.

(Negative No. J-6249 Copyright 2003 Canadian Museum of Civilization)

11

Waffles Go Hollywood-1941

This 1941 Universal Pictures publicity still is of Kentucky born Actress Una Merkel. The caption accompanying the photo reads, "After completing her featured role in Universal's riotous comedy, 'Cracked Nuts', Una Merkel entertained the cast with a waffle breakfast party and, (you guessed it) the recipe included, cracked nuts!" Sure she did. The waffle iron used as the prop is a Porcelier Scalloped with Wildflowers model. (Photo Copyright 2003 by Universal Studios. Courtesy of Universal Studios Publishing Rights, a Division of Universal Studios Licensing, Inc. All rights reserved.)

The First Traveling Waffle Salesman [1]

Undated photo of John Kleimback with examples of two sets of his early waffle iron grids
dated 1891 and 1904. These cast iron grids were heated over gas burners.
(Photo courtesy the Northumberland County Pennsylvania Historical Society)

In 1891 John Kleimbach, a German immigrant, came to the coal town of Shamokin Pennsylvania, took up residence in the Mansion House Hotel and began working for Elmer Barr, the hotel's owner. In his spare time, Kleimbach fashioned a pattern for a large rectangular waffle iron for the hotel's kitchen, capable of producing twelve waffles at once. The project interested Barr who accompanied Kleimbach to an iron foundry in nearby Danville where a pair of cooking grids was cast. Barr purchased gas burners, installing them in a special stove and Kleimbach began baking waffles.

His early success in the hotel waffle business encouraged Kleimbach to install a waffle baker in a wagon and go on the road. John became a welcome sight to other German immigrants residing in the surrounding communities, who longed for a treat from the "Old Country." Kleimbach sold his waffles for a penny apiece or ten cents a dozen. He soon began hiring kids to sell them on commission and in 1893 took his waffles to the Chicago World's Fair where they were a sensation.

In later years, the hotel owner, Elmer Barr and his brother went into the waffle business themselves, traveling to fairs and social gatherings throughout Pennsylvania. Over a hundred years after their inception, waffles are still a popular taste treat at Pennsylvania's country fairs.

As a footnote to the above story, the author cannot resist including the following. Having lived for some years in Pennsylvania, I thought I was familiar with all of the many varieties of unique taste treats available at that state's country fairs until I discovered a new type of high protein waffle being served at one such fair in central Pennsylvania. After ordering a Belgium type waffle with ice cream from one of the several venders there, I was perplexed when biting into the waffle by an unexpected crunchiness . Close examination of the much anticipated treat revealed a generous portion of baked flour weavels. The flour must have been left over from the Chicago World's Fair of 1893. So much for waffles at country fairs. I now enjoy mine exclusively at home where I have more control over the ingredients.

[1] Information courtesy, Jack Pensyl, Librarian for the Northumberland County Pennsylvania Historical Society.

Electric Waffle Iron Development

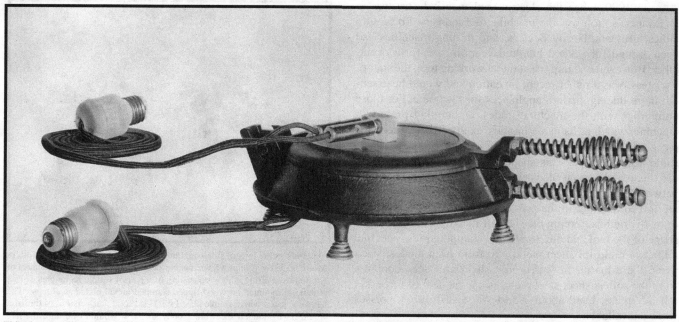

This photograph taken in 1911 at General Electric's Schenectady works shows the company's efforts to produce a practical electric waffle iron. The awkward spring insulating feet and other off-the-shelf hardware items indicate that this is probably an early prototype. GE didn't market a waffle iron until after it purchased Edison Electric in the mid-1920s. (Photo Copyright 2003 The Schenectady Museum, Schenectady, NY. All rights reserved.)

Electric Waffle Irons

Late Comers To The Appliance Scene

The first electrically heated appliances were laundry irons, toasters, and grills introduced to the marketplace shortly after the turn of the 20th century. These were soon followed by electric coffee makers, urns, space heaters, hot plates, soldering irons, curling irons, and stoves. Each of these devices was mechanically simple and the jobs they had to perform were straightforward and not very difficult to accomplish: a toaster just had to hold a piece of bread in proximity to an open heating element; a coffee maker or urn needed only to heat a small container of water; a space heater had to radiate thermal energy into a room with just a modicum of efficiency from a simple open heating element; and a soldering iron or hair curler had to impart a modest amount of heat into a relatively small metal rod.

None of these devices required much in the way of technological innovations in order for them to accomplish their tasks. Consequently turn-of-the-century engineers had little difficulty coming up with designs that both worked to one degree or another and were economically feasible to manufacturer. Electric waffle irons, on the other hand, presented special design challengers.

A great deal of heat must be generated to bake a waffle in a reasonable amount of time. The six or eight hundred watts of energy must be distributed evenly over two large cooking surfaces. Additionally, the entire appliance must withstand the potentially damaging by-products of the baking process-hot grease, and scalding steam. Although Simplex Electrical Company created several electrically heated waffle iron models beginning around 1905, none were very safe, practical, or popular. It would take nearly fifteen more years before manufacturing technology had advanced sufficiently to make possible a practical affordable electric waffle iron. Due to their greater complexity and the demanding job they're required to perform, waffle irons were and still are more expensive than most other small electric appliances. Here's how they were perfected.

15

Metal Working Technology or...
How they learned to turn stuff into things.

In 1900, when the electric appliance industry was in its infancy, so too was the machine tool industry. To be sure lathes, grinders, boring devices, and milling machines had been around for several hundred years in one form or another. However, one important metal working tool, the stamping press, was a rather recent invention and would be essential in producing modern appliances for the home. For those unfamiliar with the machine trades, a stamping press is a machine, which as its name implies, exerts a great force on a piece of sheet metal, usually quite rapidly, to press it into some desired shape. This shape is dictated by the tool and die (male and female blocks of metal) installed in the press between which is placed a sheet of metal. The tool and die are forced together in the press either by mechanical means or by hydraulics, forcing the sheet of metal to conform to the shape of the tool and die. In effect a stamping press acts like a kind of mold for sheet metal. To form even modest sized parts like a toaster or waffle iron shell with deep contours from the softest sheet steel requires a great deal of force and a heavy press. Until about World War I such heavy presses were unavailable.

Turn-of-the-century durable consumer goods were nearly always fabricated from leather, wood, cast iron, cast brass, or cast aluminum. Large parts for wagons or early automobiles like frames, fenders and body panels were usually made of wood or leather. On more expensive automobiles, large curved panels were often made of malleable sheets of aluminum, hand hammered or beaten to shape over wood

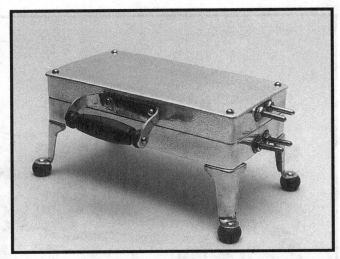

Materials technology in small appliances is displayed in this small **Landers Model E-931** waffle iron from the late teens. The top is a simple flat sheet of aluminum covering a body consisting of a pair of simple rectangles of cast aluminum mounted on wood-tipped stamped nickel plated steel legs. The handle is wood with a simple plated steel bracket. Later versions of this iron would have stamped sheet brass body shells. It wouldn't be until the late 1920s before Landers and many other appliance makers would switch to stamped carbon steel body shells.

forms by skilled craftsmen called panel beaters, then tacked to a wood framed body structure. Medium size sheet metal parts like headlight housings or dashboards were stamped from sheet aluminum or brass, materials ductile enough to be formed by the small stamping presses available at the time. Due to the much greater force required to shape steel and a lack of stamping presses powerful enough to form any but the smallest pieces, steel was reserved for small parts like screws, small plates, and angle brackets.

The need for improved stamping capability brought on by World War I caused a rapid advancement in the development of tool and die technology and the creation of presses strong enough to form relatively large steel parts. By war's end, presses capable of stamping out large automobile body panels and fenders were readily available. (It took until 1937 however before Ford Motor Company could announce that it had a press large enough to form an entire car roof from a single piece of steel.) No longer were designers limited to simple flat panels. By the early 1920s, steel parts for larger household appliances like stoves, refrigerators, and washing machines could be deep drawn and shaped into relatively complex forms. Attractive small appliances could also now be made of inexpensive stamped carbon steel rather than having to be cast and machined from brass, aluminum, or iron.

By the late 1920s manufacturers had metal working technology capable of producing complex shaped articles like this **Beardsley & Wolcott Model W2014** waffle iron. Even at this time many items were still made from sheet brass, an easier material to deep draw in stamping presses than sheet steel.

A foundry worker today would recognize everything in this heavily retouched photo taken in the National Stamping and Electric Works foundry room, Chicago, around 1900. The rectangular objects on the floor are steel mold frames, referred to in the foundry trade as flasks. One half of the flask assembly is placed on a table and partially filled with special fine grain casting sand. A replica of the part to be cast, usually a wood pattern, is placed in the sand. Passageways are created through the sand to the exterior of the flask for molten metal to enter and for gases to exit. Three of these vent openings can be seen in the assembled flasks in the foreground. The upper section of the flask is stacked onto the sand-filled lower half and packed solidly with additional sand until it is full. The flask halves are then carefully separated, the pattern is removed from the sand and the sand-filled flask halves, now with a void in the shape of the pattern within the sand, are brought together again. The flasks are tipped up slightly on one end to facilitate the escape of gases from the three vent holes provided as the molten metal is poured into the large hole visible in the uncovered flasks, visible to the right rear. After the brass solidifies, the mold halves are split and the sand cleaned from around the casting. The three young men in center of the photo are handling the ladle used to carry and pour the molten metal from the furnace into to the flasks. A round sand-sifting screen hangs from a peg on the wall at left near the sand tables where the flasks are packed. Foundry work was and still is hot, dirty, and dangerous. At this time this foundry was producing small cast brass pieces used in gas lights. Later the company would be one of the first to produce electric lighting fixtures. Additional early photographs of this factory and its offices can be found under National Stamping and Electric Works in the company history section. (Photo courtesy Mrs. Barbara Gent)

Three vintage stamping presses are visible in this circa 1910 photo taken inside the National Stamping and Electric Works in Chicago. The workers seated on packing crates with heads perilously close to the spinning belt pulleys are stamping the small bell shaped pieces seen in the barrel and boxes. These brass stampings were later nickel-plated and assembled to a support to become the top for a gasoline fueled lamp, one of the company's main products at this time. One such lamp minus its glass globe can be seen hanging from an overhead pipe in the center of the photo. (Despite the fact that this building had been fitted with natural gas lights and later with electricity, the managers probably felt it was more economical to burn gasoline in company made lamps for illumination rather than paying gas or electric bills.) The stamping presses seen here, like most of the machinery in factories for a hundred years prior to this time, were powered by one or more steam engines located in the factory's coal fired boiler room. Power from the engines was applied to an elaborate system of revolving overhead shafts. Leather or canvas belts transferred power from the steam engines through pulleys to the shafts and then back down to the machinery on the factory floor. The large heavy belt pulley on each of these presses acted as flywheels storing energy to even out the cyclic demand for power created by the machine as it stamped and then released each part. Changes in this belt and shaft power system began to appear at about the time this photo was taken. Steam engines were gradually being replaced by large electric motors which, like the steam engines, were hooked by belts to the overhead shaft system. These open belts and pulleys were a constant danger. Floor clutter and poor illumination seen here and typical of all early factories only added to the perils. During World War I factory deaths actually exceeded American military battlefield deaths. Although a modern day OSHA inspector would have a field day in this factory, this was the norm back in "The Good Old Days." By the mid-1920s small but powerful electric motors were available that were efficient and compact enough to be installed directly onto the machinery, making the dangerous and very energy inefficient pulley and shaft power systems obsolete. (Photo courtesy Mrs. Barbara Gent)

Metal Finishing Technology or...

How they learned to keep things from turning back into stuff

Protecting appliance parts from oxidation corrosion or other physical damage like scratching and abrasion requires that they either be painted or plated. Nickel plating was in common use on many goods by the late 1800s and was a much more durable finish than paint, which was susceptible to abrasion and heat damage. Nickel plating is an electrolytic process whereby a thin layer of nickel is deposited on the surface of a metal item by means of a low voltage electric current. If an item to be Electro-plated is iron or steel it is usually copper plated first to enhance the cohesion of the nickel to the article. Nickel, being relatively soft, is easily polished, but is also easily scuffed or scratched. In addition, over time, the initial warm silver-gold luster of nickel tends to tarnish to a cloudy white.

Manufacturers spent years trying to develop a finish that was both more durable than nickel and would retain its initial bright shine. In 1925, the plating industry introduced Chrome plating to automobile and appliance makers. This tarnish proof tough new plating with its bright silver-blue luster was touted as a miracle finish more scratch and scuff resistant than nickel and never needing polishing. Consumer goods with the new chrome plating were customarily sold at this time at premium prices usually 25% or more than comparable nickel plated items.

Chrome plating can not be applied directly to iron. steel, copper, or brass. For chrome to adhere to ferrous (iron or steel) items they must first be copper plated, then nickel plated. Copper and brass pieces need not be copper plated but like ferrous ones must be nickled. After the nickel has been applied it must be polished and cleaned before the chrome is deposited in a very thin layer over it. The chrome plating step itself is a sensitive one involving close and careful monitoring and control of the plating solutions and the electrical current used to deposit it on the nickel substrait. Unfortunately, manufacturers unaccustomed to this exacting process initially had a difficult time obtaining consistent results. Even today it is not uncommon to have uneven results. Early chromed appliances often suffered premature plating failure evident by the characteristic rust blisters and peeled plating all too commonly seen on them today. It took until the mid-1930s before chrome plating reached acceptable quality levels and not until the 1950s could the process be considered perfected.

In 1913 British metallurgist Harry Brearley invented a tough rust resistant chromium iron alloy which he called "Rustless Steel." Throughout the 1920s Henry Ford spent millions and was in the forefront in an effort to develop inexpensive machining processes for "Stainless Steel," the name adopted in America for England's "Rustless Steel." By the late 1920s Ford Motor Company had perfected deep drawing techniques that allowed Ford to use stainless steel for the radiator shell, door handles, hub caps, and other trim items

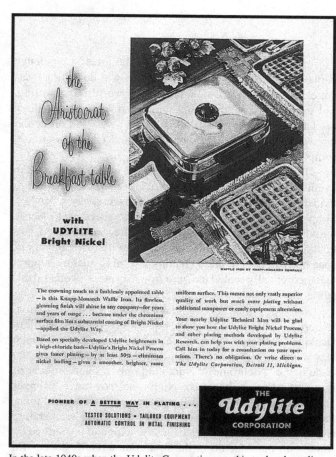

In the late 1940s when the Udylite Corporation ran this trade ad, appliance manufacturers were still struggling to produce consistently high quality chrome plating for their products. Udylite offered an apparently superior nickel substrate process under the chrome. Most surviving examples that the author has seen of the **Knapp-Monarch Model 29-150** featured here, do in fact have unusually nice finishes.

on his 1930 Model A. Although Ford had reduced manufacturing costs for Stainless Steel enough to make it a viable material for automobile applications and in aircraft, medical devices, and commercial kitchens, the manufacturing cost remained too high for it to be a practical choice for small consumer appliances. Even if it had been economically feasible, it's doubtful that Stainless Steel would have been used in small appliances in any case. Appliance makers were designing goods intended to last only a few years at best and Stainless Steel would have been considered over-kill. By the time Stainless Steel did finally become economically viable, tough new inexpensive plastics had been developed that were not only as well suited to many appliance applications as Stainless Steel but unlike steel could be molded cheaply and easily into very complex shapes.

Heating Element Development or...
How they learned to build an electric fire.

At the turn of the 20th century the greatest challenge in making electrically heated appliances was designing heating elements that were safe, reliable, powerful, long lasting, and inexpensive. Considering the materials and technology available to engineers in 1900, this was a very tall order and for waffle iron designers, one that would take years to accomplish.

In 1900, heat producing resistance wire was most often an alloy of iron, which was electrically inefficient, prone to oxidation and corrosion, and softened excessively when hot. Simplex Electric, credited with the first successful electric toaster/grill around 1904, used iron wire encapsulated in a thick enamel coating. This was baked to the wire and appliance body in a thick mass creating a solid insulating support that theoretically sealed the wire from oxygen and other damaging elements.

In 1905, after several years of joint experimentation, Albert L. Marsh, a Michigan metallurgist and William Hoskins an Illinois inventor/entrepreneur patented a tough new alloy of nickel and chromium, to which they gave the trade name "Nichrome." Containing only a small amount of iron and being carbon free, Nichrome was much stronger and more long lived than earlier thermal wire. Hoskins Manufacturing Company was formed to produce high temperature electric laboratory furnaces using the wire and is credited by some with manufacturing the first commercially successful electric bread toaster in 1907 derived from these furnaces. Hoskins eventually sold the Nichrome patent to General Electric who had tried unsuccessfully for years to create its own thermal wire. Until the Marsh patent ran out in the mid-1920s, GE charged all other manufacturers twenty-five cents per appliance for the right to use it.

Early "Nichrome" was a major improvement over iron alloy wire in both electrical efficiency and physical strength. However, unlike its modern counterpart, it still retained a small ferrous component that was particularly susceptible to corrosion when exposed to cooking steam generated during waffle baking or bread toasting. Such corrosion sometimes produced high resistance hot spots that would melt the wire, causing premature failure of the heating elements.

A major consideration in baking waffles electrically is the considerable amount of heat that must be distributed evenly over a large surface area. It wasn't difficult for a large coal or wood-fired cook stove to impart 600 or 800 watts of thermal energy into a traditional cast iron waffle maker, but it was a quite another matter for turn-of-the-century engineers to design electric elements robust enough to accomplish this.

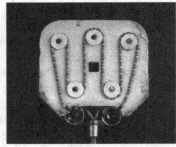

1920s Fitzgerald heating element. Nichrome wire is wrapped onto asbestos cord that serpentines around asbestos spools; element is sandwiched between asbestos sheets inside appliance.

Designers had to devise a safe and inexpensive method of supporting several feet of red-hot wiring while at the same time isolating it electrically inside a metal housing. In 1900, the only solid insulating materials available with the necessary heat tolerant properties were asbestos, mica, porcelain, and refractory cement or brick clay. However, each had shortcomings and certain limitations that made them all less than ideal for appliances.

Discounting the health hazards of asbestos that were unknown in the early 20th century, this fibrous mineral is physically weak, difficult to work with, and absorbs moisture-something present in abundance in a baking environment. Damp asbestos promotes corrosion of wiring left in contact with it.

Sheet mica arms radiate from stamped metal hub to support spring wound Nichrome wire; asbestos sheet spreads heat evenly. 1920s **Bersted Model 65**

Mica, a mineral with excellent insulating properties and can withstand high temperatures, is brittle, difficult to machine, and, in a moist environment, deteriorates over time.

Ceramics have good insulating properties but require expensive molding techniques to form into useful shapes. Being brittle they are also materials susceptible to heat and shock stress.

Refractory materials such as high temperature cements and brick clays are inexpensive, easy to form, and have ideal heat transfer characteristics, which seems to make them an ideal solution for producing a simple and inexpensive heating element. Manning-Bowman engi-

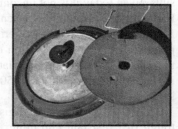

An early 1920s Manning-Bowman clay-matrix heating element removed from back of cooking grid. Spring wound Nichrome wire is suspended within the clay pancake on right.

neers in the early 1920s certainly thought so and designed that company's first waffle irons with clay-matrix elements of various shapes and sizes. These all worked surprisingly well. Although relatively slow to reach operating temperature, the great mass of clay created a thermal reservoir that prevented rapid changes in temperature when cold batter was poured onto the grids. The clay bed also distributed the heat evenly, eliminating cooking grid hot spots common to other early types of elements. However, moisture absorption problems plagued the embedded wiring causing it to corrode and fail prematurely. The company abandoned the clay matrix design by 1930.

Early 1920s **Westinghouse Type A** waffle iron. Each strip is a flattened thin walled metal tube housing a length of wide ribbon Nichrome wire sandwiched between insulating sheets of mica.

Most firms settled on heating elements consisting of ribbon-type Nichrome wire wrapped onto a hard asbestos or mica sheet. This flattened wire coil was then sandwiched between pairs of similar sheets that helped distribute the heat and separated the wiring from the metal of the appliance's shell. This type of element, first developed for small laundry irons, worked well in that application where the wire was sealed from moisture and needed heat only a small surface. The design was generally unable to produce enough heat when used in any but the smallest waffle irons and tended to have insufficient thermal mass. Although used in toasters for many years, mica heating elements were discontinued in American- made waffle irons, hot plates and grills by 1930.

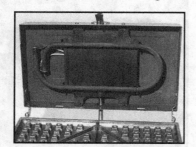
"Calrod" heating element inside early 1930s **GE Model 149G22** grill/waffle iron. Removable grid (not installed here) sits in contact with rod for best heat transfer; slow to heat but they last forever.

In 1913 General Electric patented a method of suspending a heating wire in a metal tube filled with a compacted magnesium or calcium oxide insulating medium. This "Calrod" heating element was first used by The Edison Electric Appliance Company in stoves and ovens and by the mid-1920s appeared in several models of the company's hot plates, grills, and waffle irons. Calrods, although slow to reach operating temperature, proved to be tough. They were sealed against moisture and, because they were able to generate a considerable amount of thermal energy, proved ideal for large appliance applications. Unfortunately, by the late 1920s, Calrod manufacturing technology was no longer cost competitive with other types of small appliance heating elements.

By the early 1930s GE went to more conventional less costly designs. "Calrods" reappeared in small appliances like broilers and toaster ovens after World War II when new manufacturing technology reduced cost and improved their response time.

In the mid-teens, Landers, Frary and Clark designed the first of a series of small rectangular waffle irons that employed a unique heating element consisting of spring-wound Nichrome wire serpentined around a number of small ceramic insulating spools strategically spaced on the back surface of the aluminum cooking grids. Lugs cast into the grids pass through the center of the spools and hold them in position. The assemblage is covered by an insulating asbestos sheet which in turn is covered by a thin steel retaining plate screwed to the back of each grid. This design worked so well that the company adapted it for use in many of its later 1920s grills and waffle irons. Because of the sturdiness of these elements, appliances equipped with them are often capable of giving reliable service more than eighty years later. By 1930, Landers did away with this over-engineered element in favor of lighter less expensive open frame designs requiring considerably fewer parts.

Incredible number of ceramic insulating spools support spring wound Nichrome wire on bottom of cooking grid of late 1920s **Landers Model E-9510** grill. Landers used a similar arrangement in its waffle irons at this time.

By the mid-1930s most appliance makers had settled on simple inexpensive open frame type elements of one variety or other. These invariably employ spring wound Nichrome wire threaded over around or through

Open frame type heating element, from **Dominion** twin **Model 1357** circa late 1930s. It's simple, inexpensive, rugged, and persists to the present.

mica or ceramic insulators that are held in position by inexpensive stamped sheet metal suspension forms. This simple design, engineered in the 1920s, is still used today in most waffle irons, grills and some toaster ovens.

Temperature Regulators or...
How they learned to handle the heat in the kitchen

The earliest heat producing electric appliances had no form of automated temperature regulation other than that achieved by balancing the amount of electric energy introduced into the appliance with the amount of heat dissipated to the environment. Non-automatic waffle irons, if properly engineered, work surprisingly well without a thermostat if kept filled with batter.

Manufacturers tried unsuccessfully for years to design a small, reliable, and inexpensive thermostat that could stand up to the harsh conditions found inside kitchen appliances. In the mid-1920s, Liberty Gauge and Instrument Company purchased the rights to a laundry iron thermostat invented by a teenage boy and became the first to produce a reliable inexpensive appliance thermostat. (Details of this story can be found elsewhere in the history of the Liberty Gauge and Instrument Co.)

Liberty Gauge's thermostat is a simple device consisting of a heat sensitive bimetal strip which, depending on its temperature, opens or closes a pair of silver electrical contacts that turn the current to the heating elements on or off. Heat from the elements bends the bimetal strip forcing one contact away from a similar but stationary contact. Varying the spacing between the contacts with a control knob attached to a cam changes the amount of heat required for the strip to open the contacts, thus changing the operating temperature of the appliance. This basic design adopted by nearly all of the major appliance manufacturers by the early 1930s is used in one form or another today to control most modern heat producing appliances.

This **Liberty Gauge & Instrument Company** waffle iron circa mid-1920s, is the first waffle iron model with a truly automatic temperature regulator. The control knob located below the lid handle is positioned along a horizontal slot to control the operating temperature. See Liberty Gauge & Instrument history for details about the young inventor of this controller.

A complex, expensive, but very effective thermostat assembly circa late 1930s, found inside the **Dominion made Model 1353** twin waffle iron. While most twin models have either no thermostat or a single controller, Dominion chose to use two in this model to regulate each cooking unit independently.

Industrial Design or...
How they learned to make stuff look better than just stuff

This 1913 Western Electric ad clearly illustrates appliances made before the era of industrial designers and styling departments. The Sturtevant vacuum cleaners were bulky cumbersome beasts while the washing machine with open belts, pulleys and gears was a safety nightmare. (1913, *National Geographic Magazine*)

Prior to the 1920s, nearly every contraption from steam engines to toilets was designed to perform a practical function either by their inventor or by mechanical engineers. These mechanical types ruled the manufacturing world and were preoccupied with just making things work. Few had any interest in art and aesthetics. The form of their creations generally followed their function. If a product like a washing machine had belts, pulleys, gears, levers, and cams, they might be hidden for safety's sake with a rudimentary sheet metal cover, but the housing would usually have a very simple functional shape created only to cover the offending parts.

Lack of styling in consumer goods prior to the 1920s can't all be blamed on the artistic insensitivity of engineers however. The available materials and the technology to form and shape them were until then somewhat limited. Two things occurred during and immediately after World War I to change all that. Manufacturing and materials technology made tremendous strides during the war and the post war economic boom created the phenomenon of mass marketing.

Prior to World War I most advertising was aimed at a local market and often amounted to nothing more than long dissertations on the technical attributes of a product. Typical

23

ad copy would often run several paragraphs and read like excerpts from an engineering manual. In the early 1920s, circulation of major magazines became nationwide and a multitude of similar goods began appearing them. Since these products usually all worked equally as well or as poorly as the competition's, copy writers became hard pressed to find ways of making their goods stand out from the rest. It became evident that the easiest way to make products seem unique was to make them look different. Thus was born the field of industrial design.

By the late 1920s forward thinking manufacturers had created styling departments staffed by professional artists whose sole purpose in life was to make things aesthetically pleasing. Product advertising soon reflected this change. Ads no longer were filled with lists of technical specifications but instead began to emphasize shape, color, finish, and design. In 1925, the Jordan Car Company even went so far as to use blatant sex appeal to try to sell its little sporty roadster. By the mid-1930s the styling department had as much influence in most large companies as the engineering department. By the 1950s industrial designers were kings of the hill and for better or worse yearly styling changes became the norm for many products.

Deco was the style of choice in the 1930s not only in product lines but in it advertising as well. This classic Art Deco graphic element was used in a 1936 GE ad for major appliances. The red robe, yellow shield, and black background are truly striking when viewed in color.

(March 28, 1936, *Saturday Evening Post*)

Knobs, Handles and Feet or...
Little things mean a lot

Nearly every household appliance has knobs, handles, or feet. In the last hundred years the styling of these essential little pieces has changed considerably, partly due to styling trends but for the most part because of the evolution of materials technology. Waffle irons are an excellent vehicle to examine some of this evolution

At the turn of the twentieth century, handles or feet found on everything that required such items, were made from some type of cast, stamped, or drawn metal, formed leather, or machined wood. Wood was inexpensive and the technology required to machine it had been perfected for at least three hundred years. Wood, being a poor conductor of heat, was the material of choice for handles of tools and appliances that got hot. The drawbacks to using wood were that too much heat could damage it and in order for it to look attractive it had to be painted or varnished. Painted wood being prone to damage by both heat and moisture was at best a mediocre material for appliance applications. Be that as it may, wood was cheap and easy to work. Wood, painted usually with black enamel, was used for almost all appliance handles until about 1925 when a not so new material called "Bakelite" began replacing it.

Painted wood handles like these of 1920s vintage could only be mass produced cheaply in relatively simple shapes due to the limitations of the material and the machines then available to shape it.

Back in 1907, in a series of experiments, Belgian born chemist, Leo Baekeland succeeded in combining phenol (carbolic acid) with formaldehyde (the smelly stuff in biology class) to produce the first synthetic plastic which was later given the trade name "Bakelite." This new phenolic resin was not only heat resistant but could be molded into intricate shapes impossible to machine. It could also be infused with colored pigments, eliminating the inherent problems with paint and making it nearly ideal for appliance parts.

Bakelite would have been perfect for appliance parts except for two factors. Pure Bakelite, it turned out, was very brittle and the new technology to mold it was quite expensive. Reinforcing fibers or wood flour fillers could be added to the resin for strength but that added to the manufacturing

cost and produced a somewhat mottled appearance. To hide the mottling, manufacturers needed to add coloring. Unfortunately, the mottling limited the color choices to black and dark shades of brown, dark green, dark blue, and an exaggerated red.

As molding technology matured the price of Bakelite came down slowly until by the early 1930s it replaced painted wood in most appliance handles and knobs. The ability to be

Easily molded Bakelite and other plastics far surpassed wood in making intricate and complex handle designs possible. Plastic was also more durable and less expensive to fabricate than wood. These examples date from the 1930s.

molded allowed designers to create beautifully stylized intricate parts impossible with wood. Except in the late 1930's when varnished wood handles were in fashion for a brief period, Bakelite continued to be the main material for most appliance handles for thirty years and became a generic name for all similar plastics.

During the 1930s the chemical industry developed several durable plastics which were more easily molded than Bakelite. Unlike the old phenolic resins, the new plastics were tough, flexible, and required no fillers for strength. Without the need to hide fillers, designers could pigment plastic parts nearly any color of the rainbow.

Unfortunately, some designers used plastics in applications for which they were ill suited. Many of the new resins also proved over time to be less tolerant of heat than Bakelite. For years premature failure of plastic parts caused many consumers to equate plastic with cheap and flimsy. It wasn't until the 1950s that truly heat-resistant plastics were developed, and by the 1960s they had successfully replaced the older resins in most appliance applications.

Bakelite is still manufactured in considerable quantities today for use in many high tech electronic applications. It is the trade name for certain of the plastics produced by Bakelite Ltd. in England and the Bakelite Corporation in America. Other technological and styling innovations are listed below in the "Waffle Iron Time Line" and are mentioned in more detail in the histories of the individual companies.

Electric Waffle Iron Time Line

1900-14

The invention of Nichrome (Nickel Chromium) wire in 1906 spurs appliance manufacturers to begin developing more electrical home appliances that produce useful heat including, stoves, hot plates, coffee makers, toasters, and flat irons. Simplex Electric Heating Company of Boston markets the first electric waffle iron, around 1906. General Electric develops waffle iron prototypes in 1911, which resemble cast iron stovetop models, but does not market any production models. Lack of 24-hour electric service for potential customers slows all electric appliance development.

1915-18

First true production model waffle irons such as Landers, Frary & Clark E-930 are introduced about 1918. All waffle irons of this period are small leg-mounted units with painted wood handles. Some are modified toasters like Chicago Flexible Shaft's Model B with waffle grids or Westinghouse's Type A waffle iron that started out as a sandwich grill. Armstrong Electric & Mgf. Co. supplies a waffle iron accessory attachment for its Perc-o-Toaster. Most waffle irons are purchased by urban dwellers able to obtain 24 hour electrical service.

1919-21

Conventional round waffle irons first appear. Most like the Russell Electric model shown here are plain and vary in size from 5 to 7 ½ inches in diameter. All are leg-mounted units . Cooking grids vary from mostly flat shallow dimples making quite thin waffles to very thick with deep dimples resembling those of old cast iron stovetop models. The earlier rectangular models persist through the 1920's.

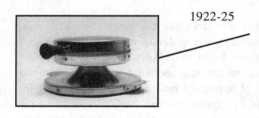

1922-25

The first pedestal models, like this Edison Electric 817Y160, appear. Leg-mounted models are phased out. Electric waffle irons begin to be sold as the wedding or Christmas gift of choice during these boom times as more homes are wired for electricity and housewives welcome ways to escape the heat of the old cook stove. Sales of traditional cast iron waffle irons plummet. Chrome plating is introduced by some manufacturers in 1925 as a non-tarnishing but more costly alternative to Nickel plating onsome small appliances.

1926-29

Liberty Gauge & Instrument Company introduces the first waffle iron with an adjustable automatic thermostat. Pedestal models predominate. Top-of-the-line examples such as this Landers Frary & Clark E-7324 have ornate metal or ceramic insert lids and pedestals with fancy fretwork cutouts. Bakelite begins to replace painted wood in handles and feet. Art Deco replaces Art Nouveau as the dominant trend in styling. It will remain in vogue until the 1950s. Total annual waffle iron production for 1929 reaches 768,000 units.[1]

1930-34

First low-profile units appear such as the Manning-Bowman 1637. Most manufacturers using various trade names for the finish offer chrome-plated models. Pedestal models, ceramic lid inserts, painted wood handles, and nickel plating are phased out. The first small grill/waffle iron combination units appear. A depressed economy lowers demand for consumer goods and prices drop significantly. Many small firms cease operations by 1934. Total waffle iron production from 1930 through 1934 is 2,876,309 units.[1]

1935-41   Tray-mounted "twin" or "double" units such as the Dominion 1353 appear. Varnished wood handles become fashionable. Heat resistant colored plastic handles begin to replace Bakelite on some models. Combination grill/waffle iron units gain a significant market share. Total waffle iron production for the period 1935 through 1938 is 2,922,015 units.[1]

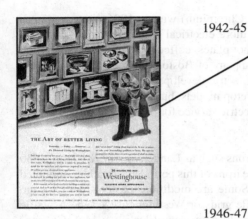

1942-45   In February 1942, The War Production Board issues Order L-41 to control production for the war effort. It forbids the purchase of materials for, or fabrication of, eighty different appliances. Small manufacturers unable to afford the retooling costs to make defense goods close their doors. Larger firms get into lucrative war work making everything from canteens and bomb fuses to wing flaps and land mines. Several manufacturers initiate trade-in and refurbishing programs to keep their dealers in business and customers happy. Silex coffee makers, manufactured primarily from unrationed glass, are the only new kitchen appliances available during this period. Wartime consumer ads like this 1944 Westinghouse example promise more and better products at war's end.

1946-47   Rationing of materials is first lifted for use in major appliances such as refrigerators and washing machines which are considered critical for health and safety. Many consumer goods are made with old tooling and are basically unchanged warmed-over prewar models like Dominion Model 1302. Shortages of strategic materials such as chrome cause manufacturers to paint rather than plate some parts. Full production of small appliances does not resume until 1947. Even so, as a result of unprecedented demand for any new appliances, a record 3.6 million waffle irons are produced during this period . Waffle iron production diminishes steadily each year after 1947 until the 1980s. Varnished wood handles are gone, replaced by traditional Bakelite or heat resistant plastics. Gone too are "twin" models.

1948-59   Super-sized, rectangular combination models, like this Westinghouse SGWB-521 (Sandwich Grill, Waffle Baker) are popular in meeting the needs of larger post war baby boom families. Early models are square and plain but by the early 1950s round corners and the bulbous look becomes the epitome in styling. Major consolidation of appliance manufacturing and the entire housewares industry begins and continues into the 1990's. Several major manufacturers sell their appliance divisions or close their doors including two of the oldest and largest, Manning-Bowman and Landers Frary & Clark.

1960 to   Minimalist styling returns as exemplified by this McGraw-Edison Model
Present   37100 from the early 1960s. Teflon-coated pots and pans imported from France in 1963 are an instant sensation creating the non-stick boom in appliances. Teflon is applied to waffle iron cooking grids in the mid-1960s. So called "Belgian" type waffles are sold at the 1965 New York World's Fair and consumers rediscover what old-fashioned waffles were like four decades before. In 1969, the author discovers that early Teflon coatings on waffle irons fail if overheated. He becomes disillusioned with his Teflon coated GE and begins looking for a waffle iron like "Mom" used to have. So begins his quest for the perfect waffle iron.

[1]   Production numbers courtesy The Association of Home Appliance Manufacturers (AHAM) Figures are approximate and include combination waffle iron/grill models.

The Companies-Their Products-Their People

The following section contains the histories of appliance manufacturers with a strong emphasis on their waffle iron and grill products, an area long neglected and of special interest to me. Also included are histories of companies that, although not appliance manufacturers themselves, were major retailers or distributors of appliances, and because of that, had a significance influence on the entire housewares industry. Wherever possible, I've included biographical sketches of the individuals directly involved with the companies.

I have made specific comments about what I believe are particularly interesting, unique, or in some cases the only waffle iron products of each firm. Occasionally a reference to the quality or performance of a model will be found. I am

an appliance restorer and as such have rebuilt over 400 waffle irons and road tested over 250 different models, often using more than one type of recipe. Although the ratings are subjective in nature, I think I'm a qualified judge of waffle iron performance.

A model number appearing in bold type in these descriptions indicates that a picture of that particular item can be found nearby. A more complete listing of waffle iron models can be found in the *Price Date & Model Guide* section. As is the case elsewhere in the book, when the reader encounters references to dates as "Early..." "mid-..." or "late..." one should assume that "early" refers to the first third of the decade in question, "mid-" the middle third, and "late" the last third of the decade.

Aluminum Goods Mfg. Co.
"Mirro"

This impressively large **Model 9358M** appears to be chrome-plated steel but is actually plated aluminum. In 1931 it sold for $9.95 placing it at that time in the medium price range. Although fairly common, examples with unblemished plating are unusual. The plating technology was in its infancy and still not perfected.

Joseph Koenig founded the Aluminum Manufacturing Company in Two Rivers, Wisconsin in 1895, a time when new aluminum refining methods had reduced its cost and made it practical for ordinary applications. Three years later, Henry Vits formed the Manitowoc Aluminum Novelty Company, also in Wisconsin. At the same time, investors in Newark organized the New Jersey Aluminum Company. Five years later, in 1903, Albert Layse set up the Aluminum Sign Company in Two Rivers Wisconsin, very near Joe Koenig's eight year old Aluminum Manufacturing Company.

By 1908 competition among these manufacturers was so intense that it had driven all them all to the brink of bankruptcy. Fearing the loss of its largest customers to bankruptcy, The Aluminum Company of America (ALCOA) stepped in and consolidated the three into one company which ALCOA called the Aluminum Goods Manufacturing Company. ALCOA became one-fourth owner of the new conglomerate and of course arranged to be the exclusive supplier of its aluminum.

In 1913, the conglomerate, headquartered in New Jersey, began making high quality aluminum cookware, at its Wisconsin manufacturing facilities under the "Viko" name. In 1917, the brand name was changed to "Mirro." Meanwhile, ALCOA was also marketing its own cookware under the "Wear-Ever" label. When the New Jersey partners in the Aluminum Goods Manufacturing Company sold their interest in the conglomerate to ALCOA in 1920, ALCOA became a one third partner and ended up accounting for more than 65% of all of the aluminum housewares made in the U.S. for the next ten years.

The Aluminum Goods Manufacturing Company became the Mirro Aluminum Company in 1957 and finally the Mirro Corporation in 1977. Today Mirro is part of Newell/Rubbermaid. Employing about 2000 people in Wisconsin. Mirro remains the World's largest manufacturer of aluminum cookware.

Over the years Mirro has manufactured everything from fishing boats and aluminum siding to pressure cookers and lawn furniture. During World War II it supplied the military with canteens. From the late 1920s to 1982, the company produced a small line of electrical appliances. Its first kitchen appliance was an electric coffee percolator, introduced in 1928. This was followed by an electric waffle iron designated **Model 9358M** pictured above. This husky looking plated aluminum iron, sold in 1931 for $9.95. Although this model heats rapidly and cooks a medium-thick waffle, quickly and evenly, aluminum was an unfortunate choice of material for the body. Aluminum's efficient heat transfer characteristics causes the base to get very hot, creating a potential burn problem, or if left unattended on a heat sensitive surface, a possible fire hazard. Due to fairly successful sales these irons are relatively common and can be obtained at reasonable prices. Their impressivly large size makes them an interesting display piece.

Armstrong Electric & Mfg. Co.
"Perc-o-Toaster" "Old South"

Model W, labeled **"Old South"** reflected the company's West Virginia southern heritage. Armstrong products uses a unique oversized non-arcing power cord connector (see insert). Replacement cords are not available. The temperature gauge is unusual, being calibrated in degrees rather than levels of browness.

Founded in 1916, by Charles C. Armstrong in Marysville, Ohio, as Armstrong's Standard Stamping Company, the firm became Armstrong Electric and Manufacturing Company when it was moved to Huntington, West Virginia, after World War I. The name was later simplified to Armstrong Products Company.

The company's first product, invented by its founder, was a combination appliance that could cook eggs, broil bacon, and brown toast, all at the table. In 1918, Armstrong marketed a second combination appliance, which made toast and brewed coffee at the same time. This Model PT "Perc-o-Toaster" could be purchased with an accessory waffle iron attachment of dubious merit designed to be inserted in a slot in the base. One wonders how the user was supposed to clean batter overflows from the interior.

In 1920, Armstrong manufactured a conventional, heavily constructed, pedestal-type waffle iron designated **Model W** and labeled **"Old South."** This iron uses a unique large pronged power connector intended to prevent arcing when the cord was attached. **Model W** was advertised as the first waffle iron to feature a built-in temperature indicator. This large easy to read gauge and the iron's substantial heating elements made the appliance a pleasure to use.

By 1930, in addition to the "Perc-o-toaster" and **Model W** waffle iron the company was manufacturing two models of table stoves and an **"automatic" coffee percolator**. The rear portion of this unique two chambered pot is filled with cold water and placed on a separate hotplate base. During the perking process, water is transferred through the coffee grounds to the front chamber. The shift in weight tilts the pot forward slightly on its base opening a micro-switch that shuts off the power.

Both the "Perc-o-Toaster" and **"Old South"** waffle iron were manufactured in considerable numbers into the 1930s. Although relatively common, these appliances are eagerly sought by collectors and command high prices. The "Perc-o-Toaster" waffle iron accessory is very common, and is often mistaken for a piece of camping cook gear or a stovetop iron. They usually sell for under $10.00.

The coffee never burns in this pot. Water is transferred from the rear to the front of this two chambered pot during the perking process. The weight of the redistributed water tips the pot forward slightly on its hotplate stand, opening a micro-switch underneath which shuts off the power at the end of the perking cycle. (Photo courtesy Dan & Vi LaBelle)

Arvin Industries

Arvin Industries was founded by Q.G. Noblitt and Frank Sparks in 1919, under the name Indianapolis Air Pump Company, to manufacture a hand operated automobile tire pump. In 1921, they changed the name to The Indianapolis Pump and Tube Company and in 1927 to Noblitt-Sparks Industries. The firm became Arvin Industries in 1950.

Arvin began as a parts supplier to the automotive industry but diversified by entering the toy business in 1924, purchasing the Dan Patch Novelty Company, a maker of children's wagons. Over the years the firm has manufactured everything from metal furniture, radios and space heaters to land mines and incendiary bombs, the last two items being their contribution to the war effort in the 1940s. Today the company is one of the major manufacturers of automobile exhaust and suspension system components

In the late 1940s and early 1950s, Noblitt-Sparks manufactured two very popular models of a large grill/waffle iron. The first, **Model 3500**, is a 1320-watt super size iron with reversible grills that convert to flat griddle plates. This rather clumsy looking sharp cornered unit was restyled in the early 1950s into the smooth lined Model 3550. Both units are identical internally, and each suffers from poorly designed grill retaining clips. Some were produced for Sears Roebuck and sold as Kenmore Model 344-6657 or Model 344-66680. All Arvin models produce large waffles of approximately 80 square inches, and do so quite well.

ARVIN LECTRIC COOK

GRILLS! FRIES! BAKES! TOASTS! — America's most versatile cooking appliance! Bacon and eggs for breakfast, toasted sandwiches for lunch, pancakes or waffles for dinner, hamburgers, steaks or chops for a crowd—they're all easy to fix with ARVIN LECTRIC COOK! Cooking area equals three 10-inch skillets; converts in seconds to fully automatic waffle baker. For any special occasion, ARVIN LECTRIC COOK is the gift supreme! See it at your dealer's —now! **$27⁹⁵**

Cooking area big enough to do 16 hamburgers at once . . .

. . . or 4 full-size sandwiches . . .

. . . or 4 generous crispy waffles!

NOBLITT-SPARKS INDUSTRIES, INC.

COLUMBUS, INDIANA

ALSO MAKERS OF FAMOUS ARVIN RADIOS

The **Arvin Model 3500 "Lectric Cook"** grill/waffle iron featured in this 1949 ad is shown grilling 18 of the world's smallest hamburgers. About as bulky as a Buick of the same vintage, the copywriter was still stretching the capability of this beast with this hamburger feat. The $27.95 price tag was, for that time period, as hefty as the appliance.

This 1948 **Model 3500** grill/waffle iron with 80 square inch cooking surface was designed to supply waffles by the acre to large post war families. Model 3550 introduced in 1950, like the automobiles of that era, had more rounded corners and a bulbous look.

33

Beardsley & Wolcott Mfg. Co.
"Torrid"

The Frank E. Wolcott Manufacturing Company of Hartford, Connecticut began making electric appliances around 1909 using the "Torrid" brand name. Soon after, a Mrs. Sutton and her sister Mrs. Bridges, co-owners of the "Silex" coffee maker patents, asked Wolcott to develop an electric heating unit for their Pyrex coffee maker. Wolcott did, and soon became involved in the sales of this unique product. In 1927, Wolcott sold a ½ interest in his company to Charles Beardsley of the Novelty Manufacturing Company, and the new organization became the Beardsley and Wolcott Manufacturing Company of Waterbury, Connecticut. In early 1929, the company purchased the Silex Company, and in June the company was again reorganized into Wolcott Inc., a holding company, with Silex a wholly-owned subsidiary. The company name was changed in 1936 to The Silex Company.

This 1926 ad for the Silex vacuum drip coffee maker appeared three years before Silex was purchased by Wolcott Manufacturing. In 1909 two Massachusetts sisters combined a Pyrex coffee pot of their own design with a Wolcott electric hot plate, to create the now famous coffee maker.

This Louis XIV design must rank as one of the most uniquely styled waffle irons of all time. Beardsley & Wolcott labeled it the **Model W2014** "Torrid Avignon." It was clearly intended to impress luncheon or dinner guests, rather than the kids on Sunday morning. The bright red and white easy-to-read temperature indicator is discreetly tucked behind the green marbleized plastic "door knocker" lid handle.

Beardsley & Wolcott continued:

During World War II Silex prospered. Their coffee maker, manufactured primarily with unrationed glass, was one of the few consumer products available during the 1942-45 period. With increased competition after the war, Silex suffered major losses for several years. In 1953, in an effort to diversify and boost sales, the company bought The Chicago Electric Manufacturing Company, a firm founded in 1902. The expanded product line successfully stemmed the red ink. Proctor Electric purchased Silex in 1960, and the company became Proctor-Silex. In 1966, the SCM Corporation acquired Proctor-Silex.

By the late 1920s Beardsley and Wolcott was well established in the appliance business, offering a medium-priced line of goods including coffee urns, percolators, toasters, grills, table stoves, and waffle irons. The waffle irons were oversized and utilitarian in appearance, but were of good to excellent quality. Most "Torrid" models came with an accurate, easy to read, red background-colored temperature gauge, usually unobtrusively located on the front or side of the units. The less expensive versions came without heat indicators. None of the models are thermostatically controlled.

Model W2014, pictured on page 34, deserves special mention for its styling. Sold as the "Torrid Avignon," this chrome plated Neo-Classical or Grecian styled unit, looks much like the proverbial lamp containing the wish-giving genie. This top-of-the-line model, with green marbleized Bakelite feet and lid handle, sold new in 1931, for $14.95. The United Drug Company sold it as the "Electrex" Model X550. Today both versions are much sought after.

In 1929 Beardsley and Wolcott offered this attractive **"Torrid"** model with painted wood handles in Cherry Red, Delft Blue, Woodland Green, or Canary Yellow for $9.95. (February, 1929, *Good Housekeeping Magazine*)

The "Torrid York" **Model WY 010** came with either red, green, blue. yellow, or black handles and matching colored "art silk" cord. Notice on this exquisitely preserved example, the lamp socket adapter still on the cord. Homes in the 1920s had few if any outlets to accomodate small electric appliances. The adapter allowed connection to be made into a light socket.

(Photo courtesy Dan & Vi LaBelle)

Ben S. Loeb Inc.

Ben Loeb was an early member of the New York Housewares Manufacturers Association, an organization that later became part of the National Housewares Manufacturers Association and is today the International Housewares Manufacturers Association. In the 1920s and 1930s, Loeb operated a small housewares manufacturing business in New York City. The only two Lobe products that have surfaced to date, are the "**Master**" waffle iron that appears to be mid or late 1920s vintage, and the plain **Model 255,** of slightly later vintage. Like many kitchen appliances before the age of industrial design, the Loeb waffle irons appear more utilitarian than stylish. The "**Master**" model works well, creating a very nice thick waffle. Any Ben S. Loeb artifact should be considered rare.

Model 255 is a plain unit with no temperature indicator and less substantial handles than the "Master" model pictured below.

Ben Loeb's "**Master**" waffle iron isn't much to look at but it cooks a nice thick waffle quickly and evenly. A second version was made with a tear drop type lid handle. All Ben S. Loeb items are scarce and quite collectible.

Bersted Manufacturing Co.
"Tru-Heat"

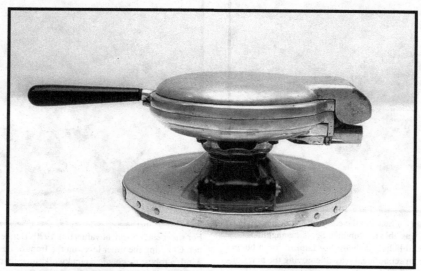

Bersted's first waffle iron, **Model 1832-A** from the early 1920s, looks surprisingly similar to Edison Electric's first model of the same era pictured on page 62. Both irons employed sealed heating elements cast integral to the cooking grids. The long handle on the Bersted was designed to prevent steam burns when lifting the lid. The Eidson iron has a small handle with a steam shield.
(Photo courtesy Dan & Vi LaBelle)

Alfred Bersted started a small machine shop operation in Chicago in 1913 and began making small appliances shortly after World War I. The appliance business grew and prospered enough to attract the attention of Max McGraw owner of McGraw Electric. In 1926 McGraw purchased Bersted Manufacturing and made it a division of McGraw Electric. Al Bersted was retained as president and ran the division for McGraw until he repurchased his old company in 1930. Bersted remained sole owner of his company until McGraw once again purchased it from him in 1948. At that time Bersted became president of McGraw-Electric and eventually CEO.

Dick Moran, who worked for Bersted at McGraw-Electric's Toastmaster Division for forty years beginning immediately after World War II, related in a speech to the Toaster Collectors Association in 2001, the following about Bersted. "Mr Bersted (he preferred Al) was 5 foot 6 inches tall, heavyset with winkley blue eyes and usually chewing on an unlit cigar. He traveled constantly and was usually in his office only on weekends or for a little while Friday afternoon or Monday morning. During the week he would tour our factories look over others for acquisition, call on our biggest customers and whatever else might teach him something for our company's benefit. Those who knew him well said he could walk into a factory and a half hour later could tell you to the dollar what it was worth in the market. Whether he was in a facory, store, or office, Al would talk to anyone. He preferred to wander through these places alone so employees would feel free to talk and give him straight answers. He never made a big deal of telling a person who he was."

Mr. Moran continues his narrative and personally vouches for the accuracy of the following most amusing incident involving Bersted. "He hated wasted time. One morning in 1957, Al flew into Midway Airport in Chicago but when he went to retrive his car from the parking garage discovered that someone had borrowed it and blown the engine. He wasn't so angry about that but his immediate thought was how was he to get back to the office in Elgin the fastest way possible. His answer was to walk next door to the Buick agency and buy a new car. The only one immediately available was an outrageous looking tri-colored model in black, red, and tan. He purchased it on the spot just to get back to the office with the least amount of wasted time."

Between 1930 and 1948, Bersted acquired the Swartzbaugh Manufacturing Company (Everhot) of Toledo, Ohio and United Electrical Manufacturing ("Eskimo" fans) of Adrian, Michigan. The history of The Bersted Company is intimately connected with that of McGraw Electric (later McGraw-Edison). Further details of this fascinating relationship can be found under "McGraw-Electric."

Early Bersted products were simple, utilitarian, and affordable, and can be characterized as the Model T Fords of the appliance world. The first waffle iron **Model A-1832** made around 1920-21, was a plain narrow-necked pedestal model with solid cast-aluminum body halves. An unusually long, thin, painted wood lid handle protrudes from the upper body. Succeeding models in the mid-1920s are tall bulky affairs often with minimal ornamentation. They have excellent heating elements, but unfortunately, only a few models have tem-

Bersted Continued:

Bersted made this utilitarian iron for Sears in the early 1920s. Somehow, one of the company's copy writers was able to convince Sears management that calling it the "**Challenge**" would help sell them. For families on a budget Bersted products like this were an economical way of enjoying the new convenience of electric appliances.

For sheer entertainment value, this 1920s Bersted /Sears Model is a prizewinner. Cranking the timer lever on the front of the base turns the power on and winds a robust mechanical clockwork timer that sounds like the ticking clock swallowed by the crocodile that chased Captain Hook in Peter Pan. At the end of the preset cooking cycle, the timer turns the power off and rings an impressively loud bell, hidden inside the pedestal. Model 240 made in the early 1930s has a similar timer and bell.

perature indicators. This makes overheating a common occurrence if the cook is not careful to monitor the iron frequently, and unplug it when necessary.

Model 68 from the mid-1920s has a built-in clockwork timer, an entertaining and humorous attempt to eliminate overheating, without resorting to an expensive thermostat. The operator sets a sliding cocking arm stop on the front of the pedestal for a desired cooking time. A cocking lever is then moved to the preset stop, winding the timer's spring a predetermined amount. This action also closes a switch that maintains power to the heating elements. At the end of the timed cycle, the power switch opens and a rather boisterous bell announces the end of the cooking cycle. Some of these models were labeled "Stewart Waffle Mould Model 20-Made by Stewart Die Casting Corp."

In the mid-1930s, Bersted adopted an extreme Deco styling motif characterized by exaggerated body shapes and distinctive ribbed triangular plastic handles which were employed on Model 217 and **Model 251**. During this period, the company apparently found itself in a pricing squeeze, and spent money on styling to boost sales, while skimping on materials. Several models appeared with stamped sheet steel grids instead of the traditional, more expensive, and much more effective cast aluminum variety. These models are interesting as collector items, but due to the poor heat transfer characteristics of the steel grids, are very difficult to use successfully.

Bersted was a very popular low-priced brand, often sold through mail-order chains such as Wards and Sears. Many examples survive today, and except for the early less common models, command relatively low prices from collectors. They usually work well however, and in good condition make a nice addition to any kitchen.[1]

Model 251 dating from the mid-1930s was one of the company's most popular models and unfortunately one of lesser quality. The eye catching brown plastic deco style handles are flimsy and the iron tends to overheat quickly. The distinctive raised shield on the lid (insert) convinced many purchasers that this was a higher quality item than was the case.

[1] Permission to reproduce certain biographical information about Al Bersted courtesy Eric A. Murrell (Editor of the Toaster Collector Association News Letter, *The Saturday Evening Toast.*

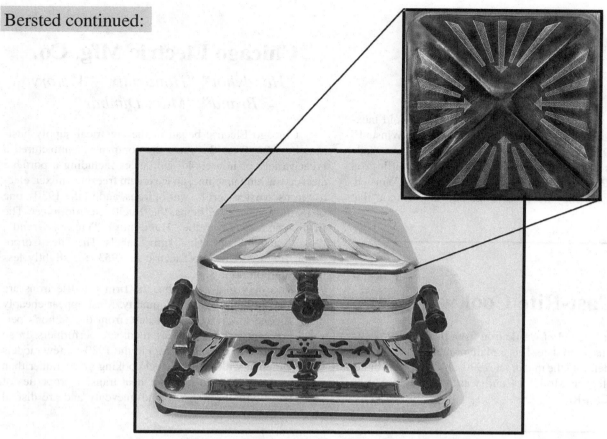

The strange herringbone design embossed in the lid of this Model 230 (insert) seems to have been created by a designer who was either in a hurry or who simply ran out of good ideas. The entire unit looks like an inexpensive knockoff of the Lindemann & Hoverson Model 317 which is pictured on page 96.

Model 207 is another Bersted attempt during the depression years, to make its products noticeable on store shelves by placing unusual designs on otherwise ordinary looking products. The distinctive chevron lid pattern and brown Bakelite handles still attract attention.

Capitol Products

"Lady Winsted"

Capitol Products was a marketing firm that sold inexpensive products made by others and labeled "Lady Winsted." In the late 1930s or 1940s, Son-Chief appears to have made two versions of a model 425 combination grill/waffle iron for Capitol Products. Both firms were located in Winsted, Connecticut and may have been one and the same at that time.

Cast-Rite Cookware

Only one model of waffle iron from this Chicago company has surfaced to date. It is a plain domed non-automatic pedestal model from the mid or late 1920s. It closely resembles a Russell Electric Model 14 and was probably made by Russell for Cast-Rite.

Chicago Electric Mfg. Co.

"Handyhot" "Handymix" "Victory Brand" "Mary Dunbar"

Chicago Electric began in the electrical supply business in 1902. Over the years the company manufactured a great variety of household appliances including a portable electric washing machine, an ice cream freezer, a mixer, electric irons, toasters, grills, waffle irons, and in the 1930s, one of its most successful items, the "Jucit" electric juicer. The firm's products carry the "Handyhot", "Victory Brand", "Mary Dunbar", and "Handymix" labels. The Silex Corporation acquired Chicago Electric in 1953, for slightly less than a million dollars.

With only one exception, the firm's waffle irons are uninspired in both design and quality. Most appear cheaply made for the low price market and, from the author's personal experience, almost all are mediocre performers. In an unsuccessful cost cutting attempt in the 1930s, a few models were equipped with pressed steel cooking grids, rather than cast aluminum. Due to the poor heat transfer properties of steel, these units heat slowly and unevenly and are dismal performers.

Model AF26 "Wafflator", a full sized stacked double was advertised as being able to make two waffles in two minutes. A clever latch assembly allows the user to open each pair of grids independently using a button in the tear drop lid handle. It's high $18.50 price created lackluster sales in 1930-31 which makes this a fairly rare collectible.

Model AFUC has heavy cast iron grids, which seem to take a week to heat and another week to cool. It does an excellent job of producing waffles that appear to have been made by an old cook-stove-type iron.

This automatic "Victory" model (half of a "Wafflator" model) is a slow but consistent performer. The easy-to-read temperature indicator in the lid is apt to become sluggish and inaccurate over time from exposure to steam and grease.

The Chicago Electric **Model AF26 "Wafflator"** deserves special mention for its unusual space-saving stacked design, duplicated only once, some years later, by the Serva-Matic Company. The "Wafflator" double-decker design may have been a good idea for producing lots of waffles quickly, but the price of $18.50 was too high. Few depression era families could afford such a princely sum, and sales were poor. Except for the **Model AF26**, which commands very high prices from collectors, most Chicago Electric waffle irons remain modestly priced.

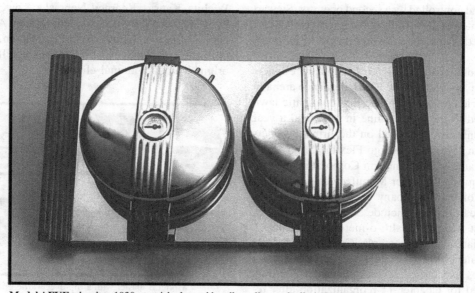

Model AFUE takes late 1930s varnished wood handle styling to the limit. Most twins are more work to use than standard models but cleaning spilled batter from the handle grooves on this model is a whole lot more extra trouble than with most.

Chicago Flexible Shaft Company

"Sunbeam"

An 1890s advertising lithograph showing the company's first product, a horse clipper. The fellow at left provides rotary power to the flywheel-type crank handle suspended on a line from the ceiling. The power is transfered to the clipper head through a flexible shaft.

Sunbeam was founded in 1893 as a partnership between J.K. Stewart and Thomas J. Clark, for the purpose of manufacturing a mechanical horse clipper that Stewart had invented. This device was powered by one person cranking a large wheel connected through a flexible shaft several feet long to a clipper head controlled by a second operator. Stewart and Clark incorporated in 1897 as the Chicago Flexible Shaft Company and added sheep shearing equipment to its product line.

In order to counter the seasonal demand for clippers and shears the company entered the home appliance arena in 1910 with an electric clothes iron. The first automatic lawn sprinkler was added to the product line in 1920 and a year later the name "Sunbeam" was used on the firm's products for the first time. In 1946 the Chicago Flexible Shaft Company changed its name to the Sunbeam Corporation.

Sunbeam acquired the Oster Manufacturing Company in 1960 and the Coleman Company of Wichita, Kansas in 1998. Today Sunbeam brands include Sunbeam®, Oster®, Mr. Coffee®, First Alert®, Health-o-meter®, Coleman®, Coleman PowerMate®, Grillmaster®, Campingaz®, and Pelouze®. In the late 1990s the company experienced some financial difficulties and closed several plants. In February 2001 Sunbeam filed for Chapter 11 reorganization after reporting losses stemming from $2 billion of debt. In November 2002 a Coleman shareholders lawsuit was pending, a management reorganization was in progress and on November

26th a federal bankruptcy judge approved Sunbeam's reorganization plan, giving nearly all of the company's shares to the major lenders, Morgan Stanley, Wachovia Corp. and Bank of America. Sunbeam as of this writing still has business units in Aurora and Bridgeview, Illinois; Miami Lakes, Florida; Wichita, Kansas; Kearney, Nebraska; Lowell, Massachusetts; Lyon, France; Tokyo, Japan, and Sydney Australia. The corporate offices are currently in Boca Raton, Florida. Incidentally, the company's Australian branch still makes the firm's original product-animal clippers.

Model B toaster with a flip-over waffle grids. Turn of the century manufacturers designed multi-purpose units hoping to convince potential customers that these do-all marvels were worth their very high cost.

(Photos courtesy Victor Vale)

Notable Sunbeam Landmarks

1910 The company enters the home appliance business with their "Princess Electric Flat Iron."

1920 The company markets the America's first automatic lawn sprinkler.

1921 "Sunbeam" is registered as the company's trade mark.

1924 The company introduces the first combination electric toaster/grill.

1925 Ivar Jepson is hired as a draftsman. Later, he was responsible for the design of all of the company's best-selling products including the "Mixmaster". Today he is acknowledged as one of the great industrial designers of all time.

1930 The company introduces the first lightweight (6 lb.) electric iron, the "Toastwitch" toaster grill, the "Wafflewitch" waffle iron, and The "Mixmaster" the first heavy-duty stand type mixer for the home selling for under $20.00. An instant sales success, production reaches 300,000 units per year by 1936.

1937 The "Shavemaster" electric razor is introduced.

1946 The Chicago Flexible Shaft Company becomes The Sunbeam Corporation.

1956 The company introduces the "Lady Sunbeam" hair dryer.

1963 Sunbeam introduces the first spray mist steam iron.

1970s Sunbeam manufactures digital clocks, fry pans, women's shavers, fans, electric scissors, and can openers.

Model F3 "Wafflewitch," with ivory colored Catalin plastic handles, was the Cadillac of waffle irons in 1930. The cooking unit pivots on a heavy support to expose an aluminum batter bowl, often mistaken for a syrup warmer. In use, the bowl does not become warm. This model came with a matching ladle (right) and was designed to impress depression-era guests with one's affluence and cooking skills.

Sunbeam introduced three premium priced appliances in 1930, the "Mixmaster" mixer, the "Toastwitch" grill, and the "**Wafflewitch.**" The "Mixmaster" was the first heavily constructed home mixer and became a phenomenal sales success. The "witches" did poorly and soon faded from the scene. (Unidentified November, 1930 magazine)

Records about the company's waffle irons either do not exist or are no longer available from Sunbeam. Information that is available comes from period catalogs, advertising, and numerous surviving examples of individual models. Chicago Flexible Shaft Company entered the waffle iron market in 1930 with its **Model F-3 "Wafflewitch."** This very stylish though rather unconventional contraption, consists of a chrome-plated aluminum body, attached to a tray-mounted pillar that suspends the cooking unit above a plated aluminum batter bowl. The cook swivels the cooking unit to one side while lifting its lid to expose the batter bowl resting

beneath on the tray base. Priced at $19.95 this appliance was definitely aimed at the luxury segment of the depression era market. In today's dollars it would have cost about $210.00. Understandably, few were sold. Today **Model F-3** is rare and commands very high prices in the collector market. Care must be exercised when purchasing this model however. Most suffer from a certain degree of plating deterioration due to the difficulty in the 1930s, of plating aluminum properly. Additionally, non-functional sealed heating units in these cannot be serviced. The company in the mid-1930s introduced a much less exotic and more affordable Model D-33 iron.

Chicago Flexible Shaft continued:

In 1940, Sunbeam introduced the **Model W-1,** the first in a series of large square waffle makers that cook a giant 80 square inch waffle. Accessory aluminum foil blanket inserts could be purchased which, when laid on the waffle grids, would convert the unit into a mediocre grill. After World War II, the W-1 was given a better-illuminated temperature indicator and became the **Model W-2.** By the early 1950s, the boxy styling of the W-2 was reworked to create the rounded **Model CG** Combination Grill/waffle iron. This model could be purchased in a single purpose waffle iron configuration or, for slightly more, as a combination unit. With 1200 watt heating elements, accurate sensitive thermostats, and a non-overflow grid design, models **W-1, W-2,** and CG are all excellent heavy-duty performers. Many can still be found in excellent condition and make very practical modern kitchen appliances, especially suited to large families.

Model W-2, circa late 1940s was one of the highest quality waffle irons ever made. With 80 square inches of cooking surface it waS also one of the largest. Other than A redsigned easier to see indicator light behind temperature control, this is identical to its predecessor the Model W-1pictured in the ad at right. Both models were made to near-commercial quality and are a pleasure to use.

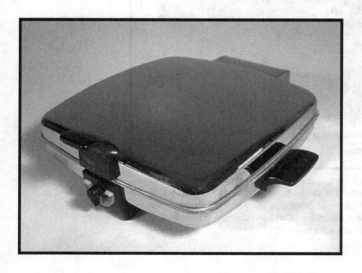

Model W-1 featured here was introduced in the early 1940s and reintroduced after World War II. More than a year after the war, when this 1947 ad appeared, new small appliances were still hard to find due to materials shortages, labor problems, and delays in shifting to peacetime production. The last line reads, "The supply is increasing-See your dealer."
(November, 1947, *Good Housekeeping Magazine*)

The **Model CG** (Combination Grill/waffle iron) circa 1950s is basically a restyled Model W-2. Like its predecessors the W-1 and W-2, the CG is of near commercial quality and makes a huge waffle. Unlike the previous models, the CG has removable grids which could be interchanged with flat grilling grids. This iron was expensive when new and today they still command higher than normal prices on the used market. It is a nice practical everyday appliance.

45

Club Aluminum Company

"Hammercraft"

Club Aluminum Company was originally organized in Chicago in 1923 as the Club Aluminum Utensil Company, for the purpose of selling Aluminum pots and pans in the home on the "party" plan, much like Tupperware was sold in later years. Club Aluminum contracted with The Monarch Aluminum Manufacturing Company for the fabrication of its goods. The firm's very substantial cast aluminum pots came with an attractive hammered finish, and a heavy tightly-fitting lid which sealed in moisture released during the cooking process, making it unnecessary to add water. The company marketed these pots as "waterless" cookware and sold them under the "Hammercraft" name. A severe downturn in sales during the depression put the company into bankruptcy in 1933. During a subsequent reorganization, they dropped home sales in favor of heavy discounting through department stores. Both Club Aluminum and Monarch survived the depression and eventually merged. Renamed Club Products, the company was acquired by Standard International Corporation in 1968.

In the mid and late 1920s, Club Aluminum sold a most unusual if not bizarre waffle iron. No model number was assigned to this bulky pedestal-type model. The unusual contraption produced a standard size round waffle with dimples on top, but with a pancake flat bottom. A plunger rod attached to the upper cooking grid protrudes through the lid. This grid assembly is able to slide upward, inside the tall domed lid, allowing for infinite batter expansion during the baking process, eliminating overflows. Lifting the lid pulls the waffle from the flat lower cooking grid. Pushing on the plunger then ejects the waffle from the lid chamber. These irons heat and cook slowly and the large dome collects most of the cooking steam making it difficult to determine when the waffle is done. This model is rare and commands higher than normal prices from collectors.

This Club Aluminum iron creates a flat-bottomed waffle with conventional dimpled top surface (insert). The thickness of the waffle is determined by the amount of batter used. The internal plunger allows for one inch of expansion, theoretically eliminating any possibility of an overflowover. Who manufactured this iron for Club Aluminum is not known.

Club Electric

In the 1920s, this Chicago based marketing company sold two bulky, non-automatic, pedestal-type electric waffle iron models manufactured for them by Bersted. The earlier Model R.I. is nearly identical to the more common **Model 07** pictured below. Labeled "Waffle Mold", each has an ornately pierced, inverted, cone shaped base, prominent identification placard, and black enameled wood handles. Bersted also made a **Model F6** "Donut Mold" for Club Electric (pictured at right) which Bersted also made for Sears and sold as their own Model 60 "Donut Mold." This item resembles a conventional pedestal-type waffle iron on the outside but with its special grids is supposed to be able to cook six triangular donut-like cakes. The author was unsuccessful in several attempts to do this. The "Club" name correctly infers that this organization, as with other companies with similar names, used a "party" or membership type selling technique popular in the 1920's, which was revitalized later with the Tupperware parties of the 1940s, 1950s, and 1960s.

Bersted made **Model F6** donut mould (upper right) circa late 1920s uses the same body shell as this **Model 07** made for Club Electric by Bersted. The waffle iron worked well for the author but several attempts to make donuts in the donut mold were only partially successful. A special batter may be required for good results.

The Coleman Company [1]

Coleman

One day in the late 1890s, schoolteacher William C. Coleman noticed in an Alabama drugstore window, a rather unusual gasoline-fueled lamp that created a brilliant white light. He concluded immediately that selling this device to rural folks accustomed to dim kerosene lanterns might be a good money making idea. He purchased a number of these "Efficient" lamps from the Gilliland Company of Memphis Tennessee and full of optimism, headed for Kingfisher, Oklahoma Territory, in January 1900. Unfortunately, just a few days before his arrival a fly-by-night lamp salesman had just fled town after fleecing a number of Kingfisher's citizens of a significant amount of their hard-earned cash. Consequently, Coleman's lamp selling efforts immediately met with considerable sales resistance. Undeterred, he set up a lighting service, the Hydro-Carbon Light Company and leased his lamps, guaranteed to work as advertised. No light, no pay! It worked, and his new business prospered.

Coleman moved his operation to Wichita, Kansas in 1901 and bought all rights to the lamp the following year. By 1905 his firm was manufacturing and marketing not only individual lamps and lanterns, but was installing entire gasoline-fueled lighting systems in rural homes that were out of reach of electricity. By the mid-1920s, the company was involved in the manufacture of numerous gasoline-fueled household goods including hot plates, cook stoves, broilers, radiant heaters, hot water heaters, and clothes irons. The firm sold most of its products through hardware and small department stores in the Midwest.

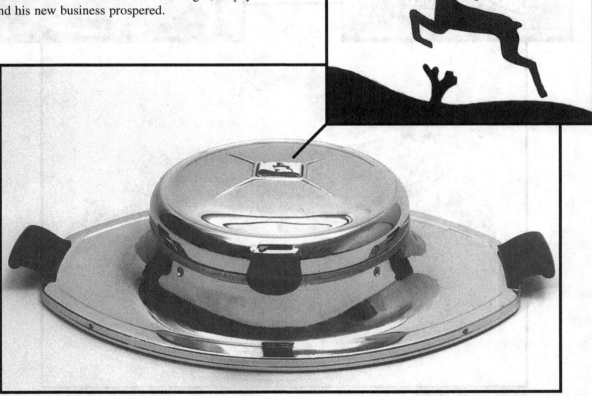

Model 17 "Aristocrat", designed by Ambrose Dean Olds, is much sought after by art deco collectors, for its classic Art Deco leaping Gazelle lid tile (insert). The over-sized heating elements tend to cause this iron to overheat if it is not monitored closely during the cooking session. The original 1930 patent drawing for this model can be found on the next page.

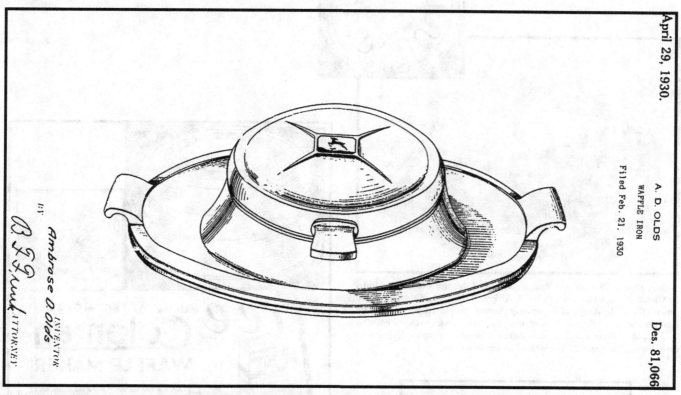

April 29, 1930.

A. D. OLDS
WAFFLE IRON

Filed Feb. 21, 1930

Des. 81,066

Ambrose O Olds
INVENTOR

B F Frick ATTORNEY

The design patent drawing for the **Model 17 "Aristocrat."** The patent was issued issued on April 29, 1930 to Ambrose Olds, a free lance industrial designer. Shortly after the patent was granted the iron went into production, but with a more smoothly curved base than is illustrated in the drawing. The $15.00 price tag was about twice the average for a waffle iron at that time. (Drawing courtesy Nancy Conway)

Seeing the increased availability of electricity to many of his customers, Coleman decided in 1929, to offer electrical appliances. Dean Olds, an industrial designer and engineer, was hired away from Hotpoint to create the designs for a series of new waffle irons. Coleman, who took a special interest in electrical projects, most likely directed the overall design effort himself. By June of 1930, the company was shipping electric toasters, coffee percolators, two burner electric hot plates, thermostatically controlled electric clothes irons, and two types of electric waffle irons, the Model 16 "Aztec" and the Model 17 "Aristocrat".

All of the company's electrical appliances were of good to excellent quality, but the unfortunate timing of their introduction, at the beginning of the depression and the high cost of production resulted in higher than average prices and disappointing sales. Production was discontinued on all electrical products by 1935 except for commercial electric coffee machines, which continued to be manufactured until 1939. Sales remained so weak on household products that it took the company over four years to dispose of its excess inventory.

As of this writing, the Sunbeam Corporation holds a 79% interest in Coleman. The company continues to produce its traditional product lines of products in Wichita, and celebrated its centennial in 2000. The Coleman Museum, located in the factory's outlet store, is an excellent place to see the complete history of this interesting manufacturer.

All Coleman electrical products including seven models of waffle irons are either scarce or rare. Two irons, **Model 16C "Aztec"** and the **Model 17 "Aristocrat"**, with its art deco leaping Gazelle lid plaque, are highly prized by collectors. **Model 19A** is probably most rare. Factory records of the Model 16SS exist, but actual examples have not surfaced. This may have been a prototype stainless steel model that was never released for sale. Complete information on all models can be found in the model and price guide section.

[1] Historical information and materials courtesy Herbert Ebendorfer, Curator The Coleman Museum, Wichita, Kansas.

Coleman continued:

Factory records indicate less than a hundred of this non-automatic **Model 19A** were produced between 1931-33. A view of the back of a cooking grid (insert) shows the design of the heating elements employed. Nichrome wire is serpentined around ceramic spool insulators, a throwback to the early 1920s when Landers Frary and Clark used virtually the same complex design in its early irons. (See pages 21 and 90 for Landers examples)

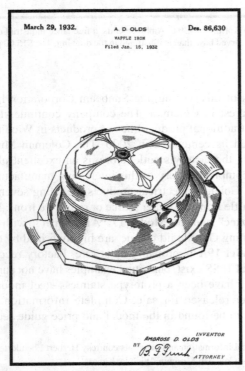

March 29, 1932.   A. D. OLDS   Des. 86,630
WAFFLE IRON
Filed Jan. 15, 1932

INVENTOR
AMBROSE D. OLDS
BY
B.F.French ATTORNEY

This design patent issued in March 1932 looks similar to the Model 19 shown above. However, the octagonal deco motif pictured in the drawing was never used by Coleman on any of its products.
(Drawing courtesy Nancy Conway)

To spur lagging sales during the depression, Coleman teamed up with Washburn Flour and Wesson Oil for this 1931 newspaper ad campaign that appeared on February 24th in The Wichita Eagle. (Material courtesy Herb Ebendorfer- The Coleman Museum, Wichita, KS)

Dominion Electrical Manufacturing Company [1]

The History of the Company

Twenty-eight year old Benjamin Shaffer had emigrated to Winnipeg from Albany, New York by 1917 and was working for, or with a Canadian relative by the name of Joseph Wolinsky. The Wolinsky family had significant real estate holdings in Toronto and owned the Marlboro Hotel in Winnipeg. Joe Wolinsky was also operating a small manufacturing concern by this time making electric hot plates. Ben Shaffer became the firm's US sales representative with an office in Minneapolis. By the early 1920s Shaffer had become convinced that the American market was more promising than the Canadian one for electrical goods, and decided to reestablish the company in the United States.

> For details about the Shaffer and Lifson families and what became of the principles after Dominion was sold, please see the segment at the conclusion of the Dominion Company history and products.

Shaffer found a partner in Minneapolis, 30 year old Nathan Lifson, who was instrumental in securing financing and acquiring property for a manufacturing facility in that city at 722 Ontario Avenue. Dominion Electrical Manufacturing Company was incorporated in March of 1921 with Benjamin and his wife Martha Shaffer designated president and vice president respectively and Nathan and his wife Sarah Jane Lifson, secretary and treasurer. (Neither woman was active in the business. Mrs. Lifson was, in fact, a renowned pianist for the Minnesota Symphony Orchestra.) Nonetheless, this incorporation was the beginning of a forty-year partnership that was to create what at one time was possibly the world's largest independent appliance manufacturer.

Dominion Electrical, named in honor of the Dominion of Canada, adopted a domino as its logo and began by manufacturing a line of small electric appliances including hot plates, toasters, grills, and waffle irons. In the mid-1920s Dominion purchased the Electrahot Manufacturing Company, another fledgling appliance maker in Minneapolis, and ex-

Dominion's first factory, built in the early 1920s at 712 Ontario Ave. W. Minneapolis. New windows and landscaping are encouraging signs that the building will be around many more years.

(Photo taken spring 2002, courtesy Dan & Vi LaBelle)

The 1933 company basketball team. The trophies show that they must have been pretty good. Left to right-Clifford Sommer, Bob Shaffer (who would become president of Dominion in the 1960s, and Tom Farrel. The others are unidentified.

Dominion continued:

panded the Dominion product line to include coffee percolators, hair curlers, soldering irons, and stoves. Although Dominion absorbed Electrahot Manufacturing, the Electrahot name was used on certain Dominion made products until the late 1930s.

By the mid-1930s, a combination of factors including a negative business climate in Minnesota, a need for a larger manufacturing facility, and a desire to be closer to the center of their markets, convinced Lifson and Shaffer to find a new location for the company. The firm, now called simply Dominion Electric Company, was moved in April 1935 to a plant at 150 Elm Street, Mansfield, Ohio where it remained for over thirty years. The company also supported a Canadian manufacturing subsidiary called Samson-Dominion Limited in Toronto.

During World War II Dominion did 100% war-related work including the manufacture of two types of bomb casings, incendiary bombs, anti-tank mines, and Pitot (air speed indicator) tubes for aircraft. For its exemplary performance the firm was presented with three service flags including the coveted Army-Navy "E."

After the war the firm continued to grow. Dominion had purchased the old Majestic Electric Appliance Company and was operating it as a separate division with 150 people in nearby Gallon Ohio. Dominion's profit sharing plan, initiated in 1942, was by the 1950s considered an industry model.

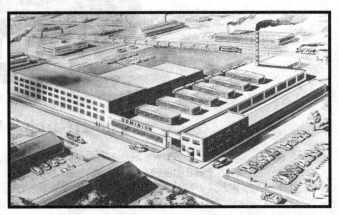

An artists rendering of Dominion's Mansfield, Ohio facilities circa 1953. Mansfield was also home to the Westinghouse Electric's small appliance division.(Courtesy Mr. Burton Lifson)

Dominion was celebrating its 30th anniversary in July 1951 when this photo was taken at the Shelburne hotel in Atlantic City. Pictured are the company's executives and sales representatives who were in New Jersey for the biannual National Housewares Manufacturers Association trade show. Seated at the table beginning fourth from left are Robert Shaffer, Benjamin Shaffer, Nathan Lifson, and Burton Lifson. (Photo courtesy Mr. Burton Lifson.)

Dominion continued:

A recession in the mid-1950s caused a temporary reduction in the company's workforce, but in March 1957, management began an ambitious $300,000 expansion that included a large new warehouse in Mansfield.

1957 however did not end up as a banner year for Dominion. The firm went through a 26-day strike in August and in November its founder Benjamin Shaffer died suddenly and unexpectedly. Following Shaffer's death, his son Robert, who had been with the firm since 1933, became vice president under Nathan Lifson, now the president and elder statesman of the business. Lifson's son Burton, who had joined the company in 1947 and held various positions including purchasing director, became vice president of operations. Sheldon Shaffer, Robert's younger brother, who had been at Dominion since 1949, became the executive vice president in charge of marketing.

Benjamin Shaffer had never believed in print or media advertising, relying instead on selling through factory representatives. In fact much of his time over the years had been occupied with direct selling to customers. With his passing, the firm changed its sales philosophy and launched a new and very successful national television advertising campaign. Dominion became a prime sponsor of such popular TV shows as *The Today Show* with Hugh Downs, *The Tonight Show* with Jack Paar (later Johnny Carson), *I Love Lucy,* and *The Real McCoys.* On television Dominion introduced a new brief case-type portable hair dryer that was such a sales success that in 1961 the firm created a separate division and built a 73,000 square foot plant in Gallatin, Tennessee to meet the demand for it and other appliances being advertised on television.

By the early 1960s, philosophical differences between the Lifsons and Shaffers culminated in the purchase of the Lifson interests in the company by the Shaffer family. Robert Shaffer became company president and Sheldon Shaffer vice president and secretary. The Shaffer brothers operated

A young Johnny Carson demonstrating a Dominion toaster oven on the Tonight Show circa 1963. Dominion sponsored a number of popular TV programs in the 1960s propelling the company to national prominence and expanding its sales significantly. Prior to this time the firm relied upon factory sales representatives to sell products.

Sheldon Shaffer Dominion's vice president of sales in 1961 is about to launch a very successful television advertising campaign with the firm's new Model 1805 portable brief case-type hair dryer. (Photo courtesy Mrs. Dianne Shaffer.)

Unprecedented demand for the company's new portable hair dryer in 1961 necessitated construction of this 73,000 square foot manufacturing facility in Gallatin, Tennessee to make them. The plant initially employed 185 women and 35 men who also produced portable mixers, portable ovens, and hot dog cookers. (Photo courtesy Mr. & Mrs. Sheldon Shaffer.)

Dominion until the company was sold to Scovill Manufacturing in 1969, at which time Dominion became part of Scovill's Hamilton Beach division.

From its inception, Dominion was a turnkey operation with a full in-house manufacturing capability. The company had its own design department, made its own motors and thermostats, and did all of its own metal working including machining, stamping, plating, and polishing. In the 1940s and 1950s, Dominion had what was reputed to be one of the best tool and die making facilities in the Midwest. Tooling made by the company in Mansfield was used in both its American and Canadian plants. In addition, the firm maintained a complete in-house printing facility to produce product instruction manuals and advertising literature. Emulating much larger corporations like General Electric and Westinghouse, Dominion even maintained an experimental test kitchen complete with a full-time home economist. The company however did not manufacture power cords and outsourced all of its plastic parts.

At its peak in the early 1960s, Dominion employed 1300 people who produced over 2 million electric appliances annually. The product line at one time or another included flat irons, toasters, waffle irons, grills, hot plates, fans, coffee makers, corn poppers, deep fryers, mixers, roasters, cookers, and hair dryers. For years the company was an original equipment manufacturer for many retail chains and participated heavily in the S & H Green Stamp program of the Sperry & Hutchinson Company. Nearly all of the company's products were of good to excellent quality, carried a one year exchange warranty, and were usually priced for the middle or upper level markets.

This plain pedestal **Model 64** was Dominion's first and came with the same black, red or green painted wood handles as the leg-mounted Model 65. Wards sold a variant of Model 64 as its top-of-the-line so-called "Blue Line" model.

An old newspaper photo of the waffle iron assembly line at the Mansfield, Ohio plant, circa late 1940s. The woman at left is fastening lid handles with flexible shaft power screw driver. Women were usually, but not always, assigned to light assembly or office work in appliance plants while parts fabrication and finishing was left to men.

(Mansfield News-Journal, September 28, 1947)

Model 65, Dominion's second, differed from the first version, Model 64 only in that it was leg-mounted rather than a pedestal-type. (Manufacturers at the time were undecided as to which styling trend would succeed.) Both came with the same body and red, green or black painted wood handles. Collectors prefer the less common red or green versions.

Dominion continued:

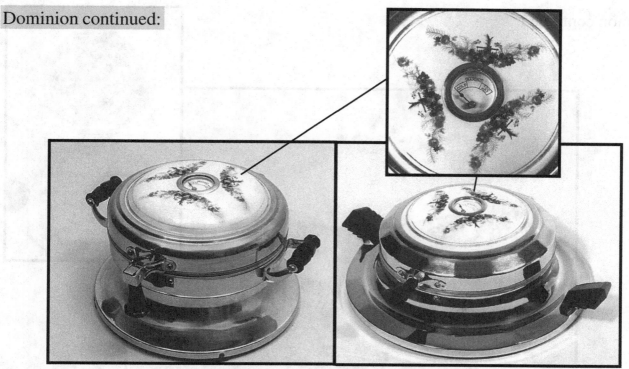

Model 67-H (left) circa late 1920s, features a perched parrot with a flower garland background repeated three times on a ceramic lid insert made by Sebring Pottery. The same insert appeared several years later on **Model 126** (right), but did nothing but make an otherwise nice deco model appear dated. Finding examples like these with both good porcelain and good plating is difficult.

From the beginning with its first model, designated **as "Style 64,"** Dominion's waffle irons were distinguished for their practical solid no-nonsense designs, rather than for their stylishness. Only a few porcelain lid insert models such as **67-H, 73, 74, 122,** and **126** from the late 1920s, and a very rare porcelain insert **Model 510** grill/waffle iron and matching waffle iron **Model 595** from the mid-1930s (pictured in the Hibbard, Spencer, Bartlett & Co. history) can be called truly eye catching. The company manufactured many ordinary models in vast quantities, often offering each model for as long as ten or fifteen years. Dominion supplied waffle irons for Sears ("Heatmaster"), Ward's ("Blue Line" and "Signature"), various department store chains such as Hibbard Spencer and Bartlett ("Lady Hibbard"), May Department Stores ("Mayd Best"), and small retail distributors including Triangle Industries ("Apollo"), Made-Rite, and Everbrite. During the depression era, the company also sold serviceable but unmarked factory seconds, a practice abandoned after the war.

Because of the great numbers produced and their general work-a-day styling, most Dominion models command lower prices than many other brands. However, almost all of the company's models work well, and in good condition can be excellent inexpensive practical every day appliances.

In the early 1930s during Prohibition, Coors Brewery of Golden, Colorado prohibited from making beer, searched for other money-making opportunities. The brewers porcelain division, a long established producer of laboratory ware such as mortars, pestles, and crucibles, turned to making inexpensive kitchenware. By punching a small vent hole in its cookie jar lids, Coors created an attractive insert for this rare unnumbered Dominion made model. Coors stopped kitchenware production in the late 1930s

[1] Family and company history, courtesy Burton Lifson, Lisa Shaffer, and Sheldon Shaffer. Certain other historical information courtesy Thomas G. Yontz Richland County, Ohio Historical Society.

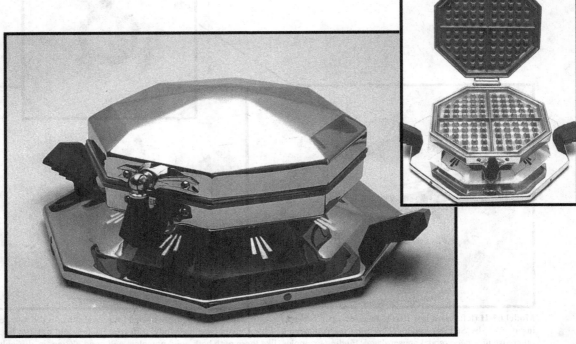

The automatic octagonal **Model 521**, circa early 1930s, has a temperature indicator light designed to shine through the deco-style cutouts in its pedestal. This eye catching iron is well made but doesn't match the quality of the hexagonal Edicraft model from which it appears to have been copied. (See picture of Edison's creation on page 167) This iron with slightly different Dominion handles can occasionally be found marked "Majestic Electric Appliance Co, Model 402." (Iron generously donated to the author by Victor Vale)

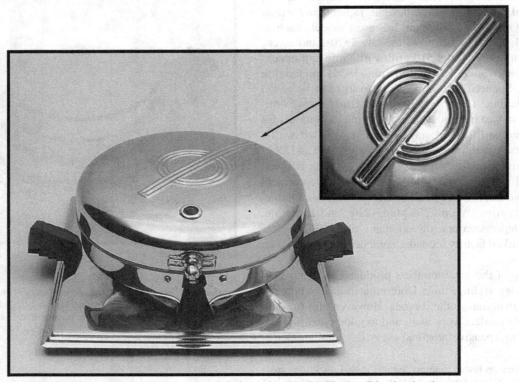

Model 596 has brown rather than the usual black Bakelite chevron handles. The deco lid embossing (insert) resembles the monogram on Dagwood's shirt in early Blonde and Dagwood comic strips.

Two variants of **Model 1302**. Both share identical body stampings and internal parts. Mid-1930s version (left) has enameled base and black Bakelite handles. A later version (right) has a chrome-plated base and varnished walnut handles.

Model 1354 with geniune walnut handles is one in a series of similar twin models the company made prior to World War II. Twins were popular for a short time until consumers realized they took more effort to use and maintain than conventional models.

Model 1315, if viewed from the front at a low angle, looks like a penguin. They work well, were priced right and sold in great numbers as Christmas or wedding gifts in the 1940s and 1950s . Model 1314 is the similar looking non-automatic version. These aren't very exciting stylistically but make a very practical addition to any kitchen.

The Shaffer Family & Dominion Electric[1]

Benjamin Shaffer is credited with founding Dominion Electric in 1917 in Winnipeg Canada and naming it in honor of the Dominion. Ben however was not Canadian but was born in Albany, New York, in 1889. He married Martha Miller who was born in New York City in 1891, one of thirteen children. Ben and Martha had four children beginning in 1908 with Robert, then Lillian, Shirley, and in 1927, Sheldon. Interestingly, the arrival of each of the four Shaffer children was evenly spaced at seven-year intervals.

Sheldon, characterizes his father as being a hard working quite extraverted person who, in addition to being intimately involved with the manufacturing operations of the firm, spent a considerable amount of time away from home visiting customers. Mr. Shaffer was a natural salesman and felt that the most effective way of selling goods was through factory sales represen-

Benjamin Shaffer

tatives. He believed that print advertising was less effective and too costly, which explains why magazine advertisements for Dominion products prior to the late 1950s are virtually non-existent. Mr. Shaffer was an active member of the B'nai Jacob Congregation in Mansfield Ohio and was a frequent contributor to welfare and civic funds in that area. He passed away quite unexpectedly on November 12th 1957 while waiting in his doctor's office for a routine examination.

Robert, nearly twenty years Sheldon's senior, went to work for Dominion straight from high school in the early 1930s. Having basically grown up in the company Bob became intimately familiar with not only the sales and managerial facets of the business but also knew the manufacturing portion as well. He worked in various managerial positions both in the sales and manufacturing segments of the firm, and after thirty years became president of the company in the early 1960s. Robert Shaffer, like his father,

Robert Shaffer

felt that a strong personal relationship with the company's sales force was critical for the success of the business. Doug Shaffer's childhood memories of his father were of many "good-byes" and "welcome homes" brought about by the almost weekly business trips his father made, with product samples in hand, from the Mansfield facility to the company's Chicago sales office.

In the late 1960s Robert saw an appliance industry being dominated by a few large concerns and felt that selling Dominion at that time was in the future best interest of the owners and employees. In 1968, after 35 years with Dominion and in failing health, Bob Shaffer retired. He passed away January 26th 1984 in Mansfield, Ohio. He is survived by three children, David, Nancy and Douglas.

Sheldon Shaffer was born in 1927 and was the youngest of the four Shaffer children. He entered Ohio State University in 1945 but left shortly after and spent two years in the Navy before returning and graduating from Ohio State in the late 1940s. He went to work for Dominion in 1949 and held several positions in the company including executive vice president

Sheldon Shaffer

and secretary of the Dominion and Shaffer Corporations. In the early 1960s Sheldon was instrumental in initiating a very successful, and, for Dominion, an unprecedented national television sales campaign. Sheldon became President of Dominion when his brother Robert retired in 1968.

After the sale of Dominion in 1969, Sheldon and his wife Dianne moved to Florida. There he became involved in volunteer work with *The Starting Place*. At the time this was a small unstructured organization with a "rap" center in a warehouse in Hollywood, Florida, devoted to helping troubled teens. *The Starting Place* today, is a large multi-faceted tax supported Florida foundation devoted to helping individuals and families torn apart by emotional and behavioral problems caused by drug and alcohol abuse (See www.startingplace.org. on the web). As its long-term director, Sheldon has been responsible for much of the growth and continued success of this much needed and most worthy organization. Sheldon and Dianne are the proud parents of three very successful children, Steven, Benjamin, and Susan.

[1] The Shaffer family history generously supplied to the author by Mr. & Mrs. Sheldon Shaffer, Mrs. Lisa Shaffer, Mrs. Laurie Ginsburg, and Mr. Douglas Shaffer.

The Lifson Family & Dominion Electric [1]

Nathan Lifson was born in 1891 on the Russian-Lithuanian border arriving in America as an infant with his parents when they emigrated in 1894. His first job as a teenager was selling newspapers on the streets of New York City. He saw action in World War I and was discharged from the Army in Des Moines, Iowa in 1918. By the early 1920s Nathan was living in the Minneapolis area and working with or for his uncle Benjamin Lifson, a successful real estate broker in that city. It was at this

Nathan Lifson

time that Nathan met and married Sarah Jane Waisbren, a talented young musician who taught piano and played in the Minneapolis Symphony Orchestra under conductor Eugene Ormandy. Nathan and Sarah Jane subsequently had three children, Anita, Burton, and Kalman.

In 1921, Ben Shaffer, wishing to move his small electric appliance company from Winnipeg, Canada to Minneapolis, met Lifson and the pair formed a formed a partnership. Nathan supplied much of the capital, and, through his Uncle Ben Lifson, the real estate in Minneapolis to set up a new manufacturing facility for the Dominion Electrical Manufacturing Company.

Lieutenant B. Lifson circa 1942

Ben Shaffer was responsible for manufacturing and sales while Nathan concentrated on the financial matters of the firm. For nearly four decades this arrangement succeeded and remained virtually unchanged until Ben Shaffer's death in 1957. During that time both men built Dominion into the world's largest independent appliance manufacturer with sales of over 2 million units a year and a workforce of over a thousand people.

In 1941, eighteen year old Burton was attending Yale University when Japan attacked Pearl Harbor. He enlisted in the army shortly thereafter and was made a lieutenant in the Army Air Force. Burton participated in four major campaigns in the Pacific Theater, rose to the rank of captain and was part of a small advanced reconnaissance group that was the first American military unit to land in Tokyo on September 3rd, 1945 only hours after the Japanese surrender. After the war he went back to Yale and graduated with an engineering degree in 1948.

The next year Burton went to work for Dominion as an engineer and eventually became vice president of operations. After the passing of Ben Shaffer in 1957, philosophical disagreements developed among the company's managers, which culminated in the Shaffer family purchasing the

Burton Lifson

Lifson's interest in the firm in 1959. (Burton's younger brother Kalman, a Harvard law school graduate, worked only briefly at Dominion in the 1950s.)

Nathan and Burton moved their families from Mansfield, Ohio to the Philadelphia area in the early 1960s and purchased a small electrical specialties firm with roots that stretched back to the turn of the century. (One of the firm's founders was a protégé of Thomas Edison.) Nathan passed away in Philadelphia in 1974 at age 83. Burton is currently Chairman of the Board of CW Industries, a company that he has grown into a world leader in the manufacture of precision electrical and electronic components for the automotive, telecommunications, marine and appliance industries. Today his firm has worldwide sales and facilities in five countries. Burton and his wife Rita have two daughters, Cynthia, and Kathy, both successful professionals in their own right. Burton is still quite active in his company and regularly commutes from his home in Florida to the corporation's headquarters in Pennsylvania.

[1] The Lifson family history and related materials generously provided to the author by Burton Lifson.

Dover Manufacturing Company

Dover Manufacturing of Dover, Ohio, was an early producer of electric flat irons and the first to attempt to build one with an automatic temperature control. The firm's 1916 "Dover-A-Besto," however, proved unreliable and was quickly taken off the market. In 1925, the company developed a "Vea No Burn Out" heating element for its percolator which included a safety fuse, a much-needed innovation at the time. In 1936, the company was purchased by the rapidly expanding Knapp-Monarch Company and ceased to exist.

Although no full size Dover made waffle irons have surfaced, a number of Model 44 toy pedestal irons have. These fully operational miniature irons appear to date from the late 1920s, and are much sought after by toy collectors. No doubt these toys were patterned after a full sized model that the company made during this period and were intended to be sold to help placate a child who wanted a new waffle iron just like mom had.

Edison Electric Appliance Co.

Hotpoint

It was 1903 and Earl Richardson was working as plant superintendent for the Ontario California Power Company. For some time he had been thinking that the power company could make more money if only it would create more demand for its product. At that time his plant, like most, generated power for lighting purposes for only a few hours after the sun went down. In his spare time Richardson designed a small lightweight electric iron as a possible demand booster and convinced his bosses to allow him to distribute a few dozen samples to selected power customers for testing. He also convinced the company to generate electricity during daylight hours every Tuesday, the traditional day to finish laundry, so the women wouldn't have to iron at night. The response to these light convenient irons was so positive that in 1904 Richardson quit the power company and, with four employees, created the Pacific Electric Heating Company for the express purpose of manufacturing the iron.

His first irons were made with a wire wound brass core which, as it turned out was not quite as good an idea as first thought. Complaints came in that the irons were failing prematurely. Women who had perfected the art of evenly heating non-electric irons on stove tops, were complaining that the center of the sole plate became too hot, scorching their laundry while the edges were too cool. Richardson's wife suggested to him that a redesigned iron should be made to heat at the point and edges, areas that she knew were particularly important for successful ironing under pleats and around buttons.

In 1905 Richardson had a redesigned model ready for testing and again placed samples in the hands of selected housewives. The response from the women to their irons with the "hot point" was overwhelmingly positive. Richardson now not only had a moneymaking product, he had a trade name. His "Hotpoint" irons became an instant success. He sold more laundry irons in 1905 than any other maker.[1] By 1918, the firm claimed in its advertising that over 3 million housewives used Hotpoint irons.

In the Teens Richardson purchased the Simplex Company of Boston, another early electric appliance manufacturer and in 1914 registered "Hotpoint" as a trademark. The Company's name was also changed from Pacific Electric

[1]   This version of the company's beginnings appears in nearly identical form in several books. I am very suspicious of the accuracy of the details mentioned in this account but to date have been unable to locate a reliable primary source to either confirm or refute them. Richardson wasn't the first to manufacture an electric iron. Simplex in Boston and American Electric Heater in Detroit were two firms that predate Richardson's Pacific Electric Heating Company.

A shortage of domestic help for the upper middle class during and after World War I prompted several appliance makers to label their products "servants." By purchasing these so-called "servants" many middle class families felt that they'd moved up a notch socially, which indeed they had. This 1925 Christmas ad shows 15 different electrical appliances available from Edison Electric that year. (December 12, 1925, *Saturday Evening Post*)

Heating Company to Hotpoint Electric Heating Company. At this time the company introduced a series of Hotpoint "El..." products including the "El Tosto" toaster, "El Tostovo" toaster stove, "El Grillo" grill, "El Perco" coffee pot, "El Eggo" egg cooker, "El Chafo" chaffing dish, "El Bako" table oven, and a heating pad called the "EL Comfo". (The world was mercifully spared the El Waffelo as it had yet to be invented. Maybe California's Spanish heritage had something to do with the names, or maybe the company's copywriter was showing the effects of too much time in the hot California sun.)

By the late Teens Richardson had purchased the rights to the Edison name (rights Edison sold to numerous companies over the years) and changed his firm's name to Edison Electric Appliance Company. In 1918, The Hughes Electric Heating Company (the firm credited with making the first electric range in 1910), the heating device section of General Electric, and the Edison Electric Appliance Company merged. George A. Hughes, founder of Hughes Electric, became the president of this new conglomerate. In 1931 the firm's name was changed to Edison General Electric Company and in 1934 this name was dropped when it became the Hotpoint division of General Electric.

Although Westinghouse and General Electric were both experimenting with electric waffle irons as early as 1906, the Simplex Electric Heating Company was first to market several crude models from 1904 to 1910. Landers appears to have been first to market a truly practical electric waffle iron around 1918, followed by Edison Electric with the introduction of its **Model 116Y23** around 1920. This small pedestal unit has unique sealed heating elements cast within solid nearly indestructible one-piece aluminum cooking grids. It was apparently a great sales success judging by the significant number of surviving examples found in working condition today.

Edison Electric introduced its second-generation waffle iron **Model 157Y112** around 1922. It employed sealed "Calrod" heating elements, updated versions of which are used in many electric ranges even today. The early Calrods were quite expensive to manufacture and very slow to heat. They proved to be trouble free, however, and were used in all of the company's waffle irons until the firm's new owner, GE, reverted to more conventional and economical open elements in the early 1930s. Edison Electric's most popular waffle iron was **Model 116Y53** (a later version was designated Model 126Y53) produced in the late 1920s.

Edison Electric Continued:

A heavy cast iron counterweight (insert), fastened under the base, allows unit to be opened fully without tipping. A small metal tab installed on some examples and visible between lid handle and upper cooking grid, is a steam deflector to keep the handle cool and dry. According to the instructions, the hinge can be disassembled with a screw driver for cleaning by the owner.

Hotpoint **Model 116Y23**, circa early 1920s, (pictured here and at upper right) was one of the first commercially successful electric waffle irons. The solid aluminum body halves have sealed heating elements cast within them. Like many early units this one requires a split electrical cord to supply power to each of its cooking grids.

By the late 1920s, in addition to household appliances, Edison Electric was manufacturing an extensive line of commercial products including large electric ranges for shipboard use and a series of heavy-duty toasters intended for restaurants, as well as commercial waffle irons like the **Model 421YA202** pictured.

A distinguishing feature of nearly all Edison Electric household waffle irons is the oversized painted wooden lid handle. Although it prevents burned fingers, it distracts from the otherwise stylish appearance of the company's waffle iron products. These waffle irons are of excellent quality and, although slow to reach operating temperature, perform well. Collectors should take note that many suffer from very thin nickel plating on the stamped brass bodies. Over-polishing will cause the brass to show through the plating. Individuals overzealous with a polishing wheel sometimes advertise examples as "rare" solid brass models. These look impressive when first polished but tarnish quickly when heated. They may be appealing to interior decorators but have little collector value.

Model 157Y112 is most likely Edison Electric's second waffle iron model. It has Greek revival decorative banding and an unattractive oversized handle that unfortunately would appear on a number of later models. "Calrod" heating elements, a new innovation in the early 1920s made this iron an excellent if slow performer.

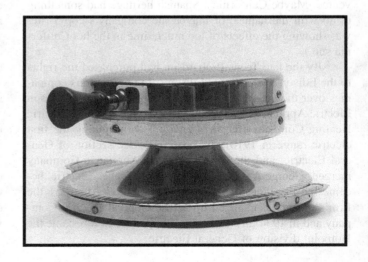

Except for its clunky lid handle the **Model 817Y160 "Simplex"** is a truly stylish early art deco unit. The narrow neck design of early pedestal models like this keep nearly all of the heat generated in the body from reaching the base. A slightly later version designated Model 126Y161 has a convenient toggle switch in the base to control the power.

Late 1920s commercial **Model 421YA202** pictured here was intended for restaurant or institutional use. Each cooking unit has its own power switch, pilot light, and clockworks timer. The timers are cocked by pressing down on the levers located below the round pilot light windows. These indicators are bright enough to be easily visible across a large busy commercial kitchen.

It's 1928, times were good for urban dwellers like this young couple depicted enjoying the good life. The husband needed a well paying job to pay for all of the new electric appliances shown. The toaster cost $9.75, the "Hedlite" space heater $10.00, the percolator $21.00 and the **Model 126Y53** waffle iron $15.00, substantial prices for the late 1920s. (1928, *Saturday Evening Post*)

Model 116Y53 was the most popular waffle iron Edison Electric ever produced. Introduced in the mid-1920s, it was manufactured for about four years. The later versions were designated Models 126Y53 and 146Y53.

By 1930 when this ad appeared in the professional journal *Marine Engineering & Shipping Age*, Edison Electric was part of GE and selling commercial kitchen equipment for shipboard use. The ocean liner pictured, is the S. S. Leviathan, the flagship of The United States Lines at this time.

Edison Electric continued:

Furnished with jade green and yellow deco handles the Edison GE "Ambasador" model pictured in this 1930 ad is arguably one of the nicest looking GE's ever made. Due to space constraints within the base, making a pedestal model, like this automatic, was quite an engineering challenge. By 1930 pedestals were being phased out in favor of low-profile designs which gave more room for bulky thermostats. Due to its high price and the shakey depression economy at this time, few of this model were sold.

(1930 *Lady's Home Journal*)

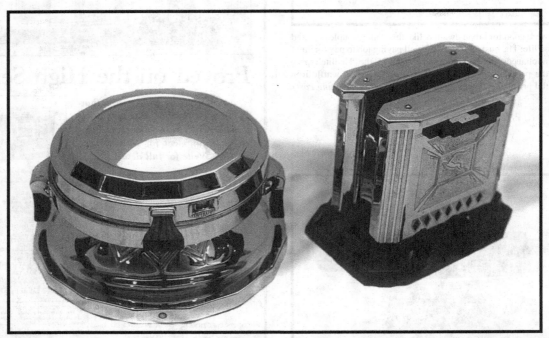

Model 129Y175 "**Ambassador**" waffle iron and **Model 129T31** toaster were stylish but costly top-of-the-line products designed to compliment each other. The iron has green and yellow marbleized Bakelite handles while the toaster, referred to by some as the "Gazelle" model, has a leaping Gazelle on the side. A Gracefully leaping animal was a popular Art Deco motif in the 1930s. A similar Gazelle decoration appears on the lid of the Coleman Model 17 waffle iron pictured on page 48.

(Photo courtesy Dan and Vi LaBelle)

Electrahot Manufacturing Company

Electrahot Manufacturing Company began in the early 1920s as Electrahot Appliances Inc. and was located at 307 5th Avenue South, Minneapolis, Minnesota. A 1920 company catalog shows three electric curling irons, two soldering irons, a nine-cup aluminum coffee percolator, and a full size four-burner electric range with oven. In the mid-1920s, Dominion Electric Manufacturing Company, also of Minneapolis, took control of Electrahot Appliances renaming it the Electrahot Manufacturing Company. Dominion ran Electrahot as a separate entity for a time but eventually merged the operations. Dominion continued to use the Electrahot name on certain products until the early 1940s.

Electrahot's first waffle iron appears to be Model 701, a small nondescript low-profile unit with a single, turned wood lid handle. A **second model** (pictured) with no model designation is identical but is equipped with an impossible-to-view open hole temperature indicator in the lid. In the early 1930s, several very stylish non-automatic waffle iron models were produced with Art Deco Bakelite chevron handles and porcelain lid inserts. Model 24P and versions of 144, 246, and **Model 247**, pictured on the next page, came with inserts made by Hall China in that company's "Silhouette" pattern. Hall also made "Tulip" pattern inserts for versions of Model 144, 217, and **247**. Hall produced a matching serving platter in the Tulip pattern and a complete dinner service in the Silhouette pattern. **Model 74**, pictured below, has a decidedly European deco-styled tulip pattern china insert made in Germany.

Because of their superior styling, most Electrahot waffle irons command higher than average prices. Those with porcelain lid inserts are sought after by both porcelain and appliance collectors. Models 24P, 144, and 246 and **Model 247** (with the Hall Silhouette pattern) command the very highest prices.

This petite unlabeled 5½-inch diameter iron is Electrahot's second model and dates from the late 1920s. The heating elements are rated at a modest 400 watts. The difficult to read temperature indicator viewed through a hole in the lid is nearly useless.

Electrahot produced two Tulip patterns for its ceramic lid models. This **Model 74** from the early 1930s has the attractive and relatively rare German-made version. Because ceramic lid waffle irons sold for premium prices when new and were aimed at a smaller up-scale market nitch than metal topped models, they are more scarce today and generally command higher prices than the all metal varieties.

Electrahot continued:

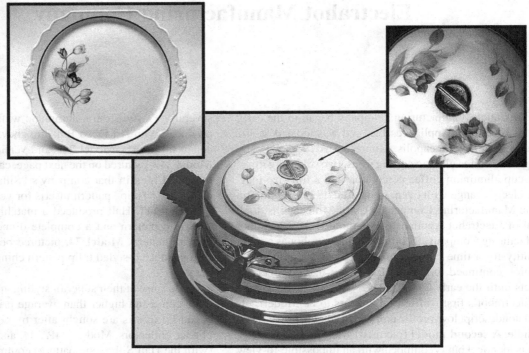

Model 247 from the early 1930s has the much sought after Hall Pottery Tulip lid. There are at least two variants of this decal. The matching 12 inch plate (upper left) is part of a serving set.

This Model 247 is equipped with a "Silhouette" pattern ceramic lid insert made by Hall Pottery. Hall used this decal on various items including dinnerware. Electrahot got a lot of mileage out of the stamping dies and handle molds for this iron. The same body and handles appear on at least half a dozen different models. Model 246 is identical except for slightly less fancy temperature indicator dial.

66

Estate Stove Company

The old Estate Stove factory, Hamilton, Ohio. Date of photograph is not known. Built in 1884, it was added to several times before being closed in 1962.
(Photograph courtesy: The Butler County Historical Society, Hamilton, Ohio)

In 1842, Lazard and Felix Kahn founded the Kahn Brothers Stove Foundry in Hanging Rock, at the very southern tip of Ohio. In 1884 they moved the business to Hamilton and in 1905 changed the name to The Estate Stove Company. For many years the firm was noted for its fancy cast iron wood, coal and gas-fired kitchen cook stoves, parlor heating stoves, and later for its "Heatrola" home heating furnaces. In the 1940s the factory covered 13 acres and the firm was one of the largest stove makers in the world. The company was purchased by RCA in 1952 and by Whirlpool-Seeger in 1955. The Hamilton plant was closed in 1962.

For a short time in the 1920s, the company manufactured a very attractive small pedestal-type electric waffle iron designated the **Model 75**. Using its years of stove making experience, the firm produced beautiful vitreous enamel finishes on these irons in white, powder blue, or apple green. Each iron came with a permanently attached cord with an in-line push button switch. The nickel-plated extremely narrow cast iron pedestal neck adds both weight and style to the iron. These waffle irons are scarce and command very high prices from appliance collectors. The blue and green versions are the most desirable.

Model 75, circa mid-1920s, is a relatively small iron made by a stove company unaccustomed to producing light-weight products. The nickel-plated cast iron pedestal neck and extra thick high quality cast aluminum grids makes this petite cooker weigh in at an impressive 9 pounds. The company also made a four slice Model 77 swinger type toaster at this time which spins all four slices simultaneously-a fun gadget to toast with.

67

Excel Electric Company [1]
Muncy Indiana

In 1921 or 1922, Jack Reichart started a small manufacturing business at 1924 South Walnut Street, Muncie, Indiana, which he called Excel Electric Company. The firm manufactured moderately priced toasters (real ones and working toys-see ad), coffee pots, tea kettles, and a "Table Well" or what today is known as a "slow cooker" or "crock pot". The firm's corn popper, which could be purchased either electrified or as a stovetop model became its most popular product. Excel stovetop poppers are reputed to have accompanied English explorer Sir Hubert Wilkins and America's Admiral Richard Byrd on separate arctic expeditions in the late 1920's.

Excel sold many thousands of these corn poppers in electric or stove top form with either red or green handles. The crank is attached to a stiff wire stirring arm that sweeps the bottom of the kettle.
(Photo courtesy Michael Sheafe, www.ToasterCentral.com New York City)

A late 1940s city directory stated that the firm manufactured electric table lamps, electric corn poppers, barbecue machines, aluminum tea kettles, coffee makers, joining hardware for cooking utensils, steel stampings, sewing cases, and novelties. No mention is made of waffle irons and, in fact, the author has never seen any that may have been made by Excel Electric.

In 1949, a polio epidemic swept the country hitting Muncie, Indiana particularly hard. At that time, so-called "Iron Lungs" were used to assist those Polio victims that were so severely stricken that their breathing was impaired. The patient lay in a sealed metal cylinder with only their head exposed. Rhythmically varying the pressure in the chamber assisted the patient in expanding and compressing their lungs, something normally done by the muscles in the abdomen.

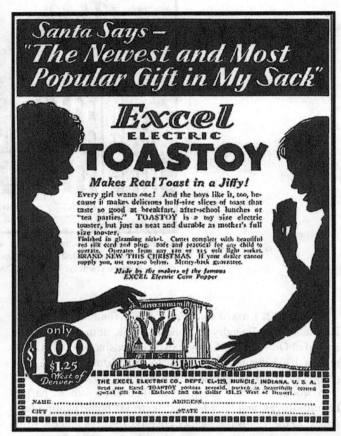

A 1920s ad for Excell's popular one dollar ($1.25 west of Denver) working "Toastoy" toy toaster. A child could toast two quarter-slices of bread and at the same time learn what the term "hot" meant.

A critical shortage of iron lungs prompted Jack Reichart to design an iron lung with the necessary pressure regulators that could be fabricated by nearly any metal shop from two fifty-five gallon steel drums and could be powered by a vacuum cleaner. Procuring empty alcohol drums saved by a nurse at a local hospital, Reichart and his twelve employees constructed numerous "Iron Lungs" testing and improved their design and sending plans to high school shops around Indiana. The heroic efforts of this little appliance company saved the lives of many children in the late 1940s. Unfortunately its founder didn't live to see the fruits of his labor or the conquest of Polio. Jack Reichart passed away in 1950 at age 64.

[1] All information and materials courtesy Michael Sheafe, New York City. (www.ToasterCentral.com)

Excel Incorporated

" Electro-Craft"

This Excel, not be confused with The Excel Electric Company of Muncie, Indiana (See Excel Electric Company), had facilities in Chicago in the 1930s and 1940s and was renamed Electro-Craft Corporation by the 1940s.

From the late 1930s to the late 1940s, the company manufactured several versions of a tray-mounted twin type waffle iron. The **Model W-50** "Brunchmaster" came with either varnished ribbed wood or dark bakelite handles, and appears at first glance to be just another inexpensive double unit mounted on a cheap tray. In actuality, the company spent its money, not on the product looks, but rather on its internal parts, and, as a result, created a very capable performer. Husky heating elements coupled with a sensitive sealed thermostat, gives this appliance the ability to make pairs of 4 ½ X 5 ¼ rectangular waffles quickly and consistently. With rounded corners, these waffles are perfect for heating in a toaster and eaten as a quick breakfast treat. The Model W-46 is the non-automatic version. Brunchmasters are fairly plentiful and are great appliances for everyday use.

The **Model W50** "Brunchmaster" is anything but a typical "Twin" unit of the late 1930s. Excel equipped it with a very expensive sealed thermostat, thus making it is one of the best performing irons of its kind ever produced. A later variant came with dark plastic handles instead of the varnished wood example pictured here. Some versions came with attractive amber-colored jeweled indicator windows while others were colorless. A Model W46 was the non-automatic version.

Finders Manufacturing Co.

This Chicago firm is best known for its broilers but in the late 1940s did produce a very utilitarian automatic waffle iron designated the Model 611 that was sold as the "Holliwood Waffler." This iron has a plain aluminum rectangular shell with generic looking Bakelite handles, control knob, and feet. It makes a 7-inch by 12-inch rectangular waffle in four sections. The company's sales slogan, as unimaginative as their waffler, was "When you buy a Holliwood you by the Best." Appliance collectors evidently like the "Holliwood" name or believe the sales pitch. Although the Model 611 is relatively plentiful, prices for it at this time usually exceed $75.00.

Firestone Tire & Rubber Co.

This well-known tire manufacturer expanded the inventory of its chain of neighborhood retail stores in the 1930s to include not only tires, but also housewares. By the 1950s, a shopper in a Firestone store could purchase everything from refrigerators and freezers, to stoves, washing machines, and a whole assortment of small appliances including vacuum cleaners, mixers, grills, toasters and waffle irons. Manufacture of these items was contracted to various makers. Samson United Corporation made a waffle iron for Firestone in the 1930s that resembled Samson's Model 331. There are very likely other irons by other manufacturers with Firestone labels.

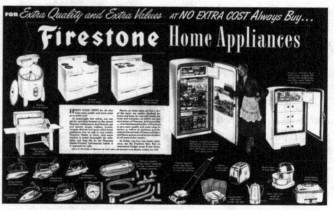

Close examination of this 1950 ad reveils that the small appliances sold by Firestone at this time included those made by Knapp-Monarch, Landers, Westinghouse, Toastmaster, Dormeyer, McGraw Edison & General Electric.

Fitzgerald Manufacturing Company [1]

"Star" "Empress" "Star-Rite" "Never Leak"

Model 528 sandwich grill circa 1920s, has handles and heating element parts borrowed from the company's waffle iron line (See the Model 538 waffle iron pictured on page 72). This was a clever way to reduce costs while adding to the product line. The designers gave no thought to maintenance when they added decorative cutouts to the base. They look great but spillage or overflows that can easily reach the interior are impossible to clean short of total disassembly.

Patrick J. Fitzgerald emigrated from Ireland in 1894 and found work as an apprentice machinist in the small western Connecticut industrial town of Torrington. By 1906 Fitzgerald saw an opportunity in the infant automobile industry and created The Fitzgerald Manufacturing Company to supply "Never Leak" gaskets to carmakers.

The auto industry prospered and so did Fitzgerald. By 1918 he opened a second plant in nearby Winsted and the company's product line was expanded to include truck horns and household electric appliances. By the late 1920s, the product line included fans, hairdryers, mixers, heating pads, hot plates, toasters, a sandwich grill, a juicer, flat irons, twenty different coffee percolators, urns, and several waffle irons. In 1927 "Never Leak" gaskets flew the Atlantic to Paris with Lindbergh in the engine of The Spirit of Saint Louis.

As with most firms, Fitzgerald suffered financial setbacks during the depression years. Its gasket division continued to make money over the years but the appliances did not and were eventually acquired by Son-Chief Electric. In 1975 the company was closed and reopened under bankruptcy protection as the Fitzgerald Gasket Company. It was sold in 1978

to the Tannetics Company of Erie, PA. which sold it to Harry Harlow in 1983. In 1986, when Harlow sold the firm's name, customer list, machinery, and dies to the Badger Cork & Manufacturing Company of Trevor, Wisconsin, Fitzgerald, after 80 years, ceased to exist.

Fitzgerald's appliance products were often uniquely styled and aimed at the medium to low end of the market. Beginning in the early 1920s, the company promoted heavily, to young married couples, what turned out to be a very popular line of waffle irons. The first was a solidly built small leg-mounted split cord model labeled the **"Star"**, which was soon superseded by a pedestal model of nearly identical design also labeled "Star".

By the late 1920s, the company was marketing waffle irons under both the "Star-Rite" and "Empress" names. A 1928 advertisement lists three sizes, the 7 ¼ inch "Family" model, the "Standard" model, and the 4 inch diameter "Junior" or "Individual" model which, according to an overzealous copy writer, was good, "for a hundred uses." The inexpensive "standard" model was sometimes labeled "Kraken Iron" or "Lightening". These petite toy-like units make a most

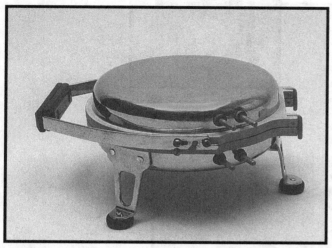

Fitzgerald's first model waffle iron, the "**Star**," circa early 1920s, isn't very stylish but is equipped with robust sealed heating elements and a unique two-position duel-purpose handle that could be used either to open the lid or to carry the iron. Like most early waffle irons of this period, a split power cord is required to connect both heating elements.

The company's second "**Star-Rite**" model waffle iron is a redesign of the first model "Star." The stylists simply replaced the legs of the first version with a pedestal-type base. The duel-purpose two-position lid handle is shown here in the carrying position.

Fitzgerld's second waffle iron model, the "**STAR-Rite**", is advertised in this 1923 ad for $9.00 . According to the copy, this little wonder cooks twice as fast as conventional non-electric cast iron models because both sides heat simultaneously. (November, 1923, *Good Housekeeping Magazine*)

71

This later "**Star-Rite**" model with an emerald green jeweled lid knob (some were sapphire blue), was the top-of-the line Fitzgerald waffle iron in the late 1920s. The tombstone-shaped "Wait for Eclipse" temperature gauge (insert) is unique but not well engineered. The diecast housing and steel internal pieces usually suffered damage from the steam generated during the cooking process. In addition, repeated heating and cooling often loosened the gauge's front plate retaining rivets, allowing the plate to fall off.

unusual round waffle, with a series of five concentric ridges rather than dimples. The **Model 538**, sold as the "Empress" model, was the company's most luxurious and came with a green or blue cut glass inlayed lid finial, and a unique eclipse-of-the-moon-type temperature indicator, which proclaimed, "Wait for Total Eclipse." The slightly less expensive Model 532 is identical except for a non-jeweled metal finial. The least expensive of this series is the Model 531, with plain metal finial and no temperature indicator.

When using the company's waffle makers, one is left with the distinct impression that they're better lookers than they are cookers. Rather than standard 660 watt heating elements, all but the first model irons were equipped with low capacity 550 or 580 watt asbestos covered heating elements which heat slowly, cook unevenly, and are prone to early failure from moisture-induced corrosion of the Nichrome wire. Most "Empress" models suffer further moisture damage to their stylish but poorly engineered die cast temperature indicator housing. The company's engine gaskets apparently worked better than their appliances, otherwise Lindbergh would have never made it into the history books.

Model 535 "Star-Rite Junior" (right) could easily be mistaken for a working child's toy when compared to the full size **Model 538**. The insert shows the unusual circular type pressed aluminum grid of the junior model. Although advertised as having a hundred uses (see ad next page) the author can only think of one.

---

[1] Historical materials courtesy Gail Kruppa, curator, The Torrington Historical Society, Torrington, Connecticut.

Forestek Plating & Mfg. Co.

"Du-All"

Forestek was located at 9607 Quincy Avenue, Cleveland in the late 1920s and early 1930s, and manufactured two models of a small multi-purpose type waffle iron that the firm called the "Du-All." The "Du-All" came with flat and dimpled interchangeable cast iron cooking grids and is equipped with expansion hinges that make it possible to use the contraption as either a sandwich grill or as a waffle iron. It creates old-fashioned style waffles much like those made by cast iron stovetop irons. The company claimed that by laying the lid back fully and installing the flat grids, the "Du-All" could be used as a double burner hot plate. Fat chance!

Forestek also manufactured an inexpensive rectangular leg-mounted sandwich grill with the same lid handle arrangement, raised lid decoration, and expansion hinges as was used on the "Du-All" pictured below. This grill was capable of heating two sandwiches side by side.

These cheaply made, crudely finished cookers could be purchased with nickel or chrome plating and with a green or black painted wood lid handle. The early examples were leg- mounted with slotted hinges and pull knob type handle. Later versions had a plain square pedestal base, rod-type hinges, and a horizontal lid handle fixed to a pair of curlicue brackets. These irons have primitive, barely adequate heating elements and dangerously exposed power wire connectors located in the base. They're great conversation pieces, but don't work well and must be used with caution due to the shock hazard present.

How about Waffles?

FOR that cozy hour after the theatre or the dance when he has brought you home . . . for Sunday's late breakfast with all the family there . . . for afternoon tea, or the weekly bridge party.. for the crowd on Sunday nights.

Waffles are so delightfully inti-

mate, somehow. They seem to fit in perfectly with so many happy occasions . . . just right for any hour of the day or night . . . light, crisp, delicious . . . with a subtle appeal to the appetite . . . and what is more important —the appetite of *man*.

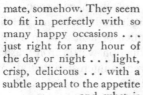

★

STAR-Rite waffle irons come in three sizes—the large family size, 7¼ inches in diameter, beautifully nickeled, $10.00. In Canada, $13.00. The standard size that is just right for serving four or

★

six—rustproof, and also in shining nickel finish, $9.00, in Canada $12.00. The Junior or individual iron for a hundred uses, $3.95, in Canada $4.95—all of them charming accessories to the smartest table.

STAR-Rite
ELECTRICAL NECESSITIES
Fitzgerald Manufacturing Company, Torrington, Conn.
Canadian Fitzgerald Company, 95 King Street East, Toronto, Ont.
Makers of Never-Leak Automotive Gaskets

This 1928 ad lists three sizes of Fitzgerald waffle irons. The large family size is priced at $10.00, the standard size is $9.00, and the "junior" model which, according to a very imaginative copywriter, "has a hundred uses," cost $3.95. The same writer suggested that whipping up a batch of waffles after an evening at the theater would be a nice romantic idea. I certainly hope he received a creative writing award for this ad.

(April, 1928, *Good Housekeeping Magazine*)

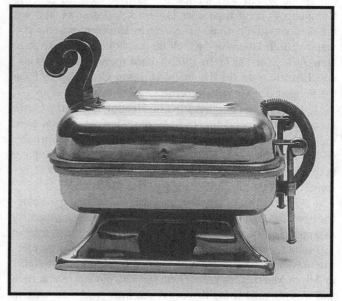

This is the more common of two versions of the "Du-All" grill/griddle/waffle iron. A leg mounted version was also produced. The curved lid handle acts as a support when the unit is opened fully and used as a pancake griddle or double hot plate.

General Electric Company

"Hotpoint"

Mr. Hotpoint is an odd little character in bright red "Long Johns" who appeared in GE advertising in the early 1930s. At that time the power industry began using "Ready Kilowatt.," a similar advertising character in the form of a lightening bolt.

During the 1870s and 1880s Thomas Edison was at his inventing zenith. The result was the creation of several separate companies including the Edison Lamp Company in Newark, New Jersey and the Edison Machine Works in Schenectady, New York. In 1889, Henry Villard, a German Emigrant and self- made financier, purchased and merged the various Edison enterprises giving the inventor cash and stock and putting him on the board of directors of the new enterprise which was named the Edison General Electric Company. A short time later Edison sold his stock and left the company to continue his career as an inventor at his private research laboratory which he had built in West Orange New Jersey, in 1887.[1] In 1892 Villard merged Edison General Electric with the Thomson-Houston Company to form the present day General Electric Company.[2]

In 1918, the Hughes Electric Heating Company (stove makers) and General Electric's heating devices section were merged into the Edison Electric Appliance Company (Hotpoint). In 1931, Edison Electric Appliance Company became Edison General Electric Company and in 1934 became the Hotpoint division of General Electric.

GE was one of the first companies involved in the electric appliance industry, producing an electric desk fan as early as 1889. The company produced an electric clothes iron in 1904 and is credited by some with producing the first electric toaster in 1909. General Electric had acquired the rights to Albert Marsh's Nichrome heating wire patents at that time and was not only using this improved heat producing wire in its toasters, but was also charging all other companies twenty-five cents per appliance for the right to use it in their products.

The first GE waffle iron may have been produced as a cast iron prototype model, around 1911. Close examination of a photo of it (reproduced on page 15) reveals a crude power plug arrangement, simple, off-the-shelf handle retaining hardware, and rather elaborate heat insulating spring-type feet. It is unlikely that this ever became a production model. Due to the very thin construction of the lid of this probable prototype, the company engineers were most likely experimenting with the newly acquired nickel-chrome alloy wire and using it in ribbon form, sandwiched between insulating sheets of mica or asbestos. In all likelihood, the company's first production waffle iron wasn't produced until after GE acquired an interest in the Edison Electric Appliance Company in 1918.

Over the years General Electric produced waffle irons with styling that ranged from mediocre to classic, and a look that generally could be categorized as middle-of-the-road conservative. However, two late 1930s examples stand out as styling classics. The automatic **Model 129Y199**, and the non-automatic **Model 119W4**. Both were designed by August Propernick in 1939, and epitomize late deco styling at its finest. Each is well made and were so popular that GE marketed variants of both well into the 1950s. The company's Model 149T81 toaster with it's cream colored plastic trim is the attractive matching piece to waffle iron **Model 129Y199**.

Except for very early models, most GE waffle irons were made and sold in great numbers and many have survived in good condition. This abundance of supply keeps prices low for most GE models. Many examples made before the 1960s are solid, easy to use appliances, which, in good condition, make a practical addition to any modern kitchen.

---

[1] Edison sold the rights to his name to numerous companies to which he was in no other way connected, and continued working at his West Orange laboratory until his death in 1931.

[2] Villard's fascinating life is detailed in an excellent biography written by his granddaughter Villard de Borchgrave entitled *Villard, The Life and Times of an American Titan*: See bibliography.

General Electric Continued:

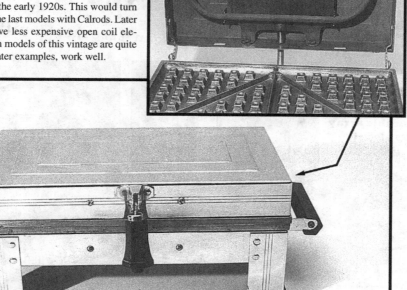

Model **149G22** grill/waffle iron circa mid-1930s, has sealed Calrod heating elements (insert) introduced by the company in the early 1920s. This would turn out to be be one of the last models with Calrods. Later GE units would have less expensive open coil elements. Combination models of this vintage are quite heavy, and unlike later examples, work well.

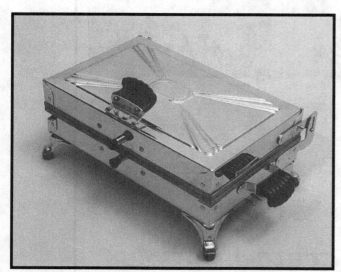

Grill/waffle iron **Model 119G19,** circa early 1930s, came with interchangeable cooking grids and scalloped handles in either ivory or black plastic. The upturned lid handle appears bent but was designed as a support, necessary when the lid is fully opened in the grill mode. The knobs located on the front are spring loaded grid release pulls.

A recipe book like this which featured one waffle concoction for each week of the year, accompanied every waffle iron that left the GE factories for over 20 years. This example with the NRA seal dates from the 1933-35 era. The blue eagle was the symbol of Roosevelt's National Recovery Administration, one of many agencies FDR created to try to pull the country out of the depression. The eagle could be used by businesses that conformed to certain federal labor and wage guidelines. The NRA was declared unconstitutional by an ultra-conservative Supreme Court in 1935.

A Christmas ad circa 1936 features the "**Raleigh**" waffle iron with ivory colored handles ($9.95) and the rather outdated looking "**Gem Box Cooker**" grill/waffle iron ($6.95). Electric heating pads like the one featured at lower left were not a new idea even in 1936, since they had been marketed since the teens. This one however, is somewhat unique. It came in a box disguised as a book. You could I suppose, hide it from heating pad burglars more easily that way. (December, 1936, *Esquire Magazine*)

It is difficult to distinguish this early 1930s GE **Model 119Y180** with Butterscotch Catalin handles from its Manning-Bowman contemporaries (see pages 103-104). Several parts are directly interchangeable between brands suggesting that GE may have contracted some production to Manning-Bowman or vice-versa. All are very good quality and make thick Belgiam-style waffles with large dimples.

The striking black accents and ivory-colored Catalin plastic handles of **Model 129Y183** sets this early 1930s automatic iron a step above the ordinary. Unfortunately the paint is easily damaged and most no longer look as nice as this never-used example.

General Electric continued:

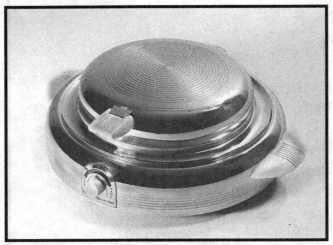

Model 119Y198, a small high quality non-automatic twin unit from the late 1930s, is a nice iron with which to make small square waffles that can be frozen and conveniently reheated later in either a toaster or microwave. This model like most GE products is plentiful.

Top quality materials, construction, and plating have contributed to a large survival rate for the early 1940s **Model 129Y199** pictured here. The handles are ivory-colored plastic. This is, in the author's opinion, one of the best waffle irons ever made. The easy-to-see illuminated red temperature indicator arrow above the control knob make them a pleasure to use. **Model 149Y199** is the identical post WWII version.

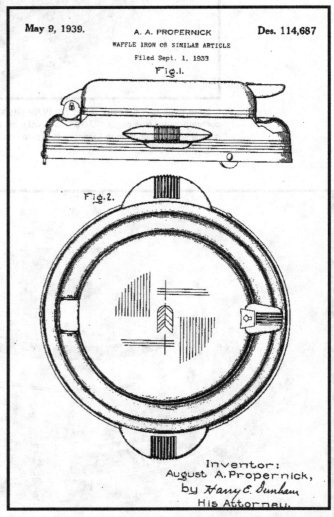

Possibly the most popular GE waffle iron ever, the non-automatic **Model 119W4 "Westport"** with brown plastic handles, was made from the late 1930s to the late 1940s. Model 119Y194, a later black handle version was produced well into the 1950s. Rare examples can be found with the same ivory-colored handles used on the Model 129Y199. This was likely the result of a shortage of brown handles during a production run. The "Westport" is a nice quality iron that works well but lacks an easy-to-read temperature indicator. The little slide indicator built into the handle is nearly useless.

This is the original 1939 design patent drawings by August Propernick for **Model 119W4** pictured at left. Only early examples of the iron were produced as drawn with no venting slits and the banding around their circumference. (Drawing courtesy Nancy Conway)

General Mills

"Betty Crocker"

During World War II, General Mills, an old established cereal grains company with the "Betty Crocker" logo, had become involved in war goods manufacturing. At the end of the war the firm was suddenly saddled with excess manufacturing capacity which prompted management to come up with some way of utilizing the machinery. In 1945 it was decided that in order to keep to the manufacturing facilities busy and to cash in on the post-war demand for consumer goods, "Betty Crocker" would enter the appliance business.

Production began in 1946 with a small pressure cooker and a clothes iron. A mixer, a coffee percolator, a toaster, a deep fat fryer, and the Model GM-6A combination grill/waffle iron had been added to the product line by 1952. The author believes that McGraw-Electric made all of the General Mills waffle irons. In 1954, after evaluating the return on investment, General Mills management decided that the firm's resources could be better utilized elsewhere and the entire appliance division was sold to McGraw-Electric. McGraw labeled some 6A irons with the McGraw-Electric as well as the Manning-Bowman label(see page 109 for photograph). In addition two versions were made for Penney's with the "Penncrest" label and designated either 4888 or 4894.

The Model GM-6A grill/waffle iron and its variants are well made, large, square box shaped units, typical of most post war waffle bakers produced by several other appliance makers at that time. The reversible grids can be used to grill on or to produce a waffle of over 100 square inches. They are fairly plentiful and, in good condition, can be a nice work-a-day appliance.

Gold Seal Electric Company

All that is known about this Cleveland, Ohio firm is from the examination of three surviving examples of the company's waffle irons. All are small, nickel-plated pedestal models, dating from the early or mid-1920s. Two have no model number, while the third is stamped **Model H-1084**. This example is identical to the unnumbered models except for the addition of decorative fretwork in the pedestal and a slightly smaller external wiring conduit. These irons make very thin crispy waffles, with surfaces that are mostly dimple. Each is fitted with either red or black painted wood handles of a complex but technologically crude design, unique to this manufacturer. Counting various screws, washers and pieces of wood, each handle consists of a nine separate pieces. The heating elements are of a common early design, consisting of ribbon Nichrome wire, wrapped on a mica sheet, and sandwiched between sheets of asbestos. Manufacturers found this type of element both slow to heat and prone to early failure from cooking moisture damage. Most abandoned the design by the late 1920s. Gold Seal waffle irons are scarce to rare and are nice examples of early appliance technology.

Great Northern Products Co.

"Tri-Plex" "Quality Brand"

The Great Northern Products Company, of Chicago, was a marketing organization that, in the 1920s and 1930s, sold the products of various manufacturers with Great Northern's own "Tri-Plex" or "Quality Brand" label. Knapp-Monarch, Landers Frary and Clark, Wear-Ever, and Bersted were four of the known original equipment manufacturers for Great Northern. Occasionally an item was labeled Great Northern Manufacturing Company.

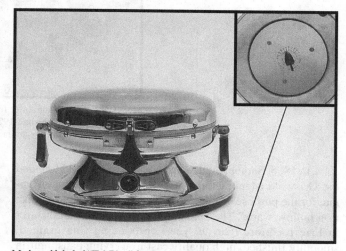

Made and labeled "**Tri-Plex**" for Great Northern Products Co. by Knapp Monarch, this early automatic model has the temperature control hidden under the pedestal base (insert). Hiding the control might be a nice styling touch but it makes adjusting the temperature difficult when the iron is hot. The oversized red jeweled indicator window in the pedestal is both attractive and easy to see.

This early 1920s Gold Seal unit has unique wood handles consisting of three pieces of machined and enameled wood and six pieces of hardware to hold them together. This iron is slow to reach operating temperature but is a good cooker. Most early models like are best purchased as a collectible rather than for regular use.

Griswold Manufacturing Company [1]
"The Line That's Fine at Cooking Time"

Model 38E is a no-nonsense, functional looking, leg-mounted waffle iron typical of the mid-1920s. It came with a permanently attached cord and a heavy armored wire conduit visible near the hinge.

In 1865, Samuel Seldon and Matthew Griswold founded the Griswold Manufacturing Company in Erie, Pennsylvania, for the purpose of making what they called, "extra finish iron hollow ware." The company was a major manufacturer in Erie for more than 90 years, producing fine grained, smoothly finished, high quality cast iron frying pans, muffin pans, griddles, and waffle irons. By World War I, Griswold, in a joint venture with the Aluminum Company of America, produced the first cast aluminum tea pot which proved very successful and was soon followed by numerous other cast aluminum cookware products.

The company was controlled and run by the Griswold family until it was sold to a New York investment syndicate in 1946. McGraw-Edison acquired Griswold in 1957 and two years later sold it to The Randall Company, a Cincinnati car parts maker. Randall combined Griswold with Griswold's long-time rival, Wagner Manufacturing Company, which had been acquired by Randall in 1952. In 1959, Griswold/Wagner was sold to Textron who, in 1969, sold the division to The General Housewares Corporation.

One of Griswold's earliest and most popular products was its cast iron stovetop waffle irons which the company continued to produce well into the 1930s. With the widespread use of electricity in urban areas by the mid-1920s, the firm saw a new business opportunity and entered the electrical appliance arena with a line of products that included, hot plates, ovens, deep fryers, and sandwich grills intended for the commercial market.

Success with its commercial electric products prompted the company, in the late 1920s, to produce the Model 1-8-E electric waffle iron for household use. This small, cast aluminum, leg-mounted iron was followed by the undecorated pedestal Model 2-8-E, the leg-mounted **Model 3-8-E,** and

pedestal Model 4-8-E. A 1931 company product catalog explained that these irons are "totally devoid of decoration to allow ease of cleanup." One wonders if the company's management may have been experiencing pricing pressure from depression era competitors and was simply reducing manufacturing costs to remain in the sales race.

Two variants of the **Model 2-8-E** may exist. One version has conventional cast aluminum grids, while a second, illustrated in a 1931 *Gage Encyclopedia of Electrical Products*, shows this model with a hearts and stars grid pattern, similar to one of Griswold's popular cast iron stove-top models. Due to the lack of surviving company records, it is difficult to state with certainty when Griswold stopped making consumer grade electric waffle irons. To date no models newer than about 1935 have surfaced. The company produced at least twenty-five commercial model waffle irons for restaurants into the 1950s.

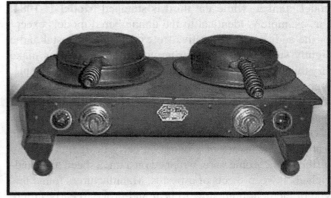

This mostly cast iron commercial **Model 150-8-E** is typical of restaurant equipment of the late 1920s. It has individual three-position temperature control switches and large green indicator lights easily visible to a busy short-order cook across a large commercial kitchen.

Griswold continued:

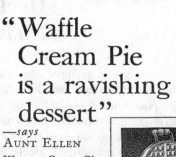

"Waffle Cream Pie is a ravishing dessert"

—says
AUNT ELLEN

WAFFLE Cream Pie piles up five waffles high, is filled with a special creaminess, topped with powdered sugar, and cut in wedges like a layer cake. Or the cream waffles themselves make fine servings, baked lightly on the Griswold Electric Waffle Baker. The Griswold gives them a delicacy in a fast, even way. Or if it is simple, hot butter-waffles you like, the Griswold bakes these beside you fresh at the table. As soon as you are ready for the next one, the next one is ready for you.

The Griswold Electric Baker is all simplicity. No ornaments of any sort. It bakes without need of turning the waffles—makes them crisscross, or bakes

How to make the mallowy cream, and how to make the very delicate waffles for the Waffle Cream Pie, are told you in detail in Aunt Ellen's recipe. Address "Aunt Ellen," Dept. E, The Griswold Kitchen, Erie, Penna.

FREE — *"The Aunt Ellen Booklet on Waterless Cooking"—with fifty famous recipes by Aunt Ellen. Among them, the recipes for Old Virginia White Meal Waffles . . . Devil's Food Waffles with Whipped Cream . . . Waffles with rice and nuts! Write for the booklet.*

four crisp hearts and a star. No grease—no smoke or smell. It is all *clean* cooking. And if you follow the easy instructions, no waffle ever sticks. Use the Baker often. The grids are pure cast aluminum, and thoroughly sturdy. Fully guaranteed. The Electric Baker comes in the design illustrated; and in a model lower in price, in which identical heating units are used. At electrical shops; hardware, department, house-furnishing stores. The Griswold Mfg. Co., Dept. E, Erie, Pennsylvania.

GRISWOLD

★   Reg. U. S. GRISWOLD Pat. Off.

© 1928

According to this 1928 ad, **Model 2-8-E** was "All simplicity. No ornamentation of any sort." Claiming that this made them easier to keep clean, the copy didn't mention that it also made them less costly to produce. This model could be purchased with either conventional grids or hearts and stars grids similar to those available for years on the company's cast iron stove-top line of waffle irons. (1928 *Good Housekeeping Magazine*)

The following are commercial models listed in the company's catalog # E39 from the late 1930s

110-8-E	160-12-E	360-A-12	660-8-E
110-12-E	310-A-8	610-8-E	660-12-E
150-8-E	310-A-12	610-12-E	1052 *
150-12-E	350-A-8	650-8-E	1066 *
160-8-E	360-A-8	650-12-E	

* Ice Cream Waffle Baker

A 1946 company issued catalog lists the following two commercial units:

Model 3112	A rectangular double unit
Model 3208	A round double unit

Griswold electric waffle irons are well made, plain-Jane affairs that were not made in great numbers. Due to the Griswold name and their relative scarcity, the company's products command higher than average prices from both appliance collectors and Griswold aficionados.

---

[1] Certain historical and model information courtesy David G. Smith, co-author of *The Book of Griswold & Wagner*- See bibliography.

Heatmaster
(Sears Roebuck & Company)

In the 1940s, Sears Roebuck replaced the "Heatmaster" label for their kitchen appliances with the "Kenmore" name. Although Sears manufactured some of their own products over the years, "Heatmaster" and "Kenmore" appliances were made by a number of manufacturers including Bersted, Chicago Electric, Dominion, Electrahot, Manning-Bowman, Porcelier, Samson United, and Whirlpool among others. See each of these individual manufacturers in the price guide for dates and values of "Heatmaster" and "Kenmore" items. See also "Sears Roebuck & Company" in this company histories section.

Hecla
(Australian)

Only one example of a waffle iron manufactured by this Australian company has surfaced to date. It is a hefty 8½-pound nickel-plated flat topped round pedestal type with no model number. The pedestal base is cast iron and resembles an old style oil lamp base. The nametag affixed to the front of the body is inscribed "Hecla, Made in Australia, 240 volts 600 watts. The company logo, also on the tag, is a profile of a smoking volcano. The heating elements are heavy strip wires insulated between sheets of mica and are very similar to those employed in Westinghouse units dating from the early 1920s.

This circa 1920s Australian made **Hecla** requires a split power cord and 240 volts to operate. The very narrow pedestal neck prevents heat transfer to the cast iron base, but it and the primitive lid handle bracket are both mechanically weak. The over-sized brass lid hinge on the other hand is excessively heavy and robust. The cast iron base looks suspiciously like an old style oil lamp base. I suspect the manufacturer was manufacturing such lamps before diversifying into electric appliances. When new the iron would have been entirely nickel-plated. Unfortunately this example has over the years lost most of its plating.

82

Hibbard, Spencer, Bartlett & Company
"Lady Hibbard" "O.V.B"

William Gold Hibbard
1826-1903

Franklin F. Spencer
1817-1890

Adolphus C. Bartlett
1845-1922

Charles H. Conover
1847-1915

Hibbard, Spencer, Bartlett and Company was not an appliance manufacturer but rather a large wholesale hardware distributor that, beginning in the 1920s, sold a great quantity of electric kitchen appliances under the "Lady Hibbard" brand name. I've included the history of the company here since, like Sears and Wards, this firm had a significant influence on the marketing of small electric appliances to the American consumer during the first half of the Twentieth Century.

The history of this wholesaler is an interesting story and should be called "The Company of Characters." William Gold Hibbard, the company founder was a native of Cortland, New York and son of a general store keeper. He moved to the Chicago area as a young man in 1849 and worked there for five years as a clerk in the Clarke-Stimson & Blair hardware store before opening a wholesale hardware business of his own in 1855 in a co-partnership with a Nelson Tuttle and a George Gray. Tuttle, Hibbard & Company prospered immediately, capitalizing on the explosive growth of Chicago fueled by the westward expansion of the country due to the California gold rush. The firm started in a small four-story building at 45 South Water Street. Two years later the first of several fires that were to plague the business destroyed this first building. The firm promptly resumed business and, even in the middle of the economic panic of 1857, moved to larger quarters at 32 Lake Street. Three years later the business had outgrown that building and moved to an even larger building at nearby 62 Lake Street.

While at the company's original address, Hibbard had become friends with Franklin Spencer who worked in the office of a stove company next door. The two men had much in common, since Spencer too was from western New York and was also a son of a general store owner. Hibbard bought

out Tuttle in 1867 and formed a new partnership with Spencer. Tuttle, Hibbard & Company became Hibbard & Spencer and its owners moved it into a fourth and still larger building on Michigan Avenue.

Hibbard and Spencer were both somewhat eccentric and in surprisingly complementary ways. Even the men's shaving habits were complimentary. Just look at their portraits. Hibbard was the autocrat of the pair while Spencer was fun loving, outgoing, and prone to making a joke out of almost any situation. After years of working together Spencer discovered that Hibbard had purchased a burial plot in a prominent Chicago cemetery. Spencer promptly bought a plot across the driveway from Hibbard's. He then informed his business partner that as close as they were in business, they would be even closer in death. Then with a big smile Spencer told Hibbard that he was about to have a contractor construct a tunnel under the road so that they would be able to get together more easily later.

Spencer's outgoing personality made him a natural salesman. He became the firm's marketing manager while Hibbard remained general manager and ran the day-to-day affairs of the business, often in a most unique manner. Fred Kelly, in his 1930 book *Seventy-five Years of Hibbard Hardware*, recounts the following about Hibbard. "He was czar and did what he pleased without having to hold conferences." Kelly continues, " Since his word was law, Hibbard sometimes used his power in ways that were amazing and amusing-almost as if he were not merely head of a business but patriarch of a tribe. If there appeared to be too many employes (sic) bearing the same name, and therefore possible confusion in payrolls or other records, Hibbard simply changed somebody's name to whatever struck his fancy. If there were an excess of

Frank Andersons, one of these might discover that he had become Frank Johnson. Two employees were named Frederickson. Hibbard ordered that one of these, employed as a carpenter should be known thenceforth, as Fred the Carpenter- though his first name was George." Sometimes employees would adopt their Hibbard name at home, which for a few heirs caused considerable legal problems later.

The Hibbard and Spencer building, located on Michigan Avenue, was quite close to Chicago's baseball park and the roof of the building made an ideal location to view games for free. Upon returning to work one fine Fall afternoon, Hibbard was surprised to find the place almost entirely deserted. He learned that nearly everyone had gone to the roof to watch the final innings of one of the closing games of the season. Hibbard quietly climbed the steep flight of steps leading to a trap door through which the crowd had gained access to the roof-and locked the door! He left his employees trapped on the roof long after the finish of the game and in fact forgot about them totally. By the merest chance he remembered to release his prisoners just before leaving for home. It was fortunate that he did. That night, October 7, 1871, the great Chicago fire occurred and the Hibbard & Spencer building was totally destroyed.

What little that was saved before the building burned was removed to Hibbard's home and business was conducted from there until a new facility could be constructed. A young clerk in the firm by the name of A.C Bartlett was instrumental in the business's recovery. His persuasive letter writing style convinced many suppliers to stick with the firm during the rebuilding process when Hibbard had little cash flow. The fire turned out to be a boon to the company. Demand for tools and hardware was immense during the rebuilding of the city and Hibbard & Spencer were there to meet that demand. After the fire, the company continued to grow and in 1877 its limited profit sharing plan dating from 1868 was expanded to include all junior members of the firm. As a result the name of the company was changed to Hibbard, Spencer & Company.

Adolphus Clay Bartlett, like Hibbard and Spencer, was from western New York but wasn't quite as idiosyncratic as his senior partners. He was however the stereotypical American success story. He went to work for the firm at age nineteen dusting shelves in the tinware department. He had what today is referred to as a "Type A" personality. Early on he set

Hibbard Spencer & Company warehouse burning during the great Chicago fire of October 7, 1871. No lives were lost but the building and most of the inventory were totally destroyed. All of the drawings in this section were commisiioned by the company in 1930 and appear in a book commemorating 75 years of the company's history.

his goals at the firm quite high and worked hard to achieve them. For years he was usually first in the door in the morning and the last to leave at night. From shelf dusting, Bartlett became a clerk, then a salesman, sales manager, and in January, 1882 Secretary of the company. The firm's name was changed to Hibbard, Spencer, Bartlett & Company and would not change again for another eighty years. Bartlett the toiler continued to rise in the business becoming vice-president, president and in 1914 was the first to occupy the newly created position of chairman of the board. Not bad for someone who literally started out sweeping floors. Bartlett, who didn't leave his hyperactivity at work, was well known in the Chicago area for his active involvement in several educational and charitable organizations and relief societies.

Another great character and the last business czar at Hibbard was Charles H. Conover. He was a man of small stature who suffered an inferiority complex because of it most of his life. He was stern, severe, and demanding, but to everyone displayed an unwavering sense of justice and fair play. He, like the three senior partners, came from western New York. He began his working career as a schoolteacher but soon found more agreeable work as a hardware salesman. His job entailed travel to Chicago where, shortly after the great fire of 1871, Hibbard hired him as a buyer. He was responsible for creating Hibbard's purchasing department and making it into one of the largest of its kind in the country. He always looked at the long-range business picture and had an "I'll show you" attitude. This gave him great success as a buyer. Falling prices never worried him. One of his favorite

Hibbard, Spencer, Bartlett continued:

expressions was: "They can't reduce prices faster than I can buy goods." In the late 1890s a price war occurred between nail manufacturers, reducing the price of kegs of nails drastically. Every time the price dropped, Conover bought nails. After the company's warehouse was filled with all the nails it could hold, Conover rented basements up and down Lake Street and filled them with nails too. After the manufactures stopped the price war and doubled their prices, Conover had in stock for Hibbard, Spencer, Bartlett & Company estimated to have been over a million kegs of nails that he could now sell for less than anyone else. A similar situation arose a few years later during a tinware price war. Conover accumulated hundreds of railcars filled with pots, pans, plates, and cookie sheets.

Conover followed Bartlett up the corporate ladder at the firm. Conover was a compulsive reader all his life and for years had a standing order at a Chicago bookstore to send him any book in which they thought he might be interested. Comparatively late in life he discovered that books he liked were cluttered with Latin phrases he didn't understand. His feelings of inadequacy kicked in, and busy as he was, he took up the study of Latin at age 60 so that he could translate the phrases. He died suddenly nine years later in 1915, shortly after becoming president of the firm.

In 1932, Hibbard, Spencer, Bartlett and Company, which had used "OVB" (Our Very Best) as a Trade mark for years, introduced a new brand name to America which they called "True Value" Hardware. The firm continued in business with that brand until 1962 when John Cotter & Company purchased the hardware part of Hibbard and its "True Value" brand name. Hibbard, Spencer, Bartlett & Company, once a giant of the hardware business ended up a forgotten real estate operation.

The company's facilities on Lake Street, Chicago, circa 1930. Employees (some on roller skates) processed all orders within 3 hours and ten minutes of receipt-an amazing feat without computers or automated conveyor systems.

From the teens onward, Hibbard, Spencer, Bartlett & Company were a major distributor of electric appliances and marketed them under the "Lady Hibbard" name. In the 1930s Dominion Electric designed a number of waffle irons models exclusively for Hibbard, which were intended for the high-end appliance market. Two pictured here are of normal Dominion quality with very striking ceramic lid inserts. They were marketed during the depression when few families had the extra cash to be able to afford such luxurious goods and today are quite scarce.

Dominion made Model 344 Grill (top) and **Model 595** waffle iron (left) with matching ceramic lid inserts could be purchased from Hibbard dealers in the early 1930s as a "Lady Hibbard" set. The cobalt blue and silver striped inserts with delicate flower decals make these real eye catchers. Dominion Electric made versions of these with all steel lids for their own dealers.

Jacks Evans Manufacturing Co.

"Aunt Sarah"

Only a single product of this Saint Louis manufacturer has surface. It is a late 1920s sandwich grill that resembles a small, round, low profile waffle iron. Recesses cast into the otherwise flat grill surfaces leave markings in the bread as it is grilled of the four suits of cards. Obviously intended for use during card game gatherings, the grill has "Another Aunt Sarah's Product" stamped on its bottom.

Justrite Electric Mfg. Co.

"Colonial Tourist"

Records for this Minneapolis company cannot be found but I strongly suspect that Dominion Electric, also of Minneapolis, purchased Justrite in the mid-1920s and until about 1930 operated it as a separate division. In the late 1920s Dominion stamped its Model #67, a full sized pedestal unit, with the "Justrite" name. Justrite, the firm or the Dominion subdivision, produced at least three different waffle iron models during the late 1920s and early 1930s. **Model 700** and Model 701 are nickel plated low profile irons with 5½ inch cooking grids that produce thin round "desert" or "party" size waffles. Could their diminutive size and the name "Colonial Tourist" stamped on the bottom, suggest the possibility that this was a travel-type waffle iron? **Model JW-1111** pictured, is a pedestal model of conventional size with a large easy to read temperature gauge and distinctive deco designs embossed in the lid. It is also equipped with stock Dominion handles. All non-pedestal Justrite irons were slow to reach operating temperature and the base of each became quite hot. **Models 700** and 701 are, in fact, capable of damaging heat sensitive surfaces.

Another variant of Justrite **Model 700**, this time photographed with a five dollar bill to illustrate its tiny size. Ity-bitty waffles anyone?

"**Justrite Style 67**," made by Dominion in the late 1920s after Dominion had acquired Justrite but before it dropped the Justrite name from its product line. This example has green painted wood handles.

This very petite Justrite **Model 700** iron is labeled "**Colonial Tourist**". Was it intended to be stuffed in a suitcase and used as a traveling waffle iron? When in use, the base becomes very hot and may damage heat sensitive surfaces. A second version has a black painted base. These are often mistaken for a children's toys but were intended for serious adult useage.

Justrite/Dominion **Model JW-111** from the late 1920s is a typical pedestal model of this era except that during use the base becomes uncharacteristically hot. A second version with an octagonally segmented top was also produced.

Knapp-Monarch Company [1]
"Therm-A-Hot" "Lady Dover" "Hostess"

Andrew Knapp founded A.S. Knapp and Company in the early 1920s to sell the "Knapp Cap," a device used to train a kid's hair to hold a pompadour shape. Founded as a sales organization in Saint Louis, the company soon acquired a Kansas City luggage manufacturer and marketed an inexpensive line of suitcases through chain and department stores and mail order houses. In 1926, Earnest Johnson, president of the Monarch Company (see *Monarch Company*) of Webster City, Iowa, approached Knapp in the hope of using Knapp's sales organization to sell Monarch home appliances. An agreement was reached that turned out to be quite lucrative for both parties. In January, 1929 Knapp and Johnson merged their companies to form The Knapp-Monarch Company. Knapp became president and Johnson vice president of the new organization. With the merger, the company's headquarters was located in Saint Louis, with luggage manufacturing in Kansas City, Missouri, and appliances manufacturing in Webster City, Iowa. In January, 1931 all manufacturing was consolidated at a new plant in Belleville, Illinois.

Knapp-Monarch acquired several companies in the mid-1930s including electric motor manufacturer Galvin Electric and flat iron maker Dover Manufacturing. In 1938 the firm also purchased the Sparklet Company. In the mid-1950s, to expand its housewares product line, Knapp-Monarch purchased all of the tooling used for the NESCO product line from the National Enameling and Stamping Company and the tooling of the Finders Manufacturing Company, makers of the "Holliwood" waffle irons and broilers.

Although Johnson died barely two years after the 1929 merger, Andrew Knapp ran the company until his death in 1961. In 1969 Knapp-Monarch became a division of the Hoover Company and Andrew's son Robert S. Knapp supervised operations of the Knapp-Monarch division for Hoover.

In the early 1920s, while running Monarch, Earnest Johnson invented the "Therm-A-Jug," a device to keep hot food hot and cold food cold. This was soon followed by the "Therm-A-Magic" percolator which sold for $12.50, two models of non-automatic toasters priced at $1.50 and $2.50, two models of the "Therm-A-Hot" table stove, and three "Therm-A-Hot" model waffle irons designated **960**, 961, and 965. (A second Model 965 was produced in the late 1930s.) All of these products were sold under the Knapp-Monarch name after the 1929 merger. Beginning in 1936, the company marketed some of its products under the "Lady Dover" name.

Through the years, the company's electrical housewares were designed for the low to mid-priced segment of the market with many carrying brand labels of various store chains. The waffle irons, with a few exceptions, often look inexpensive and plain. **Models 967** and 968 have decidedly interest-

ing deco styling. The **Model 960** (sometimes labeled simply "Therm-A-Hot" or "Hostess") is interesting for no other reason than it's diminutive size. It's 8 ½ inch overall diameter and tiny 300 watt heating elements allowed the unit to make a "party size" or "desert" waffle just 5 ¼ inches across.

Model 960 photograhed with a dollar bill for size comparison. These tiny irons required smaller easier-to-manufacture heating elements than those required for full sized units. They were popular for a short period during the 1920s but lost favor when consumers realized how much additional work was required to produce an adequate supply of waffles. Today they make nice decorator pieces.

Knapp-Monarch is the only known manufacturer to have produced a quad waffle iron, the Model 980-0. It was manufactured for only a short time in the late 1930s and early 1940s. At first glance it looks like a conventional wood handled tray mounted twin unit of the period, but closer examination reveals that each cooking unit is actually a small pair of stacked units. The operator, if he is a trained juggler, can make four small party sized waffles simultaneously in this contraption.

Cooking performance of Knapp-Monarch irons varies from mediocre to very good, depending on the model. Except for very early examples that are historically important and somewhat scarce, most models of Knapp-Monarch waffle irons are common and command low prices in the collector market.

[1] Earnest Johnson materials, courtesy, Ketta Lubberstedt, Reference Libraian, the Kendall Young Library, Webster City, Iowa.

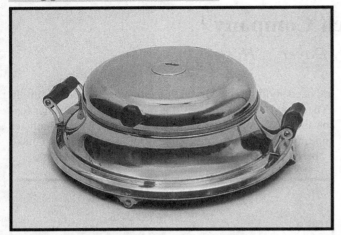

Model 967 was made shortly after the Knapp and Monarch merger in 1929. Because the base becomes quite hot during use, taller than normal feet were necessary to elevate the units away from heat sensitive surfaces.

Marked only "Faultless Appliance Company," this is actually a Knapp-Monarch product dating from the early 1940s. K-M also made a twin model at this time for "Faultless with the same lid and handle design.

Model 29-150 with a temperature control on top, is a typically large, square, late 1940s iron. A half-sized rectangular version (Model 29-515) and a round version (Model 29-501) were also made using the same handles and temperature control.

It was 1949 when this ad appeared and 15 years since Claudette Colbert made *It Happened One Night,* with Clark Gable. Knapp-Monarch used her and several other movie personalities to hawk their appliance line in the late 1940s. This ad gave Claudette a chance to plug her latest movie, *Bride For Sale.* The **Model 29-510** waffle iron in the ad turned out to be more successful than the movie.

Landers, Frary & Clark

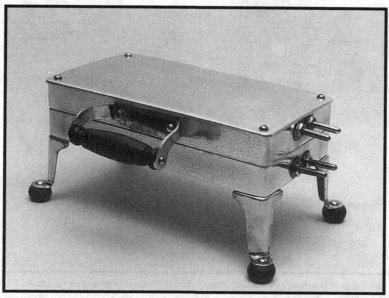

Model E931 was the first in a series of small, high quality, rectangular waffle irons manufactured by Landers from the late-teens to the early 1930s. The grids and body shells are one piece polished aluminum castings each with a flat aluminum cover and a sheet mica heating element inside. More refined later models pictured on the following pages, have nickel-plated stamped brass housings and improved heating elements. The cute feet are painted wood knobs. Some of these irons are found with the lid handle sloped downward like this example while most have their handle oriented upward. I suspect they were installed either way at the whim of the production foremen or may have been reinstalled differently by owners at some point. The legs slide off for ease of cleaning.

In 1832 at age 21, George M. Landers went to work in New Britain, Connecticut, as an apprentice to Josiah Dewey who owned a small foundry there. By 1842 he was in partnership with his former boss and their firm Dewey and Landers was manufacturing small metal hardware products such as furniture castors and cabinet latches. Dewey died in 1847 and Landers ran the business by himself until 1853 when he created a new partnership with one Levi Smith. The pair formed a stock company under the name of Landers & Smith Manufacturing Company. The firm expanded its product line to include window and show case hardware, railroad car trim items, and baby buggies. Landers & Smith prospered and in 1862, acquired Frary, Clark & Company. The combination became Landers, Frary & Clark.

By the end of the civil war, the Landers, Frary and Clark product line included scales, balances, faucets, molasses gates (valves), screws, wrenches, harness straps and fittings, meat hooks, and metal toys. Five years later it had also become one of the largest cutlery companies in the world. The firm continued to grow and add to its product line, adopting the "Universal" trade name in the 1890s along with the slogan "The trade mark known in every home." Indeed, by the turn of the century the "Universal" name was on everything from hatchets to ice skates and mousetraps to meat grinders.

By the mid-1920s, the Landers work force would peak at over 3000 employees. By this time the firm was manufacturing over 4000 separate items and offered major appliances including water heaters, washing machines, and electric ranges. It was estimated at the time that at least one "Universal" product was in 60% of all American homes. A few of the firm's products were so popular they took on lives of their own. For example, The "Universal Identical" food chopper, introduced in 1897, remained in production nearly unchanged until 1955.

Landers weathered the depression years as well as the other large appliance makers and in 1941 spent $2,000,000 to retool for defense work. It manufactured everything from mess kits to bayonets and artillery shell fuses during the war. In 1945 the company spent an additional $3,000,000 to convert its plants back to peacetime production.

This two-page ad illustrates the wide range of electrical goods available by the late 1920s from Landers Frary & Clark. Top left is waffle iron **Model E9914** for $9.95; lower left is the "**Marie Antoinette**" **Model E9574** for $14.95. At bottom right is the "Oven Cooker", an early insulated crock pot or slow cooker which could be unplugged and carried to work for a hot meal. (June, 1929, *Saturday Evening Post Magazine*)

In the 1950s the firm sold off the cutlery and major appliance divisions and purchased several other manufacturers including the Standard Products Company, the Dazy Corporation, and Ever-Bright Limited of Canada. Management problems developed in the mid-1950s and through a series of complex stock manipulations by outside investors, local control of the company in New Britain was lost by 1959. In early 1965, company executives shocked the housewares industry by announcing that, after a hundred and twelve years, Landers, Frary and Clark was closing its doors. The assets, inventory, and equipment were purchased by General Electric's Housewares Division, which continued to use the "Universal" name for only a short time.

Landers was one of the first companies to manufacture electric home appliances with the 1908 introduction of an electric coffee percolator and followed in 1912 by the "Thermocell" electric iron. By the late teens, the company was producing electric hot plates, toasters, grills, and the **Model E 931** and E 3931 electric waffle irons. These were followed by the Model 9311 (a 931 with embossed lid), **Model E 930** (that's correct) and the 9300 series of similar rectangular tray-mounted units. Advertised as "…made with a no stick surface" and "…never needs greasing," these waffle makers were a great sales success. After more than 80 years, many of these robust little units, with their unique split green cords, are still able to cook little square waffles very nicely- and without sticking.

Model E9311 is a refined version of Model E931 pictured on the previous page. It has an embossed aluminum lid, flat plastic feet, and better heating elements than its predecessor.

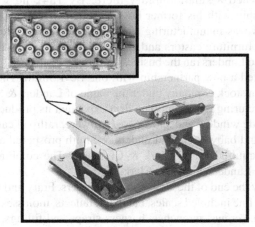

Third generation tray-mounted **Model E930** was introduced in the early 1920s. These units contain robust well-engineered heating elements (insert).

90

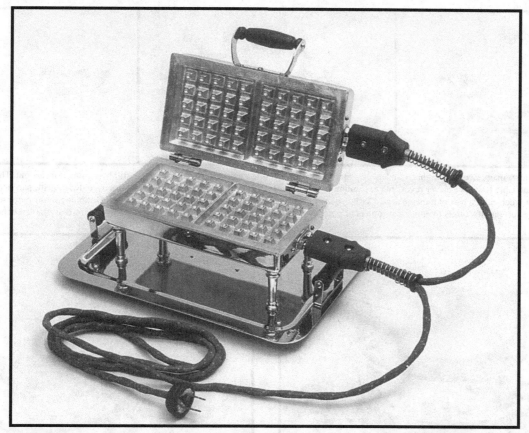

Model E9305 was the fourth and final version of the company's early split-cord rectangular units. Except for aluminum grids, the entire appliance including the attached tray and support legs are nickel-plated brass. All of these small rectangular models work well and are really fun to use.

Model 3904"Thermax" with strap legs is clearly a transition model between the company's earlier tray-mounted rectangular units and its later pedestal models. Slightly later Model 3914 and the Model E9914 "Thermax" pictured in the ad on opposite page are identical except for Cabriole-styled legs.

"Universal" was not a name normally associated with high style, but the company did make several models of waffle irons that are real head turners. Models E6304, **E 6824**, **E 6904**, and E 6924 are rare examples of Landers' irons with porcelain lid inserts. Models E 9324 and **E 7234**, though not porcelain types, stand out as two of the company's best styling efforts. Sold in the late 1920s and early 1930s as "deluxe" waffle irons in the "Old English Pattern," each is chrome plated with ivory colored handles. Not mentioned in any ad copy, is the indicator light hidden inside the pedestal of **Model E 7234.** When the unit is operated in a darkened room, the eerie red glow emanating through the pedestal cutouts reminds one of a flying saucer in a 1950s science fiction movie.

Possibly the most unusual and rarest of the Universal waffle irons is the **Model E 9350** pictured on page 92. A combination grill/waffle iron, this model is converted from one function to the other by literally turning it inside out. The company's designers must have spent many sleepless nights creating this odd contraption with its complex hinge.

91

In the late 1920s, after many sleepless nights, Landers designers figured out how to convert a waffle iron into a grill by turning it inside out. The secret is in the removable lid detachable base and clever reversible expanding hinge. This truly rare **Model E9350** can be used as a sandwich grill, pancake griddle (right), waffle iron or in a pinch can be part of a magic act… "Now you see a waffle iron…Presto…Now you see a griddle." Designing multi-purpose appliances was a common method for manufacturers to entice consumers to purchase what at that time were very expensive but never-before-available kitchen gadgets.

Model **E6824** is one in a series of beautifully styled ceramic lid models produced by Landers in the late 1920s and early 1930s. Models E6304, E6904, E6924 (at right), and E7234 share the same lid and body design . All work every bit as good as they look.

Landers used but one multi-colored flower pattern for all of its ceramic lid models. The **Model E-6904** pictured here is the non-automatic version of Model E6924. Without the temperature control and indicator window, of the automatic version and with ivory-colored handles, I believe this is the nicest looking of all the ceramic models.

In the 1930s, the "Universal" name appeared on several heavy-duty commercial waffle irons intended for the restaurant trade. Little information is available about the company's commercial products. Since compared to other brands few appear for sale they appear not have been too popular.

In the late 1920s, The Winchester Arms Company contracted with Landers to have Winchester labels attached to a number of bottom-of-the-line Model E 9533 waffle irons. Today, these "Winchester" examples often fetch prices well into three figures, from Winchester collectors. Current collector prices for other Landers, Frary & Clark waffle irons vary widely. Due to their plain designs and abundance, many are still to be found in the $5-25 price range. A few scarce, stylish, or exceptionally well preserved examples can reach over $100. Almost all "Universal" waffle irons, regardless of price, are good performers. The early rectangular tray mounted models from the 1920s are some of the most well made waffle irons ever and are great fun to use.

The top-of-the-line "Old English" automatic **Model E7234** with ivory-colored Catalin plastic handles was marketed in the early 1930s for the princely sum of $17.50. An impressively large red indicator bulb located inside the pedestal shines through the cutouts producing an erie effect in a darkened room. Model E7324 was the non-automatic version.

UNIVERSAL
"The Electric Ware Beautiful"

De Luxe Waffle Iron "Old English" Pattern

Chromium Plate, $17.50.   Others to meet every purse, $8.45 and up

The highest and lowest priced articles bearing the trade mark

are alike in quality, workmanship and lifetime service.

"The Secret of Perfect Waffles" and valuable recipes are given with our
attractive Cook Book, "Household Helps"—sent free upon request

LANDERS, FRARY & CLARK, NEW BRITAIN, CONN., U. S. A.

The elegance of this 1931 ad belies the fact that America was at this time in the throes of a depression. The $17.50 price for the **Model E 7324** "Old English" iron shown, adjusted for inflation, is equal to $167.00 today. This and the automatic version, Model E 7234, pictured on the preceeding page, came with ivory Catalin plastic handles. By 1933, when the economy hit bottom, few families could afford these fancy models making them scarce collectibles today. (February, 1931, *Good Housekeeping Magazine*)

Model E7704, circa mid-1930s, looks much like a flying saucer prop from a 1950s science fiction movie. Although it's quite eye catching, the protruding elevated base and small lid handle creates a very real burn hazard if one isn't careful while using it. This unit, being non-automatic and with very efficient heating elements, must be watched carefully as it tends to overheat if not unplugged at regular intervals. Model E3274 is nearly identical while Model E7724 is the automatic version.

Automatic **Model E2024,** dating from the mid-1930s, is another example of Landers tasteful styling in a medium priced product. The handles, feet, and temperature control knob are walnut-colored brown Bakelite.

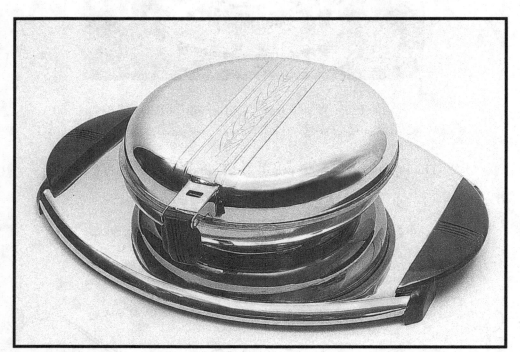

Model EA3001 from the late 1930s continued a popular styling theme for Landers. The brown Bakelite handles in several modified but recognizable forms and the embossed "Coronet" wheat lid pattern were used on several models of automatic and manual waffle irons or combination waffle iron/ grills including Models EA3000, 3201, 3601, 3602, and Grill Model E1370. All of these models are quite attractive and work well. The tray on this model is easily detached for quick cleaning.

94

Liberty Gauge & Instrument Company

This Liberty Gauge iron is, from a technological stand point, one of the most significant appliances ever made. It was the first waffle iron equipped with a modern automatic adjustable thermostat (insert). This thermostat design is still used in heat-generating appliances today. When the correct temperature is reached, the thermostat lights a red signal lamp behind a jeweled window in the base.

Despite its very short life span, Liberty Gauge had a profound influence on the development of the modern appliance industry. Several Cleveland businessmen organized the company as a machine shop to manufacture war goods during World War I, thus the patriotic "Liberty" name. When the war ended in 1918, the company suffered a sharp decline in business and the owners scrambled to find a new niche for their enterprise. J.A Zimmer, one of the principles, hit upon the idea of entering the hot new growth industry of electric appliances.

In 1921, Liberty introduced its first product, an inexpensive electric hot plate. It was an instant success, selling over 200,000 units in the first year. In 1925, Joe Myers, a Jackson, Michigan inventor, approached the company with a new clothes iron he had designed with what turned out to be the first reliable adjustable temperature control found in any appliance. Nine years prior, at age 14, Joe had invented the controller and incorporated into his mother's iron. The Liberty version of the iron was introduced at the 1926 Philadelphia electrical trade show. Here it caught the attention of Philadelphia appliance maker Proctor and Schwartz, who had been unsuccessful in developing a trouble-free thermostat of its own for a toaster. In 1928, after lengthy negotiations, Proctor and Schwartz purchased Liberty Gauge outright for $200,000, and incorporated Liberty's thermostat technology into its own products. Joe Myers went with Proctor and Swartz and headed the research department until his retirement in 1953.

To date, only one model of Liberty waffle iron has surfaced. Some were made for Montgomery Ward and have a tag that reads "Montgomery Ward Automatic Signal Waffler." The much-vaunted thermostat in this waffle iron is a clever but crude affair, consisting of a large virgin silver electrical contact, welded to the free end of a heat sensitive bimetal strip. A second contact attached to a similar but plain steel strip is pressed against the first contact to a greater or lesser degree by a simple sliding control lever protruding from the front of the unit. These contacts when closed, complete the circuit to the heating elements. As the temperature-adjusting slide is moved to the "darker" position, the contacts are squeezed together more tightly. Greater heat is then required to bend the bimetal strip enough to separate the contacts and shut off current to the heating coils. This simple controller works well, making these waffle irons good performers. By the late 1920s this inexpensive and reliable thermostat design was adopted by the appliance industry at large to control most heat-generating products and is still used today.

A Liberty waffle iron in good working condition is a rare industrial artifact, illustrating an important step in the evolution of modern home appliances. So few have surfaced that a true market value cannot be established at this time.

Lindemann & Hoverson Company [1]

"L & H Electrics"

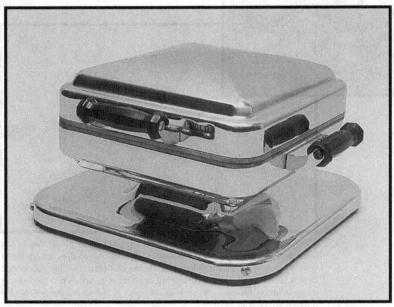

A late 1920s appliance with a by then dated early 1920s appearance. Looks aside, *Model 151* is a well made quality waffle iron that works as well as any modern example.

Albert J. Lindemann was born in Hamburg, Germany in 1845 and immigrated to Milwaukee with his parents in 1863. After graduating from high school he became a journeyman tinsmith in southern Illinois. In 1875 he moved back to South Milwaukee where he opened a retail hardware, tinware, and stove store with his father. In 1892 [2] A.J. Lindemann formed a partnership with H.C. Hoverson and the pair incorporated the A.J. Lindemann & Hoverson Company. Lindemann was President and Hoverson was Secretary of the corporation. Although Hoverson retired from the company in 1896, the firm would retain his name for another 62 years.

The company had an 80 X 150-foot five-story factory constructed at 189-191 Hanover Street, Milwaukee, where it began manufacturing conventional coal and wood-fired cook stoves. By the late 1890s, the company numbered 200 employees and was marketing gasoline fueled stoves, a series of unique combination solid fuel/natural gas stoves, and the "Kerogas" stove, an efficient clean burning kerosene range. (The "Kerogas" was sold until the 1950s to farm families unable to obtain either gas or electrical service for cooking.)

By the mid-1920s L&H had a sprawling four block long plant on Cleveland Avenue in Milwaukee covering ten acres and employing over 1000 workers. The facility included an iron and brass foundry, sheet metal shops, machine shops, a porcelain enameling plant, a wick weaving shop, a research and Chemical laboratory, a power plant, a warehouse, and loading docks capable of accommodating 30 rail cars simultaneously. In 1925 the company opened a new eight-story office complex in downtown Chicago. By this time L&H was manufacturing a complete line of full size electric ranges, and a line of small electric appliances including three toaster models and two models of waffle irons. (The bread ejecting mechanism on the L&H Model 202 toaster was licensed from Rutenber Electric.)

The company discontinued small appliance manufacturing in the 1930s but continued producing a complete line of full sized gas, electric, and solid fuel cooking ranges and gas and electric water heaters into the 1950s. A devastating labor strike in the late 1940s lasting two years, signaled the decline of this once prominent Milwaukee company. It became a part of Chilton Metal Products Company of Chilton, Wisconsin in 1958.

For years Albert Lindemann was noted in the Milwaukee area for his great interest in that city's education system. In the early part of the century he was instrumental in drafting compulsory education laws for young men in the trades and was one of the founders and administrators of the Milwaukee Trade School. He also served for years as a member and President of the Milwaukee School Board. Lindemann was

Lion Electric Appliance Corp.[1]

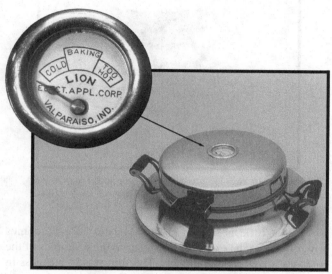

This iron is the only example of this company's products that has surfaced to date. It's not much to look at but is a surprisingly good cooker. The author would like to hear from anyone with more information about Lion Electric and its other products.

Lindemann & Hoverson, like many appliance manufacturers, spent the war years making goods for the military. This 1944 ad in the *Milwaukee City Directory* promises a return to quality consumer goods after the war.

also in the forefront of worker safety. He insisted that all L&H facilities be clean, well lighted, and adequately heated and ventilated. For some years the L&H factory was considered a model facility for worker safety. Lindemann remained active in his firm until 1939, when his son Eugene took over as President. Albert Lindemann passed away in 1941 at age 87.

Waffle iron **Model 317**, pictured on the preceeding page, is automatic, equipped with a preset non-adjustable thermostat, and a wheel-type temperature indicator located adjacent to the handle on the front of the lid. Because of its inefficient ribbon wire heating elements, the iron is slow to reach operating temperature. Once to temperature however, the thermostat maintains the temperature correctly for the entire cooking session. A nearly identical non-automatic Model 315 was also produced with either a dial-type gauge in the top of the lid or with no gauge. All L & H irons are of excellent quality and produce thick 6½-inch square waffles.

Valparaiso, Indiana, a quintessential midwestern manufacturing and farming community that bills itself as both the "Turkey Capital" and the "Popcorn Capital" of the world, was home to Orville Redenbacher of popcorn fame. In the late 1920s it was also home to the Lion Electric Appliance Corporation. The only record of this little firm with the impressive name is a phone listing in the Valparaiso city directory for 1930. By the mid-1930s, the company appears to have been moved a few miles north, to west Chicago. The only item produced by this firm that has surfaced is the small low-profile waffle iron pictured above. This inexpensively made unit heats quickly and the responsive easy-to-read temperature gauge makes it a surprisingly nice iron to use.

[1] Information courtesy Bonnie Cuson, Curator for The Historical Society of Porter County, "Old Jail Museum", Valparaiso, Indiana.

[1] Historical information courtesy Steve Daily, Curator of Research collections, Milwaukee County Historical Society, Milwaukee, Wisconsin.

[2] Various sources give founding dates for the firm of 1892, 1894, and 1896. The author believes 1892 is most probable.

Majestic Electric Development Company
"Grideliere"

Model 150, circa 1922, with original lamp socket adapter and box. An artifact this old with original instructions, hang tag, and accessories, is of great historical value to researchers.

Model 151, Majestic's second generation grill/waffle iron, dates from the mid-1920s and weighs an impressive 9 pounds. The awkward looking lid handle serves as a support when the lid is fully opened and the grids are reversed for use as a pancake griddle (insert).

Model 11508 "Grideliere" and all subsequent models came with a "Catalin" plastic lid handle in several colors and a dome type temperature indicator which doubled as the griddle support.

What little is known about Majestic Electric comes primarily from the examination of surviving examples of the company's well-made products. The firm was in business in Philadelphia, Kansas City, and San Francisco in the early 1920s under the name Majestic Electric Development Company. Its main product line was electric heating devices including radiant space heaters ("The Best In Creation for Heat Radiation"), electric fireplace logs, and two models of an on-demand electric hot water heater that was installed on faucets much like a modern day water purifier.

By the early 1930s the firm had become Majestic Electric Appliance Company and was marketing at least two toaster models (66-T and 462). It had by then closed the Philadelphia operation but maintained offices in Minneapolis, Kansas City, and San Francisco. The company was likely purchased by Dominion Electric at this time. Two nearly identical models of a distinctive octagonal waffle iron have surfaced recently (see page 56). One is marked Dominion Minneapolis. The second with silghtly different handles, but ones used on other Dominion irons, is labeled Majestic Electric, Minneapolis. A 1947 newspaper article about Dominion Electric of Mansfield, Ohio briefly mentions that, "The Galion division known as the Majestic Electric Appliance Company, Inc. employs some 150 persons." It can be assumed that Dominion had purchased Majestic Electric and was operating it in the late 1940s as a separate division in the nearby town of Galion, Ohio. Dominion records do not indicate what became of Majestic.

At least five versions of Majestic Electric's waffle iron/pancake griddle were marketed from the early 1920s to the mid-1930s. The first model labeled **Type 150**, is a plain tray-mounted combination unit with a permanently attached cord and reversible grids. The flat top was advertised as being useful as a plate warmer while one's waffle is baking. Four subsequent refined versions are large, round, very heavy, pedestal models. All are labeled **"Grideliere"** and are non-automatic combination models. They are converted from waffle maker to pancake griddle by installing the cooking grids with the flat surfaces exposed. The lid is then opened fully and, depending upon the model, rested on its handle or temperature indicator housing. Instructions that accompanied these units cautioned not to cook bacon, sausage, sandwiches, or similar foods as to do so will cause problems with grease seeping into the enclosed heating elements. Virtually every example the author has encountered had in the past frequently been used to cook greasy foods. So much for reading instructions. In addition to the **"Grideliere"** appliance, Majestic also marketed at least two electric toaster models, the 66-T and the 462.

Except for the first **Model 150,** all of the waffle irons take a very long time to reach operating temperature and it seems a week to cool down. They also tend to overheat if not monitored closely. If treated properly they do make attractive useful appliances. However, it is best to purchase a low mileage or professionally restored unit in top condition. Opening the sealed body halves of the later models for servicing is definitely not recommendedas they are filled with large quantities of loose asbestos insulation.

Manning-Bowman Company

"Homelectrics"

Manning Bowman marketed its first electric waffle iron, Model 1605, in the early 1920s. It was the first of several similar models. Excellent heating elements assured fine performance and nice styling produced strong sales. The entire body and tray like most small appliances of this vintage was fabricated from brass and then nickel plated. See the patent drawing and an advertisement for this iron on the next page.

Manning-Bowman Company, one of the first houseswares manufacturers in the United States, was founded in 1849 in Cromwell, Connecticut as Thomas Manning and Son. Manning's son Thadeus took on a partner, Robert Bowman, in 1864, and the new company was incorporated as Manning-Bowman and Company. The firm produced "Britannia" ware, planished (toughened, polished) tinware, and porcelain enamelware. In 1872, they merged with the Meriden Britannia Company, and moved to Meriden, Connecticut, where they remained for over eight decades.

Over the years, Manning-Bowman became involved in supplying the hotel and restaurant trades with numerous cooking devices, only later adding household cooking items to its product line. Shortly after the turn of the century, the company was one of the first to manufacture electrical appliances for the home. By the teens, they, along with Landers, Frary and Clark, were the leaders in the portable appliance industry, and remained so until after World War II. In 1952, Manning-Bowman was sold to McGraw-Electric, which continued using the Manning-Bowman name into the mid-1950's.

Manning-Bowman began making electric waffle irons in the early 1920s and apparently was quite successful as evidenced by the large number of early models that have survived. First generation units like the **Model 1605** pictured above, have heavy heating wires imbedded in a large thick refractory clay matrix, an effective method of spreading heat evenly over the entire cooking grid. The quality of the materials, plating, and craftsmanship of these early irons is superb and all of the early models work well. The waffle grids on most of the company's models were designed to create a very thick, Belgian type waffle, with large dimples similar to those made by many cast iron stovetop waffle irons of the day.

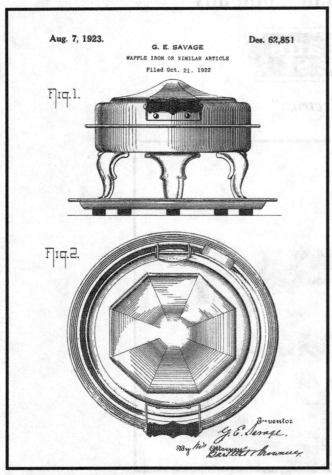

The 1923 design patent drawing for **Model 1605**. The crude lid hinge depicted in Figure 2 was refined for production. Although this was designed more than 80 years ago, these irons still work well even by today's standards. (Drawing courtesy Nancy Conway)

In the mid-1920s, Manning-Bowman was one of the first to offer chrome-plated appliances, which were advertised as having a non-tarnishing "Aranium" finish. In 1928, the firm introduced an economy line of appliances labeled "Homelectrics." Quoting from the 1928 company catalog, "The price (on 'Homelectrics') has been kept down to a moderate figure by the omission of manufacturing refinements which while they enhance the appearance of the appliance, do not add to the everyday utility." In essence, these were high quality "plain-Jane" models. This product line disappeared by the mid-1930s.

Because most Manning-Bowman models are plentiful, styling rather than rarity dictate current values for the company's products. A case in point is the unique and attractive Deco styled **Model 6060 "Twin-o-Matic"** stacked double iron. Created by industrial designer Karl Ratliff in 1937, it was heavily advertised and even featured at the New York

The **Model 1605** waffle iron cost $15.00 in 1923, more than an average day's wages. The Model 1225 toaster was $8.00. Electric appliances were a new luxury at this time and unaffordable for many. (1923, *Ladies Home Journal*)

Manning-Bowman continued:

World's Fair in 1939. Except for the war years, this model, and the less expensive non-automatic Model 5050 "Twinover," remained in production well into the1950s, making them among the company's most popular waffle irons. Although quite plentiful, they are often erroneously labeled "rare" by sellers who generally ask higher than average prices for them.

Manning-Bowman was known for superb styling rather than for cutting edge innovation. Most waffle iron models were manufactured in great quantities for many years with only minor styling variations. Since the company was a supplier for several large retail chains, department stores, and various sales organizations, it is not unusual to find Manning-Bowman products labeled with the brand names of Sears Roebuck, Montgomery Ward, Penney, The Jewel Tea Company, Affiliated Retailers of New York, and others. Most of the company's products are stamped with both an "Article number" and a "Serial number." The serial number is the actual month and year of manufacture and was used by the factory to resolve claims on its one-year product warranty. Nearly all Manning-Bowman products are well made and stylish, making most very practical additions to any kitchen.

What a difference a fancy ivory colored teardrop handle can make to the looks of a waffle iron. **Model 1703,** circa late 1920s, like it's predecessors, has excellent heating elements that work well. A new feature introduced for the first time is a built-in temperature gauge visible in lid. Automatic temperature regulation was still be a few years in the future.

ELECTRIC SERVINGS
are simplest, freshest — and hottest

If there is any food in the world you want piping hot, it is toast and waffles. . . . The very second a piece of toast is made on an electric toaster, it can be buttered and eaten. No delay, no carrying, to lessen its fine crispness. And the very moment a waffle is lifted from the electric waffle iron, it can be split into fours, and buttered or syruped while still so hot it well might burn one's finger!

Manning-Bowman Table Appliances are to help you live life pleasantly —and more at your ease. The delicate toast, the crunchy waffles are made and served fresh where you are. Coffee in percolator urns can be brewed and served fresh—at its best.

Need we point out the

beauty of these Manning-Bowman Table Appliances? Note that the waffle iron has no handles to mar its round design. This is because you can lift it by the tray at any time—the tray is always cool. . . . At breakfasts, luncheons, suppers, repeatedly, homes are using these Manning-Bowman Table Appliances more and more. They are electrically built for just such steady use. Ever welcome as wedding or anniversary gifts. There are also lower-priced designs with the heating elements the same. The little book, "From Breakfast to Midnight Bridge," gives several fine menus and recipes for electric cookery. May we send you a copy? It is free. Manning, Bowman & Co., Meriden, Conn.

7-cup Percolator 3112/7. Price, $19.

Manning-Bowman
Electric Appliances
Wholesale distributors in Canada — Northern Electric Company, Ltd. Canadian prices on application.

Model 1616 was the company's second generation waffle iron and the first in a series of similar pedestal models. The designers basically took the body from Model 1605 and placed a pedestal tray under it. The octagonal domed top would appear on succeeding models for about five years. These early MB waffle irons are quite robust and work very well. All however require a power plug on the cord which can connect to a pair of unique spade-shaped pins on the iron.

Model 1616 cost $15.00, a princely sum in 1928. The matching Model 1228 "Tip & Turn" toaster was a more modest $6.00. The waffle iron was touted as having a base so cool it needed no carrying handles. The pedestal's attractive fretwork in fact does ventilate the base keeping it as cool as advertised.

(April, 1928, *Good Housekeeping Magazine*)

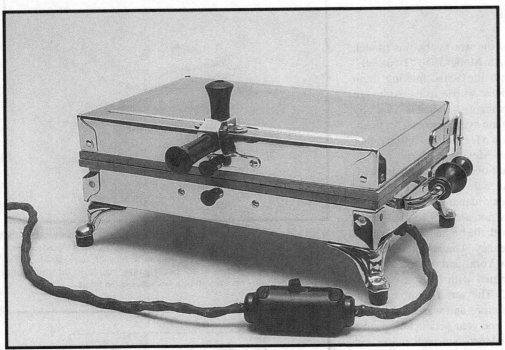

This 1930 **Model 515** combination grill/waffle iron appears to have too many lid handles but in fact the knob pointing straight up acts as a support when the lid is opened flat and the unit is used as a grill. This appliance weighs in at a hefty 8 pounds and came with a permanently attached cord with in-line power switch. This is a typical example of the first combination type models and is much better constructed than later examples of this type. Because separate flat grids were supplied for grilling rather than flipping the waffle grids over, the seasoning required for making waffles is not damaged during a grilling session. Flipping multi-purpose grids for grilling on newer units destroys the seasoning on the waffle-making dimpled side.

The Model 516 "Cook-All" was the second generation combination unit and derived from Model 515 pictured at top. It could be purchased in the mid-1930s with an assortment of internal cooking grid accessories designed for baking, grilling, cooking, and frying. This was a top quality product but its high price made it unaffordable for most families during the depression. Their classic Art Deco styling make these quite collectible. (Photo courtesy Dan & Vi LaBelle)

Manning-Bowman continued:

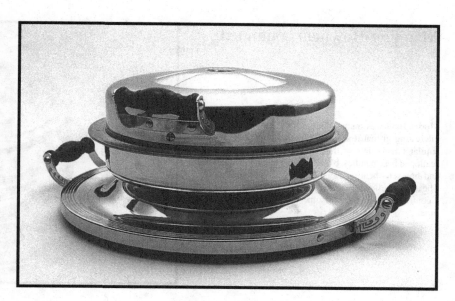

By the time **Model K-44** was introduced in the early 1930s the pedestal-type waffle iron was considered outdated. This very low profile pedestal was the last of its type from Manning-Bowman. The next models would be the new deco styled low profile integrated base units.

Model 1618 with off white wood handles is the first of the more modern looking low profile models. However, it still retains the Art Nouveau decorations popular through the 1920s. Manning-Bowman was not quick to change its styling but when it did, it was nearly always superb. The lid handle on this model looks like a cabinet knob and sticks up at an awkward angle . A fancy cut glass spacer was inserted between the lid and knob to insulate the painted wood from the potentially damaging heat.

Model K-1635, circa early 1930s, has attractive green and yellow marbleized Bakelite handles. Being automatic at this early date meant that it was a top-of-the-line model. A similar and equally stylish unit was produced with a plain lid.

103

Manning-Bowman continued:

Model 1637 was manufactured in the mid 1930s and is interesting in that it shares a great number of parts with similar GE models of this vintage, including the black scalloped base handles, black ceramic tear drop lid handle and bracket, heating elements, and temperature gauge. The author believes that Manning-Bowman may have had a contract to manufacture some of GE's products at this time.

Model K1038 is from the early 1930s. It's a typical low profile model of this period but with very untypical orange and black handles. Later deco styling efforts by the company were more appealing.

The Art Deco look exemplified in **Model 725** from 1935 was the most popular styling from the early 1930s until World War II. This model came with either bright red or black beaded plastic handles. The red handled version is more desireable to collectors.

Model 1649 is a late 1930s-early 1940s model with varnished walnut handles. Other companies used walnut at this time but Manning-Bowman pieces seem to have the best grade of wood. The circular design in the lid is a motif the company modified and used on several models including Model 2182 pictured below.

This **Model 2182** was made for Montgomery Ward and shares the same circular lid design found on two other models pictured on the page. The ivory-colored plastic handles make this a rather attractive appliance. Manning-Bowman made appliances for various retailers over the years. The quality of these units is every bit as good as the examples labeled Manning-Bowman.

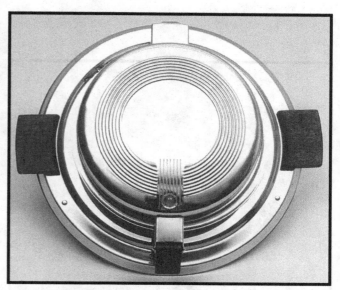

Model 1657 of late 1930s vintage is another iron with walnut handles. Natural wood on appliances was popular for a few years prior to World War II, but after the war most manufacturers returned to Bakelite or modern heat resistant plastics developed for the war effort. Model 1656 is the less expensive non-automatic version of this style. Both produce thick Belgian-style waffles with little effort required from the cook.

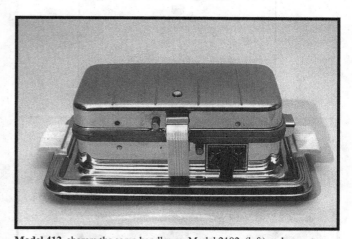

Model 412 sharers the same handles as Model 2182 (left) and same tray as Model 2525 (left). It is a well made automatic model manufactured in the late 1930s and early 1940s. The unusual feature of this unit is the fact that it bakes two separate waffles under the same lid. The thermostat assembly on MB units of this vintage are quite accurate and maintain a fairly steady heat. The temperature control visible on the front of the unit looks like a generic-type volume control knob borrowed from an old radio. For Manning-Bowman it is uncharacteristically utilitarian in appearance.

Model 2525 is a non-automatic twin model made to compete with Dominion Electric who dominated the twin-type waffle iron market prior to World War II. Consumers soon realized that these twin models were a lot more work than those that made a single larger waffle. Most were discontinued shortly after the war when the post war baby boom required larger waffles for larger families.

Manning-Bowman continued:

Model 1646 from the mid-1930s exemplifies Manning-Bowman's knack for great deco styling. The handles and feet are a rich chocolate brown-colored Bakelite. This model like most of the company's irons is a great cooker as well as being a great looker. Model 1648 is identical in body and tray design but has less durable wood handles painted black.

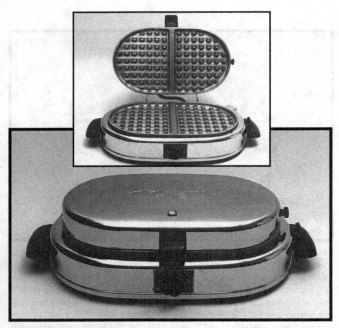

Model 423 is a well made combination waffle iron/grill dating from the early 1940s. It is one of the few waffle irons capable of making oblong waffles (insert). Separate flat grids must be installed to convert this to a sandwich grill. This example is labeled "Affiliated Retailers of New York" a retailing organization that was based in New York City in the 1930s and 1940s. It has the same ugly radio control knob as that found on Model 412 pictured on previous page.

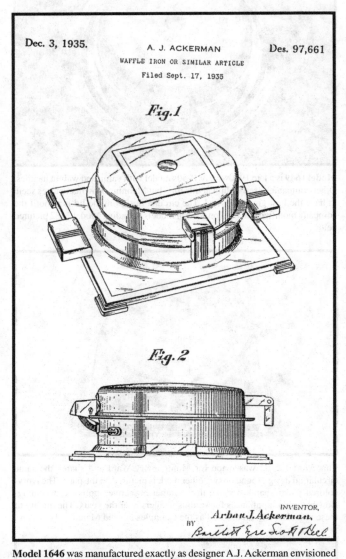

Dec. 3, 1935.   A. J. ACKERMAN   Des. 97,661
WAFFLE IRON OR SIMILAR ARTICLE
Filed Sept. 17, 1935

Fig.1

Fig.2

INVENTOR,
Arban J. Ackerman,
BY

Model 1646 was manufactured exactly as designer A.J. Ackerman envisioned in his 1935 patent application, reproduced here. This was a styling transition away from a decade of art deco and towards the sleek 1940s minimalism.
(Drawing courtesy Nancy Conway)

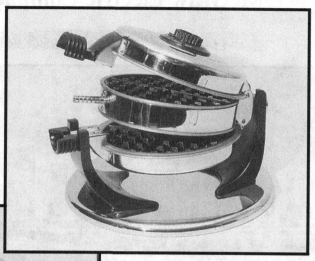

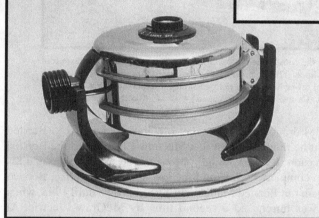

Manning-Bowman hit the sales jackpot when they introduced the **Model 6060** "Twin-O-Matic" in 1939. Though heavy and bulky, the futuristic styling continued to make this a popular item into the 1950s.

With two-tone cream and chocolate brown handles, **Model 1160** epitomizes the minimalist styling of the 1940s. Ford Motor Company used the exact same color scheme and handle design for the interior trim of the 1940 Ford standard models. (I know because I own this waffle iron and a matching 1940 Ford coupe.)

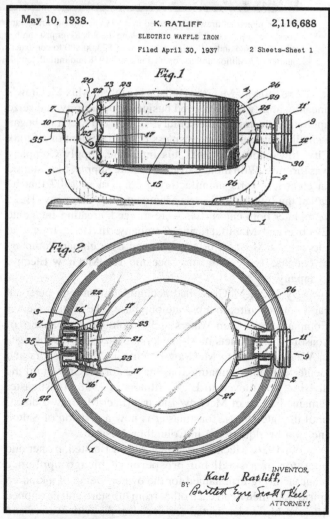

Model 1646 "Twin-Over" (the non-automatic version of Model 6060) was modified in production slightly from this 1938 Karl Ratliff patent drawing. The prongs for the power cord plug were given a protectice socket.

McGraw Electric Company [1]

This architectural drawing appeared in a 1937 newspaper article announcing the construction of McGraw Electric's new 123,000 square foot Toastmaster plant on 25 acres of land along the Fox River just south of Elgin Illinois. The town, hard hit by the depression, attracted McGraw by providing land and collecting donations of $23,000.00 to construct water and sewer lines and a railroad siding. The plant, built at a cost of a quarter of a million dollars, opened in early 1938 and initially employed 600. (Courtesy George F. Waters)

The Story of McGraw-Edison is a tale of Max McGraw's uncanny ability to see a good business opportunity and seize upon it. At the turn of the century, 17 year old McGraw began a small electrical supply business in the basement of a Sioux City, Iowa store. By 1903, his Interstate Supply Company was thriving. With money from Interstate Supply, Max started an electrical parts manufacturing concern in 1907 that he called the Interstate Electric Manufacturing Company. Three years later both enterprises were merged, creating Interstate Electric and Manufacturing Company. In 1912, Interstate Electric and Manufacturing purchased The Lehman Company of Omaha. The combination became The McGraw-Electric Company.

By 1926, McGraw had accumulated enough personal capital, to acquire, in a private purchase, The Waters-Genter Company from Glen Waters and Harold Genter, makers of Toastmaster products in Minneapolis. Max sold his interests in Waters-Genter to McGraw-Electric in 1929. Waters and Genter continued running Toastmaster for McGraw until the division was moved to Elgin, Illinois in 1938. Toastmaster remained a part of McGraw-Electric (later McGraw-Edison) until the late 1990s. Toastmaster is now a division of Salton Inc. and headquartered in Columbia, Missouri.

In 1926, McGraw also met Alfred Bersted, owner and operator of a small but prosperous Chicago appliance manufacturing firm named for the owner. Being of a kindred spirit, both men liked each other from the start, and developed a friendship which lasted for decades. As with Waters and Genter, Bersted agreed to sell his business to McGraw and operate it for Max, as a subdivision of McGraw-Electric.

By 1930, the depressed economy had reduced appliance sales dramatically. One day McGraw mentioned to Bersted that he thought it best that McGraw-Electric sell the Bersted division. Bersted thought the same and promptly bought his old company back from McGraw at a fire sale price. Bersted again ran Bersted Manufacturing as his own until 1948, when it was purchased a second time by McGraw-Electric. Al Bersted came with that purchase and was made President of McGraw-Electric and eventually Chairman of the Board.

Max McGraw was a shrewd businessman with an uncanny ability to see business opportunities and exploit them. He was fond of saying, "Never buy a company unless it's making money or seems about to go broke." This simple business philosophy worked well for him. In fifty years he was able to build a one person electrical supply business into an industrial empire.

The 1950s was a period of major expansion for McGraw-Electric beginning in 1952 with the purchase of The Everhot Company and appliance giant Manning-Bowmann. Two years later McGraw acquired the appliance division of General Mills. In 1957 McGraw bought the venerable old Griswold Manufacturing Company, the Fairchild Camera Company, Ingraham Time Products, and Thomas A. Edison Inc. When McGraw purchased Edison's old company and changed his company's name to McGraw-Edison, Max became fond of relating that his own name finally appeared ahead of Edison's on the New York Stock Exchange. In addition to the company's mentioned above. McGraw also acquired Clark Water Heater, Buss Fuse, Speed Queen, Albion humidifiers, Tropic Aire, Village Blacksmith, Allover Clippers, Duracrest, Spartan Bottle Warmers, Eskimo, Coolerator, Zero, and Halo Lighting.

McGraw-Electric continued:

The old McGraw factory, still in service over six decades after Max McGraw had it built. Over a hundred clockmakers were employed in the plant making timers and delicate heating elements. During World War II their precision skills were used to make anti-aircraft shells and fuses. In the 1950s the plant made Toastmaster, Manning-Bowman, Penney and General Mills products. McGraw-Edison left Elgin in 1965. The complex is now called the Elgin-O'Hare Commerce Center.
(Photo courtesy Jeffrey Larson, Chicago, Ill. February, 2002)

Although McGraw was a no-nonsense aggressive businessman, he seemed to have had a loyal following of subordinates. For years both Al Bersted and Glen Waters had cordial relations with Max while they ran the Bersted and Toastmaster divisions for him. Surprisingly, Max the empire builder was also something of a nature lover and conservationist. When he built his new plant in Elgin, Illinois in 1938, he also purchased 2000 acres of land in the area and turned it into a protected wetlands. In the late 1940s every Toastmaster toaster that was built in the plant had to make four perfect pieces of toast before it was boxed for shipment. The factory used over a thousand loaves of bread daily for this final test and inspection process. Much of the resultant toast was trucked to Max's wildlife preserve where it was fed to the water fowl that were happily residing there.

McGraw died of cancer at the Mayo Clinic in 1964 at age 81. Today, McGraw-Edison though no longer manufacturing household appliances, still is involved in nearly all other facets of the electrical manufacturing industry. Even though McGraw was heavily into appliance making for years, he never saw fit to hire an in house home economist. The Toastmaster division finally hired one in 1975.

Over the years, in addition to the Toastmaster brand, McGraw-Electric and later McGraw-Edison, made waffle irons under the "Fostoria," "Lady Winsted," "Twin Star," "Capitol," "Penncrest," "General Mills," and "Manning Bowman" labels. These are honest, work-a-day type waffle irons most of which, from a stylistic point of view are anything but exciting.

[1]   Certain historical information courtesy George F. Waters, Dick Moran, and Eric A. Murrell, Editor of *The Saturday Evening Toast*, the newsletter of The Toaster Collector's Association.

Formed wire legs also serve as carrying handles on this **Model 363** grill/waffle iron, a clever way of producing a nice looking appliance at minimal cost. Many McGraw products like this one appear to be of better quality than they really are.

Model 6A from the late 1950s, has 1400 watt heating elements, the most powersful of any non-commercial waffle iron. This versions of this model were made for Manning-Bowman, General Mills, and J.C. Penney (Penncrest).

109

Metal Ware Corporation
"Empire" and "Empco"

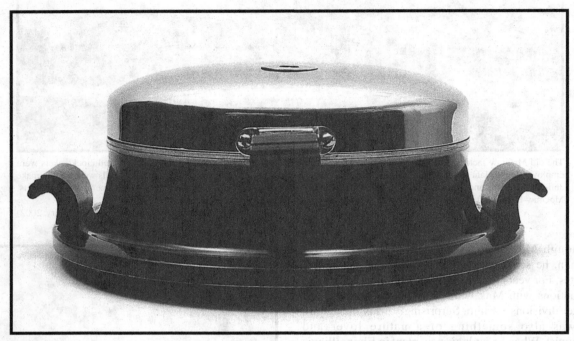

Metal Ware **Model 718** is unusual for its fancy curved handles. At first glance they appear to be molded Bakelite but in fact are intricately machined from wood and painted black. The black painted base contrasts with the chrome-plated lid. Though eye catching, paint is not a very durable finish. During operation the black color conducts considerable heat from the grids to the body making necessary extra tall feet beneath this unit to raise it sufficiently high above heat-sensitive surfaces to protect them from damage.

Joseph Koenig, the founder of Mirro, started the Metal Ware Corporation in 1920. Koenig sold the firm to the Drumm family in 1931. Today members of the Drumm family operate the company from three plants in the Two Rivers, Wisconsin area. It is part of the NESCO Corporation and manufacturers appliances and cookware under the NESCO® name, Open Country Camp Cookware® and American Harvest® brand names.

In 1916 the Metal Ware Corporation was the first to patent a valveless pump for a percolator which could work in less than three minutes and which is still used in most percolators today. In the early 1930s, the company marketed thirteen different percolators or percolator sets under the "Empire" or "Empco" labels ranging in price from $3.25 to $20.00. They also produced a Model S-59 toaster for $4.00,

a Model S-74 Sandwich Grill for $15.00, a Model S-49 Sandwich Toaster for $4.50, and a Model S-52 Toaster-Stove for $2.50. The company also made an impressive working toy electric range which included burners capable of boiling water, and a functional oven.

In the 1930s the company also made a Model S-75 tray-mounted, three-section, rectangular waffle iron and a conventional round pedestal unit designated Model S-76. Both units were sold under the "Empire" label, were non-automatic, came with six-foot cords, and had a list price of $10.00. These irons are uncommon and the author has not seen either model for sale. The **Model 718** non-automatic "Empire" iron pictured above appears to date from the early or mid-1930s. It and all of the company's other products are scarce to rare.

Mid-City Manufacturing Company
"Jiffy" or *"Jiffey"*

Whether the "**Jiffy**" was designed as a toy or a true kitchen appliance is open to debate. The fact remains, they're cute and with a real power cord and heating elements they work, albeit not very well.

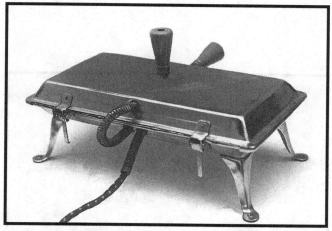

Put expandable rod-type hinges on the back of a Jiffy, a funky knob on top, and flat grids inside and you still have a cheap Mid-City appliance, but one that can toast sandwiches or grill pancakes. These came in various configurations as can be seen below. (Photo courtesy Dan & Vi LaBelle)

In the late 1920s and early 1930s, this Chicago company produced several models of very small inexpensively made cooking appliances that can easily be mistaken for children's toys. These products may be found unmarked, or labeled, "Jiffy," "Jiffey," "Jiffy Electric," "The Jiffy," "Mid-City Mfg. Co.," or "Central Flatiron Mfg. Co. Johnson City, N.Y."

The firm's waffle irons are equipped with pressed sheet aluminum cooking grids riveted into a nickel-plated undecorated stamped steel body shell mounted on four thin pressed metal legs. Six variations of the same basic iron were produced. One version is equipped with an oversize red, green, or black painted wooden knob lid handle. A second type is fitted with a metal bale-type combination lid lifter and carrying handle. Both versions are approximately 5½ inches square and have permanently attached power cords. A third variant of the square model with knob type lid handle is equipped with a detachable power cord. Two different rectangular models were produced These resemble two square models side by side and measures 5½ by 11 inches. They were equipped with either a bale type handle or colored wooden knob. Both rectangular versions have permanently attached cords. The company made a limited number of combination sandwich grill/pancake griddles by modifying the rectangular double waffle iron with flat cooking grids.

The great number of surviving examples of this company's waffle irons indicates that the firm met with considerable sales success with them during the early depression years. Unfortunately, most found today suffer from some degree of plating deterioration. All make a small, very thin wafer type waffle, with shallow indistinct dimples. Great care must be exercised when using these poorly designed irons, as they tend to overheat and being top heavy, tip over backward when the lid is placed in the fully open position.

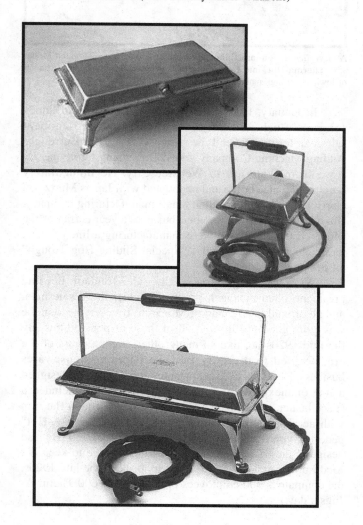

Monarch Company [1]
"Therm-A-Jug" "Therm-A-hot"

A clever leg design turned this otherwise utilitarian early Monarch Model 950 "**Therma-Hot**" into a rather nice looking appliance. Not bad for a bunch of Iowa hog trough makers! (See Story)

In January, 1917, twenty-eight year old Ernest Sidney Johnson, flush with money earned as the pre-eminent salesman for the Oliver Typewriter Company and Burroughs Adding Machine Company, moved his young family across Iowa from Waterloo to Webster City. He immediately purchased a nice home and negotiated with James Mertz and Harry Hotchkiss to buy their small manufacturing company. Jim and Harry had started their business a year earlier as the Monarch Company and were manufacturing a line of sheet metal chicken feeders and a "Special Sliding Hog Trough" all designed by Mertz.

With the completion of the sale, Johnson became president, plant manager, production chief, head salesman, and all around handy man of Monarch. By every account he was quite good at fulfilling all of these responsibilities. By the mid-1920s he, like so many other entrepreneurs of the era, decided to diversify into the booming housewares business. He was a talented inventor and personally designed a line of inexpensive electrical appliances that included a space heater, a hot plate, a toaster, a curling iron, a flat iron with accompanying ironing board, and a "Therm-A-Hot" pedestal type waffle iron he designated **Model 950**. He also designed the "Therm-A-Jug", a thermos device to keep hot food hot and cold food cold. (At its peak in the late 1920s, the company's 300 employees produced over 600 Therm-A-Jugs a day.)

In 1926, Johnson made arrangements with Andrew Knapp, president of the Knapp Company, a Saint Louis based luggage manufacturer, to use the Knapp sales organization to sell Monarch goods. This arrangement worked so well that three years later, on January 7th 1929, by mutual agreement, the companies were merged to form the Knapp-Monarch Company. Andrew Knapp became president and Earnest Johnson became vice president of the new organization. Manufacturing continued in Webster City and at Knapp's luggage plant in Kansas City, until January 1931, when all manufacturing was consolidated into one facility in Belleville, Illinois. The Johnson family, which now included three children then moved to Saint Louis.

Sadly, just nine months later, on September 21st, 1931, Ernest Johnson died of pneumonia, following a gall bladder operation, at age 52. He was buried in Webster City, the place he always felt was home. The conclusion of the Knapp-Monarch story may be found under "Knapp-Monarch" elsewhere. The old Monarch Factory that was located between Des Moines and Wilson Avenues, just north of the railroad tracks in Webster City, stood vacant until 1937, when Beam Manufacturing reopened it to produce its famous "Doodle Bug" motor scooter.

[1] Historical information courtesy Ketta Lubberstedt, Reference Librarian, Kendall Young Library, Webster City, Iowa.

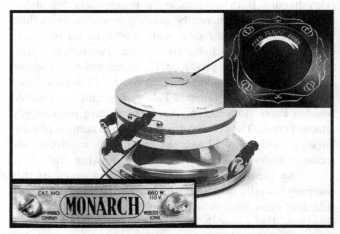

Model 965 is a well made pedestal unit and the last waffle iron model made in Webster City, Iowa in the late 1920s. By 1931 everything made by the then new Knapp-Monarch Company came from Belleville, Illinois.

Montgomery Ward Company

A Wards waffle iron circa late 1920s. Though it has no model number, it's marked "Ward Blue Line," the label used on the company's top-of-the-line products. Wards was strictly a retailer who contracted to have products manufactured for them. This particular waffle iron was made by Dominion Electric in Minneapolis.

In 1872, Aaron Montgomery Ward, a traveling dry goods salesman, began selling to farmers in the Midwest through a one page list, which in effect was the first mail order catalog and predated Sears Roebuck by over 14 years. In 1875, Ward was the first with a "satisfaction guaranteed or your money back" offer. At its peak, the "Monkey Wards" catalog was over 240 pages thick and became the shopper's bible for rural residents all across America.

The company became publicly owned in 1919 and opened its first retail stores in the 1920's. It lost ground to Sears in the 1950s by delaying moves to new suburban centers, a strategic blunder from which the company never fully recovered. In 1968 Wards merged with the Container Corporation of America to form Marcor. Mobil Oil bought controlling interest in the ailing firm in 1974 and became sole owner two years later. In 1985, Ward unveiled a new specialty store concept and discontinued its catalog business.

In 1988, Ward was purchased by GE Capital Corporation who arranged a leveraged management buyout through their Kidder Peabody subsidiary. In 1991, the new management reopened the company's catalog sales division. However, faced with new aggressive discount competitors like Wal-Mart and Target, sales were sluggish and Ward filed for bankruptcy reorganization in 1997. General Electric recapitalized the company but in December, 2000, Ward closed its 250 stores and filed for Chapter 11-bankruptcy protection.

Wards appliances were manufactured by various companies including Dominion, Electrahot, Liberty Gauge, Manning-Bowman, and Porcelier and in later years carried either the "Hankscraft" or "Ward" label. For details about individual Ward models see these various companies in the price guide.

Another Dominion product made for Wards, this **Model 375** non-automatic unit with pie crust base and walnut handles dates from the mid-late 1930s. Ward appliances are rarely exciting to look at but generally work well.

Generic looking **Model DE-2197** (DE=Dominion Electric) with black Bakelite trim is from the 1940s. It's automatic and a bit above average in quality. Items like this aren't too collectible but make good inexpensive everyday appliances.

National Stamping and Electric Works [1]

An artist's rendering of National Stamping's 3212-3246 West Lake Street facilities, circa 1920s. This 64,000 square foot building was the former Lindstrom Smith Company appliance factory purchased by National Stamping in 1921. It replaced National Stamping's smaller antiquated factory at 424 South Clinton Street. Interior pictures of that older factory can be seem later in this article.

Frank L. Kohlhase was almost an American-born native son, but his parents timing was a little off. He was actually born in Stettin, Germany, August 16, 1861. Just four months later the family immigrated to the United States, settling in Indiana. There as a teenager Frank made money as a duck hunting guide in the state's marshlands. In 1876 the Kolhase's moved to the Chicago area where Frank entered the metal trades first as a moulder and later becoming a machinist and an electro-plater. He secured a job as a machinist with the A.D. Foster Company, but was soon made a foreman. He rose to superintendent, and eventually became general manager of the company.

Frank L. Kohlhase
1861-1932

In 1897, Kohlhase left the Foster Company and founded his own firm, National Stamping Works for the purpose of manufacturing metal household specialties. The firm was located initially in a small factory building at 133-139 South Clinton Street (today 118 S. Clinton), Chicago. (Several photographs of the interior of this facility can be found later in this article.) As the company grew it was relocated within the city at least twice. City directories from 1914 to 1921 list an address of 424 South Clinton, three blocks from its original location. Several pictures inside this facility can also been seen later in this article and in the section "Electric Waffle Iron Development." In 1921, National Stamping purchased the electric goods manufacturer Lindstrom, Smith Company and in so doing acquired Lindstrom's large factory building at 3212-3246 West Lake Street near Garfield Park, pictured above. This factory covered 64,000 square feet and at its height employed about 300. It would be National Stamping's permanent address for the next 26 years.

National Stamping Works initially fabricated small metal stampings, metal spinnings, and miscellaneous brass castings. It also made tooling for industry, did job lot plating and polishing, and custom machining. By 1900 the firm was manufacturing gaslight fixtures as well as gasoline and battery powered lanterns. Around 1910 National Stamping Works was manufacturing several electric related products and in recognition of its expanded capabilities, "Electric" was added to the company name.

As electricity became more widely available and with the acquisition of the Lindstrom, Smith Company in the early 1920s, National Stamping and Electric entered the electric appliance industry in a big way. The company was organized into two divisions. The Lindstrom, Smith division, with its

114

The company's first office, circa 1900, when it was still called National Stamping Works. The company was located at 133 South Clinton Street at this time. Seated in front at a very battered secondhand desk is the company's prim looking bookkeeper. The company secretary is manning a vintage typewriter, center, and a young Frank Kolhase, the company founder, is at the roll top desk with the company telephone. The secretary and Mr. Kolhase must have gotten along well as this lady appears in pictures taken fifteen years later. Hung about the room are various gas light fixtures, the main product of the firm in its early days. A "Fisher Girl" advertising calander can be seen on the wall at right. These were all-American girls drawn by the popular illustrator of the day, Harrison Fisher. They predated Charles Gibson's Girls by about a decade. In order to eliminate glare, the photographer used an old trick of covering the exterior windows with paper and igniting flash powder in a holder for all of the illumination for the photo.

"White Cross" brand, produced a wide variety of electrically operated products including irons, toasters, grills, hair dryers, vibrators, curling irons, heating pads, electric combs, violet ray machines (medical quackery devices in vogue at the time), sewing machine motors, vacuum cleaners, and battery operated lanterns. The second division, Acorn Brass Manufacturing Company, produced cast and stamped hardware and machined items.

By the mid-1920s the firm was manufacturing two different models of a double burner hot plate as well as a space heater, a coffee percolator, a vacuum cleaner, two different cabinet type kerosene stoves, and a $9.00 waffle iron designated the **Model 156**. A dealer's brochure indicates that by 1930 the company offered six different waffle iron models (**156, 254, 255, 257, 258, 259**) and two, three-piece matching serving sets. The following year the company offered three "White Cross" electric toaster models, ten different coffee percolators, two coffee urns, two table stoves (hot plates), and the same six waffle irons that appeared in the company's 1930 brochure. The deflation of the depression years is clearly illustrated by a 17% drop in price for the **Model 156** iron from $9.00 in 1926 to $ 7.50 in 1931.

Frank Kohlhase died December 27, 1932 at his winter home in Saint Petersburg Florida. He was 71. His son Edwin, who had attended Northwestrn University and who had worked for Western Electric, AT&T, and Union Special Machine before coming to work for his father in 1921, assumed the presidency of National Stamping and Electric Works in 1933. He continued to operate the business until he passed away in

Edwin A. Kohlhase
1898-1945

September 1945. After that, National Stamping struggled. It was finally sold in 1947 to the Eureka Williams Company of

National Stamping continued:

In 1900, at about the time this picture was taken, National Stamping's main product was gas light fixtures, seen here being assembled by seven teenaged boys. This was probably the cleanest safest and least noisy place in the factory. Until the 1920s when moving assembly lines were installed in factories, most production was done in batches. Barrels and crates of parts like those seen here would be brought to one location and the product would be put together and packed by hand a few at a time. Until child labor laws were enacted during the depression, much of the lighter factory work was done by what we refer to today as adolescents. Prior to that time there was no such catagory for children.

Detroit, whereupon National Stamping and Electric Works and its "White Cross" brand ceased to exist.

Details of the inner workings of the firm are nonexistent, but a wartime Chicago Tribune article dated June 16, 1944, indicates that it, like many small appliance makers, it was struggling at this time,. The article announced that the War Production Board was about to allow the Chicago firms of National Stamping and Electric, Chicago Flexible Shaft (Sunbeam), Waage Manufacturing, Gilson Manufacturing, the Lawrence M. Stein Company, as well as the Rochester, New York firm of Samson United, to manufacture a limited number of laundry irons for civilian use. To qualify for this special work each company had to have fewer than 100 employees. According to the same article, due to the critical shortage of labor for defense work in the Chicago area, only unskilled female labor could be used to produce the irons there. The article went on to say that the Office of Price Administration also required that the irons be priced no higher than their selling price at the time of Pearl Harbor. Sunbeam was allowed to produce 162,500 irons, Samson United was allocated 98,500, and National Stamping was allowed 8,800. In the article, B.A. Graham, President of Sunbeam at the time, expressed concerns that high wartime costs and these price restrictions might preclude any possible profit if they were made in Chicago. Whether these irons were actually produced by any of the companies is unknown.

Compared to other brands, prices of "White Cross" products when new were in the low to medium range. From personal inspection, **Models 156, 250**, 254, and **668** waffle irons leave the impression that they are inexpensive bargain basement items. **Model 668**, from the late 1930s and early 1940s, appears to be an inexpensive look-a-like copy of the very popular General Electric Model 119W4 of the period. Instead of GE's nicely molded brown plastic handles, the "White Cross" model has inexpensive brown painted wood handles that look as though they were created in a junior high school wood shop. The **Models 156** and **250** have inadequate heating elements that heat the grids slowly and unevenly. Model 254, however, deserves special mention. For this model, the engineering department used the excellent heavy-duty heating element designed for the company's 1925 hot plate and created a nice waffle iron around it. The result was an iron that works very well and contrasts sharply with many of the company's other models.

[1] Historical information courtesy Lesley Martin, research specialist, The Chicago Historical Society. Family and additional company history courtesy Mrs. Barbara Gent. Waffle iron references are the author's.

116

Most of the employees here are teenagers except for the pre-teen in front. This is a machine room at the company's 133 S. Clinton address, circa 1900. In the left foreground is a hand operated arbor press used to bend small metal parts. The large weight on the press's handle assisted in the bending process when the handle was thrown. The dangerous belt-driven machine the boy has his hand on is a small stamping press. The teen at right is seated in front of a hand operated riveting press. Also visible is a metal shears at the far end of the table, a drill press at left, and a small lathe right center. The young fellow in center of picture is grasping a long handle used to engage and disengage the overhead power shaft which drives his lathe.

Although the company was producing some electrical products by 1915 when this photo was taken, here they are manufacturing hand pumped suction type carpet sweepers. A finished example can be seen leaning against the pillar at right center between the supervisor and someone who appears to be a salesman. These sweepers were actually a suction pump operated by grasping the wood handle and pulling and pushing the tube. A pile of handles with diaphragms attached can be seen over the right shoulder of the young man holding a small paintbrush in the foreground. Although this old factory had at some point been retrofitted with a sprinkler system, a fire bucket still hangs from the pillar behind the salesman.

As the firm grew, so too did the office staff. This is the company's 424 South Clinton Street facility around 1915. This office was nearly as spartan as the company's first one pictured previously. Barely visible at very far right is the telephone operator /receptionist. (The author, while restoring the photograph under high magnification, counted five telephones in the room, a significant number for that time.) The large dark cabinet against the far wall behind the woman seated at right is the company safe. Mr. Kolhase and his secretary, first photographed in 1900, are seated in the far corner. The woman at front center appears to be the poster lady for the most harried billings clerk of the year award. The photographer again covered the windows with paper to cut glare.

National Stamping continued:

The young man in right foreground in this circa 1915 photo taken in the South Clinton Street factory, is installing a power cord on some type of electrically powered device. A pile of these cords with screw-in-type porcelain plugs can be seen draped over a box in center background. What this product is remains a mystery. Examples on the bench have a faucet type spigot sticking out of the side near the top. Could this be the base of some type of water heating device? The supervisor in the background is standing behind a partially assembled item that looks like a metal cabinet on cabriole legs. The cabinet has a large hole punched through its back panel. If anyone thinks they know what these products are, the author would like to know.

This factory issued photo, circa 1920s, shows one of the company's Kerosene fueled stoves. These were popular with families in rural areas where electricity or gas service was unavailable. The reservoir at left was filled with fuel, which flowed by gravity to each burner. The odor from this contraption operating in a closed room in winter must have at times been overwhelming. Odor or not, it was a lot nicer than chopping wood or lugging coal and emptying ashes.

National Stamping continued:

What appear to be water heater tanks are being fabricated in this 1915 photo. Two workers in the background are holding soldering irons and were probably "sweating" (soldering) pipefittings to the tops of the tanks. Close examination of the faces of the workers in this and several other photos from the same vintage, indicates that many of them seem to be Italian immigrants. Although the factory was originally plumbed for gaslights, it has also been wired with a rudimentary electric lighting system as evidenced by the knob and tube wiring along the ceiling at left and the drop cords. However no light bulbs are installed in the sockets. Illumination is still being supplied by natural gas burned from the ends of the pipes located above the workers at left. Each pipe is capped with a silk mantle like those found in Coleman lanterns. Hanging on the far wall are cardboard patterns which were used to trace the correct shape of various parts onto sheet metal stock.

Opposit the tank assembly operation , seen in upper photo, is this row of soldering stations. The men appear to be fabricating burner assemblies. The man wearing the vest and holding a cigarette must have been the leadman of the group as he also appears at center rear in the tank assembly photo. He's sporting rather classic high-heeled shoes like those worn by Flamenco dancers. On the wall between the third and fourth men from the left can be seen an open flame burning from a rickety-looking gas line that feeds the soldering iron heaters on the workbench. Three mantel capped gas pipes hang from the ceiling but are not lit. One of the company's gasoline fueled lanterns, minus it's shade, hangs from an overhead water pipe, and is being used for supplemental illumination. The long crates on the floor contain sections of threaded pipe.

The South Clinton Street office staff, circa 1919. The old office appears to have received a face lift, due in part to some heavy handed darkroom retouching by the photographer . (I think as a personal joke he took the time to enhance some cracks in the far wall which are visible below the right ceiling beam.) The ornate old tin ceiling appears to have been plastered over since the 1915 photo of the same room was taken (see page 118). There are also new light fixtures and a few pieces of new furniture. The uncomfortable wire chairs are still in evidence however, and the wood floors are still barren of carpeting. One of the company's gasoline lamps with a light-colred shade can be seen on the far roll top desk. Although the firm was manufacturing some electrical goods by this time, these non-electric lamps were popular in rural areas where electric power was still unavailable. Within two years the company would move to newer larger facilities near Garfield Park. As a small aside, the author noted while restoring the National Stamping pictures, that clean floors was not a high priority at the company either in the offices or the factory. Every picture shows a dirty or littered floor.

National Stamping attempted to make models that looked expensive but were still affordable. To achieve this, the company often cut corners on materials. This unnumbered model from the mid-1920s was equipped with inexpensive thin stamped sheet aluminum grids instead of the heavier and more costly cast variety. Performance suffered due to the resultant poor heat distribution.

Model 156, like several other "White Cross" irons of 1920s vintage, has a base that gets unusually hot for a pedestal-type iron. These irons were equipped with extra tall feet to prevent damage to heat sensitive work surfaces.

The **Model 156** waffle iron is featured in this "White Cross" holiday ad for 1926 along with an iron, toaster, percolator, space heater, and heating pad. Such items in the retail trades were given the designation "Lamp Socket Appliances" because in many homes of the period, wall outlets were few and far between. Small appliances were usually sold with adapters allowing them to be connected to the more plentiful lamp sockets. Such an adapter can be seen peeking from behind the waffle iron.

(December, 1926, *Liberty Magazine*)

National Stamping continued:

Model 250 with its ivory colored wood handles could easily be mistaken for a Landers made product of this late 1920s period. Though non-automatic, it is above average in both looks and quality. The large easy to read dial-type temperature gauge in the center of the lid is a definite aid for the cook.

NEW TWIN WAFFLE IRON

No. 666

New Twin Waffle Iron

Waffles without waiting for all when this new White Cross twin waffle baker is used. Bakes two waffles at the same time quickly. Each waffle is full size and baked evenly because of the special White Cross oven type heating elements. Cast aluminum no-stick grids, size 5" x 5¾", which require no pre-treatment before use. Heat indicator on each grid indicates correct baking temperature. A matched appliance with the new modernistic engraved design on the base and cover. Finished in bright, sparkling chrome with walnut colored lifting and side handles. Complete with Underwriters' Approved detachable cord set.

Waffle Irons

Beautifully styled series of waffle irons with leaf design on top and carried through with the matching metal overlay on each walnut handle. Cast aluminum no-stick grids require no pre-treatment before use. Full expansion hinge with concealed connecting nickel wires. Nichrome heating elements distribute heat evenly both top and bottom for uniform baking at all times. Finished throughout in brightly polished chrome. The timing lever on automatic models can be set for whatever type of waffles are desired and then signal light tells when grids are sufficiently heated for pouring the batter and again when waffle is baked ready for serving. Non-automatic models have heat indicator to show correct baking temperature.

No. 565   Large automatic waffle iron with 8¼" cast aluminum grids and butter groove.
No. 569   Same as above but without batter groove.
No. 563   Large non-automatic waffle iron with heat indicator, 8¼" grids and batter groove.
No. 568   Same as above but without batter groove.

No. 565

No. 568

Cat. No.	Item	Watts	Std.	Lot	Weight	Code
666	Twin Waffle Iron	660	3	18		ZIJFA
565	Large Auto. Waffle Iron	660	3	18		ZIJJO
569	Automatic Waffle Iron.	660	3	21		ZIJOJ
563	Large Non-Auto. Waffle Iron	660	3	18		ZIJGE
568	Non-auto. Waffle Iron	660	3	15		ZIJLY

Models 565 and 568 illustrated on the right in this 1940 winter catalog have solid walnut handles with classic-looking brass Roman-style laurel wreath inlays. The author has never seen either of these models. The very common Model 666 illustrated at top is a lower cost twin model with painted wood handles. (Winter 1940, Pittsburg Electric Supply Company catalog)

Model 265 is without a doubt the most stylish waffle iron National Stamping ever produced. The large raised lid design (insert) shouts Art Deco. Being a well-engineered automatic model, its performance matches its good looks.

Whether by accident or design, this "White Cross" Model 668, circa late 1930s, looks very much like General Electric's very popular Model 119W4 of the same period (see page 78). A close examination however, reveals inexpensive painted wood handles, simple heating elements, and thin grid castings, making it far inferior in quality to the GE model.

Nelson Machine & Manufacturing Company [1]
"Mastercraft" "Bel Air"

This early 1930s toaster, one of Nelson's first products, looks and works surprisingly like a "Star" model made a few years earlier by Fitzgerald. A twist of the knobs turns the bread. Not many of these were produced as Nelson may have been infringing on Fitzgerald's patents.

(Toaster courtesy Michael Sheafe, www.ToasterCentral.com)

Christian B. Nelson, one of eight children, was only able to complete the sixth grade before having to go to work to help support the rest of his cash-strapped Norwegian family. By the 1920s he was working as a machinist making pressure cookers for the Presto Company in Eau Claire, Wisconsin during the day while going to school at night.

In 1931 Nelson incorporated the Nelson Machine and Manufacturing Company in the state of Delaware and on December 8th registered the company with the Secretary of State of Ohio. The articles of incorporation list the company's location as Lakewood, Ohio and the purpose of the business as being, "To manufacture, buy, sell and otherwise deal in metal specialties and electrical appliances of all kinds..." C. B. Nelson was designated president of the corporation and his wife Harriette was secretary. On papers dated 1935, the location of the principal business office is listed as 7933 Ewald

Road, Cleveland.

Harry and Peter Nelson, two of Christian's brothers and both machinists, worked in various capacities for the firm for some years. Harry was also 1/3rd owner of the firm. Peter's three sons, John, William, and Robert all worked for the company. John became manager of the firm's plating operation while his brother Bill became the company office manager. Robert was a machinist like his father and uncle. Christian was the company's general manager, engineer, designer, and chief salesman, until a stroke in 1972 forced his wife Harriette to take charge. She operated the firm until 1979 when it ceased operations. At its peak in the mid-1970s Nelson Machine and Manufacturing employed about 100 workers.

One of the first items produced by Nelson in the early 1930s was a very inexpensive clothes iron aimed at the low

Heavy well made heating elements installed in an inexpensive plain looking shell, created an affordable appliance that works well. Nelson got many miles from the mold that made the plastic handles seen on this iron with no model number. The same handles in either ivory or brown were used on many of the company's products for years.

end of the then depressed consumer market. The iron, which sold for about a dollar, was so successful that the company expanded into lower cost toasters, waffle irons, pop corn poppers, and coffee percolators. Many of these items were sold through Sears, Wards, Penney, and other department stores and also in so-called "5 & 10¢" stores like S. S. Kresge, F. W. Woolworth, and W. T. Grant.

During the war years C. B. Nelson was able to secure several cost plus defense contracts for his company and the firm prospered. However after the war, when the company was forced back into a competitive environment, it faced severe price competition from rival appliance makers. To cut costs and eliminate labor union pressures, the firm was reorganized and in January 1948 moved into the old Empire Steel Mill in Ashtabula, Ohio where it remained until its closure in the late 1970s.

By the 1960s, Nelson was manufacturing pop-up toasters, electric griddles, fry pans, crock pots, and a very popular deep fryer model of which about 200,000 were made annually. One of C. B. Nelson's greatest talents was an uncanny ability to design products which could be used to exploit particular market niches that were of little interest to large manufacturers like GE, Westinghouse, or McGraw-Electric. For example, in 1968 he crafted a clever charcoal-type picnic grill that was designed to be stamped from inexpensive steel barrel lids. The low material cost allowed Nelson to price the grills well below those of the competition.

The quality of Nelson waffle irons as with many of its other products ranges from average to poor, reflecting C. B. Nelson's cost driven design philosophy. Performance characteristics vary from very good for **Model 451**, to absolutely abysmal in the case of **Model 511**. In a January 1949 *Consumer Reports* article on waffle irons, the magazine said of the Nelson **Model 250**, "This waffle iron ran too hot to make a satisfactory waffle unless the cord was unplugged during the baking." The article further stated, "For one willing to accept the inconvenience of unplugging the cord and also the small size of the waffle, this iron can be considered 'acceptable' because of its low price." That $4.95 low price did not include a cord, nor did the company issue a guarantee. Nelson often did not label its products, or simply used the capital "N" overlain with a lightning bolt illustrated under the title to this article. A few items can be found labeled "Mastercraft" or "Bel Air." Most Nelson products are lacking

Nelson Machine continued:

Model 250, (insert) with black painted base, cost slightly less than **Model 350** with its chrome-plated base. Both versions look inexpensive but cook reasonably well.

(Model 350 photo courtesy Dan & Vi LaBelle)

Model 511 grill/waffle iron from the 1940s has no rivals in the category of worst performer. It overheats very quickly, its ill-fitting grids warp when hot, and it cooks thin waffles very unevenly. To add injury to insult (pun intended), the thin plastic lid handle gets hot enough from escaping steam to cause burns.

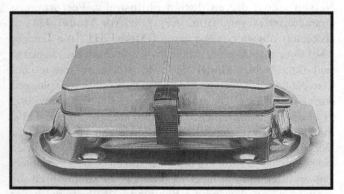

Model 200 sandwich grill, circa late 1940s is a typical low cost "Plain-Jane" Nelson product of this period. However, it does make nice grilled cheese sandwiches, but then to me there is no such thing as a bad grilled cheese sandwich.

Is this bulky looking waffle iron Nelson-made? It measures an impressive 12 inches across the base, 5 inches high, and probably dates from the mid-1930s. The iron is totally devoid of markings to indicate who made it but the black plastic handles and temperature dial look very similar to those used on some Nelson products (see iron pictured on preceeding page). A similar version of this iron came with rectangular black plastic handles.

126

Perfection Electric Products Company [1]
"Excelsior" & "PEPCO"

The Perfection Electric factory shortly after it was erected in 1920. This building housed the company's entire operation including the business office, laboratory, and a well equipped tool and die room. Stamping, plating, assembly, and shipping were all done on site.

On January 19, 1920, seven prominent citizens of New Washington, Ohio, met in the third floor auditorium of the grand old 1881 high school building, to organize the Perfection Electric Products Company and cash in on the hot new post war growth industry of electric household appliances. In attendance that day was George Hoffman, L.P. Uhl, Frank Spillette, M.M. Kibler, C.T. Seitter, Henry Kruesheld, and J.H. Donaldson. These gentlemen were all convinced that New Washington, situated on two rail lines midway between Cleveland and Toledo, was an ideal location for an appliance manufacturing facility. They knew of the abundance of unskilled labor available from the recession plagued local farming populous, and were confident of attracting many into their factory with a promise of steady wages. Those board members of German decent, were also confident that friends or relatives, with training in the machine and metal working trades, could easily be convinced to leave war ravaged Germany for the promise of Midwest American prosperity. The first order of business that day was planning for the construction of a factory, followed by the appointment of Henry Kruesheld as plant manager.

Construction began on a small masonry factory in April, 1920. A minor setback occurred in June when a strong spring windstorm blew across the flats of northern Ohio and damaged the gable ends of the partially completed machine shop and office building. In September, advertisements for girls to work in the assembly section of the factory appeared in editions of the *New Washington Herald*. Shortly before Christmas, the same paper announced that production at the factory had started with 36 employees. They were men and women, with names like Heydinger and Alspach, Durnwald and Zucker and included machinists and toolmakers, platers and press operators, assemblers, typists, and clerks. In January, the *New Washington Herald* proudly reported that the first shipment

of appliances had left the factory by horse "dray," for one of the two train depots in town.

For three years the company produced high quality toasters, electric irons, sterilizes, egg cookers, hot plates, and waffle irons, but a major business slump occurred in early 1924, resulting in a plant shutdown that April. Frank Spillette replaced Henry Kruesheld as plant manager and production resumed in July of 1925. In 1926, in a second attempt to revive the business, the board of directors replaced Spillette with Charles Lucas. Due to heavy debt loads, the firm was unable to meet interest payments on its loans, and ceased operations in 1927. The factory was later occupied by a succession of firms including the Ohio Soya Company and the Perfect Rubber Company. Sadly, the old building was completely destroyed by fire late in the afternoon of December 18th, 1947. [2]

During its short existence, Perfection Electric produced a Model 4-7-A "Excelsior" toaster and two models of waffle irons, each labeled "**Excelsior**." The first, a petite 6-inch diameter leg-mounted unit, came with a white porcelain enamel finish, a non-expanding lid hinge, and a power socket located on the front under the lid handle. The heavy-duty over-engineered heating elements in this appliance take a very long time to reach operating temperature, but work well and likely have a service life of several hundred years. The second "**Excelsior**" was introduced in 1922 and was furnished with a stylish tray. The power connector this time was located on the back along with the push-down-to-operate-type lid handle. Appliance collectors should consider any Perfection Electric product a rare industrial artifact.

[1]   Historical information and materials courtesy Joseph R. Blum and the New Washington Historical Society, New Washington, Ohio.

[2]   New Washington was home to a second waffle iron maker in the 1920's. See "Reynolds Aluminum Company" for details.

Perfection Electric continued:

One windy Midwest morning in the early 1920s the entire staff was assembled behind the factory for this photo. The gentleman in suit and vest at front left is Henry Kruesheld, the plant manager at this time. All but two of the women are dressed in smocks for factory work. Several workers are teenagers. Some of the men are recent imigrents from war-torn Germany.

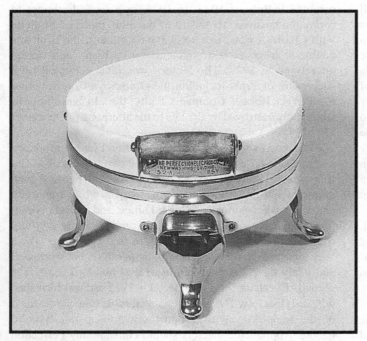

Perfection's first waffle iron model with baked white enamel finish was built during the infancy of the electrical appliance industry when designers were still unsure what an electric waffle iron should look like. In this instance they placed the power cord connector in front where it was sure to be in the way of the cook.

WAFFLE RANGE COMPLETE WITH NICKEL TRAY. LIST PRICE $18.00 EACH.

EXCELSIOR
ELECTRIC WAFFLE RANGE
A New Style Waffle Range

"*Excelsior Electric Waffle Range*" is what this 1922 ad called the company's second waffle iron model. It is like no other waffle iron ever made. The lid handle was mounted above the hinge ostensibly to prevent steam burns when opening the top. Pressing down on the handle opened the lid. A quarter turn of the cooking grids allowed their removal for easy cleaning. (January 1922, Electrical Merchandising)

128

Porcelier Manufacturing Company [1]

Porcelier used six different Colonial Silhouette patterns on its waffle irons. Two are shown here. Upper left and on iron "Introduction"; upper right "Proposal." These decals are multi-colored in contrast to the "Piano Lesson" decal (not shown) which is black and white.
(Iron photo courtesy Kelly Singer)

The Porcelier Manufacturing Company began in East Liverpool, Ohio, in 1927, as a small maker of vitreous china products. By1930, the company was reincorporated and moved to Greensburg, Pennsylvania, a small town twenty miles southeast of Pittsburgh. At it's peak in the 1940's, Porcelier produced porcelain bowls, mugs, pitchers, lamps, lighting and bathroom fixtures, novelty items, and a complete line of porcelain kitchen appliances including electric coffee percolators, toasters, sandwich grills, and waffle irons. The company had metal working facilities and manufactured many of the metal parts for their electrical items in-house. The firm closed its doors in July, 1954, primarily a victim of the increased use of plastics instead of costly ceramics, by competitors, in electrical fixtures, appliances, and other household goods.

The company manufactured waffle irons from 1934 to about 1940 offering customers a choice of either an automatic thermostatically controlled model or a slightly less expensive non-automatic unit, which came with a built-in temperature indicator in the lid. The entire internal elements of these irons were unique to Porceleir and were designed by one Emil Walder with his patent assigned to Porcelier in the mid-1930s. Throughout production, the design was not changed, making precise dating of individual units difficult.

Porcelier's electrical appliances were classed in the luxury goods category and were sold through traditional retail outlets, or through the larger mail-order companies such as Sears (Heatmaster) and Wards (Hankscraft). The waffle irons were marketed individually, or as part of a matched set that

Scalloped with Wildflowers
Colonial Silhouette (Man and woman in colonial dress) in following poses...

Introduction	(Lady with fan/gent bowing)	*Minuet*	(Couple dancing)
Bouquet	(Gent presenting flowers)	*Proposal*	(Gent proposing)
Acceptance	(Gent kissing lady's hand)	*Refusal*	(Lady turned)

(Irons with the six decals listed above came with handles of various colors)

Piano Lesson   (Lady at harpsichord with woman instructor in Black & white)
Serv-All   (Cream body with platinum or red and black deco lines)
Barock-Colonial   (With plain, gold, red or blue "dots" or bumps. The blue is most rare, plain may not exist,
            as certain collectors believe they are due to paint worn or removed from other versions)
Basketweave with Wild Flowers   (Produced with either square or round handles)

Porcelier continued:

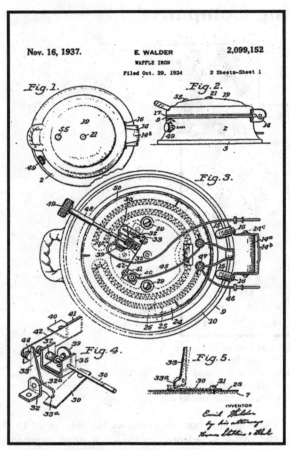

The 1934 patent drawings (not granted until 1937) for the various components of the Porcelier automatic models. These irons are complex and as a consequence were expensive to build.

Basketweave Wild Flowers models like this were made with either rounded base handles like this one or with squared-off handles.
(Photo courtesy Kelly Singer)

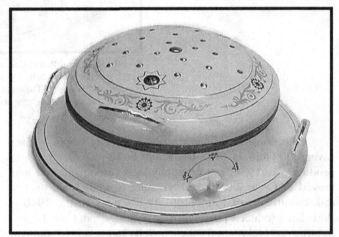

Barock-Colonial automatic models like this can have gold, red, blue, or plain dots or bumps visible on lid. Blue is least common. Plain versions are thought by some authorities to be the result of worn paint. (Photo courtesy Kelly Singer)

Serv-All models have cream-colored bodies with either platinum, red, or black accent lines.

could include a batter pitcher, syrup "jar" (pitcher), a toaster, a sandwich grill, and a coffee percolator with sugar bowl and cream pitcher. Although over a hundred different patterns appeared on Porcelier products, just fifteen were applied to the appliance line of goods. These are listed on the preceeding page in order from most rare to most common.

By appliance industry standards, Porcelier was a very small "niche" producer. Due to the high cost of manufacturing porcelain-bodied appliances, the company had a difficult time keeping prices competitive during the depression years. Consequently comparitively few of their kitchen appliance products were ever produced and sold.

Due to low production volume and the fact that porcelain-bodied appliances are easily damaged in use, surviving examples of Porcelier waffle irons are scarse to rare and active trading in them is limited. The majority are found with heat stress cracks in multiple locations. Most models in average condition with original cord sell for well over $100 and it is becoming increasingly common for those in excellent condition to fetch over $300.

[1] Information about models and rarity courtesy Kelly Singer and Jeff Gordon.

Precision Manufacturing
"Rainbow"

Whoever thought up the name for this company either had a great imagination or a wonderful sense of humor. The 1940s products of this Dover, New Jersey firm were anything but precision-made. At first glance, the company's **Model 80W** "Rainbow" waffle iron appears to be an inexpensive throwaway, but what this appliance lacks in looks it more than makes up for in performance. It cooks a moderately thick, 7 inch diameter waffle more quickly and evenly than many more expensive looking irons. However, it has one annoying shortcoming-the steeply sloping base insures that any batter overflows end up on the counter or tabletop. The author has seen just one model each of the company's unnumbered toaster and waffle iron.

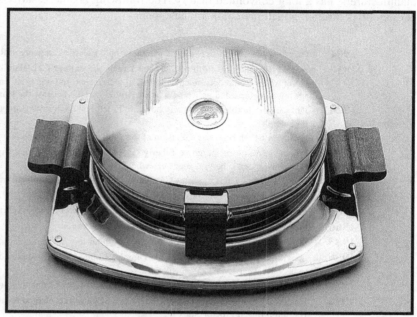

Model 80W, a bargain basement special from the late 1930s or early 1940s, is a surprisingly good cooker. Inexpensive irons of this type are generally poor performers and usually quite frustrating to use. This is a pleasant exception.

Precision Mold & Foundry Company Inc.

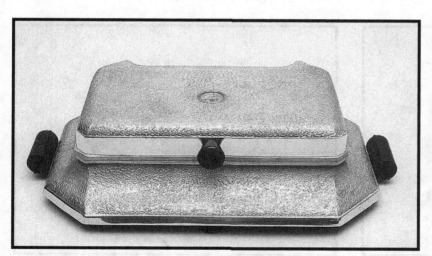

Made by a Los Angeles Aluminum foundry during the silent film era, this cast aluminum iron was one company's way of cashing in on the booming market for home appliances in the 1920s. Disguising itself as a single unit, it actually makes a pair of waffles side by side under one lid.

Precision Mold and Foundry of Los Angeles, like many small manufacturers in the 1920s, diversified into the new growth industry of the decade, electrical appliances. They produced an attractive and unusual dual waffle iron that masquerades as a single unit. Being a foundry product, the **Model 101** has a heavy two piece all cast aluminum body in a stylish hammered finish with attractive polished edges. This iron works very nicely, but with cooking grids cast integral to the body shell, the entire unit becomes exceedingly hot during use, even to the point of charring it's Bakelite handles. This one-of-a-kind appliance is rare and very collectable.

131

Proctor & Schwartz Company

Founded in 1885 as the Philadelphia Textile and Machinery Company, Porctor & Schwartz, like many other appliance manufacturers, has a long convoluted history. The following is a necessarily sketchy chronology of the major transitions and permutations through which the company has gone.

1904 Fred Osius and William Horlick form the Arnold Electric Company in Racine, Wisconsin.

1910 Arnold Electric hires farm boy Chester Beach and cashier L.H. Hamilton, who perfect a strong high-speed electric motor which would operate on either AC or DC current, and was small enough to power drink mixers, knife sharpeners, sewing machines, and polishing wheels. Arnold Electric became the Hamilton Beach Company.

1920 Philadelphia Textile & Machinery becomes Proctor and Schwartz Company with facilities at 7th Street and Tabor Road, Philadelphia.

1922 Hamilton Beach becomes a division of the appliance conglomerate Scovill.

1928 Proctor & Schwartz purchase Liberty Gauge and Instrument Company and become Proctor and Schwartz Electric Company. (See "Liberty Gauge" elsewhere)

1929 Frank Walcott creates the Silex Company, which specializes in coffee makers.

1953 Silex purchases the Chicago Electric Manufacturing Company.

1960 Proctor and Schwartz and Silex merge to form the Proctor-Silex Corporation.

1966 Proctor-Silex becomes a division of the SCM Corporation.

1983 SCM sells Proctor-Silex division to Wesray Appliances.

1986 Scovill sells Hamilton Beach to Glen Dimplex Limited. Wesray Appliances and Wear-Ever Aluminum Company merge to become Wear-Ever/Proctor-Silex Inc.

1988 Proctor-Silex division is sold to the North American Coal Company of (Cleveland) Ohio (NACCO).

1990 Hamilton Beach division of Scovill is sold to NACCO and is merged with the Proctor-Silex division to form a subsidiary-Hamilton Beach/Proctor-Silex Inc.

Proctor & Schwartz styling resembles that of Toastmaster and could be characterized as utilitarian or commercial. Internally, all of its irons use the same parts. The thermostat control on these units though overly complex, is quite sensitive and accurate, making the irons a pleasure to use. An interesting innovation, the "Glow Cone" indicator window first appeared on Proctor & Schwartz toasters and waffle irons in the early 1930s, and continued to be used into the 1950s. This small cone shaped Pyrex window magnified the light emanating from the heating elements, signaling the status of the appliance. The prism effect of the cone, makes it quiet easy to see, even in a brightly-lit room.

Although Proctor and Swartz waffle irons can be considered uncommon or even scarce, their plain styling keeps prices for them low. In good condition they make a very nice every- day type of practical appliance.

Model 698 like all Proctor and Swartz models is a well-engineered quality appliance. It may not win any styling awards but it's a real pleasure to use . This is a Sears "Heatmaster" example from the mid-1930s.

Model 1516 has stylish deco-type handles and lid emossing. Missing is the antique-looking radio knob temperature control common to earlier Proctor irons, replaced by a smaller more streamlined modern one. Proctor & Schwartz models all share the same internal parts.

Reynolds Aluminum Company [1]
"RACO" Ware

A rather decrepit looking Reynolds foundry circa 1916. Compare this with the second photo on the next page, taken in the mid-1920s. Landscaping was obviously not high on the list of company priorities.

In 1911, a group of civic leaders calling themselves the New Washington Industrial Association of New Washington, Ohio, encouraged the formation of the Reynolds Aluminum Company (no relation to Reynolds Metals) by supplying a foundry building. In 1912 it was very likely only the second aluminum foundry in America when it began casting aluminum hollowware. The firm's pots, pans, skillets, kettles, stove top waffle irons, and roasters all bore the "RACO WARE" name. Over the years, other cast aluminum kitchen items were added, including sugar scoops, sausage stuffer tubes, and butter paddles. One of the company's most successful products turned out to be a line of polished cast aluminum running board step plates, a popular automotive accessory in the 1920s and 1930s, installed on running boards to protect them from foot wear.

Reynolds was modestly successful during the teens and twenties but, like many small companies, suffered a series of setbacks after the stock market crash of 1929. The firm was moved to the Chicago area in the early 1930s, and then sold to a succession of owners. Unfortunately, it did not survive the depression.

In the early 1920s, Reynolds produced a nicely polished cast aluminum electric waffle iron, and with it became the first of two companies in New Washington to manufacture electric appliances (see the Perfection Electric story). The

"RACO" waffle iron closely resembles those made by Landers and Westinghouse during this period. In fact the split power cord appears to have come from the same supplier that provided Landers Frary & Clark with cords for its small rectangular irons. "RACO" waffle irons should be considered rare industrial artifacts.

[1] Historical information and materials courtesy Joseph R. Blum and The New Washington Historical Society, New Washington, Ohio.

The primary product of Reynolds was cast aluminum cookware like this stove-top-type waffle iron which in this case is missing its base. The ball-socket-type hinge allowed the iron to be turned without having to be lifted completely from its base. The large cast trademark leaves no ambiguity as to the manufacturer.

133

The same factory as pictured on the previous page five years later. The facility has a new addition on on the front, which appears to have doubled the size of the building. Notice the new but still unpaved streets. The single awning by the front enterance is a nice touch but the landscaping committee still hadn't gotten around to weed control.

(Photo courtesy Joseph Blum and The New Washington, Ohio Historical Society)

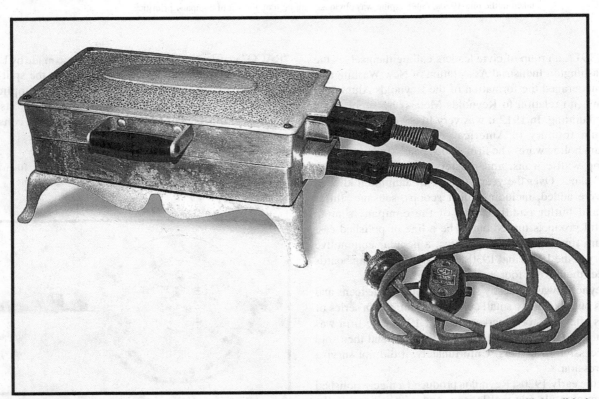

This rare Reynolds electric waffle iron model has heavy cast aluminum body shells and lid which, when new, were most likely polished. The unique skirted legs are nickel-plated steel. The cumbersome split power cord was typical of early 1920s. waffle irons.

(Photo courtesy Joseph Blum)

Robeson Rochester Corporation
"Royal Rochester"

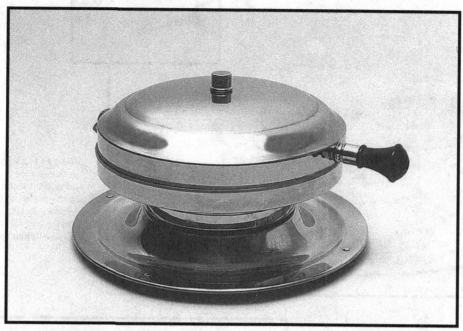

A late 1920s **Model 6468** was for some reason named the "Dictator", a designation also used by Studebaker for one of its car models at the time. Ten years later during the Nazi era, copywriters would have never considered the name.

The Robeson Rochester Corporation was formed in 1922 with the merger of the Robeson Cutlery Company, a knife manufacturer founded by M.F. Robeson in upstate New York in the 1870's, and the Rochester Stamping Company, a small New York pot and kettle manufacturer that began in 1888 as the Rochester Stamping Works. First noted for their well made and nicely styled coffee percolators, by 1931, Robeson Rochester was marketing an extensive line of porcelain and metal products including flat irons, tea pots, casseroles, coffee urns, percolators, and waffle irons. The company's porcelain products were sold under the "Royal China" or "Royal Rochester Royalite" names and were guaranteed never to be affected by heat or cold. The Fraunfelter/Ohio China Company made all of the ceramic parts for Rochester's electrical goods until Fraunfelter went into bankruptcy in 1939. From the 1930s through the 1970s Robeson Rochester was bought, sold, and divided several times and at present exists as Robeson Industries Corporation.

The Waffle iron line of products was introduced in the late 1920s and continued through the 1930s. The less expensive models were non-automatic and designed with metal lids while the more costly came with Fraunfelter-manufactured porcelain inserts in six patterns. In order of popularity these were "Golden Pheasant," "Red Poppy," "Black Leaf and Myrtle," "Orange Luster," "Royal Bouquet," and "Modernistic."

Waffle irons could be purchased separately or as part of a matching serving set that could include a coffee percolator or urn, a very stylish tapered batter bowl, a ladle, a syrup pitcher a sugar bowl, and a cream pitcher. A rare waffle keeper was made in the "Golden Pheasant" pattern. It resembles a shallow chaffing dish held in a four-legged nickel-plated metal stand. A walnut serving tray was also offered in the late 1930s. Waffle iron/grill Model 250, produced in the late 1930s, was the only dual-purpose model made by the company. During the depression years Robeson Rochester products were considered top of the line luxury goods and, by industry standards, were not produced in very great quantities.

Collectors should be aware that the firm's early chrome-plated models often suffer from deteriorated finishes, due to the inadequacies of the chrome plating technology available at the time. Nearly all Royal Rochester waffle irons were well engineered and all are able to do a credible cooking job. Non-automatic models are more common than those with thermostats. All Royal Rochester waffle irons should be considered uncommon or scarce, but none are rare. The ceramic insert models are highly sought after by both porcelain and appliance collectors, with the "Modernistic" pattern the most desirable and fetching the highest prices.

135

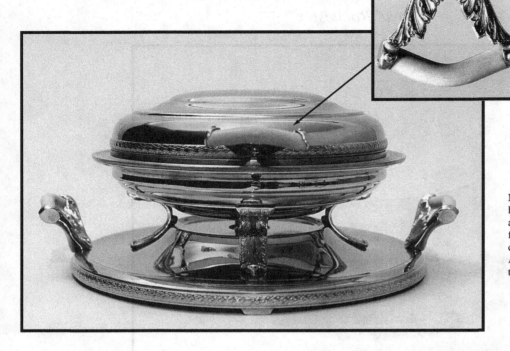

Model **E6472** with curved imitation bone handles still looks classic. Few were made and today in nice condition this model fetches higher than average prices from collectors. Beardsley and Wolcott 's "Torrid Avignon" model of the same vintage has the same styling(see page 34).

Model **12310** with a Celtic-type lid design looks elegant. The sliding tab temperature indicator incorporated into the lid handle on this and several other models was good styling but made them nearly impossible to read. This is an automatic model with the slide-type temperature control in front.

Given the genteel name The "Berkley," **Model E6469** from the late 1920s was one of the most ordinary irons Rochester made. At $7.25 it was also the least expensive. At that time it was considered by retailers to be a mid-priced model.

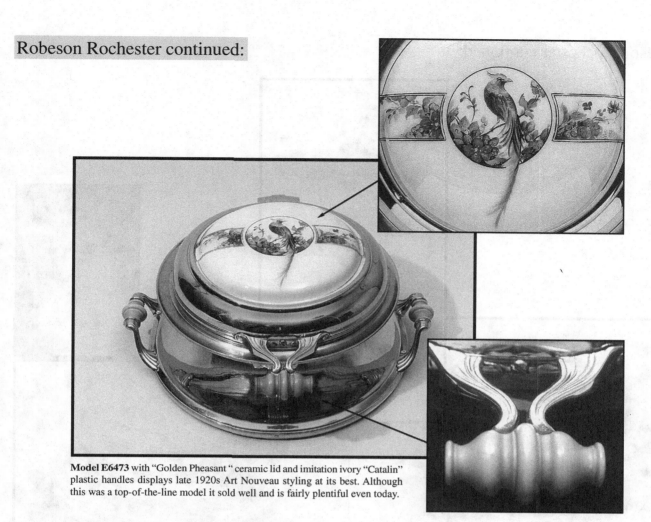

Model E6473 with "Golden Pheasant " ceramic lid and imitation ivory "Catalin" plastic handles displays late 1920s Art Nouveau styling at its best. Although this was a top-of-the-line model it sold well and is fairly plentiful even today.

The beautifully sculpted "Golden Pheasant" batter bowl (above) and shallow chaffing dish (right) are part of a matching set intended to go with **Model E6473** as well as the firm's Model 12820. Preheated, the chaffing dish can serve as a waffle keeper. Rochester also offered a matching syrup dispenser and coffee urn.

Model 12840 (left) with ivory-colored painted wood handles and later **Model 12920** (right) with black bakelite fittings, each have the same attractive Deco "Red Poppy" ceramic lid insert. Matching accessories like a batter bowl and the syrup pitcher pictured above could be purchased for these irons. Rochester had changed from an alphanumeric model designation system to a five-digit numbering system by 1930.

Rock Island Manufacturing Company [1]
"RIMCO"

On February 1st, 1907, the Secretary of the State of Illinois issued a license of incorporation to Carl E. Shields, Frank G. Young, and C. J. Larkin. With $50,000 of capital stock, the trio founded the Rock Island Tool Company in the western Illinois city of Rock Island. According to the papers of incorporation the purpose of the business was the manufacturing of high quality vises. Shields was made president and treasurer of the new firm, positions he would hold for the next nineteen years.

Three years later, the same three gentlemen reorganized the corporation by purchasing its assets including the manufacturing plant at 1st Street and 15th Avenue. The 30 plus employees of the former tool company became employees of the new Rock Island Manufacturing Company, or "RIMCO." A major expansion of the company's product line and manufacturing facilities was initiated at this time. By 1912, in addition to a complete line of vises, the firm was also manufacturing grinding wheels, livestock fountains, feed grinding mills, and various agricultural hand tools. The company's foundry was also making Sad irons (cast iron clothes pressing irons) which became so popular that within five years Rock Island Manufacturing was reputed to be the world's largest Sad iron producer. By World War I, the firm had expanded into the automotive accessories field and had a work force of approximately 200 people.

In 1918, in a move to enter the rapidly growing electric appliance field, Rock Island Manufacturing absorbed the Loetcher-Ryan Manufacturing Company of Dubuque Iowa, an electrical specialties manufacturer. Loetcher-Ryan was dissolved and its manufacturing equipment was moved to Rock Island's plant. The company's first effort at making electric household goods was a line of electric irons.

Resigns as Head

CARL E. SHIELDS.
Carl E. Shields, 1420 Forty-seventh avenue, Rock Island, has resigned as president and treasurer of the Rock Island Manufacturing company to become the manufacturing head of the American Nokol company, Chicago.

By 1922, the firm occupied a 12-acre industrial site on the banks of the Mississippi River and employed over 250 people. In January 1926, Carl Shields resigned as president and treasurer of the company to become manufacturing head of the American Nokol Company, a major Chicago manufacturer of oil-fired home heating equipment. During the nineteen years of Shield's leadership, Rock Island Manufacturing had grown from a small foundry operation of 30 employees to a diversified manufacturer employing over 400, with sales in excess of a million dollars annually.

Company records after this period have not surfaced and further information is sketchy at best. The Rock

Rock Island continued:

An aerial photo of the 12 acre Rock Island factory campus circa mid-1920s. The facility had 150,000 square feet of floor space and was located on the banks of the Mississippi River, visible at upper right. Notice the rail siding into the front of facility to receive materials and ship finished products. Could this be part of the fabled Rock Island Line?

Island City directory for 1928 lists a Horton W. Stickle as president of the firm; in 1934, Herbert R. Butz is listed as president; in 1936 and again in 1937 a Stanley H. Schubert is listed as president or manager. The company was apparently in financial trouble during these depression years and after 1937 was no longer listed in the city's directory. The office of the Secretary of State, Springfield, Illinois shows that the business was "dissolved involuntarily" on 31 October, 1958. In all likelihood the company had been inactive for some time prior to this, and this final action was probably taken to settle the books and pay off creditors. The author would be very interested in hearing from anyone with information about the final years of Rock Island Manufacturing Company.

As of this writing, only two models of the company's waffle irons have surfaced. **Model 88-A** dates from the early or mid-1920s, and **Model M-11** from the late 1920s or early 1930s. **Model 88-A** is a high quality well made iron, while **Model M-11** appears to have been designed for the low priced market. Both models work well and are a pleasure to use.

[1] Historical information and materials courtesy Judy Belan, Director Archivest, The Rock Island County Historical Society, Moline, Illinois.

The styling of the early 1920s **Model 88A** with cabriole legs was not very different from its contemporaries, but the quality was quite superior to most. Heavy-duty heating elements makes this model a very competent performer.

Model M-11 is a surprisingly good performer for an inexpensive appliance. The low stick grid design helps prevent Sunday morning cooking disasters.

140

Rogers Electric Laboratories Company [1]

Although the author has been unable to find a great deal about the Rogers Electric Laboratories Company, the biographies of the company's founder and his wife are interesting ones. Fred Joseph Langer was born in Vienna, Austria in 1868, one of four children and the second son of Franz Langer, a prosperous German industrialist. His mother died when Fred was just three. His father, fulfilling a deathbed promise to his wife, immigrated with the children to America in order that the two boys could avoid mandatory military service in Germany.

Fred J. Langer

The family settled in Cleveland in 1872. Ironically, Frank, the older son, joined the army shortly after arriving in America. He served three years on the western frontier, was honorably discharged, but died tragically on the homeward journey when he drowned in the Missouri River near Yankton, South Dakota. His father, devastated by the loss became distraught, lost interest in life and passed away in 1883.

Fred, now an orphan at age 15, continued his public school education in Cleveland and worked his way through the Cleveland Spencerian College, a business school. He went to work for the Reed Brothers Co., a wholesale millinery business where, over a period of years he worked his way up to a senior management position. In 1896 he married twenty-six year old Mary E. Eyerdam.

Mary was the eldest of six sisters and one brother. Her father Adam Eyerdam, another successful German emigrant, with significant real estate holdings in Cleveland, wished for his only son to follow him into the business world. However, upon the untimely death of the son, Mary's father decided that she, being the oldest daughter, would fulfill the lost son's role. Her father tutored her in the ways of the business world. At 15 Mary began working for a milliner by the name of Mrs. Shaw and attended the Cleveland Business College. Upon her marriage to Fred Langer, she and her new husband became business partners, opening their own millinery business. Fred was the behind-the-scenes manager while Mary did the selling and trimming in the shop.

In a few years the Langer's hat business grew to one of the largest and most exclusive of its kind in Cleveland, catering to a wealthy clientele. During this time, Fred invented several devices including a steamer for removing wrinkles from clothing, hats, and accessories and a dying machine for refurbishing soiled or worn garments, hats, and hat accessories. Over the years Fred and Mary prospered. He became director of a bank, the treasurer of a savings and loan, and was owner/manager of a real estate company. Then in 1912, Fred decided to get involved in the new field of electric appliance manufacturing.

He and George D. Rogers co-founded Rogers Electric Laboratories Company and set up shop at 1459 West 6th Street NW, Cleveland. Langer was president and Rogers vice-president. A Mr. P.C. Greenwell was secretary/treasurer. This arrangement leads one to believe that Rogers had the idea and the other two gentlemen had the monetary resources. A 1920 directory lists the same officers but has the business at 2056 East 40th Street. By 1930 the company had moved to 2015 East 65th Street. Apparently Rogers had been bought out by Langer and Greenwell since a Leo G. Haessely was now listed as vice-president instead of Rogers. In 1935 the firm had again moved and was at 1890 East 40th Street.

Fred Langer died on May 1, 1935 at age 66. His wife Mary became president of Rogers Electric and a Frank Dietz was vice-president. Leo Haessely, formerly the vice-president became secretary/treasurer. A 1940 directory has the company at 1814 East 40th Street. Haessely is now listed as president, Dietz is still vice-president, and one Anna Mahon is secretary. Mary Langer is now the company's treasurer. No records of the company after 1940 have been found. One can surmise that the business closed during the war years and did not reopen. Mary Langer passed away in Euclid, Ohio, December 2, 1956. There is no record of Fred and Mary Langer having had children.

The author has seen only three examples of products made by Rogers Electric, each being waffle irons of 1920s vintage. Two are pictured on the next page. The company's waffle irons were fitted with either red, green, or blue-painted wood handles, and have heavy cast iron cooking grids that produce a thin waffle consisting mostly of dimples. Each iron has a permanently attached power cord connected to exposed screw terminals under the base. The company manufactured a less expensive model iron without carrying handles for a Cleveland retailer named H. Cook Inc. That model has a single green lid handle and matching green silk covered power cord. Any Rogers Electric Laboratory appliance is rare and should be considered highly collectable. Care must be exercised when using the waffle irons due to the shock hazard present with the exposed power cord connectors.

---

[1] Historical information courtesy Ann K. Sindeler, Western Reserve Historical Society, Cleveland, Ohio.

This very primitive waffle iron from the early 1920s was manufactured during the infancy of the electrical appliance industry. Although it tends to overheat and cooks the center of the waffle more than the edges, it does a credible cooking job for an iron of this vintage. The handles on this and most examples are wood, painted apple green. A few examples have been found with with handles painted red or blue-green.

This model, made for H. Cook Inc. (a retail outlet), has neither handles nor feet on the base. All else is identical to Roger's standard model seen above, including a power cord permanently attached to exposed electrical contacts located under the pedestal.

Russell Electric Company
"Hold Heet"

This late teens or early 1920s Russell Electric with no model designation was one of the first electric waffle irons on the American market. The only concession to styling was the cabriole-type legs. Lack of style does not preclude the fact that this iron cooks very nicely.

Located in Chicago in the 1920s, Russell Electric was the first appliance maker to exploit drugstores as outlets for small household electrical goods. In the early 1920s, Russell Electric approached various drugstore chains with the idea of selling an inexpensive electric curling iron. It was an immediate success and was soon followed by a heating pad, a drink mixer, and in 1925, the very first chrome-plated flat iron. By the late 1920s, the firm was manufacturing toasters and at least two waffle iron models marketing them under the "Hold Heet" name.

The firm's first waffle iron (pictured above), made in the mid-1920s, has solid cast aluminum body halves with cooking surfaces designed to make a thin waffle with large flat dimples. The upper body half is capped with a nickel-plated brass plate fastened rather crudely to the body with four round-head screws. The iron is supported on four cabriole-style pressed steel legs that are removable for cleaning. The series wired heating elements are made from Nichrome ribbon wire insulated between sheets of mica.

A second model waffle iron, made in the late 1920s, is labeled "**Catalog Number 14**." Unlike the company's first model, this unit is equipped with a modern-type pair of 660 watt heating elements, employing spring-wound heating wire suspended on mica sheets that radiate from a central pressed metal support. This design works well, heating the grids quickly and evenly, and was also employed in waffle irons of this period made by Samson United. One example of **Model 14** has been found labeled "Cast-Rite Cookware," a Chicago housewares company.

Early Russell Electric Company waffle irons were not made in great numbers and are scarce today. Prices vary depending on condition but are generally above the average for this type of collectible.

From a distance **Model 14** appears rather plain, but closer examination reveals subtle Art Deco embossing. This iron probably dates from the mid-1920s. An unadorned version was made for a retailer called The Electric Products Company.

143

Russell Electric continued:

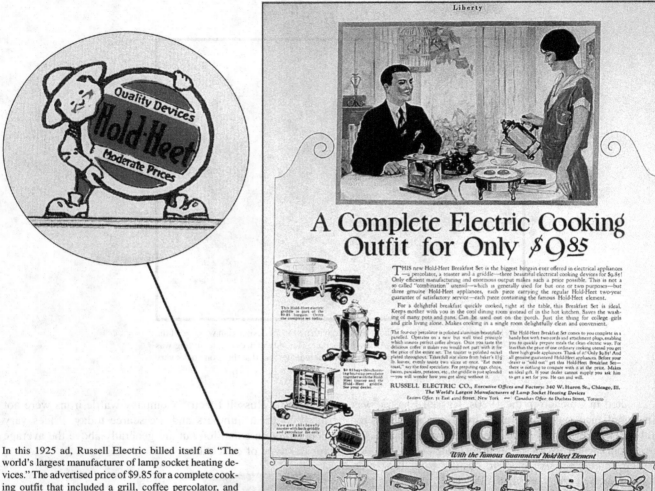

In this 1925 ad, Russell Electric billed itself as "The world's largest manufacturer of lamp socket heating devices." The advertised price of $9.85 for a complete cooking outfit that included a grill, coffee percolator, and toaster was a real bargain considering that the company's waffle iron was listed at $12.00.
(August 29, 1925 Liberty Magazine-Courtesy of Michael Sheafe-www.ToasterCentral.com)

This plain but elegant looking domed iron has no model designation. It probably dates from the mid or late 1920s. See "*Super Maid Cookware Corporation*" for a classic tear-drop-handled version of this iron made by Russell Electric for that retail organization.

144

Rutenber Electric Company [1]
"Marion" "Flip Flop" "Reco"

The Rutenber Factory Complex
Marian, Indiana, circa 1922.

Edwin A. Rutenber had business interests in Indiana as far back as September, 1902 when he organized the Western Motor Company to manufacture four and six-cylinder car and truck engines in Logansport. In July, 1912 the company was reorganized in Marion, Indiana as the Rutenber Motor Company. At that time Rutenber sold his interest in the company and announced that he was about to organize a new company in Logansport-this time to manufacture electric appliances.

On September 12, 1912, Rutenber Electric Company was incorporated with Edwin Rutenber as president. James Digan was named vice president and James Delong was secretary-treasurer. The firm's first product was an electric clothes iron followed by a table stove and a soldering iron. By 1914 the company was producing an extensive line of products including a three burner electric range, a combination grill/stove, one and two burner electric hot plates, an oven, eight sizes of reflective electric space heaters, and the previously-mentioned clothes iron. These products were all sold under the "Reco" brand name.

In early 1916, the Marion Association of Commerce, a local trade group, invested $50,000 in the company with the stipulation that the firm be moved to Marion. By July of that year Rutenber Electric was operating in a new factory at 201 East Charles Street, Marion. With this larger facility the company was able to expand its product line to include toasters, griddles, and so-called "nickel in the slot" automatic popcorn machines. The "Lak-Tro-Pop-Corn" popper, as it was called, was intended for arcades and other public places. By 1921 Edwin Rutenber, the firm's founder, had sold his interest in Rutenber Electric and had started yet another enterprise, the Marion Fence Machinery Company.

Model 60
RECO TOASTER
PRICE - - $2.90

This neatly designed electric toaster is just as good as it looks, made for hard ware, as well as an ornament for the table. The body of this toaster is made of three stampings that are nickel plated and highly polished. The keep-hot rack is embodied in our design, is not a loose piece, but made in one unit. Owing to the fact that we have eliminated wire racks and other small loose parts, the *"Reco"* toaster is the easiest toaster made to keep clean.

Model 60 Vertical toaster complete, nickel plated with separable plug and attachment packed in substantial boxes, only $2.90.

THE RUTENBER ELECTRIC COMPANY
LOGANSPORT, INDIANA, U. S. A.

A pre-1916 factory-issued dealer sales flier for the nickel-plated Model 60 "Reco" toaster, packaged "in substantial boxes, only $2.90." The company was still located in Logansport, Indiana at this time.

Model 25
1 BURNER, 3 HEAT HOT PLATE
Watts 600—Volts 110
PRICE - - - - $7 50

Single burner Hot Plate with three heat switch and 7 ft. cord. The plate is 8¼ inches in diameter, supported in a cast aluminum frame which is highly polished. There is no other device on the market that has so desirable a finish as that on the "Reco" Hot Plate.

Aluminum once polished will never tarnish or peel like an article finished in nickel.

Every woman has found this stove a convenience as it can be attached to any lamp socket in any room or on the porch. This model plate is being used successfully by Surgeons, Drug Stores, Hotels, Cafes, Laboratories and other places where sanitary devices are desired.

THE RUTENBER ELECTRIC COMPANY
LOGANSPORT, INDIANA, U. S. A.

Another pre-1916 ad flyer from the Rutener factory. This early hot plate was being sold not only for household use but for drug stores, hotels, cafes, and even laboratories. Whoever held the patent for the three-way switch on this item must have made a fortune. The same switch was used almost unchanged on appliances made by numerous manufactruers well into the 1950s.

Throughout the 1920s Rutenber Electric prospered. The firm changed its brand name to "Marion" and expanded its product line to include a coffee urn and thirteen models of electric ranges. An aggressive marketing campaign was initiated in 1922 in an ambitious attempt to boost the firm from a regional to a nationally recognized brand. At the time, Rutenber Electric was reputed to be the third largest electrical goods maker in the country. However, lack of sufficient capital to compete against giants like General Electric and Westinghouse on a nation-wide basis, doomed the company's expansion efforts from the start.

During the 1930s, the firm's work force of about one hundred employees, produced percolators, sandwich grills, waffle irons, and a large selection of full-size electric ranges that were marketed primarily in the Midwest. During World War II, when appliance manufacturing was suspended by government order, Rutenber supplied metal footlockers to the navy.

From the Teens through the 1940s, nearly every appliance manufacturer including Rutenber offered electric space heaters . This was the era before insulated houses when most rooms had at least one area that was uncomfortably chilly in winter.
(October 4, 1919, *Saturday Evening Post Magazine*)

An early 1920s ad shows two fashionably dressed young ladies extolling the virtues of not having to handle the hot toast to turn it in the Marion "Flipflop" toaster. (May, 1922, *The House Beautiful Magazine*)

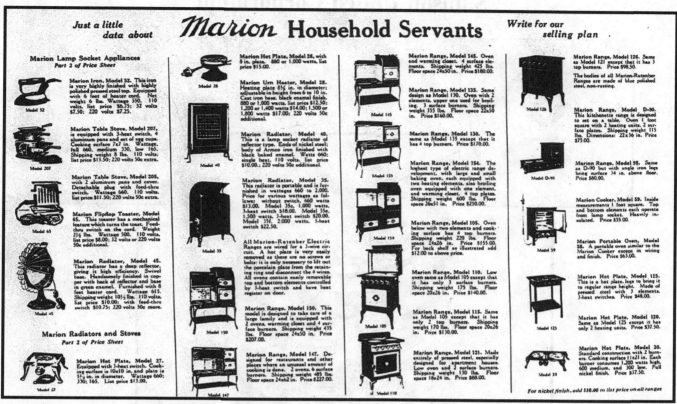

Just a little data about ***Marion*** **Household Servants** *Write for our selling plan*

Marion Lamp Socket Appliances
Part 2 of Price Sheet

Marion Iron, Model 52. This iron is very highly finished with highly polished pressed steel top. Equipped with 6 feet of heater cord. Net weight 6 lbs. Wattage 550. 110 volts, list price $6.75; 32 volts $7.50; 220 volts $7.25.

Marion Table Stove, Model 207, is equipped with 3-heat switch, 4 aluminum pans and set of egg cups. Cooking surface 7x7 in. Wattage: full 660, medium 330, low 165. Shipping weight 8 lbs. 110 volts, list price $13.50; 220 volts 50c extra.

Marion Table Stove, Model 205, with 2 aluminum pans and cover. Detachable plug with feed-thru switch. Wattage 660. 110 volts. list price $11.50; 220 volts 50c extra.

Marion Flipflop Toaster, Model 65. This toaster has a mechanical feature which turns the toast. Feed-thru switch on the cord. Weight 2¼ lbs. Wattage 500. 110 volts. list price $6.00; 32 volts or 220 volts 50c additional.

Marion Radiator, Model 45. This radiator has a deep reflector, giving it high efficiency. Swivel base. Handsomely finished in copper with back of reflector and base in green enamel. Furnished with 8 feet heater cord. Wattage 615. Shipping weight 10½ lbs. 110 volts. list price $10.00; with feed-thru switch $10.75; 220 volts 50c more.

Marion Radiators and Stoves
Part 2 of Price Sheet

Marion Hot Plate, Model 27. Equipped with 3-heat switch. Cooking surface is 10x10 in. and plate is 5½ in. in diameter. Wattage 660; 330; 165. List price $13.00.

Marion Hot Plate, Model 26, with 6 in. plate. 880 or 1,000 watts, list price $15.00.

Marion Urn Heater, Model 28. Heating plate 8½ in. in diameter; adjustable in height from 6 to 10 in. Cast iron base, black enamel finish. 880 or 1,000 watts, list price $12.50; 1,200 or 1,400 watts $14.00; 1,500 or 1,800 watts $17.00; 220 volts 50c additional.

Marion Radiator, Model 40. This is a lamp socket radiator of reflector type. Ends of nickel steel; body of Armco iron finished with black baked enamel. Watts 660; single heat. 110 volts. list price $10.00.; 220 volts 50c additional.

Marion Radiator, Model 35. This radiator is portable and is furnished in wattages 660 to 2,000. Price for various wattages as follows: without switch, 660 watts $13.00. Model 35c, 1,000 watts, 3-heat switch $18.00. Model 35e, 1,500 watts, 3-heat switch $20.00. Model 35f, 2,000 watts, 3-heat switch $22.50.

All Marion-Rutenber Electric Ranges are wired for a 3-wire circuit. A hot plate is very easily removed as there are no screws or bolts; it is only necessary to lift out the porcelain plate from the retaining ring and disconnect the 4 wires. All ovens contain easily removable top and bottom elements controlled by 3-heat switch and have heat register on door.

Marion Range, Model 150. This model is designed to take care of a large family and is equipped with 2 ovens, warming closet and 4 surface burners. Shipping weight 435 lbs. Floor space 24x50 in. Price $207.00.

Marion Range, Model 147. Designed for restaurants and other places where an unusual amount of cooking is done. 2 ovens, 6 surface burners. Shipping weight 485 lbs. Floor space 24x62 in. Price $227.00.

Marion Range, Model 145. Oven and warming closet, 4 surface elements. Shipping weight 425 lbs. Floor space 24x50 in. Price $180.00.

Marion Range, Model 135. Same design as Model 130. Oven with 2 elements, upper one used for broiling. 3 surface burners. Shipping weight 355 lbs. Floor space 22x50 in. Price $160.00.

Marion Range, Model 130. The same as Model 135 except that it has 4 top burners. Price $170.00.

Marion Range, Model 154. The highest type of electric range development, with large and small baking oven, each equipped with two heating elements, also broiling oven equipped with one element, and warming closet. 4 top plates. Shipping weight 600 lbs. Floor space 26x51 in. Price $250.00.

Marion Range, Model 105. Oven below with two elements and cooking surface has 4 top burners. Shipping weight 220 lbs. Floor space 24x26 in. Price $155.00. For back shelf as illustrated add $12.00 to above price.

Marion Range, Model 110. Low oven same as Model 105 except that it has only 3 surface burners. Shipping weight 175 lbs. Floor space 20x26 in. Price $140.00.

Marion Range, Model 115. Same as Model 105 except that it has only 2 top burners. Shipping weight 170 lbs. Floor space 20x26 in. Price $130.00.

Marion Range, Model 121. Made entirely of pressed steel, especially designed for apartment houses. Low oven and 2 surface burners. Shipping weight 130 lbs. Floor space 18x24 in. Price $68.00.

Marion Range, Model 126. Same as Model 121 except that it has 3 top burners. Price $98.50.

The bodies of all Marion-Rutenber Ranges are made of blue polished steel, non-rusting.

Marion Range, Model D-90. This kitchenette range is designed to set on a table. Oven 1 foot square with 2 heating units, 2 surface plates. Shipping weight 115 lbs. Dimensions: 22x36 in. Price $75.00.

Marion Range, Model 95. Same as D-90 but with angle iron legs bring surface 34 in. above floor. Price $80.00.

Marion Cooker, Model 59. Inside measurements 1 foot square. Top and bottom elements each operate from lamp socket. Heavily insulated. Price $55.00.

Marion Portable Oven, Model 58. A portable oven similar to the Marion Cooker except in wiring and finish. Price $63.00.

Marion Hot Plate, Model 125. This is a hot plate, too high to bring it to regular range height. Made of pressed steel with 3 elements. 3-heat switches. Price $48.00.

Marion Hot Plate, Model 120. Same as Model 125 except it has only 2 heating units. Price $37.50.

Marion Hot Plate, Model 30. Standard construction with 2 burners. Cooking surface 11x21 in. Each burner consumes 1,200 watts high, 600 medium, and 300 low. Full nickel finish. Price $37.50.

For nickel finish, add $10.00 to list price on all ranges

Even as early as 1922, when this factory flyer was issued, Rutenber offered a wide range of electrical goods from "lamp socket appliances" to full size electric ranges. Due to the lack of financial resources the firm was never able to compete successfully on a national scale with large manufacturers like GE and Westinghouse, but in many parts of the midwest for years "Marion" was the dominant major appliance brand.

By the mid-1950s, Rutenber was in financial difficulties, unable to compete successfully against the major manufacturers of large appliances. Sadly, on March 4, 1958, The Marion Chronicle announced that Active Products Corporation, a bathtub, sink, and lavatory manufacturer, had purchased Rutenber's assets souly to obtain the firm's facilities for applying the porcelain enamel finish to its steel products; an ignominious end to a proud old company.

The February, 1931 *Gage Electrical Encyclopedia* catalog, shows the company's Model 67C "Flip Flop" Toaster priced at $5.25 and the **Model 77 AC "Marion"** waffle iron (pictured at left) at $10.25, making the latter a mid-priced product at that time. The only concession to styling in this unusually bulky waffle iron, is a series of simple diamond cutouts around the pedestal base. What it lacks in looks the iron more than makes up for in performance. Although it has no thermostat, if kept full, it is self-regulating and will not overheat. The pedestal cutouts also manage to keep the base pleasantly cool.

The company's mid-1930s Model 777 waffle iron has striking red Bakelite handles and is a superb example of Art Deco styling at its best. This model is much sought after by both Deco and appliance collectors, and commands premium prices.

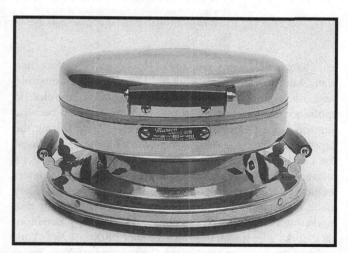

Model 77, circa late 1920s was the first of two waffle iron models Rutenber produced. The heating elements are rated at a modest 500 watts which, as it turns out, is just right to make this non-automatic iron self-regulating. Even without a thermostat, it never overheats, provided the cook keeps it filled with batter. This iron with a temperature gauge is sometimes found with a "Supreme Waffle Iron label."

[1] Certain Historical information and materials courtesy of the personnel of The Indiana History Room of The Marion Public Library and Director Barbara Love. Additional materials are from the collection of Louis E. Ebert, Marion, Indiana. Information about Marion history provided by William F. Munn, English Department, Marion High School.

Samson United Corporation

A late 1920s Samson model with ivory-colored wood handles, and parrot on a swing/Chinese lantern ceramic lid insert (upper left). A similar decal can be found on several versions of early Dominion made models. A Samson model with the same body was manufactured with the orange-colored flowers lid insert pictured at upper right. Neither of these models was given a model number.

Samson Cutlery Company of Rochester, New York, like many kitchenware manufacturers, recognized an emerging business opportunity during the 1920s and entered the electric appliance business at that time. Samson Cutlery became Samson United Corporation in the early 1930s. During the depression years, the company produced some of the finest Art Deco styling found on any appliances. Samson was an original equipment manufacturer for various retail chains including Firestone, Macy's, Red Seal, and Walgreen. They made a great number of irons labeled "Seneca" for that marketing company which was situated in nearby Brighton, New York. Records at the Department of State of New York indicate that a "Samson United Corporation of New York" was incorporated in Queens County New York on October 5th, 1953 and dissolved by proclamation on December 15, 1972. Whether this was a reincarnation of the earlier Samson United Corporation cannot be determined at this time. If anyone knows more about either Samson United, please contact the author.

Samson waffle irons are simple in mechanical design, well made, and nearly always tastefully styled. Many, such as the **Models 128** and **178** came with ceramic lid inserts, or as with **Model 331**, had plated lids embossed or painted with an attractive Art Deco motif. Very distinctive swirled deco-type handles, designed by John A. Salvia in 1935, appear on waffle iron **Models 379** and **433**. These distinctive handles and a deco-styled swirl lid design can also be found on the **Model 233** waffle iron/grill, making it one of the most stylish of combination models. Certain ceramic insert waffle irons were sold as part of a set which could include a matching coffee percolator with sugar and creamer.

A unique waffle extractor mechanism was incorporated into several late 1930s waffle irons including, Models 330 and **379.** A heavy "U"-shaped wire embedded in the lower cooking grill (see photo page 150) is activated by the hinge mechanism when the lid is opened and supposedly lifts the waffle from the cooking surface. Although a great sales gimmick, it was poorly designed, troublesome, and prone to failure. However, for collectors, this feature makes a wonderful conversation piece. Samson waffle irons with non-functioning heating elements are serviceable only if a working element can be salvaged from another unit.

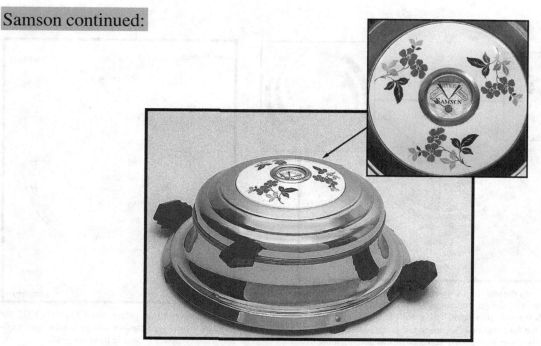

Model E128 from the late 1920s has a Hall-made poppy flower ceramic lid insert. Another version of this model has a plain pea green ceramic insert. A model labeled "Seneca E1128" looks identical. (See Seneca page 153)

Model E178 is yet another variation of Model E128 pictured above. With a delicate multi-colored Hall wildflower insert it is the least common version. Samson, like many manufacturers, utilized simple design changes to one body to create several models for the least cost.

Model E130 from the early 1930s with painted lid design is basically another variation of Model 128. It retains the same heating elements, handles, and base.   (Photo courtesy Dan & Vi LaBelle)

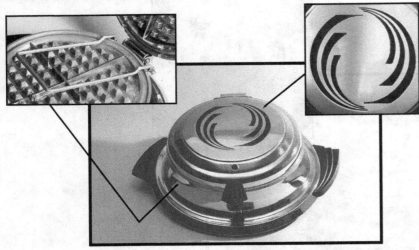

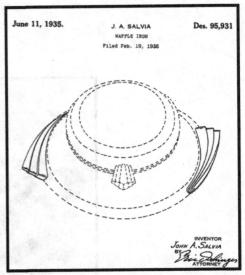

Model 379 from the mid-1930s was the first of several Samson models to use the swirl design element pictured in the patent drawing at right. This is the only iron made with a built-in waffle ejector, activated when the lid is opened (see insert). It is supposed to raise the waffle from the lower grid. Poorly designed, it was nothing more than a short-lived sales gimmick.

John A. Silva design patent dated June 11, 1935 for Samson's swirl-type handles used on at least three models of the company's waffle irons and grills.

(Drawing courtesy Nancy Conway)

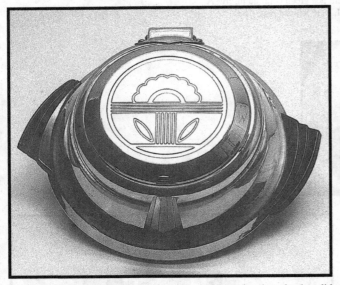

Model 233 grill/waffle iron from the mid-late 1930s is one of the most stylish combination units ever produced. The design was also used on waffle iron models 232 and 379. The paint on many of these usually suffers some deterioration. Few of these swirl models were manufactured making them all quite collectible. Those in excellent condition command premium prices from collectors.

Model 331 with swirl handles attracts attention, but what does the deco lid design represent? A flower? A tree? A nuclear mushroom cloud? The mushroom cloud is not likely as this was made a decade before the Atomic Bomb was created.

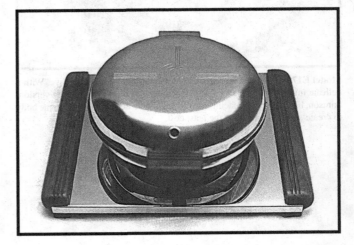

Samson surrendered to more conventional styling with **Model 5382** pictured at right. Natural wood handles like those found on this piece first became popular around 1935 but lost favor after WWII. This model dates from the early 1940s. A twin version was also produced with this styling.

(Photo courtesy Dan & Vi LaBelle)

150

Sears Roebuck & Company
"Energex" "Heatmaster" "Kenmore"

A late 1920s Sears "Challenge" waffle iron which can be seen advertised in the company's 1927 catalog (see page 152). Until the 1930s Sears did operate several of its own manufacturing facilities, but left appliance making to outside venders. This and a number of other waffle iron models were made for Sears by Bersted.

Sears Roebuck and Company began almost by accident in 1886, when a Chicago jewelry wholesaler sent a shipment of pocket watches to a Minneapolis store that refused to accept the order. Richard Warren Sears, working as a railroad station agent in North Redwood, Minnesota saw the shipment being returned and sensed a money making opportunity. He purchased the lot from the wholesaler at a deep discount and sold the timepieces to other station agents up and down the line. This first venture at retailing proved so profitable that Sears immediately opened a full time retail business in Minneapolis, which he called the R.W. Sears Watch Company.

In 1887 Sears moved his company to Chicago and expanded into servicing the watches he was selling. He advertised for a watchmaker and hired a black gentleman from Indiana by the name of Alvah Curtis Roebuck. By 1893 Roebuck was a partner and the firm became Sears Roebuck & Co. Two years later and 20 years after Montgomery Ward, Sears produced its first mail order catalog. Roebuck sold his interest in the firm soon after. Years later when he fell on hard times, Roebuck was rehired by Sears and worked for the firm as a clerk for a number of years.

Although, Sears Roebuck and Company was primarily a retail organization, the firm did become involved in manufacturing certain of its products. The company divested itself of its manufacturing plants in the 1930s when the firm's Chairman, Robert Wood, saw this as a way of raising capital to build stores in newly created retail environments called shopping malls. At no time did Sears manufacture electric kitchen appliances.

Sears first sold electric appliances under the "Energex" and "Challenge" labels. In the 1930s "Heatmaster" became the company's label and remained so until the 1940s when it was changed to "Kenmore". These products were made and labeled for Sears by outside suppliers including Arvin Industries, Bersted Manufacturing, Chicago Electric, Dominion Electric, Electrahot, Manning-Bowman, Porcelier, Proctor & Schwartz, and Samson United. With just a few exceptions Sears models are plain, utilitarian, and very functional. As such they do not command very high prices in the collector arena. Many, however, make nice everyday working appliances.

A single page from the 1927 Sears catalog illustrates the wide array of small electric kitchen appliances the company offered even at a time when many rural homes still weren't wired for electricity or had substandard service. The waffle irons shown were Bersted-made and intended for "110 volt city current" only. Somehow, an appliance named "Challenge" is a little scary.

(1927 Sears Roebuck & Co. *General Merchandise Catalog*)

Seneca

Two different Poppy decals were used to decorate the ceramic inserts found on the **Model 60-A**. Both versions pictured here are believed to have been supplied by Hall Pottery. Never over-tighten the insert retaining knob! The author learned this lesson the hard way while testing this iron after restoration. Heat expansion of the metal body stressed the insert, shattering it explosively. This was a design defect and apparently a common problem in the past. Replacement inserts were made in sufficient quantities that new ones can occasionally still be found.

This Brighton, New York marketing company sold several very attractive waffle iron models made by Samson United from the late 1920s to the mid-1930s. All of these waffle irons are simple in mechanical design, using a minimum of parts and fasteners. The heating elements are spring wound Nichrome wire embedded in a refractory clay matrix that is housed in a pressed metal ring. This type of heating unit works well but is prone to premature failure from moisture absorbed by the clay either during use or from prolonged storage in a damp environment. Once damaged the heating elements are not serviceable.

The **Model E1127 is** without a temperature indicator and is a less expensive version of Model 1131. Model 1133, a combination grill/waffle iron, has unusually nice deco styling for this type of unit. The oddly designated **Model 60-A** and Model 1128 are the only Seneca models with ceramic lid inserts. Both have permanently attached power cords. The lid insert of **Model 60-A** has a red poppy flower motif, nearly identical to one used at the time by Samson United.

Model E1127 from the mid 1930s was the most common unit sold by Seneca. The deco-styled Chevron handles were used on many of this company's products. Before purchasing any Seneca models for use, be certain that it works. The sealed heating elements are prone to moisture damage over time and are not serviceable.

Serva-Matic Corporation

Apparently, some folks back in the late 1930s or 1940s were just as impatient to put waffles on the table as some of us are today. The Serva-Matic **Model DW-46** (**D**ouble **W**affle-46) was this company's less complex answer to Manning-Bowman's popular rotating "Twin-o-Matic" double model of the late depression period. Little is known about this Chicago company. The idea of stacking one iron on top of the other did not originate with Serva-Matic. About ten years earlier Chicago Electric introduced a similar but more stylish stacked model which they designated **Model AF-26** (see page 40). Unlike the Serva-Matic, which has alternating hinges, the Chicago Electric unit has a single compound hinge on one side. Neither company had much sales success with their odd contraptions although Manning-Bowman's Twin-o-Matic double unit was a best seller, due in part to an extensive ad campaign.

During the late 1930's, Serva-Matic sold a more conventional automatic single unit designated Model AW-48 (**A**utomatic **W**affle-48) which is basically the upper part of the stacked model mounted on four legs. All Serva-Matic models are rare and interesting collectibles.

Model DW-46, circa late 1930s-early 1940s. "DW" in the model number stands for **D**ouble **W**affle iron. Using the same tray and lid, the company also produced a single unit designated Model AW-48. (Presumably "AW" meant **A**utomatic **W**affle iron.)

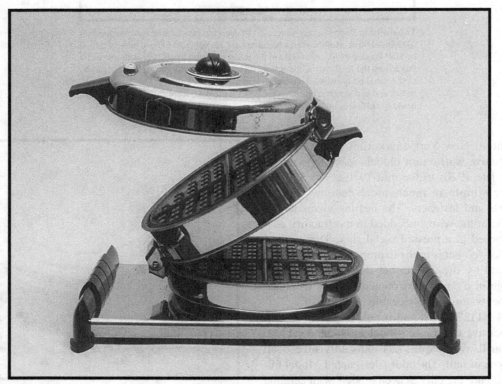

This stacked twin **Model DW-46** with a radio knob-like temperature control, dates from the late 1930s or early 1940s. It was another attempt at cooking lots of waffles in a short period of time. Not a sales success, it is scarce today. The author's example has a broken foot. Brittle plastic was a poor choice of materials for the tray end parts.

Simplex Electrical Company [1]

In 1840, a firm which would later known as Morss & Whyte was formed in Boston. In 1845 Charles A. Morss became an active partner in the venture and in 1868 became sole owner. The company manufactured screens, railings, light structural iron, and fine wire mesh called wire cloth. In 1885 the firm, which now numbered fifty employees, moved into a brick factory in Cambridge, Massachusetts. In 1923 Morss & Whyte was sold to the Newark Wire Cloth Company of Newark, New Jersey and ceased to exist.

On March 16, 1895, four descendents of Charles Morss, with $150,000, incorporated the Simplex Electrical Company and began operations in the old Morss & White factory on Franklin Street in Cambridge. The company officers were Everett Morss, president, Philip Morss Vice president, Henry A. Morss secretary/treasurer, and Everett Morss Jr., son of the president, on the board of directors. They opened a Boston office at 201 Devonshire Street.

The new firm began by manufacturing insulated wires and cables for electrical purposes, including power and phone line, interior wiring, and underwater and underground cables. The business would eventually become known as the Simplex Wire & Cable Company. By 1900 the business had diversified, forming a division called the Simplex Electric Heating Company which concetrated on the manufacture of heat-generating electrical appliances. One of this division's first products was a small flat iron that sold for $5.00 in 1905 (see ad below). The company also made several versions of a very

crude tabletop electric waffle iron (see photo page 156) which could be ordered either nickel-plated or in black enamel. In early 1917 Simplex Electric Heating Company was sold to Edison Electric Appliance Company. The Simplex name was carried on a few Edison Electric products for only a short time.

Simplex Wire & Cable Company still exists. After a series of five mergers beginning in 1960, Simplex Wire & Cable became part of Starplex Communications Inc. in 1997. It then became Simplex Technologies Inc. in 2000 and Tycom Integrated Cable Systems Inc. in 2002. Now part of Tyco International Ltd., the firm makes high technology wire and fiber optic cable products. However, another ownership change may be in the works for Simplex. Tyco's so-called "blow and go" CEO resigned in June of 2002 during a government probe of personal stock transactions amid allegations of tax evasion and shady business dealings. Because of this turmoil, Tyco stock has recently tumbled 73% in value in six months.

Simplex waffle irons are most likely the very first ever made that were heated by electricity. They are quite crude, electrically dangerous, and today are scarce but not rare. Examples in good condition normally fetch over $100.00 in the collector market.

[1] Historical information courtesy the Bostonian Society, Boston, Massachusetts.

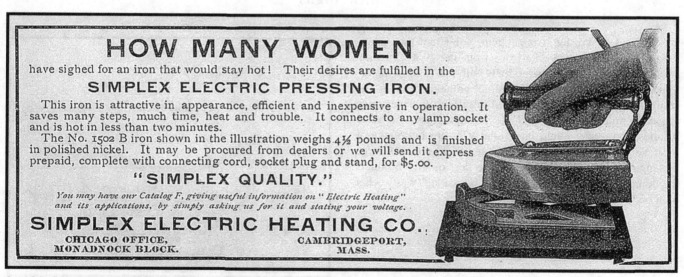

One of the first products of Simplex Electric Heating Company was this small electric flat iron. This 1905 ad says that the iron weighs just 4 ½ pounds, heats in two minutes, and including stand and lamp socket adapter, costs $5.00. What a labor saver for women used to having to heat and reheat their irons on a stovetop!

Dating from about 1905, this Simplex may be the first model of an electric waffle iron ever manufactured. Heating elements were cast into the grids which are heated in the open position (bottom view). Batter is poured onto the rear fixed grids. The front grids are then flipped (top), activating large exposed electrical contacts seen on right that control routing of power to the heating elements. Electrical safety was obviously not a consideration at that time.

(Photos courtesy Larry Lobel)

Son-Chief Electrics Inc.
"Magic Maid" "Speed Master"
"Black Angus"

Based in Winsted, Connecticut, Son-Chief Inc. manufactured toasters and waffle irons from the 1930s into the 1960s, labeling some of its products with the "Magic Maid," "Speed Master," or "Black Angus" names. Most of the company's products were designed to sell in the lower price range. Simple stampings and inexpensive plastic or wood handles, like those found on **Model 975**, are hallmarks of most Son-Chief products. The 950 and 9150 series of large rectangular grill/waffle irons are the best quality products the company made and for the very occasional waffle chef on a budget, may be a good choice.

Model 975 "Speed Master" with natural wood handles, is a typical non-automatic iron from the late 1930s, designed to sell in the low price range. Son-Chief also made a look-a-like Model 9180 combination grill/waffle iron at this time. None of its products are exciting enough to be collectible.

Stern-Brown Incorporated [1]
"Super Star"

Stern-Brown was incorporated in New York County New York on August 11, 1927. The firm's original address was 257 West 17th Street, New York City. A 1934 New York City business directory lists a David Brown as the firm's president and an Irving Edelman as treasurer. Apparently the company was capitalized by the issuance of 200 shares of privately held stock.

In the early 1930s Stern-Brown marketed a Model 90 toaster and as many as five different hot plates which the company called table stoves. By the late 1930s the firm had moved a few miles east to 42-24 Orchard Street, Long Island City, New York, and was manufacturing low-to-medium-priced waffle irons and waffle iron/grill combination units. By the great number of surviving examples of the company's products from this period, one can safely assume that Stern-Brown had found a comfortable and lucrative sales niche. Records of the company's activities in the New York City area after this period seem to be non-existent. However, a Stern-Brown waffle iron/grill labeled **Model 210** appears to be a typical model of 1950s vintage. Records at the Department of State for New York state states that the firm was "voluntarily dissolved on December 2, 1975."

The Stern-Brown name rarely appears on any of the company's products and many are also devoid of a model or catalog number. Instead nearly all are labeled "Super Star." Some earlier waffle irons carry the name "Thermo Waffle" and the very popular waffle iron/grills are sometimes marked "Master Grill." Several of the company's early model waffle irons were fitted with rather utilitarian, molded, brown Bakelite handles, while the later products came with either brown or black Bakelite or varnished wood fittings. A large draping "M" motif was formed into the doors of its toaster and the lids of the earlier waffle irons creating a hint of styling on otherwise plain items. Very late model waffle irons and grills either had no lid decoration or an inverted "U". For less expensive type waffle irons, most Stern-Brown models do a credible job of cooking, and in good condition, can be a useful everyday appliance. Due to their abundance and unexciting appearance, most "Super Star" waffle irons and grills sell for very modest prices in the collector market.

[1]   Certain historical information courtesy Michael Scheafe, New York City (www.ToasterCentral.com) . Other records from the New York Department of State.

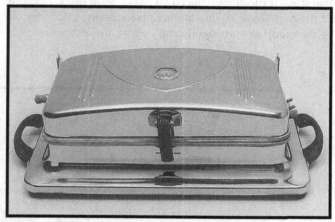

"Master Grill" grill/waffle iron dates from the late 1930s or 1940s and shares the same style handles and "M" lid motif as the "Thermo-waffil" (not a misprint) model at lower left.

The large drapery-style "M" stamped onto the lids are typical of earlier Stern-Brown models as are the classic 1930s suitcase-style brown Bakelite handles. The quality of most Stern Brown waffle irons is only fair.

Model 210 "Superstar" grill/waffle iron dates from the 1950s and is indistinguishable from combination units of other manufacturers of the period.

Super Maid Cookware Corporation

This Chicago-based company sold two nearly identical versions of a rather attractive, high quality, pedestal-type waffle iron in the mid to late 1920s. Neither is labeled with a model designation. The handles of both are turned wood, finished with an eye-catching green and white marbleized paint. Each model differs from the other only in the style of the lid handle. One has a teardrop-hanging handle while the other has a simple knob. Each is equipped with the same well-engineered robust heating elements.

A slightly smaller pedestal iron with similar styling and of about the same vintage was produced with black handles and clearly labeled "Super Maid Cookware" on the lid hinge. It is nearly identical in appearance to, and is equipped with the same heating elements as Russell Electric's Model 14 (see page 143). This leads the author to believe that Russell Electric produced all Super Maid irons. Because of their attractive styling and relative scarcity, prices for all of these artifacts are significantly above the average.

Russell Electric probably made this iron for Super Maid Cookware. The green and white marbleized wood handles are attractive but the thick paint coating used to create the effect was easily damaged. The unique heavy-duty ceramic plate heating elements found inside (see insert) were quite expensive to manufacture and resemble an element found in many hotplates.

Superior Electric Products Corporation [1]

SUPERLECTRIC

Superior Electric was founded in 1922 by 30 year old Edmund Lawrence Haas and incorporated by him in Saint Louis, Missouri in 1923. Shares of stock were issued to his wife Anna and to at least one of his three children, a daughter Marian. The firm was located first at 2204-08 Pine Street and later at 1300-1310 13th Street, Saint Louis. In 1938, labor troubles in the city motivated Haas to move the company about a hundred miles south to the small town of Cape Girardeau on the Mississippi River. The following year, when Haas' son Edmund left the firm for a military career, Haas convinced his new son-in-law Joseph Quatmann to step into his son's place as the firm's purchasing agent. Quatmann worked in

> For details about the two men most responsible for the success of the company, see the segments at the conclusion entitled "*Superior Electric-The War Years*" and "*The Men Behind Superior Electric.*"

that capacity until 1946, when he purchased the business from Haas when the founder retired. Mr. Quatmann owned and operated the company for twenty-two years until his own retirement in 1968.

Superior Electric occupied two plants in Cape Girardeau. The first site was at 1507 Independence Street. The business was then moved to a building on Nash Road in the Cape Girardeau industrial park. Both facilities still exist. The Thorngate Company, a men's clothing manufacturer, occupies the Independence Street building. At its peak in the mid-1960's, Superior employed approximately 125 employees. In 1968, the business was sold to United Industry Syndicate

Superior Electric managers at the 1939 company picnic. Fourth from right is company founder and president Edmund Haas. Far right is the president's son Edmund William Haas, who at that time was the firm's purchasing agent. (Photo courtesy Mrs. Cathi Stoverink.)

Employees and their families at the Superior Electric Company picnic during the summer of 1939. Squatting front left is Cape Girardeuau Mayor Tooke and Mr. and Mrs. Edmund Haas. (Photo courtesy Mrs. Cathi Stoverink.)

of New York, a conglomerate with strong interests in the automobile parts business. The new owners continued to manufacture appliances under the "Superior Electric" name until 1982, when the Cape Girardeau plant was closed.

Over the years Superior produced a full line of portable electric appliances, including hot plates, percolators, toasters, grills, waffle irons, and fans. Most of the its products were made for the medium-to-low-price market and sold under the "Superlectric" name. Designs for the company's very earliest Toasters (Models 55 and 66) circa mid-1920s, may have been purchased from the Permway Electric Manufacturing Company of Saint Louis. In the 1930s, Superior modified certain items slightly for Lehman Brothers Silver-ware Corporation, a large retailer who sold goods under the "Kromaster Products" label. Superior also had contracts with Sears at various times to produce products with the "Sears" or "Kenmore" labels. During World War II, the company struggled to survive due in part to war-time manufacturing restrictions. Details of the firm's wartime experiences can be found in the sidebar "Superior Electric-The War Years."

Superior's early products such, as its **Model 632** waffle iron were undistinguished in both looks and quality, but by the 1930s, the styling department had created a product look best described as extreme deco. The combination of sharp

Cape Girardeau Mayor Tooke left with Mr. and Mrs. Haas at the 1939 company picnic. They sure knew how to party in the good old days! Can you imagine what an avid appliance collector would give for a Superior Electric party hat!?! (Photo courtesy Mrs. Cathi Stoverink.)

angular designs embossed on the plated parts and multifaceted jutting chevron handles, produced an eye-catching effect, which made depression-weary shoppers take notice of "Superlectric" items on store shelves.

Model 45 hot plate illustrates the company's penchant for using classic Art Deco styling elements in it's early 1930s products. This robust appliance came with a nicely sealed heating element and is an eye-catcher even today.

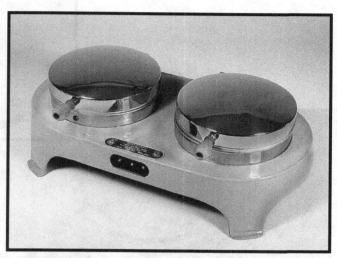

Model 750 with an institutional green vitreous enamel finish dates from the mid-1920s which makes it one of the earliest non-commercial twin models. With a 12-pound cast iron base it is also one of the heaviest. A unique elongated three-pin socket allows a normal cord to power either one or both units depending on which side of the socket is connected. This design was invented by Alvin Waage of Waage Electric Inc. and continues to be used on some of that firm's modern soldering equipment.

The **Model 750** waffle iron from the late 1920s or early 1930s deserves special mention as being possibly the earliest non-commercial twin model produced by any manufacturer. This unusual cooker is finished in a pale green vitreous enamel that covers an impressive 12 pound cast iron base. A decade would pass before twin units became popular and then only for a short time just prior to World War II.

In 1939, waffle iron **Models 706** and **708** were introduced with futuristic "Buck Rogers" type red plastic handles with chromed disc spacers (see page 162). A Model 755 Grill/Waffle Iron and two toaster models, designated 66 and 66-A, were also marketed with these same eye-catching handles. All such items are rare and command very high prices from both vintage appliance collectors and Art Deco aficionados.

The quality and performance of many vintage "Superlectric" waffle irons is average, but their styling is often outstanding. On occasion however, the styling department seems to have run amuck, as with **Model 606** (see page 162). In this case an old-fashioned Victorian style floral lid insert installed atop a sleek deco body created a design that appears a bit schizophrenic. At times the designers would also create a new model inexpensively by simply designing different handles for an older model. A good example is **Model 702** (page 162) with its unusual wooden ball handles. It's really a Model 722 in disguise. The company's Model 155 grill/waffle iron was similarly modified with at least three different handle configurations.

Most vintage Superior Electric waffle irons with Deco styling command above-average prices today. The "Buck Rogers" **Models 706** and **708**, in good clean condition can sometimes reach astronomical prices.

[1] Historic information and materials courtesy Mrs. Cathi Stoverink. Waffle iron materials courtesy the author.

This excellent quality late 1920s **Model 632** was made for and labeled *"Renfrew Electric Products Limited,"* a retailer located in Renfrew, Ontario, Canada.

Model 606 (left) with an attractive but sedate Victorian style flowered ceramic lid (insert) looks oddly schizophrenic with deco style chevron handles. **Model 707** (right) has the same body and handles but sports a more appropriate all metal deco-styled lid.

In the late 1930s the design department created several different models inexpensively by creating various handles for the same body and lid shell configuration. A bizarre look was achieved with wooden ball handles on this **Model 702.**

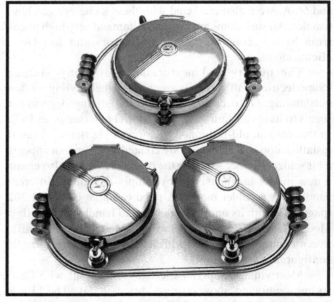

Model 708 (top) and **twin Model 706** are examples of a series of appliances the company produced in the late 1930s with "Buck Rogers" deco handles made of alternating chromed discs and bright red plastic spacers. Two toaster models (66 and 66-A) were produced with the same chrome and plastic handles and complimented these waffle irons. All of these appliances are much sought after by collectors. (Photo courtesy Dan & Vi LaBelle)

Superior Electric-The War Years

In 1942 the War Production Board issued Order L-41, which prohibited manufacturers from making most civilian goods. At the outbreak of war, smaller manufacturers like Superior Electric were just recovering from a decade-long devastating economic depression. Many could ill afford to invest in new machinery necessary to qualify for military contract work. Many closed their doors for the duration. The majority of these never reopened for business after the war.

The following illustrates the difficulties and frustrations these small manufacturers experienced while trying to survive the war years from 1942 through 1946. It is a summary of information gathered during a September 1996 telephone conversation between Joseph H. Quatmann, retired owner of Superior Electric and his daughter Catherine Quatmann Stoverink. Mr. Quatmann was hired as the company's purchasing agent in 1939 and held that position during the years recounted below. In 1946 he purchased the company and was the firm's president until his retirement in 1968. Mr. Quatmann passed away in 2000. This is a story of one man's efforts to keep a company alive during very trying times.

Joseph Quatmann's "Dishpan"

Because of war-caused business shut downs in the Cape Girardeau, Missouri area, unemployment was high and Superior had no problem finding people to hire at the beginning of the war. The company was, however, quite limited in what it could do. Plating of parts was not possible because nickel, an essential ingredient in the process, was classified by The War Production Board as a strategic war material and rationed for military use. Although the company could service return goods, it was not allowed to sell any existing inventory in case the armed services might have a need to commandeer it. Employment in the factory dropped in 1942 from 150 to about 14.

Quatmann, as part of his duties as purchasing agent, bid on numerous government contracts in an attempt to keep the factory running and the remaining people employed. He felt "fortunate" when the company was finally awarded a contract to manufacture some clothes irons for the Navy and another for hot plates for a few shipyards. Toward the end of the war Quatmann submitted a bid on a Navy contract for an item designated for security reasons on the paper work as a "dishpan." Although the part indeed resembled a very small dishpan, the military's specifications for manufacturing tolerances were so exacting it was obvious that it wasn't a dishpan at all. Quatmann could only guess at what it really was. In any case the bid was rejected for being too high and the navy split the contract among three other firms.

In desperation Quatmann went to the offices of McQuay-Norris, the Saint Louis agency in charge of military contract procurements, to see if there was a segment of the "dishpan" project Superior might be allowed to work on as a subcontractor. The agent wasn't sure but agreed to give Quatmann the names of the three prime contractors so Quatmann could find out for himself.

While Quatmann waited for the names, the agent happened to receive an urgent call from a very angry Naval Commander who had just received a load of defective "dishpans." He told the agent in no uncertain terms that he wanted someone who could make him good "dishpans" and he wanted good ones now. The agent told the Commander about Superior Electric and Quatmann. The officer replied, "send him right over."

The commander grilled Quatmann at length about the equipment and processes available at Superior, how many "dishpans" Quatmann thought Superior could make in a day, and when the Navy might expect delivery. After some fast figuring, Quatmann told the officer that once the factory was tooled up, the punch presses could most likely produce 64,000 "dishpans" a day with deliveries beginning in February. The Commander told him to immediately submit another bid through the McQuay-Norris agency.

When the agent at McQuay-Norris received Quatmann's new bid, he called Superior and told Quatmann that he was summarily rejecting it because it was of all things, too low! He then informed Quatmann that the part was made from very tough heat-treated steel, punishing to stamping presses and the expensive stamping dies. The agent was certain that high maintenance costs and an unavoidably high parts rejection rate would cause Superior to lose money at the quoted price. He told Quatmann that if Superior ended up having to close its doors it would not be good for the careers of either of them. Convinced, Quatmann submitted a higher bid.

Even though he hadn't signed an official contract Quatmann was anxious to get started. He convinced Al Aug, the very skeptical plant manager, to take a chance and tool up ahead of time to make the "dishpan." The presses had to be carefully set up for a multi-step operation. The pan was stamped round from a piece of hardened steel, then formed to a bowl shape and finally holes and a notch were punched at an angle around the lip. Fortunately the contract did come through and due to the preplanning, production was able to begin without delay.

When the first load of parts was finished, the McQuay-Norris purchasing agent in St. Louis made the three hour trip to Cape Girardeau to inspect them and insisted on taking them back with him immediately. It turned out that punching angled holes accurately through hardened steel was nearly impossible. In order to maintain accuracy, the expensive hole punching dies, as predicted, had to be replaced every few days something the other companies had tried to avoid. Superior's production eventually reached the promised 64,000 units a day. At such a high output level it became too difficult to keep an accurate count and the parts were finally invoiced by the barrel weight.

Subsequent heat treating and plating by other companies after the parts left the Superior factory caused dimensional changes to many of the parts. The subsequent high rejection rate was at first attributed to Superior. When a government contract umpire held up payment to the company for the rejects, Quatmann called the Saint Louis purchasing agent forcefully reminding him that the parts were to specifications when they left Cape Girardeau and Superior was not responsible for any subsequent changes. He also warned that if the company wasn't paid quickly it would have to shut down operations and an angry navy commander would likely plague the agent yet again. A call soon came into Superior from an admiral who said that he would personally see to it that the bills were paid and for Superior to continue making the part. The admiral was true to his word and the company continued pounding out the admiral's "dishpans" for the remainder of the war.

Each time he had occasion to meet in Saint Louis with the people at McQuay-Norris, Quatmann was given the red carpet treatment, but was never told what Superior was actually making for the war effort. Throughout the conflict, Superior's then-owner Edmund Haas, insisted that his company not make anything that killed people. Dishpans it seemed caused him no concern. Only after the war did the Superior people learn that engineers at Johns Hopkins University had developed the so-called "dishpan" that they had all worked so hard to produce. It had to be made precisely

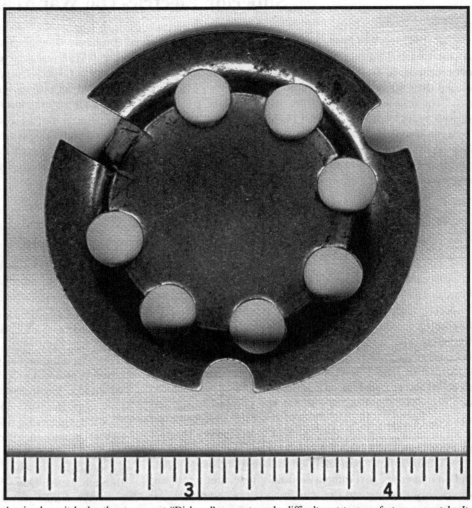

As simple as it looks, the top secret "Dishpan" was extremely difficult part to manufacture accurately. It became a major factor in the allied victory in World War II. The scale is in inches.
(Photo courtesy Mrs. Cathi Stoverink.)

from very tough steel because it was the base plate for the super-secret newly developed proximity fuse used in anti-aircraft and artillery shells. Each pan held the fuse's components and not only had to fit precisely inside the warhead but had to withstand an estimated 20,000 tons of force when the round was fired.

Few women worked at Superior during the war. Although two operated some of the heavy dangerous punch presses, none worked in plating or polishing, since these departments were considered much too dirty and the work too miserable for women. Most of the company's female employees were given less physically demanding assembly jobs or office work. (For the record, one of the foremen had to be let go for, in Quatmann's words "getting a little cute" with the two Rosy-The-Riveter-type press operators.)

In 1946, when the ban on plating was lifted, Superior returned to producing much more mundane items beginning with flat irons. The company continued in business in the Mississippi River town of Cape Girardeau until 1982.

The Men Behind Superior Electric

Edmund Lawrence Haas (1892-1981), like many pioneers of the appliance industry was of German extraction. He married Anna Maria (Jimmie) Fox. The couple lived in Saint Louis and had three children, Marian, Edmund, and Bobby. The younger son died when hit by a truck at age six. Haas' surviving son Edmund worked at Superior from 1936 to 1939 as a purchasing agent for his father, but the father/son combination in the workplace was not a comfortable fit for either. In 1939 at age twenty-five Edmund decided to enlist in the army and pursue a military career. That left Superior Electric short one purchasing agent and also left Haas no heir-apparent willing to take over the company in the future.

Meanwhile, Haas' daughter Marian had fallen in love with bright, good looking, ambitious, and sensitive, Joseph Quatmann IV. Joe came from a well-established Saint Louis family and after high school was destined for college. The depression intervened however, wiping out the Quatmann family savings and Joe's college career. Instead he went to work after school hours for Purina Mills, stuffing envelopes with Tom Mix movie promotion trinkets for kids who had clipped the necessary coupon from the company's breakfast food boxes. He soon worked his way into the marketing department, traveling extensively for the company visiting Purina feedstore owners from New England to Florida. His mission was to show how to increase sales with better product displays. Having an interest in photography, Joe also worked for a time in Purina's photo department.

Edmund L. Haas
1892-1981

In 1939, immediately after Marian and Joe were married, the couple moved to Peoria, Illinois where Joe went to work for the Oberketter Photo Studio. A few months later a phone call from Marian's father convinced Joe that there was a brighter future for him at Superior Electric. The newlyweds moved back to Cape Girardeau where Joe went to work for his father-in-law. Joe Quatmann purchased Superior Electric in 1946 when the firm's founder Edmund Haas retired. He operated the business until his own retirement in 1968. Of the seven Quatmann children, only Ted worked at Superior. He started "on the line" and became a supervisor before the business was sold in 1968.

Interestingly, neither Edmund Haas nor Joseph Quatmann was what one would consider a natural born corporate type. Although each man possessed a strong Victorian work ethic and for years spent many long hard days running Superior Electric, neither was extraverted and both grew to feel that the business was an all-consuming burden. Quatmann related to his daughter Catherine that the company's founder, more than once, made a U-turn on his commute from Saint Louis to the factory, unable to face the problems of the day.

In 1967, Joe Quatmann suffered a skull fracture in a fall, requiring a month long hospital stay. According to his daughter Catherine, during this hiatus from the stress of the factory, her father decided to re-prioritize his life. The following year he sold the company, retired, and never looked back. He said later that the sale of the business was as if a huge weight had been lifted from his shoulders. He and his wife Marian traveled; he pursued his many hobbies, and for years did volunteer work for the local hospital and the parish church. Joseph Quatmann passed away in 2000 at age 87.

Joseph Quatmann IV
1913-2000

Swartzbaugh Mfg. Company

Everhot

Swartzbaugh Manufacturing Company was founded in 1884 as the Peerless Cooker Company of Buffalo, New York. The firm's first product, invented by the company founder Charles E. Swartzbaugh, was a low pressure steam cooker for use on wood or coal burning stoves. In the late teens Swartzbaugh designed what he called a "Fireless Cooker" which might be considered the forerunner of the modern crock-pot or slow cooker. Food would be partially cooked over a stove in heavy aluminum pots, which would then be placed inside a sealed insulated chest where the cooking process would be completed with the residual heat from the pots.

In the teens the firm was moved to Ohio and renamed The Toledo Cooker Company. By 1918 the "Fireless Cooker" was given a built-in electric warming unit. In 1925 this product was replaced by the "Everhot Electric Cooker," a six quart capacity electrically heated thermos-type cooking jug.

By the early 1930s the company was manufacturing hot plates, broilers, space heaters, and waffle irons under the "Everhot" label and under contract to larger firms including GE and Westinghouse. In 1951, due to major labor troubles at its plants, Swartzbaugh Manufacturing sold the "Everhot" name and all tooling to McGraw-Electric and ceased to exist as a separate entity.

The most unusual of its waffle irons is the Model 4 "Waf-Fil Baker." Dating from the early 1930s, this rectangular contraption has oblong-shaped grids, which create four hot dog bun-like waffles that are ideal for holding scoops of ice cream or other condiments.

Model 858 "Roasterette" circa 1940s. This mini-roaster could also bake, slow cook and be used as a thermos to keep food hot at picnics or luncheons. The firm was noted for its floor model roasters large enough to cook a full-size turkey. Sales of large roasters dropped as kitchen space shrank in the 1950s and built in ovens became popular. (Photo courtesy Dan & Vi LaBelle)

Thomas A. Edison Inc. [1]

EDICRAFT.

Products are created and built in the Laboratories of Thomas A. Edison.

In 1887, with funds obtained from major inventions created in previous years at his Menlo Park laboratory, Edison opened his West Orange, New Jersey research laboratory as a place devoted to the "rapid and cheap development of inventions." At its peak, as many as 200 were employed there to invent-to-order, "useful things that every man woman and child wants… at a price they can afford to pay." West Orange became the first modern industrial research and development facility and the model for the later Bell and Westinghouse laboratories. Edison died in 1931 at age 84, but his company, Thomas A. Edison Inc., continued to exist until 1957 when it was acquired by McGraw-Electric.

Much of the activity at the West Orange laboratory was involved with the improvement of existing technologies rather than with pure research and inventing. Such was the case with the "Edicraft" line of appliances, developed in the late 1920s to cash in on the burgeoning growth of the electric appliances industry. This was the first and only instance when Edison, who was in his eighties and very deaf by this time, was involved directly in making electric appliances. The firm's manufacturing division produced one model of a clamshell-type toaster, a sandwich grill, a waffle iron, a combination grill/waffle iron, and a model of a percolator urn called the "Siphonator." All of these appliances were well engineered (some say over-engineered) and of the highest quality, but Edison's timing was inopportune. The depression struck shortly after their introduction in 1929, just as demand for high priced luxury goods plummeted. It was nearly impossible to sell waffle irons for $23.50 and the "Siphonator" for $87.50, at a time when a good used car cost about $50.00. As a consequence of the poor sales the company discontinued appliance production by 1934.

The Edison-made waffle iron was designated **Model 104000** and the waffle iron grill combination, **Model 103000**. The combination unit (see page 168) is a husky looking leg-mounted type equipped with interchangeable flat or dimpled cooking grids. Both irons employ a non-adjustable, hermetically sealed, bimetal thermostatic switch that Edison labeled the "Birka Heat Regulator." Upon close examination this precision controller appears to have an unlimited life expectancy.

Thomas Edison Inc. continued:

The **Model 104000** waffle iron (pictured below) is a robust, chrome-plated pedestal-type, with a striking Deco-styled octagonal body and base. It works nicely to create unique three- part six-sided waffles with diamond-shaped dimples. Everything about this and the other "Edicraft" appliances from the fasteners to the plating speaks of quality. Interesting manufacturing innovations were used in the entire appliance line including the extensive use of rivet fasteners and modern high temperature plastic which would not appear again in other appliances for another decade.

Because of the relatively small number produced and because of the Edison name, all Thomas A. Edison Inc. appliances command very high prices from both appliance collectors in general and Edison aficionados in particular. It is not unusual for Edison Toasters to sell in the thousands of dollars with other Edison items approaching that level.

[1] Certain historical information courtesy Doug Tarr, Curator, National Park Service, Edison National Historic Sight, West Orange, New Jersey.

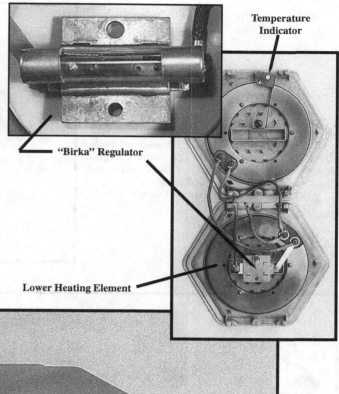

Temperature Indicator

"Birka" Regulator

Lower Heating Element

Waffle iron Model 104000 circa early 1930s, is top quality inside and out. The insert above shows the sealed heating elements and "Birka" temperature regulator, which is fastened in a pocket , cast into the lower grid. Edison used optical grade mica sheets to electrically insulate this hermetically sealed controller. All of this quality came at a steep price during a time when only the well off could afford the $23.50 cost. The unique design, its scarcity, and the Edison name make this one of the most sought-after vintage appliance of all time.

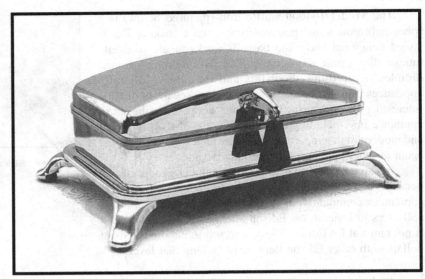

Model 103000 Edicraft sandwich grill is one of the most robust units of its type ever produced. One version is strictly a grill while this later variant is a waffle iron-grill combination unit. It contains the same "Birka" temperature regulator as the Model 104000 waffle iron.

(Photo courtesy Dan & Vi LaBelle)

This 1930 Christmas ad has "Rita" giving Edicraft appliances as Christmas gifts. Her husband must have been a high powered executive with a substantial income. The combined cost of these three items during this depression period would have equaled the cost of a very nice, low mileage, used car. (In fact, a friend of the author purchased a luxurious nearly new Auburn touring car in New York City from heiress Barbara Hutton for $100 at this time.)

(December, 1930, *Good Housekeeping Magazine*)

Toastess Corporation

Toastess Corporation was located in Pointe-Claire, a suburb of Montreal, Canada and sold two very similar non-automatic models of a combination grill/waffle iron in the late 1940s or early 1950s. One is Model 51 and the other **Model 551.** The latter, pictured below, is the more common of the two and is quite plentiful. Both units are noteworthy in only one respect-they have a very attractive flower and leaf design embossed into the lid. A slightly later automatic version of the Model 551 was marketed as Model 562. A fourth, Teflon-coated Model 575 with a mustard yellow body and chrome-plated base, was produced in the 1960s. The author suspects that other versions were also produced, possibly in avacado or blue.

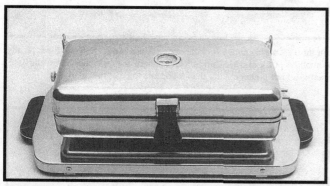

Model 551 is a plain generic grill/waffle iron from Canada. At least two very similar models were produced, one having decidedly 1930s styled Bakelite handles. This plastic-handled model probably dates from the 1940s.

United Drug Company
"Electrex"

The United Drug Company of Boston was a sales organization, not a manufacturer. In the late 1920s and early 1930s, using the "Electrex" brand name, the firm marketed several models of Beardsley and Wolcott-produced waffle irons. Most "Electrex" models look similar to the **Model X532** pictured below. They came equipped with an attractively colored wood lid handle and a pair of metal carrying handles riveted to the base. For a complete description of a most unusual "Electrex" Model, see Beardsley and Wolcott Model W2014 on page 34, which was also sold by United Drug Company as its "Electrex" Model X550.

Model X532, shown here with a standard 7 ½" waffle for size comparison, could be mistaken for a toy were it not for its quality construction. This iron makes a petite 5 ½" diameter "desert" or "party" sized waffle, a popular treat during the late 1920s when this product was marketed.

Utility Electric Company

Toastswell

The "Toastswell" trade name implies toasters, and in fact commercial toasters were this St. Louis company's main product line. The firm was founded in the late 1920s and located on Tower Grove Avenue, Saint Louis. Standex International purchased the company from the Pavelka family in 1994. On March 1, 1997, Star Manufacturing International Inc. purchased the Toastswell assets from Standex and now manufactures its products under the "Star" name at 10 Sunnen Drive, Saint Louis.

The company's first waffle iron, dating from the late 1920s, is an ordinary, unadorned, pedestal model with painted wood handles. The example pictured below has green handles. A company issued catalog, circa 1940s, lists numerous Toastswell waffle irons and waffle iron/grill models (see price guide pages 224-225), but only the **Model 830** waffle iron surfaces regularly today. It is a substantial, well-made, low profile unit with rounded lines reminiscent of automobiles of the same 1940s vintage. The very sensitive and accurate temperature controller used in this iron enables it to produce consistently well-cooked waffles with little trouble. Due to the low profile design, special care must be exercised in avoiding being burned by the protruding body, which becomes very hot during use. The company made at least one commercial twin model in the 1940s or 1950s, the CWB, which presumably stands for **C**ommercial **W**affle **B**aker.

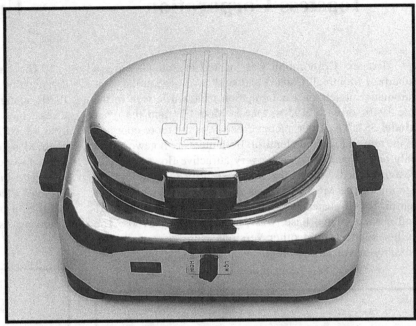

Made in Saint Louis in the 1940s, this pudgy looking cartoon-like **Model 830** has the typically rounded styling of automobiles of the era. Measuring 5 inches high and 10 inches across the base, this unit is more substantial and of higher quality than it appears to be at first glance.

THE *Toastswell*

COMBINATION WAFFLE IRON AND SANDWICH TOASTERS

With - - A NEW WALNUT TRAY

Utility Electric offered a variety of waffle irons in the early 1940s including this **Model 961** combination unit with walnut tray and crystal dishes. Notice the same styling motif as found on Model 830 above. The author has not yet seen this model. (October 1940, factory issued catalog)

The non-automatic pedestal model at left is typical of those of late 1920s vintage. It has painted wood handles (in this case green) and an embossed flower motif on the lid. It's probably Utility Electric's first model but has no model designation. (Photo courtesy Dan and Vi LaBelle)

Waage Electric Inc. [1]

Alvin Henry Waage founded Waage Electric in New York City in 1908. The firm operated in three lofts at 54 Park Place until it was relocated to its present address in Kenilworth, New Jersey. Alvin Waage had three children, Clark, Avis and Ruth. The son, Clark Alvin Waage, succeeded his father as president of the firm and was responsible for the company's move to New Jersey in July 1951. During the late 1930s and 1940s Waage also had a manufacturing facility in the Chicago area. Clark Waage, a native of the Flatbush section of Brooklyn, passed away in 2001 at age 85. Today, his son Marc is president of the company.

Over the years Waage Electric has manufactured flat irons, commercial and domestic waffle irons of various types, corn-dog cookers (A waffle-type iron designed to accept hot dogs around which is poured a special cornmeal-type batter. The iron cooks the meat and bakes the batter simultaneously.) For years the company has manufactured commercial and domestic soldering equipment. Today the firm continues to offer a complete line of commercial soldering equipment including soldering irons, solder baths, solder pots, and related manufacturing equipment. Company sales are worldwide.

This Waage sandwich grill came with a most unusual deco base. The body of this unit looks amazingly similar to the Canadian-made Westinghouse Model H326640 of the same period which can be seen on page 185.

(Photo courtesy Dan and Vi LaBelle)

[1] Information courtesy Marc Waage, President, Waage Manufacturing.

This rare Waage waffle iron looks like most of its contemporaries from the late 1920s until one looks under the body. Four thin rod supports located there attach the body to the base. This unique design is a clever way of isolating the heat to the body. If readers know of other Waage waffle iron models, the author would like to hear from you.

Waters-Genter Company [1]
"Toastmaster"

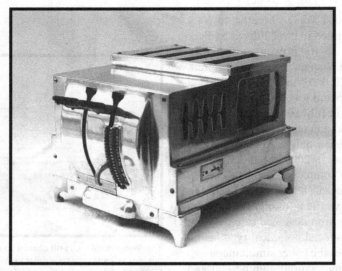

Toastmaster's mainstay product for the first ten years was the **Model 1D1** four slice commercial toaster produced from 1921 to 1932. It sold in the early 1930s for $100, a cosiderable sum at that time. The company also made an enormous 8-12 slice version designated Model 1F1. That monster could toast more than 525 slices of bread per hour. Brownness of the toast was determined by setting a stop on the machines to one of 11 positions. Either or both levers would be pushed down, lowering the bread and cocking a mechanical timer. One of the five heating elements can be seen through the mica window at the right. The company developed its first domestic toaster, the Model 1A1, from the commercial models. (Photo courtesy Dan & Vi LaBelle)

Twenty-five year old Glen Waters, arrived in Minneapolis in 1919 from Miller, South Dakota looking for a business opportunity. There he made contact with two entrepreneurs, Simpson and Furber, who were seeking financing to produce a very large commercial bread toaster which they aimed to sell to hotels, restaurants, and clubs.

> For more details about Glen Waters and his family please see the segment entitled *"The Glen Waters Story"* at the conclusion of the Waters-Genter Company history.

The men had demonstrated their toaster at the Hotel Appliance Convention that year and had convinced the prestigious Childs Restaurant chain to install and test three prototypes in their Minneapolis restaurant. These tests showed that the savings in unburned toast and the need for one less kitchen worker more than offset the $85.00 cost of each unit. By December 1919, Childs' management had ordered two more units for their New York City restaurant. In addition, the convention display had prompted the sale of units for New York City's Hotel Astor and the Union Club.

Waters calculated that the cost to manufacture each toaster was $20.00. The $65.00 profit margin convinced him that this could be a very lucrative deal and agreed to supply the cash to start full-scale production in exchange for 7% of the preferred stock in the new company and 25% of the common stock.

At the same time, Walter Strite, a Stillwater, Minnesota mechanic, designed and patented the first automatic toaster for domestic use and approached Waters with the hope of selling the patent rights to his smaller automatic machine. Waters purchased Strite's patent agreeing to give the inventor 5% of any proceeds from the sales of this toaster. These patents were unsuccessfully challenged by General Electric and remained in force until their expiration in the mid-1930s.

In 1920 production commenced on the large restaurant toaster, now modified and using the automatic features designed and patented by Strite. A year later Harold "Moose" Genter infused the company with additional capital and the firm became known as the Waters-Genter Company. Genter held the title of treasurer and was responsible for financial and sales matters while Waters concentrated on manufacturing.

The Waters-Genter commercial toasters were a sales success and by the mid-1920s were being used in a number of major hotels and restaurants around the country. Certain models could process as many as eight slices of bread at a time. In the busy and usually understaffed commercial kitchens of the day, the toaster's automatic feature saved time

Waters-Genter continued:

Toastmaster **Model 1A1**, the first automatic pop-up domestic toaster, used the same operating principal as its commercial predecessor pictured on previous page. The operator preset the cycle time, cocked a timer with the lever on right, then lowered toast with left lever. (Photo Courtesy Dan & Vi LaBelle)

but alienated a large portion of the Minnesota business community with his pro-labor stands. Olson remained in power for three terms until his untimely death of stomach cancer at age 44, in 1937. His successor, Elmer Benson, more leftist (some say communist) than Olson, scared an already skittish Minnesota business community so badly that the management of a number of companies decided to move their operations out of the state. The Wells Lamont Glove Company and Dominion Electric both of Minneapolis were two of the first to go. Toastmaster wasn't far behind.

In late 1937, McGraw announced that he had commissioned the architectural firm of Olsen and Urbain to design a $250,000 manufacturing and office facility to be built in south Elgin, Illinois. Toastmaster moved into the new plant in 1938 and remained there until 1965 (See *McGraw-Electric* section for photos of this facility). At the time of the move Waters and Genter both left Toastmaster to pursue other interests. Toastmaster remained a division of McGraw-Electric and later of McGraw-Edison until 1980 when executives of the firm, in a leveraged buy-out, turned the portable appliances division into the Toastmaster Corporation. In the mid-1980s Maytag acquired Toastmaster. The company was once again recreated with a leverage buy-out in 1987 and was sold to Salton Corporation in the late 1990s. Today, Toastmaster is headquartered in Columbia, Missouri.

by eliminating the need to monitor the toasting process and saved money by preventing a great deal of burned bread.

In 1925 the company registered the "Toastmaster" name and the following year used it to introduce the firm's first automatic household toaster, the Model 1A1. This was basically a simplified scaled-down version of the Strite commercial toaster. That year, Max McGraw, founder of McGraw Electric Company (see *McGraw-Edison*), acquired Waters-Genter for himself in a private purchase. In 1929 he transferred his private interest in Waters-Genter, to his McGraw Electric Company. Waters and Genter both retained their positions with the company and ran Waters-Genter for McGraw for nine more years.

In 1931, a young populist by the name of Floyd Olson successfully ran for governor of Minnesota on the Farmer Labor ticket. He became a very popular pro-labor governor,

In a letter from his Chicago office to Waters and Genter dated August 12, 1930, McGraw made it official that the company would be introducing the first new toaster model since the 1A1 and that a **Model 2C1** domestic waffle iron would also be produced. He voiced great optimism about the sales potential of both products and expected the company to dominate the domestic waffle iron market as it had the toaster market. As it turned out, McGraw wasn't a very good fortuneteller. An internal company financial statement dated March 2, 1933, covering the years 1927-1932, shows that the firm lost money making both commercial and domestic waffle irons during most of this six year period. Toaster sales kept the company profitable during the early depression years with waffle iron production used to diversify the product line and absorb some of the fixed costs associated with toaster manufacturing.

173

Waters-Genter continued:

The **Model 2C1** has a large, red jeweled ready light and a provision for the timer to automatically switch the heating elements into a warming mode after the waffle is cooked. A stationary knob on the front panel is intended as a thumb grip to assist in cocking the stiff timer lever. Because the operating temperature of the iron is non-adjustable, a small control lever is provided to change the running speed of the timer. In 1935, with the introduction of the company's **Model 2D1** and in all subsequent models, a conventional, less complex, adjustable bimetal thermostat controller replaced the costly mechanical timer.

From the beginning, Toastmaster built its reputation not on styling, which could be considered utilitarian, but rather by making consumer products of near-commercial quality that would last for generations. From 1971 to 1997 Toastmaster produced the most popular waffle iron ever made, the Model W252. Due to their popularity when made, and their high survival rate, collector prices on most Toastmaster products remain modest. From among the several hundred waffle irons the author has used, without a doubt, the most entertaining has been the windup, ticking time bomb, **Model 2C1** with its big red warning light.

[1]   Information about the company and personalities courtesy George F. Waters, Rochester, Minnesota. Information about models and dates of production courtesy Dawn Spires, Archivist, Toastmaster Corporation.

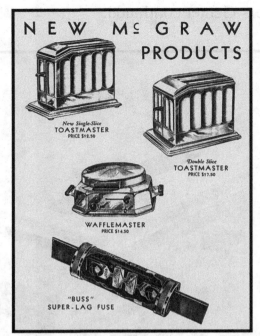

Max McGraw enclosed this new products flyer in an announcement to stockholders in August 1930. Illustrated top to bottom is the Model 1A2 toaster ($12.50), Model 1B2 Toaster ($17.50), the new Model 1C1 waffle iron ($14.50), and the "Super-Lag" fuse. This fuse was a unique slow-to-blow cartridge type with a replaceable fuse link, and manufactured by the Buss Fuse division of McGraw-Electric. (Courtesy George F. Waters & Dan & Vi LaBelle)

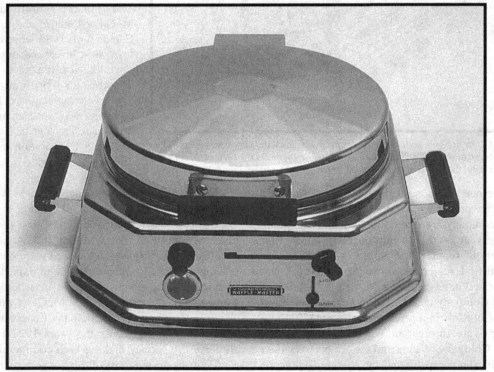

Model 2C1 "Waffle-Master" was equipped with an adjustable clockworks timer wound with a sliding knob located on the right front. The stiff nature of the timer spring required that a stationary knob on the left above the indicator light be used as a grip to assist in the winding process. When the cooking cycle was completed the iron automatically went into a warming mode. The same ticking "time bomb" timer was used in the company's toasters at this time.

Here's a Christmas Gift That's Never Been Given Before

So You Can't Go Wrong — No Matter To Whom You Give It

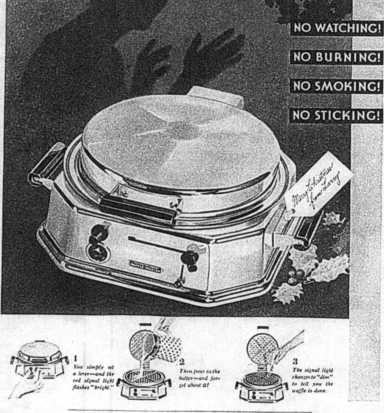

NO WATCHING!
NO BURNING!
NO SMOKING!
NO STICKING!

This Amazing New Waffle-Iron Makes Waffles AUTOMATICALLY

HERE'S something new, something smart, something marvelous—a Christmas gift that's never been given before! That you can't go wrong in giving —no matter to whom you give it.

An amazing new waffle-iron that makes waffles *automatically!* That banishes all the guesswork; all the burn, stick and bother from waffle making!

It comes as another unique electrical invention from the people who invented automatic toastmaking— from the inventors of the famous Toastmaster.

It is called the *Waffle-Master,* is completely automatic *and makes waffles entirely without the use of grease.*

All You Do Is Set A Lever

All you do is set a lever. When the iron is at just the right heat for the batter, a tiny red signal *tells you* that it is.

Then you pour in the batter, close the iron—*and forget about it!*

When the waffle is done—done to just the marvelously golden brown you want—the signal light changes again to *tell you* that it's done.

You don't open the iron, or even think about it, from the time you pour in the batter to the time you are signalled that the waffle is done.

1 *You simply set a lever—and the red signal light flashes "bright."*

2 *Then pour in the batter—and forget about it!*

3 *The signal light changes to "dim" to tell you the waffle is done.*

Waffles More Profitable Than Ever Before

Many leading Restaurants, Cafeterias, Sandwich Shops and Counter Services report demand for waffles increasing very fast. Now made profitably with Strite Automatic Waffle-Baker—a Toastmaster product. Send postcard for facts about it. No obligation, of course.

No watching. No burning. No sticking. No underdone waffles. The whole operation is automatic.

Won't Stick — Won't Burn

Another important point is that WAFFLES cooked in this device *will not* stick. Yet—you use no grease.

Another is, that waffles *will not* burn. For when one is done, the Waffle-Master turns the current down from "high" to "low" heat *automatically.*

You can take the waffle out, or leave it in to keep it hot, just as you like.

See The Waffle-Master

If you like waffles, but have had bother making them

—see the Waffle-Master. You, like thousands of others, will call it wonderful.

Now on display at most stores carrying electrical devices throughout the United States and Canada.

WATERS-GENTER COMPANY
219 N. Second St., Minneapolis, Minn.
A Division of the
McGRAW ELECTRIC COMPANY

WAFFLE·MASTER
A TOASTMASTER PRODUCT

Makes Waffles Automatically

Although Liberty Gauge and Instrument Company introduced the first thermostatically controlled automatic waffle iron in 1926, it took until 1930 for Toastmaster to create its first automatic waffle iron, the timer controlled **Model 2C1 "Waffle-Master."** Illustrated at lower left in the ad is the **Model 2AT "Strite"** dual restaurant unit. (December, 1930, *Saturday Evening Post Magazine*)

175

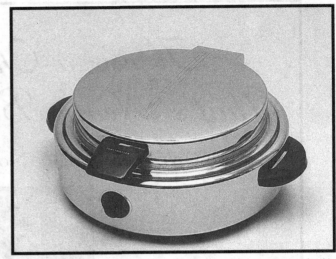

With the introduction of **Model 2D1** in 1935, a conventional bimetal thermostat with a single knob control replaced the complex mechanical timer of the company's first waffle iron model. Gone too was the reassuring Toastmaster ticking. This model continued in production until it was replaced by Model 2D2 in 1939.

Model 2D2 was introduced in 1939 and except for the war years remained in production until 1959. While none of the Toastmaster's waffle irons were beauty contest winners, all were heavy-duty appliances of near-commercial quality.

In 1938 "Uncle Hank" would have had to pay $12.50 for the **Model 2D1** waffle baker illustrated. It would have been a good deal for the newlyweds provided Uncle Hank didn't show up for waffles too often. 1930s Toastmaster products were top quality and their higher cost reflected it. These irons like toastmaster toasters, if given reasonable care, can last for generations.

This 1955 McGraw-Electric dealers fact sheet lists all of the features of the company's popular Toastmaster **Model 2D2** and explains how the unit's unique glass rod thermostat control unit detects expansion of the aluminum cooking grids in order to determine their temperature.

The Glen Waters Story [1]

Glen Waters was born in Miller, South Dakota in 1885. His father William, like many young men after the civil war "went west" to seek his fortune and became one of the first homesteaders on the open prairie of South Dakota. For a number of years William successfully brokered real estate around Miller and in the process accumulated a significant amount of land for himself. By the turn of the century the Waters family was prosperous enough to allow Glen to attend The University of Chicago and study law.

After graduating, the young Waters returned to South Dakota to practice law and like his father, deal in real estate. In 1912, he ran successfully as a republican for state senator from the twenty-third district. and represented Hand and Hyde Counties for two terms. While serving in the state senate he married Carolyn Belle Waite, a local girl who had just returned from college in California. At the end of Glen's second term, a restless Carolyn pleaded with him to please "take me away from here."

In the late teens, the couple moved to Minneapolis where Glen decided to leave the law profession and become a manufacturer. His rationale for the change was that as a lawyer his income potential was limited because he could only charge for his time. A manufacturer could make money around the clock with a factory that could produce in ever increasing volume whether he was present or not.

In a lengthy 1919 persuasive letter to a friend and former business associate in Pierre, Waters outlined in some detail what he thought might be three potentially lucrative manufacturing propositions for the two of them. The first was to go into business with two gentlemen by the name of Simpson and Furber who wanted to manufacture a heavy duty rear suspension assembly designed to convert Model T Ford cars into light farm trucks. He related to the friend that the same men also had plans to manufacture special wheel rims which were designed to give heavy vehicles added traction in mud and snow. Near the end of the letter, almost as an after-thought, Waters mentioned that Simpson and Furber, were also developing a large heavy automatic electric toaster intended for commercial use. He went on to tell the friend that he was definitely pursuing this opportunity for himself whether the friend wanted to do so or not. (See the Waters-Genter Company history)

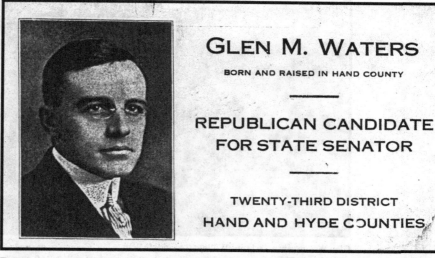

GLEN M. WATERS
BORN AND RAISED IN HAND COUNTY

REPUBLICAN CANDIDATE
FOR STATE SENATOR

TWENTY-THIRD DISTRICT
HAND AND HYDE COUNTIES

Twenty-seven year old Glen Waters handed out business cards like this while running for state senator in South Dakota in 1912. He was successful in his first political venture and was re-elected for a second term before the family moved to Minneapolis in 1918. (Courtesy George F. Waters)

Waters' friend didn't take advantage of any of the opportunities but Waters formed a long-lasting partnership in the early 1920s with Harold "Moose" Genter (pronounced with a hard "G"). Harold received the "Moose" tag for his large physical presence. Their relationship, though friendly, was strictly businesslike. The Waters-Genter Company that they formed was sold to Max McGraw in 1925 and both men worked together for McGraw for twelve more years.

Waters' relationship with McGraw was a very cordial one evidenced by a letter from Waters to McGraw dated December 28, 1929. In it Glen thanked McGraw for a Christmas gift to the Waters family of a game called "The Devil Among the Tailors." The letter goes on to say, "My association with you for the year just drawing to a close have (sic) been very pleasant indeed, and I am looking forward to the next and succeeding years with anticipation to the continuation of this pleasure."

The "Toastmaster" name was most likely created by Waters, Genter, and other managers tossing product names around a table at a meeting. Waters never took credit for either the "Toastmaster" or "Waffle Master" names. Although the company placed copyrights on these, Waters always regretted not putting a trademark on other "master" names. Shortly after the name "Toastmaster" became a marketing success a number of other firms including Sears ("Heatmaster") and Sunbeam ("Mixmaster") copied the name idea for their products.

Glen Waters continued:

Glen Waters center and sons William ("Muddy") Waters left, George right, and George's faithful Springer Spaniel "Whiskers". This photo was taken in the late 1920s on the family's 160 acre farm north of Minneapolis. Glen purchased the property for use as a private recreation area for family members and friends.

(Photo courtesy George F. Waters)

Glen Waters examining a rock sample in his home workshop in the late 1930s. He was an avid mineral collector and pursued this hobby avidly for years.

(Photo courtesy George F. Waters)

Waters with shotgun in a duck boat with a guide, hunting water fowl in the Canadian Delta Marsh. Date unknown. (Photo courtesy George F. Waters & Dan & Vi LaBelle)

Glen Waters continued:

A 1937 family portrait taken in Minneapolis in 1937. Mr. and Mrs. Glen Waters are seated and petting a rambunctious "Cocoa" the family's second Springer Spaniel. Standing are sons Bill (left) and George. Shortly after this picture was taken Mr. Waters sold Toastmaster to McGraw-Electric. Two years later he created the Waters-Conley Company.
(Photo courtesy George F. Waters)

When McGraw moved Toastmaster to Illinois in 1938, Genter was eager to leave the company to pursue other interests. He subsequently made a fortune by creating a new industry- the coin operated laundry machine rental business. Waters was less anxious to leave McGraw Electric and seriously considered moving with the company to Illinois. However, his family's desire to remain in Minneapolis persuaded Glen to quit Toastmaster. An avid amateur mineralogist, he invested heavily in gold mine stock, which during the 1938 recession lost him a major portion of his assets.

Although Waters in 1938 no longer worked for McGraw Electric, he was still on the company's board of directors. During the board's meeting that year he mentioned to another member, General Robert Wood, chairman of Sears, that he was interested in getting back into manufacturing. Wood told Waters that Sears was getting out of manufacturing to build shopping mall stores and that he should look into purchasing the Sears-owned Conley Company which was for sale in Rochester, Minnesota.

For years, The Conley Company had made windup record players for Sears. When Waters bought the company in 1939, it became the Waters-Conley Company and shortly after converted to making "Phonola" electronic phonographs. During World War II, the firm worked with the Mayo Clinic in Rochester to develop medical monitoring equipment for the Army's Air Force flight medicine research.

Glen and Carolyn Waters had two children, William "Muddy" Waters and George Franklin Waters. After graduation from Harvard at the outbreak of World War II, Bill, the oldest son, enlisted in the Army and became a lieutenant-navigator in the Army Air Force. Early in the war the army ferried Lockheed A-28 Hudsons (a heavier military derivation of Amelia Earhart's plane) from the states to the China-Burma-India Theater of Operation for use in logistics support in the war against the Japanese in China. In July 1942, while navigating one of these Hudsons on a flight to the far east, Bill was killed when the plane's engines failed and it crashed on takeoff from Kano, Nigeria.

George Waters graduated in the accelerated program from Harvard in 1943, and like his brother became a lieutenant in the Army Air Force. By happenstance he became an air freight officer in Karachi, in the China-Burma-India Theater and met General Wood (of Sears fame) who was senior logistics officer for the army at the time and was on tour to India. Following the war George went to work for his father at Waters-Conley, married, and had three daughters. In 1954 when his father retired, George purchased the medical instruments part of Waters-Conley and ran it as Waters Instruments Inc. until he too retired in the 1980s. Today George enjoys his retirement with his wife Jean in Minnesota and Florida.

During World War II the war department gave the Army-Navy "Award of Excellence" to industries that met or exceeded certain production goals and quality standards. The award consisted of a banner allowed to be flown over the plant and lapel pins for the employees. The Waters-Conley Company is being given its banner in this 1945 photo. From left to right are Glen Waters, president of the firm, Minnesota Congressman August Andreson, unidentified Naval and Army officers and an unidentified trade union representative.
(Photo courtesy George F. Waters)

Three generations of the Waters family circa 1955. Glen Waters right center is holding his granddaughter Anne. At left, is daughter-in-law Jean, Mr. Waters' wife Carolyn, granddaughters, Brenda and Dain, and at far right son George.
(Photo courtesy George F. Waters)

Glen Waters passed away in 1965. He had been born with Hip Dysplasia during the so called "Gilded Age," in an era when this very painful often debilitating condition was inoperable. It was the Victorian Era when, if a person in polite conversation was asked, "How are you today?", was expected to respond, "Fine thank you" no matter the true state of affairs. His condition caused Glen to walk with a noticeable shuffle his entire life, but no one close to him can ever remember him complaining about it, slowing down because of it, or in true Victorian fashion even mentioning his affliction. Despite his physical problem or perhaps because of it, Glen Waters was an over-achiever responsible for making "Toastmaster" a term synonymous with toasters and a household word familiar to millions around the world.

[1] Information for this piece is derived from correspondence and interviews generously given to the author by George F. Waters in 2001-2002.

George Waters today, holding an example of his father's first automatic toaster designed for home use, the Toastmaster Model 1A1.
(Photo courtesy Dan & Vi LaBelle)

Wear-Ever

Wear-Ever was incorporated as the United States Aluminum Company in 1900 and became a subsidiary of The Pittsburgh Reduction Company, an Aluminum refiner, which later became the Aluminum Company of America (ALCOA). At the same time, the Pittsburgh Reduction Company formed a marketing subsidiary-the Aluminum Cooking Utensil Company, the purpose of which was to sell the products manufactured by Wear-Ever. In 1903 this sales organization adopted the "Wear-Ever" name for the aluminum cookware they sold. By the 1920s, ALCOA, with its "Wear-Ever" and "Mirro" brands, controlled two thirds of all aluminum cookware manufacturing in the world. Today, Wearever does not hyphenate its name and is part of the Mirro Corporation.

In the late 1920s, Wear-Ever manufactured two versions of the Model 909 aluminum waffle iron in its New Kingston, Pennsylvania plant near Pittsburgh. In an effort to use as much aluminum as possible, the engineers at Wear-Ever made the unfortunate decision to use sheet aluminum stampings to form the entire shell of the unit. The result is a waffle iron with a body that, due to the excellent heat conductivity of aluminum, gets excessively hot during use. With repeated heating the aluminum losses its temper and softens drastically. Discounting these shortcomings, it otherwise does a credible job of cooking. The author suspects that these irons were given a brushed

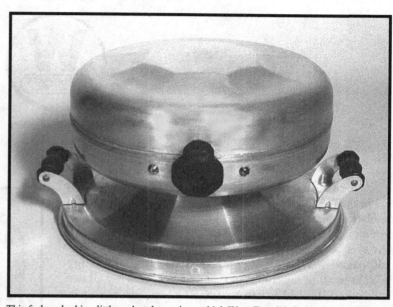

This forlorn-looking little pedestal-type iron which Wear-Ever labeled its **Model 909** has strikingly beautiful black and red marbleized painted wood handles. The use of aluminum for the body shell was a poor choice of materials but understandable since Wear-Ever was part of an aluminum refining and manufacturing empire. A second version of this iron was produced with a dial-type temperature guage in top center of lid.

finish when new. A nearly identical second version of this iron was made with a large dial-type temperature indicator in the center of the lid. Their unique orange, black, and red marbleized wood handles are very attractive, making this model a sought-after collectable.

This turn of the century catalog shows some of the Wear-Ever products available during the era of the non-electric kitchen. The stovetop waffle irons are advertised as having stay-cool "Alaska Handles", a generic term for the spring coil variety commonly found on stoves at the time. This type of handle can still be found on commercial electric waffle irons.

Westinghouse Electric & Mfg. Company
"Every House Needs Westinghouse"

The story of George Westinghouse is a fascinating one, the details of which fill volumes. His first endeavor, Westinghouse Air Brake Company, was founded in 1869 and would be the first of over 60 Westinghouse companies. At his peak, Westinghouse was the largest private employer in industrial history. He was an entrepreneur, industrialist, inventor, and probably the greatest engineer the United States has ever produced. In his lifetime he personally held over 360 patents. By 1907, Westinghouse had lost controlling interest in all of his companies, and in 1911 severed all ties with them. He died in 1914, at age 68, and was buried in Arlington National Cemetery. Four years later, he was granted his last patent, posthumously.

The Westinghouse Electric Company, later called The Westinghouse Electric and Manufacturing Company, was formed in 1886. In bold and contentious competition with backers of Thomas Edison's direct current system, Westinghouse and his engineers created the modern day alternating current power distribution system. Westinghouse entered the electrical appliance field early on, marketing the first electric fry pan in 1911. In 1912 the company was again first with a flat toaster grill and soon after, borrowing the legs, body, and heating element designs from this grill, marketed what was one of the first practical electric waffle irons, the **Type A** pictured below.

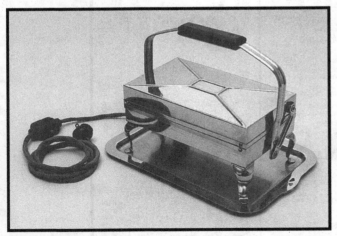

Type A irons have a heating element patent date of 1906 on the bottom but the iron itself wasn't made until the late-teens. They came nickel-plated with a permanently attached art silk-type power cord, detachable legs for easier cleaning and a tray. The tray is usually missing from surviving examples.

In the early 1920s Westinghouse was one of the first to include a waffle recipe booklet with each of its electric waffle irons. These attractive multi-colored early editions illustrate the **Type A** model in action.

182

Westinghouse continued:

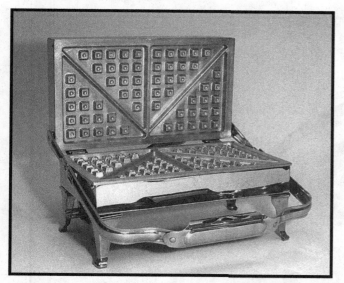

Model WA-4, the second rectangular model by Westinghouse utilizes the same 1906 heating elements, body shell and removable legs as the earlier Type A, but unlike its predecessor has a detachable cord and an all metal pull down lid handle. Westinghouse was quite successful in selling these early models which makes finding them fairly easy. Modern cords will fit them.

In 1924, the company introduced an automatic non-adjustable clothes pressing iron employing a very clever, sturdy, compact, bimetal disc-type thermostat. This "Klixon" controller, so named for the sharp clicking sound it produced, was later incorporated into the company's top-of-the-line waffle irons, including Models CPC-2, CBCA and **CBC-4**. The first version of this thermostat was prone to early failure from steam damage to the bare steel parts. Later versions were silver-plated and worked quite well, maintaining an even factory preset temperature.

Westinghouse became one of the dominant appliance manufacturers of all time. According to the February, 1931 issue of the *Gage Electrical Encyclopedia*, the company offered six models of waffle irons, ranging in price from $8.95 to 18.50, six toasters, and a phenomenal sixty different coffee pots, percolators, and urns. In the 1970s, Westinghouse's appliance division was sold to Scovill Manufacturing, which then sold the large appliance division to White Consolidated Industries. White-Westinghouse continues to make appliances.

Model WD-4 circa mid-1920s retains the complex pull down lid handle design of previous models. The handle works well for carrying purposes but opening the lid to remove a waffle during the baking process can be a struggle. The company abandoned such a handle design after this model.

Large multi-colored Westinghouse ads were always attention getters and this 1922 Christmas example is no exception. Many illustrators of the period favored the square-jawed look in men. The gentleman pictured here purchasing a **Type A** waffle iron looks strikingly similar to artist J.C. Leyendecker's classic Arrow shirt men. (December 1922, *Lady's Home Journal*)

Westinghouse waffle irons are generally of good to excellent quality and perform well, with styling that ranges from plain to elegant. The much sought after Hall "Fuji" pattern, ceramic base Models CBCA and **CBC-4** epitomize the Art Deco styling of the twenties and thirties. The extremely low profile Models WD-414, WF-24 and **WSA-24,** are wonderful examples of the sleek post-deco styling of designer Joseph Harms, accomplished by the use of nicely engineered slim line type heating elements. In the late 1930s, waffle irons were one of the wedding gifts of choice, and for a time, Westinghouse offered Models WS-14 and **WSA-14,** which could be ordered with a special enameled monogram letter insert in the center of the lid. That extra cost option is rarely found on these depression era models.

Some Canadian-made (Hamilton, Ontario) Westinghouse models like **H32640** have European deco styling not found on their American-made counterparts. Most Westinghouse waffle irons, in good condition, command higher-than-average prices from collectors for both their styling and quality.

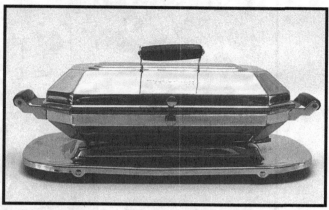

An early 1930s product of Westinghouse's Hamilton, Ontario manufacturing facilities, **Model H32640** grill/waffle iron has styling unique to products designed expressly for the Canadian market.

Model CBC-4 with a Hall made "Fuji" pattern ceramic base is equipped with a non-adjustable "Klixon" bimetal temperature controller located under the lid. When cycling it sounds like a very large toy clicker. Less common versions of this iron came with cream-colored or "sanitary white" lid handles rather than the black version pictured here.

• LUCKY woman! ... to get a Westinghouse *Dual-automatic* Flavor Zone Range! Changes heats *automatically* during cooking; banishes watching; brings hours of freedom each day.

• NEW! Lower cost ... this beautiful antique-silver cleaner. Phenomenal efficiency. $29.95. Also a marvelous motor brush model and the handy, versatile "Duster-Cleaner."

• NEW LIGHT on an old subject! Westinghouse miniature MAZDA Lamps will last to illuminate many Christmas trees for the same quality reasons that make their bigger brothers first choice of discriminating buyers for general lighting.

DO YOUR
Christmas Shopping
THIS EASY WAY

STEP inside a Westinghouse store and shopping problems vanish! Practical gifts .. shining chromium and gaily painted porcelain .. marvelous electrical efficiency. And though they bear a world-famous name, thrifty prices are the rule.

• The wonderful new Westinghouse Vacuum Coffee Maker brews coffee the way experts recommend. Hot water is drawn over the coffee just once, making a clear, fragrant, full-flavored brew. Colorful china base and "Glasbake" heat-proof vessels. Makes 2 to 7 cups automatically, costs only $9.95.

• *Fully-automatic,* heat-indicating waffle iron. Beautifully - decorated china base, gleaming chromium top. Only $9.95. Others as low as $6.45.

• GIFT OF GIFTS! What a thrill, to find a real Westinghouse *Dual-automatic* Refrigerator in her kitchen on Christmas morning! Hermetically-sealed mechanism, backed by a 4-year Service Plan. Christmas Thrift Offer makes it surprisingly easy to buy.

• NEW *fully-automatic* Westinghouse Ironer irons *everything* in record time. Far easier to use. Combines many features including down feed, two open ends, totally-enclosed motor, duplex control. Portable and floor models. An ideal gift as low as $79.50.

• An iron every woman will want ... the DeLuxe Adjust-o-matic. Fatigue-proof, sloping handle; soft sponge-rubber grip. Lighter, faster, fully adjustable-automatic. $7.75.

• Complete urn sets in many striking designs, including dainty decorated china with stunning inlaid, stain-proof Micarta trays. From $19.95.

• New toasters in period design, finished in never-tarnishing chromium. Operate on the famous "Turnover" principle ... turn toast without touching. Many as low as $2.95.

Westinghouse
ELECTRICAL
GIFTS
Electricity to operate them is the cheapest thing you buy

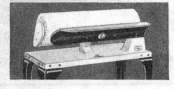

• The Westinghouse 2-for-1 Warming Pad Set is new, different, a delightful gift. Pads bring quick relief from pain ... warm comfort on cold nights. Automatic, non-radio-interfering. Both for $6.95. Also single pads as low as $3.95.

In using advertisements see page 6

For December 1932, Westinghouse offered Christmas shoppers a selection of appliances with Hall-made ceramic bodies including a coffee percolator, a coffee urn set, and the **Model CBC-4** waffle iron in the Hall "Fuji" pattern. The $9.95 price was a real bargain for this automatic model and reflected the deflation of the early depression years.

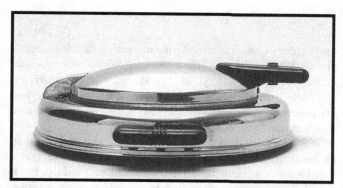

In the late 1930s when most consumer goods were still tall and rather boxy, **Model WSA-24** was low, sleek, and radically new looking. The low 3½ inch profile was made possible by ultra thin heating elements, a compact thermostat, and the temperature control and indicator light incorporated into the handle. The 1939 patent drawing for this model is reproduced at right.

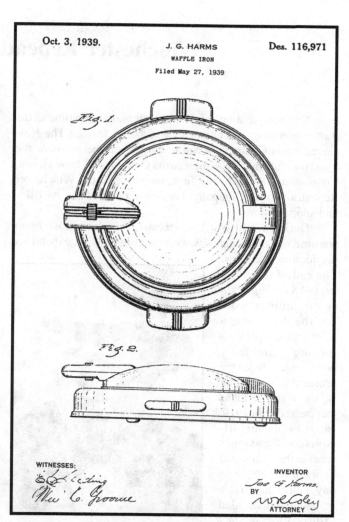

Joseph G. Harms, a Westinghouse designer, was awarded a patent in October 1939 for his ultra low profile waffle iron design. After more than 60 years the iron still looks contemporary. (Drawing courtesy Nancy Conway)

Model SGWB-521 (Sandwich Grill-Waffle Baker) is a good quality, nicely styled, combination unit that Westinghouse sold in great numbers from the late 1940s through the mid-1950s. The Grill sold for $30.00. The waffle grids pictured cost a few dollars extra. Combination units with separate waffle grids like this one are much preferred to models with flip-over -type grids. With the latter, the seasoning on the waffle grid side is destroyed each time it is flipped and used as a grill.

In the late 1930s when this **Model WSA-14** was made, waffle irons were the wedding gift of choice. This and the similar but non-automatic Model WS-14 could be ordered with a special monogrammed lid medallion. It's unusual to find one with a monogram today since depression era shoppers were reluctant to spend the extra money for a monogram. The beautifuly colored deep ruby red glass used in the indicator window was manufactured in Checkoslovakia.

Winchester Repeating Arms Company

Yes, believe it or not, Winchester was at one time in the waffle iron business. Oliver F. Winchester formed The New Haven Arms Company when he purchased the assets of the bankrupt Volcanic Repeating Arms Company of New Haven, Connecticut in 1857. The firm, later named the Winchester Repeating Arms Company, became renowned for its rifles and sporting guns.

During World War I Winchester, in order to cash in on wartime military contracts, borrowed heavily to expand its production facilities. The end of hostilities in 1918 brought an end to military work for the firm and a dramatic drop in its income. Suddenly management faced the prospect of defaulting on the wartime loans that came due in 1919. In a bold but ill-advised business scheme that amounted to Robbing Peter to pay Paul, the firm's management decided to diversify its product line. Between 1919 and 1921, the arms

Oliver F. Winchester
1810-1880

maker in a joint venture with Kidder Peabody, purchased eleven smaller profitable companies involved in making everything from razors to roller skates. The hope was that income siphoned from these enterprises would cover Winchester's wartime debts. (Remember, this was the aptly named period called the "Roaring Twenties.") The company's plan worked, at least for awhile.

Winchester merged with the Simmons Hardware Company in August 1922 and became the Winchester-Simmons Company. In a second poorly conceived move, the new firm opened retail stores in Boston and Springfield, Massachusetts, Providence, Rhode Island, New Haven, Connecticut, Troy, New York, and New York City. The stores proved unsuccessful from the start and were sold just two years later at a loss totaling an incredible 2.3 million (1924) dollars.

During the 1920s, in addition to firearm-related items, Winchester-Simmons tried manufacturing and merchandising a complete line of sporting goods including ice and roller skates, football, baseball, and basketball equipment, fishing tackle, and camping gear. Then in 1926 the company acquired the Whirldry Corporation and tried marketing that firm's spin-dry washing machine. At the same time Winchester was also making or selling safety razor products, kitchen cutlery, a complete line of carpentry and mechanic's tools, assorted dry cell batteries for telephones, radios, and flash lights, and was manufacturing radiators for vehicles.

By early 1929 Winchester's debt load was so great that the company was forced to reorganize. The stock market crash that October sealed the firm's fate and in January 1931 Winchester-Simmons went into receivership. After a series of reorganizations and major divestitures, Winchester became part of the Olin-Mathieson Chemical Company. Olin invested heavily in Winchester's core business of arms making and had the company back on solid financial footing by the late 1930s.

Winchester played a critical roll in supplying small arms to the military during World War II. The company produced over half a million M1 rifles and about three-quarters of a million M1 carbines, a weapon that the company had designed in-house just prior to hostilities. In the 1960s the firm moved away from civilian weapons production and became highly dependent on military work. A very unprofitable contract to produce the M14 rifle for the Vietnam War put the company into debt once again. A consortium of former Winchester managers purchased the arms business in 1980 and called their new enterprise the U.S. Repeating Arms Company.

In the late 1920s, Winchester-Simmons contracted with Landers, Frary and Clark for an electric waffle iron. Landers modified its inexpensive Model E9533 for Winchester by riveting a "Winchester W36" name plate to the front of it. For reasons the author cannot comprehend, Winchester collectors are regularly willing to pay several hundred dollars for this example of an unexciting waffle iron that would otherwise sell for about $10.00.

What do you have when you take a $10.00 Landers, Frary & Clark **Model E9533** and put a "**Winchester W36**" name placard on it? To certain Winchester artifact collectors you have something worth from $200 to $300.

The Odd, Unusual, and Strange

Krue Sheld
Electric & Mfg. Co.
(*Newark, NJ*)

Above are before and after restoration pictures of a Krue Sheld unnumbered model probably dating from the early-mid-1920s. Nothing is known about this Newark, New Jersey company other than the firm's designer was quite clever in reducing the cost to manufacture this item. The lid and base are symetrical dome-shaped stampings which required just a single die to produce. The quality of the unique heating elements is superb and the relief cast into each dimple assures easy release of the waffle from the grids. If anyone knows anything more about this company, please contact the author.

Nova
(*Belgium*)

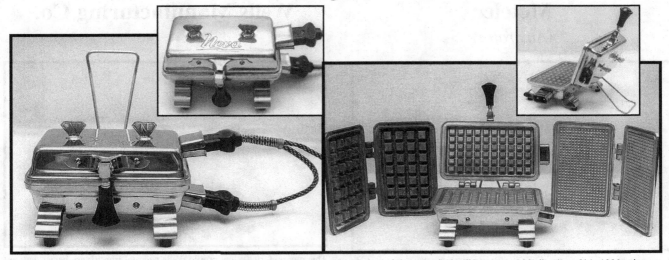

Only one model waffle iron by this Belgium company has surfaced to date. This petite unit has a typical split power cord indicative of it's 1920s vintage. If the cord is wired so that the heating elements are connected in series, the iron will operate on the European standard of 220 volts. When the elements are connected through the cord in parallel the iron can be operated with 110 volts. Three interchangeable cooking grids were available that are fastened to the body shell halves with large wing-nut-type screws embossed with the letter "N". This model is of excellent quality, quite rare, and an outstanding example of early electric appliance technology in Europe. (Photos courtesy Dan & Vi LaBelle)

Honor
(*Belgium*)

This late 1920s brochure illustrates the "Honor" brand waffle irons made in Fontaine-l'Évêque. Belgium. Much like the Nova pictured on page 189, the Honor could be purchased with various types of grids. In the brochure each grid is rated at "number per minute." (Up to an unbelievable four waffles per minute) Five different models are illustrated here. Few of these appear on the American market but when they do, they create considerable interest from collectors.

Metelec
(*Australia*)

Wells Manufacturing Co.

It's difficult to date this **"Metelec" Model N/18/W1-1** but its probably early 1950s. It came from Tasmania and requires 220 volts, standard for Australia. The conspicuous armored conduit contains the power wires from the top element and a ground wire to connect the body shell halves. At least two different handle styles exist for this iron.

This rare mid-1920s low profile Wells pedestal iron is very heavy-duty except for poorly designed handle brackets. The company became well known in later years for high quality commercial restaurant products.

R. RØNNING
(*European*)

This European-made "**R. Rønning**" iron was found in Canada. The 11-pound cast iron grids make an unusual segmented waffle with pyramid-shaped dimples. 120 volt sheet-mica-type heating elements, last used in American-made units in the early 1930s, makes dating difficult, but it's most likely circa 1950s.

L. Dahle
(*Spokane, Washington*)

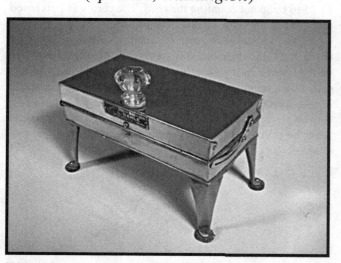

This crudely made small rectangular iron was manufactured by the L. Dahle Company of Spokane Washington probably in the early 1920s. The upper body shell is hand formed and folded sheet brass. The lower body is crudely cast aluminum. The legs are diecast (potmetal). The lid handle is an off-the-shelf glass cabinet knob. Nothing is known about the company at this time.

Unknown

This unmarked all aluminum iron has what appears to be generic kitchen cabinet knobs and handles. The feet are the same knobs used on the lid and internal fasteners seem to be surplus aircraft items. I suspect this was someone's post World War II attempt to cash in on the appliance shortage of the late 1940s.

The Rarest Waffle Iron
(*Do Not Try This At Home!*)

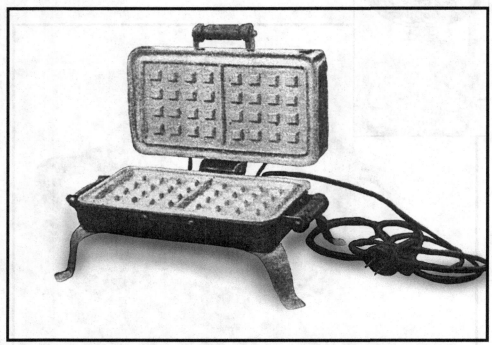

California junior high school students each fabricated everything but the cord for their 1933 waffle iron shop projects. Never underestimate the ability of kids. If anyone discovers one of these, the author would like to know about it. (June, 1933 *Industrial Education Magazine*)

I'm sometimes asked what's the rarest waffle iron that was ever made. That's easy. According to the June, 1933 issue of *Industrial Education Magazine*, the industrial arts students at the Lathrop Junior High School in Santa Ana, California, shunned the ordinary middle school tie rack, bird house, or napkin holder shop projects and went for the gold, constructing from scratch, actual working electric waffle irons.

These kids did everything from turning and painting the wood handles to fabricating the heating elements for their little waffle-making wonders. They even built all the equipment and molds necessary to cast the aluminum cooking grids and to form and nickel-plate the sheet steel bodies. According to the article, each waffle iron iron cost a grand sum of $1.25 to build not counting the cord. The cord was purchased ready-made and cost an additional quarter.

No mention was made of quantities produced, but I'll bet at least one example still survives somewhere, ready to be discovered in a junk store or attic or maybe at a garage sale. When found, it will doubtless be the most unique waffle iron in existence and an enduring tribute to one Burton H. Rowley, a depression-era California shop teacher, who can never be accused of underestimating the abilities of his students.

Model, Date & Value Guide

1900-1970

Using The Model Date & Value Guide

Model Number

Manufacturers' designated models of their products with numerous systems of letters, numbers, or combinations of both. These often were stamped on the bottom of the item as "Article Number," "Catalog Number," "Serial Number," or "Series Number." For simplicity all are referred to here as "Model Numbers." Names or phrases appearing in quotes following model numbers appear as such on the item. Letters in parenthesis following a model number may or may not be present on the item.

Years of Manufacture

Production dates assigned to products are derived from company literature, advertisements, original sales receipts, owner's manuals, or by comparing an item of unknown age to one of known vintage. During the depression years slow sales often resulted in models appearing in catalogs and advertising for as long as ten years after production was halted. Manning-Bowman was the only firm who, for warranty purposes, stamped the date of manufacture on its products. Dates followed by a (?) may not be accurate due to lack of dating evidence.

Scarcity

"Scarcity" is noted on a scale from 1 to 5. The numbers are based on the frequency that the author has encountered a particular model and may have little to do with actual numbers produced or how many actually still exist. Models designated with a 1 are uncommon while 5 means they are very common. There are few "rare" models. Most were produced by the tens of thousands even during the depression.

Price New

Prices shown here are published prices when the item was new and are footnoted as to source of this information. To convert to modern day equivalent dollars, you may wish to use the conversion formula found in the section "*What Did They Cost in the Good Old Days?*"

Model #	Approximate Years of Manufacture	Scarcity	Price New	Value Range
156	Mid-1920s-Early 1930s	4	$ 7.50 [1] -9.00 [2]	$ 10-25
250	Early 1930s	1		Not Established
254	Early 1930s	2	6.00 [1]	15-35

The Value Range

Values listed are based on several years of monitoring asking prices at estate sales, flea markets, internet auctions, antique stores, garage sales, and in thrift stores on the east coast and in the Midwest. "Not established" means a model has appeared so infrequently that a value cannot be reliably assigned. **Values are for pieces that are moderately clean, in good working order, with no evidence of rust, corrosion, or significant plating damage, with no missing, broken, or damaged components, and include a cord in useable condition.** NOS (New Old Stock) lightly used or professionally restored pieces command significantly higher prices than those shown. Original boxes and instructions also add to values. **Values listed should be used strictly as a rough guide only and are in no way intended to set or influence prices.** What an antique or collectible is worth is what a buyer and a seller both agree it's worth, not what this book says its worth! The final set price can depend on any number of factors, including supply, demand, method of sale, condition, location, season of the year, and in the case of certain collectors, the phases of the moon. I'm only half joking. Mental outlook and emotion are often significant factors in the final price paid for an item. Ask any auctioneer. Do not let your emotions or this guide overrule common sense and reason when purchasing or selling any item. Neither the author nor the publisher of this book is in any way responsible for possible losses incurred in any sales transaction.

WAFFLE IRON MODEL DATE & VALUE GUIDE

Adco

Model #		Approximate Years of Manufacture	Scarcity	Value Range
326	(Bersted made)	Mid-Late 1920s	1	$ 10-25

Affiliated Retailers Inc. *"Armaid"*

See: *"Knapp-Monarch Company"*

Aluminum Goods Manufacturing Company *"Mirro"*

Model #	Approximate Years of Manufacture	Scarcity	Value Range
9358M	Late 1920s-Early 1930s	2	$ 35-50

AMCH Industries Limited (Montreal, Canada)

Model #		Approximate Years of Manufacture	Scarcity	Value Range
700	"Montreal Canada"	Mid-Late 1930s	1	$ 5-20

Armstrong Electric & Mfg. Company *"Perc-o-Toaster" "Old South"*

Model #		Approximate Years of Manufacture	Scarcity	Price New	Value Range
PT	"Perc-o-Toaster"		2		$ 75-200
	Nickel	1918-1932		$ 11.85 [1]	
	Chrome-Ivory	Late 20's-1932		16.85 [1]	
PT	Waffle iron accessory	1918-1932	3	7.50 [3]-7.80 [4]	2-10
W	"Old South"- or "500"		2		35-75
	Nickel	1920-1932		9.85 [1]	
	Chrome	Early 1930s		10.85 [1]- 13.20 [2]	

[1] List price, February, 1931, *Gage Electrical Encyclopedia.*
[2] Retail price, 1931, Miller Brothers Hardware Co. Richmond, Indiana, *Catalog #10.*
[3] List price, January, 1922, Belknap Hardware & Mfg. Co. Louisville, KY. *Catalog # 68*
[4] List price, 1925, Belknap Hardware & Mfg. Co. Louisville, KY. *Catalog # 78.*

Arvin Industries Inc. *"Arvin"*

Model #		Approximate Years of Manufacture	Scarcity	Price New	Value Range
3500		1947-1950	3	$ 27.95 [1, 3, 4]	$ 5-25
3550 (S)		1950-1955	3	29.95 [2]	5-30
3640		Late 1950s	1		5-30
6613	Kenmore 344-6613	Late 1940s	2	21.95 [1]	5-25
6657	Kenmore 344-6657	Early 1950s	2		5-25
66680	Kenmore 344-66680	Early 1950s	1		5-25
66681	Kenmore 344-66681	Early 1950s	1		5-25

[1] List price, January, 1949, *Consumer Reports Magazine.*
[2] Advertised price, 1951, *Ladies' Home Journal.*
[3] Advertised price, April, 1949, *Better Homes & Gardens Magazine.*
[4] Advertised price, November, 1947, unidentified magazine advertisement.

Beardsley & Wolcott Mfg. Company *"Torrid"*

Model #		Approximate Years of Manufacture	Scarcity	Value Range
No #	"Penimaid-Electric Appliance-J.C. Penney Co."			
		Late 1920s-Early 1930s	1	$ 10-35
W0310	Nickel or Chrome	Late 1920s-Early 1930s	2	15-35
W2014	"Torrid Avignon"	Late 1920s-Early 1930s	2	75-160
WY010	"Torrid York"- Came with red, green or black wood handles and matching colored cord, Nickel or Chrome plated, with or without temperature gauge. Also made for United Drug and labeled X544			
		Late 1920s-Early 1930s	2	25-75

Ben S. Loeb Inc. *"Master"*

Model #		Approximate Years of Manufacture	Scarcity	Value Range
No #	"Master Waffle Iron" with red or black handles			
		Mid-Late 1920s	1	Not Established
255	Blue handles	Late 1920s	1	$ 25-35

Bersted Manufacturing Company *"Tru-Heat"*

Model #		Approximate Years of Manufacture	Scarcity	Price New	Value Range
No #	1st model-See text	Early 1920s	1		$ 40-75
6A	"Fostoria"	Early-Mid-1950s	3		10-35
20-	Sear product prefix- Use numbers following this prefix which are listed below				
55	Sears 20-55	Early-Mid-1930s	1	$ 3.29 [6]	10-25
60	"Donut Mould"	Early-Mid-1920s	1		25-50
64	20-64"Challenge"	Late 1920s-Early 1930s	1		10-35
65	Sears "Challenge"	Mid-Late 1920s	2	4.95 [7]	10-40
66		Mid-Late 1920s	3		5-30
68	Sears	Mid-Late 1920s	1		35-75
69		Mid-Late 1920s	2		25-60
202		Early-Mid-1930s	2		5-25
203		Mid-Late 1930s	2	4.30 [3]	5-25
205	"BMC Mastercraft"	Late 1930s-Early 1940s	2		10-35
207		Mid-Late 1930s	2		25-50
211	steel grids	Mid-1930s	3		5-20
212	steel grids	Mid-1930s	3		5-20
214	Black, green, or red handle- Sometimes labeled "Lightning"-Updated Model 65 Two different lid handle configurations-Knob type or long cylindrical turned wood with mounting bracket				
		Mid-Late 1920s	2	4.45 [5]	10-35

Bersted continued:

Model #		Approximate Years of Manufacture	Scarcity	Price New	Value Range
215	Black or green handles-Also labeled "Great Northern Products Co."				
		Early-Mid-1920s	2		$10-35
217		Mid-1930s-Early 1940s	2		10-35
224	Black or red handles				
		Mid-Late 1920s	3		10-35
226		Mid-Late 1920s	3		10-35
227		Mid-Late 1920s	2		10-35
228		Mid-Late 1920s	3		10-35
230	.	Late 1920s-Early 1930s	2	$ 8.50 [1]	10-25
231		Late 1920s-Early 1930s	2		10-35
232	Sears "Challenge"	Early 1930s	2	2.49 [2]	15-35
239		Early 1930s	3		5-35
240	Version # 1 with windup timer-some are labeled "Stewart Die Casting Corp. Model 20"				
		Late 1920s-Early 1930s	2	15.00 [1]	35-75
	Version # 2 with large painted wood handles, square temperature gauge in lid				
		Mid-1930s	2		5-25
241		Late 1920s-Early 1930s	2		5-25
243		Early 1930s	1		10-35
245		Mid-Late 1930s	2		10-35
246		Early-Mid-1930s	2		15-35
250		Mid-Late 1930s	4		5-35
251		Mid-Late 1930s	4		5-35
255		Mid-Late 1930s	4		5-35
255	Canadian	Late 1930s-Early 1940s	2		10-35
260		Late 1930s-Early 1950s	5		20-40
261		1960s (?)	4		5-25
310	Grill	Early-Mid-1930s	1		15-45
313		Mid-Late 1930s	2		10-25
320		Mid-Late 1930s	2		10-25
324	Grill	Mid-Late 1930s	2	4.50 [3]	5-25
330		Mid-Late 1930s	2		5-25
332		Mid-Late 1930s	2		10-35
350	Grill	Mid-Late 1930s	1		5-25
351		Mid-1930s-Early 1940s	3		5-30
361		Late 1950s	2		5-35
363	Two variants	1960s (?)	3		5-35
475	Kenmore 303.6475	Late 1930s-Late 1940s	3	5.95 [4]	5-35
486	20-486"Heatmaster"	Late 1920s-Early 1930s	1		5-35
684	20-684"Heatmaster"	Early 1930s	1	4.85 [6]	5-25
685	20-685"Heatmaster"	Early 1930s	1		5-35

[1] List Price, February, 1931, *Gage Electrical Encyclopedia*.
[2] Sale price, 1932, Sears Roebuck sale flyer.
[3] Wholesale price, 1938, Vonnegut Hardware Company Catalog.
[4] List price, January, 1949, *Consumer Reports Magazine*.
[5] Wholesale price, mid-winter 1927, Butler Brothers Wholesalers catalog, 495 Broadway, NY, NY.
[6] Retail price, 1934, Sears Roebuck Co. *General Catalog*.
[7] Retail price, 1927, Sears Roebuck Co. *General Catalog*.

Butler Brothers *"Crest Line"* (New York Wholesalers)

Model #		Approximate Year of Manufacture	Scarcity	Value Range
K6XFC-M511	Dominion made	Early 1930s	1	$ 10-35

Capitol Products Company *"Lady Winsted"*

Model #		Approximate Year of Manufacture	Scarcity	Value Range
425	Flat or curved lid-probably made by Son-Chief			
		Late 1930s-1940s	4	$ 5-25

Cast-Rite Cookware
See: *"Russell Electric"*

Chicago Electric Mfg. Co. *"Handyhot-Handymix-Victory-Hatfield-Mary Dunbar"*

Model #		Approximate Years of Manufacture	Scarcity	Price New	Value Range
AF	Toy-like model	Late 1920s	1		Not Established
AF26	"Wafflator"	Late 1920s-Early 1930s	1		$150-300
AFU		Late 1920s-Early 1930s	1		5-25
AFUC	Steel grids	Early 1930s (?)	3		5-25
AFUE	Also "Heatmaster" 305.6469	Late 1930s-Early 1940s	5		5-25
AFUE	with ribbed lids and marked "Hatfield"	Late 1930s-Early 1940s	1		5-25
AFUF	Also "Sterling", "Heatmaster", or "4602"	Late 1930s-Early 1940s	2		5-20
1400		Late 1930s-Early 1950s	2	$ 13.60 [2]	5-25
1401		Late 1930s-Early 1950s	4	14.95 [1]-21.80 [2]	10-30
1402		Late 1930s-1940s	2		5-25
1405		Late 1930s-Early 1950s	3	20.40 [2]	5-30
1723		Late 1930s-Early 1950s	1	16.30 [2]	5-25
1724		Late30's-Mid-50's (except war yrs)	4	19.05 [2]	5-30
5400	"Sterling"	Late 1930s	1		10-30
5701	"Sterling"	Late 1930s-Early 1940s	1		10-30

[1] Price on original sales tag.
[2] Catalog price, 1951, Jensen-Byrd Co. Wholesale distributors of General Hardware, Spokane, WA. *Catalog #51.*

Chicago Flexible Shaft Company *"Sunbeam"*
(Name changed to Sunbeam Corporation in 1946)

Model #		Approximate Years of Manufacture	Scarcity	Price New	Value Range
CGL-2		Early-Mid-1960s	1		$ 5-20
CG-(1)	Waffle iron/Grill	Early-Mid-1950s	4	$ 33.50 [6]	15-60
CG-6	Canadian	Early-Mid-1950s	1		Not Established
CGW	Waffle iron only	Early-Mid-1950s	3	29.75 [6]	10-50
D-33		Early-Mid-1930s	2		20-50
CS-1	Late W-2 variant	Early 1950s	1		15-50
F-3	"Wafflewitch"	Early 1930s	1	19.75 [1]	100-400
GP	Grill plates for Model CGW			4.75 [6]	Not Established
W-1		1940s	2	24.50 [2]	20-40
W-2(A)		Late 1940s-Mid-1950s	5	24.50 [4,5,7]- 28.75 [3]	15-50
WB-B		Late 1960s	1		5-20

Accessory Pieces:

W-2A	Sandwich grids (foil- #22-2469)		1	(2 pair) .50 [3]	Not Established

[1] List price, February 1931, *Gage Electrical Encyclopedia.*
[2] List price, January 1949, *Consumer Reports Magazine.*
[3] "Fair Trade Item" price, August 8, 1954, Janney, Semple, Hill & Co. dealers catalog.
[4] List price, late 1940s Raybro Electric Supplies Inc, dealers catalog.
[5] List price, 1949, Baker & Hamilton Wholesale Hardware Co. catalog.
[6] Catalog price, 1953(?) Morely-Murphy Co. Distributors of Hardware & related fines, Green Bay, WI. *Catalog # 1951.*
[7] Catalog price, 1949, W. Bingham Company, Cleveland, Ohio. Retail catalog.

Club Aluminum Company *"Hammercraft"*

Model #		Approximate Years of Manufacture	Scarcity	Value Range
No #	Plunger Top-Probably Bersted	Mid-Late 1920s	1	$ 25-50
F6	"Donut Mold"-Bersted Model 60	Mid-Late 1920s	1	25-50
R.I.	Probably Bersted	Mid-1920s	2	15-35
07	Probably Bersted	Mid-Late 1920s	3	15-35

Coleman Company

Model #			Years Made	Total Made [1]	Price New	Value Range
16	"Aztec"	Nickel	1930-33	7032	$ 8.85 [2]	Over-$35
16 C	"Aztec"	Chrome	1931-33	2367	9.90-10.80 [2] 15.00 [3]	Over-$35
16SS	Probably experimental stainless steel model		1931	213	Unknown	Not Established
17	"Aristocrat"	Leaping gazelle model	1930-33	5649	11.85-15.00 [2,4]- 18.00 [3]	100-200
17A	"Aristocrat"	Four point lid design-No gazelle	1930-33 (?)	Unknown	Unknown	Over-$50
19A	No name	Chrome-non-automatic	1931-33	99(?)	Unknown	Over-$50
19C	No name	Chrome-automatic	1931-33	1518	9.90 [2]	Over-$50

[1] Production numbers are taken from Coleman factory records which are fragmentary and sometimes conflicting. 213 examples of Model 16SS appear in production records, but are not listed in any other records. The total of 99 units for Model 19A seems very low and is probably inaccurate.
[2] Prices taken from various factory issued advertising literature 1930-33.
[3] Retail price, 1931, Miller Brothers Hardware Co. Richmond, Indiana, *Catalog #10.*
[4] Retail price, 1932, Belknap Hardware & Mfg. Co., Louisville, KY. *Catalog # 86.*

Dominion Electrical Manufacturing Company *"Justrite"*

Model #		Approximate Years of Manufacture	Scarcity	Price New	Value Range
No #	Low pedestal model with ceramic lid insert-three pheasants on rose branches				
		Late 1920s-Early 1930s	1		$ 25-50
No #	Rosebud pattern ceramic lid insert by Coors Ceramics-See photo in Dominion section				
		Mid-Late 1930s	1		50-75
DE-P-104	Ward products prefix-Use numbers following this prefix which are listed below				
	"Gem, Newark Appliance Inc."- Retail sales organization, Newark, NJ.				
		Late 1930s-Early 1940s (?)	2		5-25
45-DE	Ward products prefix-Use numbers following this prefix which are listed below				
46	Sandwich/waffle Queen				
		Early 1930s	2	$ 12.50 Nickel [9]	
				13.50 Chrome [9]	10-35
64	Green handles	Mid-1920s	1		20-50
65	Black handles	Late 1920s	3		20-50
	Green handles	Late 1920s	2		25-60
	Red handles	Late 1920s	1		30-65
67	"Justrite"	Late 1920s	2		20-45
67-H		Late 1920s-Early 1930s	2		30-60
68		Late 1920s-Early 1930s	3		25-50
73		Late 1920s-Early 1930s	3		35-60
74	Ceramic insert Nickel	Late 1920s-Early 1930s	3	11.00 [1]	35-60
	Chrome	Early 1930s	2	12.00 [1]	35-60
86-DE	Ward products prefix-Use numbers following this prefix which are listed below				
90		Late 1930s-Early 1940s	3		5-25
93-DE-	Ward products prefix-Use numbers following this prefix which are listed below.				
94-DE-	Ward products prefix-Use numbers following this prefix which are listed below.				
120		Late 1930s-Early 1940s	3		5-25
121		Early-Mid-1930s	3	13.45 [6]	10-30
122		Early-Mid-1930s	1	14.80 [6]	35-75
126		Early 1930s	2		35-60
135-A		Late 1930s	4		15-30
141	"Triangle-Apollo"	Early 1930s	2		10-35
148		Mid-Late 1930s	3		10-30
149		Mid-Late 1930s	2		20-45
188		Mid-Late 1930s	1		10-35
303-	Sears products prefix-Use numbers following this prefix which are listed below.				
307-	Sears products prefix-Use numbers following this prefix which are listed below.				
310	Modern Mode Sandwich Queen Grill				
		Early-Mid-1930s	2	14.50 [6]	10-35
310	Modern Mode Waffle Iron				
		Early-Mid-1930s	2	17.90 [6]	15-40
316		Late 1940s-Early 1950s	4		10-25
321	"Lady Hibbard"	Late 1930s-Early 1940s	2		10-25
327	"Lady Hibbard"	Late 1930s-Early 1940s	2		10-25
344-	Sears products prefix-Use numbers following this prefix which are listed below.				

199

Model #		Approximate Years of Manufacture	Scarcity	Price New	Value Range
344	"Lady Hibbard"-Ceramic lid insert Waffle iron/Grill)				
		Late 1930s	1		$ 35-75
366	Sears "Heatmaster" 307-366. See Model 590				
369	Ward 93-DE-86-5154				
		Late 1930s-Early 1940s	4		5-25
374		Late 1930s-Early 1940s	2		10-25
375	Ward 93-DE-86-5153				
	Sears "Heatmaster" 307-2006				
		Late 1930s-Early 1940s	3		15-25
377	"Triangle-Apollo", "Heatmaster", "5160 Ward 93-DE-86", or "Modern Home Appliance Co."				
		Late 1930s-Early 1940s	2		10-35
381	"Mayd Best"	Late 1930s-Early 1940s	2		10-35
399		Late 1930s-Early 1940s	3		5-20
402	Majestic Electric	Early-Mid-1930s	1		15-50
423	"Lady Hibbard"	Late 1930s-Early 1940s	3		10-35
425	"Lady Hibbard"	Late 1930s-Early 1940s	2		5-25
427	"Lady Hibbard"	Late 1930s-Early 1940s	2		5-25
443	"Lady Hibbard"	Late 1930s-Early 1940s	2		10-35
507	"Lady Hibbard"	Early-Mid-1930s	1		5-25
510	Ceramic Insert	Early-Mid-1930s	1		35-75
	Metal lid w gauge	Early-Mid-1930s	2		10-35
511	Heavy Combo unit	Early-Mid-1930s	1		15-45
521	Waffle-o-matic	Early-Mid 1930s	1		35-50
530		Early-Mid-1930s	1		5-25
555	Sears "Heatmaster" 307-555, Ward 93-DE-86. See Model 369				
567		Late 1930s-Early 1940s	2		5-20
569		Late 1930s-Early 1940s	4		10-25
582		Late 1930s-Early 1940s	2		10-25
583		Late 1930s-Early 1940s	3		15-35
587	"Everbrite-Canada"	Late 1930s-Early 1940s	2		10-25
588		Late 1930s	2		10-25
589		Late 1930s	2		10-40
590	Wood or Bakelite handles- Also Sears "Heatmaster" 307-366				
		Late 1930s	3		20-35
591		Late 1930s	2		10-35
592		Late 1930s	3		10-25
595	Ceramic Insert	Late 1930s	2		35-75
596		Late 1930s	3		20-35
620		Late 1930s	3		5-20
623		Late 1930's	2		5-20
625		Late 1930s	2		5-25
680	"Heatmaster"	Early-Mid-1930s	3		10-25
722 (S)		Mid-1930s	2		20-35
1120	"Modern Mode" Waffle iron accessory set for Models 121 & 122. Included cut crystal glass batter and syrup pitchers with Lily of Valley designs & black glass lids, small black glass pitcher tray, & large octagonal serving tray with central flower pattern and maroon edge banding				
		Early-Mid-1930s	1	$ 21.60	
1186		Early-Mid-1930s	1		10-35
1204		1940s-Early 1950s	2	10.95 [5]-13.50 [7]	5-25
1207A	Ward 2217L	Late 1930s-Late 1940s	3		5-25
1208A	Ward 2215L or Sears Style #307	Late 1930s-Late 1940s	4		5-25
1210		Late 1930s-Late 1940s	3		15-30
1214		Late 1930s-Late 1940s	4		5-20
1218	"Grid-A-Bout"	1940s-Early 1950s	3	13.95 [5]-15.95 [7]	5-20
1220		Late 1940s-Early 1950s	2		5-20
1222		Late 1940s-Early 1950s	2		10-35
1224		Late 1940s-Early 1950s	2		10-35
1225 (C or O)		Late 1940s-Mid-1950s	3	21.95 [7]	10-35
1226	Teflon coated	1960s (?)	2		10-25
1251	Teflon coated	1960s-1970s (?)	2		5-20
1301		Late 1930s-Late 1940s	5		5-35
1302		Late 1930s-Late 1940s	5		5-35
1302	Black base	Possibly 1945-46	1		35-50
1305		Late 1930s-Late 1940s	5		5-25

Dominion continued:

Model #		Approximate Years of Manufacture	Scarcity	Price New	Value Range
1306	Ward 2212L	Mid-1930s-1940s	5		$ 5-25
1307	Sears 307-6472	Late 1930s-1940s	2		5-25
	Sears 1307.64602 or 307.36132	1940s	2		10-35
1308	Sears 307-6473	Late 1930s-1940s	2		5-25
1309	Ward 2211L	1940s	4		5-25
1311	"Grid-O-Matic"	Late 1940s-Early 1950s	3	23.95 [5]	10-30
1314		Late 1940s-Early 1950s	4	$ 8.95 [5]	10-30
1315 (A)		Late 1940s-Mid-1950s	5	10.95 [5]-13.50 [3, 7]	15-35
1316		Late 1940s-Mid-1950s	5		5-35
1317		Late 1940s-Mid-1950s	2		5-35
1350	Sears 307-6471	Mid-1930s-Early 1940s	4		10-35
1351	Sears 307-6470	Mid-1930s-Early 1940s	3		10-35
1353		Mid-1930s-Early 1940s	3		20-40
1354	Ward 2213L	Mid-1930s-Late 1940s	4		20-40
1355	Chrome tray	Late 1930s-Late 1940s	4		15-35
	Black tray	1945-46	1		20-40
1356		Late 1930s-Late 1940s	4		15-35
1357	Ward 2216L	Late 1930s-Late 1940s	3		10-35
1360		Late 1930s-Late 1940s	3		20-35
1362		Late 1940s-Early 1950s	4		5-25
1380		Late 1940s-Early 1950s	2		10-35
1881	"Heatmaster"	Early-Mid-1930s	1		10-35
1886	"Heatmaster"	Early-Mid-1930s	1		5-20
1933	"Heatmaster"	Late 1930s-Early 1940s	2		5-20
1938	"Heatmaster"	Late 1930s-Early 1940s	2		5-20
1941	"Heatmaster"	Late 1930s-Early 1940s	2		5-20
1943	"Heatmaster"	Late 1930s-Early 1940s	2		5-20
1944	"Heatmaster"	Late 1930s-Early 1940s	2		10-25
1962	Sears 307-1962	Late 1930s-Early 1940s	3		5-20
2105	Ward 25-DE-2105	Late 1930s-Early 1940s	1		10-35
2006	Sears 307-2006	Late 1930s-Early 1940s	2		15-25
2109	Ward DE-2109	1940s-Early 1950s	3		10-25
2110(D orM) Ward		1940s-Early 1950s	2	19.95 [2]	5-25
2194	Ward 94DE-2194	1940s-Early 1950s	2		5-25
2197	Ward 45DE-2197	1940s-Early 1950s	3		10-35
2198	"Made-Rite"	Late 1930s-Early 1940s	2		5-25
2211(L) Ward		1940s	2	8.49 [2]	5-25
2212	"Made-Rite"	Late 1930s-1940s	2		5-25
2212 (L) Ward		1940s	2	6.25 [2]	5-25
2213 (L) Ward		Mid-1930s-Late 1940s	4	9.95 [2]	20-40
2215 (L) Ward		Late 1930s-Late 1940s	4	8.49 [2]	5-25
2215 (L) Ward		Late 1930s-Late 1940s	4	8.49 [2]	5-25
2216 (L) Ward		1940s	2	12.50 [2]	10-35
2217 (L) Ward		Late 1930s-Late 1940s	3	10.95 [2]	5-25
2218	"Made-Rite"	Late 1930s-Early 1940s	2		5-25
2221	"Made-Rite"	Late 1930s-Early 1940s	2		5-25
2361	Ward DE-2361	1940s-Early 1950s	4		10-25
2363	Ward DE-2363	1940s-Early 1950s	2		5-25
3011	"Everbrite"-Canada	Late 1930s-1940s	1		5-20
3215	Ward	Late 1930s-1940s	1		5-20
5102	Also "620"	Late 1930s	3		5-20
5103		Late 1930s	1		5-25
5126	Ward 93-DE-86-	Last 1930s	1	3.98 [8]	5-25
5129		Late 1930s	2		5-25
5134	Ward 93-DE-86-	Late 1930s	1	3.45 [8]	5-25
5139	Ward 93-DE-86-	Late 1930s	2	4.95 [8]	10-35
5145		Mid-Late 1930s	2		10-35
5146		Mid-Late 1930s	2		25-40
5153	Ward 93-DE-86-	Late 1930s-Early 1940s	3		15-25
5154	Ward 93-DE-86-	Late 1930s-Early 1940s	4		15-25
5160	Ward 93-DE-86-	Late 1930s-Early 1940s	3		15-25
5161	Ward 93-DE-86-	Late 1930s-Early 1940s	3		15-25
5460	Kenmore307.5460	1940s	2		5-25
6450	Sears "Challenge" 307-6450	Late 1930s-Early 1940s	1		5-25
6454	Kenmore307.6454	1940s	3		10-25

Dominion continued:

Model #		Approximate Years of Manufacture	Scarcity	Price New	Value Range
6457	Sears 307.6457	Late 1930s-Early 1940s	1		$ 10-25
6460	Kenmore307.64601	Late 30's-Late 40's (except war yrs)	3	9.50 [2]	5-20
	Kenmore307.64602	1940s	2		5-25
6461	Heatmaster307-6461	Late 1930s-Early 1940s	2		5-25
6464	Kenmore307.6464	1940s	2	14.50 [2]	5-20
6470	Sears 307-6470	1940s	2		10-35
6471	Sears 307-6471	Mid-1930s-Early 1940s	4		10-35
6472	Sears 307-6472	Late 1930s-Early 1940s	2	6.50 [4]	5-25
6475	Kenmore303.6475	(Made by Bersted. See Bersted Model 475)			
6479	Kenmore307.6479	1940s	2		5-25
6484	Sears 307-6484	1940s	2		5-25
6491	Heatmaster 307-6491	1940s	2		5-20
6601	Challenge307-6601	Late 1930s-Early 1940s	1		5-20
6604	Sears 307-6604	Late 1930s-Early 1940s	2		5-20
6612	Sears 307.6612	Late 1930s-1940s	2		5-20
6613	Kenmore344-6613	See: "Arvin Industries"			
6614	Heatmaster307.6614	Early 1940s	2	$ 7.50 [4]	5-20
6616	Waffle grids for Model 307.6614			1.80 [4]	2-5
6618	Kenmore307.66181	Late 1930s-Late 1940s	2	14.25 [2]	5-25
6618	Kenmore307.66182	1940s except war years	2		5-25
6619	Sears 307-6619	Late 1940s-Early 1950s	2		5-25
6657	Kenmore 344-6657	See: "Arvin Industries"			
6668	Kenmore	Late 1940s-Early 1950s	2		10-25
6676	"Hoover"	Late 1950s-Early 1960s	1		10-25
7473	Sears 307-6473	Late 1930s-Early 1940s	2		5-25
46010	Ward K-76 or DE-46010 or 6-46010 1940s-Early 1950s		2		5-20
64650	Kenmore 632-64650	Early 1960s	1		5-25
64700	Kenmore 632-64700	Mid-1960s (Teflon)	1		5-25
64810	Kenmore 632-64810	Mid-Late 1960s (Teflon)	1		5-25

[1] List price, February, 1931, *Gage Electrical Encyclopedia*.
[2] List price, January, 1949, *Consumer Reports Magazine*.
[3] "Fair Trade Item" price, August 8, 1954, Janney, Semple, Hill & Co. dealer's catalog.
[4] Retail price, Spring-Summer, 1942, Sears Roebuck & Co. General catalog.
[5] Catalog price, 1949, W. Bingham Company , Cleveland, Ohio; Retail catalog.
[6] List price, 1934, Factory issued advertising brochure.
[7] Catalog price, 1955, Belknap Hardware & Mfg. Company Louisville, KY.; Dealer's catalog.
[8] Catalog price, 1938, Montgomery Ward; Retail catalog.
[9] Prices in original Dominion owners manual.

Dover Manufacturing Company (Dover, Ohio)

Model #		Approximate Years of Manufacture	Scarcity	Value Range
44	Working child's toy	Late 1920s-Early 1930s	2	Over $ 40

Edicraft

See: *"Thomas A. Edison Incorporated"*

Edison Electric Appliance Company *"Hotpoint"*

Model #	Approximate Years of Manufacture	Scarcity	Price New	Value Range
116 Y 23	Early-Mid-1920s	2	$15.75 [4]	$ 30-65
116 Y 53	Mid-Late 1920s	5	10.50 [2] – 15.00 [3]	10-35
116 Y 85	Mid-Late 1920s	1	8.05 [2]	10-35
116 Y 161	Mid-Late 1920s	3		20-35
116 Y 177	Mid-1920s-Early 1930s	2	15.75 [5]	10-25
117 Y 112	Early-Mid-1920s	2		10-35
119 Y 146	Mid-Late 1920s	1		10-35
119 Y 155	Late 1920s-Early 1930s	1		25-50

Edison Electric continued:

Model #		Approximate Years of Manufacture	Scarcity	Price New	Value Range
119 Y 156		Late 1920s-Early 1930s	3		$ 25-40
126 Y 53		Late 1920s	4	$ 15.00 [1]	10-35
126 Y 151		Late 1920s	3		10-25
126 Y 161		Late 1920s	2		10-40
127 Y 176		Late 1920s-Early 1930s	3	14.50 [5]	10-35
129 Y 175	Ambassador model	Late 1920s-Early 1930s			2
25-50					
129 Y 178		Late 1920s-Early 1930s	3		15-40
146 Y 53		Mid-Late 1920s	4		10-35
146 Y 85		Early-Mid-1920s	2		10-35
147 Y 156		Late 1920s-Early 1930s	3		10-40
147 Y 158		Late 1920s-Early 1930s	3	12.00 [5]	10-35
149 Y 156	Lennox model	Late 1920s-Early 1930s	2	12.00 [5]	15-35
149 Y 158		Late 1920s-Early 1930s	3		10-35
157 Y 112		Early 1920s	2		35-50
216 Y 112		Early-Mid-1920s	2		35-50
816 Y 162	"Simplex"	Early-Mid-1920s	1		35-50
817 Y 160	"Simplex"	Early-Mid-1920s	2		35-50

[1] Advertised price, 1928, *Saturday Evening Post*.
[2] Wholesale price, mid-winter 1927, Butler Brothers Wholesalers Catalog, 495 Broadway, NY, NY.
[3] Advertised price, December 1925, *Saturday Evening Post*.
[4] Wholesale price, 1925, Belknap Hardware & Mfg. Co., Louisville, KY, *Catalog # 78*.
[5] Wholesale price, 1932, Belknap Hardware & Mfg. Co., Louisville, KY, *Catalog # 86*.

Electrahot Manufacturing Company

(Became part of Dominion Electric in mid-1920s but name was retained until late 1930s)

Model #		Approximate Years of Manufacture	Scarcity	Value Range
No #	Small low profile-possibly second model-See Electrahot history for photo			
		Mid-Late 1920s	2	$ 20-35
No #	Donut Maker	Late 1920s	1	35-50
24 P	Hall Silhouette pattern	Early 1930s	2	100-200
48		Early 1930s	3	20-40
62		Late 1930s	4	5-25
74	German tulip pattern	Early 1930s	1	75-125
75		Early 1930s	2	15-35
91-38		Early 1930s	1	10-25
140		Early 1930s	2	10-25
144	Rose pattern	Early 1930s	1	35-75
	Tulip pattern	Early 1930s	3	35-75
	Hall Silhouette pattern	Early 1930s	2	100-250
148		Early 1930s	3	10-35
	Taller 4" high version	Early 1930s	2	10-35
149	Mixed flower pattern	Early 1930s	2	35-75
	Tulip pattern	Early 1930s	2	35-75
	Metal lid version with temperature gauge-Sometimes labeled "Junior"			
		Early 1930s	2	10-35
172	(Mixed flower pattern	Early 1930s	2	35-50
217	Tulip pattern	Early 1930s	3	35-75
228	"Hibbard, Spencer, Bartlett & Co."	Early 1930s	2	10-35
229		Early 1930s	2	5-25
246	Hall Silhouette pattern	Early-Mid-1930s	2	75-200
247	Hall Tulip pattern	Early-Mid-1930s	3	35-75
	Matching Tulip pattern ceramic waffle serving plate		1	25-35
	Hall Silhouette pattern	Early-Mid-1930s	1	75-200
256		Mid-1930s	3	20-35
266	Made for "Hibbard, Spencer, Bartlett & Co."			
		Mid-1930s	2	25-40
268	Made for "Hibbard, Spencer, Bartlett & Co."			
		Mid-Late 1930s	2	20-35
282		Early-Mid-1930s	1	10-35
283		Early-Mid-1930s	1	10-35

Electrahot continued:

Model #		Approximate Years of Manufacture	Scarcity	Price New	Value Range
287 (S)		Early 1930s	2		$ 10-35
307	Sears-"Heatmaster"	Early 1930s	2		10-25
368		Late 1930s	2		5-25
369		Late 1930s	2		5-25
370		Late 1930s	2		5-25
375		Late 1930s	3		20-35
508 (S)	Two variants	Early-Mid-1930s	3		20-40
527		Early-Mid-1930s	3		20-35
533	Wildflower ceramic insert	Early-Mid-1930s	1		25-50
587	Twin	Late 1930s	4		10-25
620		Late 1930s	2		5-25
621		Late 1930s	1		10-35
623		Late 1930s	2		5-20
625	Two variants	Late 1930s	3		5-25
630		Late 1930s	2		10-35
634		Early-Mid-1930s	4		25-45
679	Sears-"Heatmaster	Early-Mid-1930s	1	$ 2.45 [2]	10-25
701		Late 1920s	2		5-25
722 (S)		Early-Mid-1930s	3		15-35
1186	Sears-"Heatmaster"or"Challenge"	Early 1930s	2		10-25
1188	Sears-"Heatmaster"	Early-Mid-1930s	2	4.45 [1]	5-25
1303	Auto version of Dominion 1306	Mid-1930s	3		15-30
1306	Identical to Dominion 1306	Mid-Late 1930s	2		5-25
1360	Identical to Dominion 1360	Late 1930s	2		20-35
1873	Sears-"Heatmaster"	Early-Mid-1930s	2		10-25
1932	Sears-"Heatmaster"	Late 1930s	1		10-25
1943	Sears-"Heatmaster"	Late 1930s	1		10-25
2023	Sears-"Heatmaster"	Late 1930s	1		10-25
5085		Mid-1930s	1		10-25
5306	Identical to Dominion 1306	Mid-1930s	4		10-25

[1] Price, 1936 Sales receipt.
[2] Retail price, 1934, Sears Roebuck *General Catalog*.

Estate Stove Company

Model #		Approximate Years of Manufacture	Scarcity	Value Range
75	White, Blue, Green	1920s	2	$ 35-150

Everbrite (National Everbrite Company Inc. NY)

See: *"Superior Electric Products Corp."*.

Ever Brite Limited (Toronto, Canada) *"Everbrite"*

Model #		Approximate Years of Manufacture	Scarcity	Value Range
587	Possibly Dominion	Late 1930s-Early 1940s	2	$ 10-25
3011	Possibly Dominion	Late 1930s-1940s	1	5-20

Excel Incorporated *"Electrocraft"*

Model #		Approximate Years of Manufacture	Scarcity	Value Range
W-46	Non-automatic	Late 1930s-Late 1940s	2	$ 5-25
W-50	"Brunchmaster"	Late 1930s-Late 1940s	3	10-35

Faultless Appliance Company (St. Louis, MO.)
See: "*Knapp- Monarch Company*" (Model 710-R and Model OM-343)

Finders Manufacturing Company (Chicago, Ill.) "*Holliwood*"

Model #		Approximate Years of Manufacture	Scarcity	Value Range
611	"Holliwood"	Late 1940s	2	$ 25-50

Firestone Tire Company
See: "*Samson United Corporation*".

Fitzgerald Manufacturing Company "*Star*" "*Star-Rite*" "*Empress*" "*Magic Maid*"

Model #		Approximate Years of Manufacture	Scarcity	Price New	Value Range
No #	"Star"- Leg mounted 1st model	Early 1920s	1		$ 35-50
No #	"Star"- Pedestal 2nd model	Early-Mid-1920s	1	$ 9.00 [2, 6]	25-40
528	"Star-Rite" Sandwich Toaster				
	Nickel	Late 1920s-Early 1930s	1	10.00 [1]	Over-$100
	Chrome	Early 1930s	1	11.00 [1]	Over-$100
531	"Star-Rite"	Mid-1920s-Early 1930s	3	9.00 [3]	10-35
532	"Star-Rite"	Late 1920s-Early 1930s	2		10-35
535	"Star-Rite Junior"	Late 1920s-Early 1930s	2		10-35
536	Nickel	Late 1920s-Early 1930s	3	9.00 [1]	10-35
	Chrome		2	10.00 [1]	10-35
538	"Empress" Nickel	Late 1920s-Early 1930s	2	11.00 [1]	25-50
	"Chrome Plate"	Late 1920s-Early 1930s	2	12.00 [1] -15.00 [4]	25-85
539	"Chrome Plate"	Late 1920s-Early 1930s	1	11.00 [5]	25-40

[1] List price, February, 1931, *Gage Electrical Encyclopedia.*
[2] Advertised price, November, 1923, *Good Housekeeping Magazine.*
[3] Advertised price, 1926, unidentified magazine advertisement,
[4] Advertised price, October, 1928, *Good Housekeeping Magazine.*
[5] Retail Price, 1931, Miller Brothers Hardware Co. Richmond, Indiana; *Catalog # 10.*
[6] Wholesale price, 1925, Belknap Hardware & Mfg. Co., Louisville, KY; *Catalog # 76.*

Force Waffle Maker (Acton, Ontario, Canada)

Model #	Approximate Years of Manufacture	Scarcity	Value Range
2464	"Force Waffle Maker, Acton, Ontario"-Probable Nelson made rectangular combination unit		
	Late 1930s-Early 1940s	1	$ 5-20

Forestek Plating & Manufacturing Company "*Du-All*"
See company history page 73 for details about models listed below.

Model #		Approximate Years of Manufacture	Scarcity	Price New	Value Range
No #	Nickel	Late 1920s	1		Not Established
	Chrome		1		Not Established
No #	Nickel	Late 1920s-Early 1930s	2	$ 4.00 [1]	Not Established
	Chrome			17.50 [1]	Not Established
No #	Double sandwich grill	Late 1920s-Early 1930s	1		$5-20

[1] List price, February, 1931, *Gage Electrical Encyclopedia.*

Model #		Approximate Years of Manufacture	Scarcity	Price New	Value Range
A2G48S or T	Teflon	1960s	5		$ 5-20
A4C44-T235	Teflon	1960s-1970s	5		5-20
A7G44-T538	Teflon	1960s-1970s	4		5-20
G37-P150	Waffle grids for models 119G37 & 129G38			$ 4.00 [7]	Not Established
14 G 4-4T	Teflon	1960s-1970s	3		5-20
14 G 42		Mid-1950s	4		10-20
24 G 42		Late 1950s	4		10-20
24 G 44		Late 1950s	4		10-20
34 G 42		Early 1960s	4		10-20
101 H 1	Commercial Twin, 220 volts, 1650 watts 1950s (?)		1		Over-200
101 H 1Y	Commercial Twin, 110 volts 1950s (?)		1		Over-50
119 G 19		Early 1930s	2	11.95 [1]	25-50
119 G 25	The Gem Box Cooker Early-Mid-1930s		2	6.95 [6]	10-25
119 G 35		Mid-1930s	3		5-25
119 G 37		Mid-Late 1930s	5		10-25
119 V 181		Early-Mid-1930s	3		20-40
119 W 4	Westport model	Late 1930s-Late 1940s	5	11.95 [3,5,7]	10-40
119 W 8	Castlegate model with- Wood handles or	Late 1930s	1	15.95 [7]	15-45
	Plastic Handles	Late 1930s-Late 1940s	5	15.95 [3,5]	10-35
119 W 10		Late 1940s	2		10-25
119 W YDES		Late -40's version of 119 W 4	5		10-40
119 Y 160		Late 1920s-Early 1930s	3		10-40
119 Y 180	Lancaster model	Early 1930s	4	6.45 [1]	35-60
119 Y 181		Early 1930s	3		15-35
119 Y 182		Early-Mid-1930s	2		15-35
119 Y 184		Mid-1930s	2		15-35
119 Y 187		Late 1920s-Early 1930s	2		25-40
119 Y 188		Mid-1930s	2		10-35
119 Y 191	Portsmouth model	Mid-Late 1930s	2	5.50 [8]	10-35
119 Y 192	Roanoke model with Ebony black Textolite handles Mid-Late 1930s		5	5.50 [6]- 5.95 [8]	10-35
119 Y 194		Early 1940s-Early 1950s	2		10-40
119 Y 197	Berkshire model	Mid-Late 1930s	3	5.95 [6]	10-35
119 Y 198		Late 1930s-Early 1940s	5		10-30
120 V	Canadian- H.E.P.C. # 929 Late 1930s-Early 1940s		1		10-35
129 G 38		Late 1930s-Early 1940s	3		10-30
129 W 9	Diana model	Late 1930s-Late 1940s	5	17.95 [5,7]	20-60
129 Y 189		Early 1930s	2		25-50
129 Y 199		Late 1930s-Late 1940s	5	17.95 [3]	20-50
129 Y 175	Ambassador model with green and yellow marblized handles Late 1920s-Early 1930s		2	18.50 [9]	25-60
129 Y 178		Late 1920s-Early 1930s	2		10-30
129 Y 183		Early-Mid-1930s	1		35-60
129 Y 193	Raleigh model with "Old Ivory" Textolite handles Mid-Late 1930s		4	9.95 [6,8]	10-40
129 Y 199		1940s except war yrs	5		20-40
139 G 38		Late 1930s-Early 1940s	5	16.95 [7]	5-25
139 G 39	Grill	1940s	2	14.95 [5]	5-25
149 G 22		Mid-Late 1930s	2		35-65
149 G 23		Mid-Late 1930s	2		35-65
149 G 37	A La Carte model	Late 1930s-Early 1940s	5	14.95 [7]	10-30
149 G 39		Late 1940s-Early 1950s	2		5-20
149 G 40		Late 1940s-Early 1950s	3	18.95 [5]	5-25
149 W 199		Late 1930s-Early 1950s	5		20-50
149 Y 183		Late 1930s-Early 1940s	2		10-40
149 Y 184		Late 1930s	2		10-35
149 Y 188		Late 1930s	2		10-25
149 Y 193	Raleigh model	Late 1930s-Early 1940s	2		10-40
149 Y 194		1940s except war yrs	2		10-40

General Electric continued:

Model #		Approximate Years of Manufacture	Scarcity	Price New	Value Range
149 Y 199	Diana model	Late 1940s-Early 1950s	5		$20-40
159 G 40		Mid-1950s	4		5-25
179 G 38		Early 1950s	5		5-25
179 G 39		Early-Mid-1950s	3	$ 16.95 [2]-16.50 [4]	5-25
179 G 40		Early- Mid-50's	5	21.95 [2]- 22.50 [4, 10]	10-30

[1] List price, 1933, Christmas advertisement, unidentified magazine.
[2] List price, December 1950, advertisement, unidentified magazine.
[3] List price, January 1949, *Consumer Reports Magazine.*
[4] "Fair Trade Item" price, August 8, 1954, Janney, Semple, Hill & Co.; dealers catalog.
[5] List price, late 1940s Raybro Electric Supplies Inc. dealers catalog.
[6] Advertised price, December 1936, *Esquire Magazine.*
[7] List price, 1949, Baker & Hamilton Wholesale Hardware, San Francisco California; catalog.
[8] List price, 1937, Brown-Camp Hardware Company, Des Moines Iowa; catalog.
[9] Advertised price, December 1929, *Ladies' Home Journal.*
[10]   Catalog price, 1955 Belknap Hardware & Mfg. Company. Louisville, KY; Dealer Catalog

General Mills *"Betty Crocker"*

Model #		Approximate Years of Manufacture	Scarcity	Value Range
GM-6A	McGraw made	1952-1954	2	$ 10-25

Great Northern Products Company *"Tri-Plex" "Quality Brand"*

Model #		Approximate Years of Manufacture	Scarcity	Value Range
No #	Green handles (Landers made model)			
		Mid-Late 1920s	1	Not Established
No #	"Quality Brand" (Bersted Model 215)			
		Mid-Late 1920s	1	$ 10-35
No #	"Quality Brand" (Wear-Ever Model 909)			
		Mid-Late 1920s	1	Not Established
No #	"Tri-Plex"			
	(Knapp-Monarch "Therm-A-Magic" model with under pedestal thermostat)			
		Late 1920s-Early 1930s	1	Not Established

Griswold Manufacturing Company

Model #		Approximate Years of Manufacture	Scarcity	Price New	Value Range
1-8-E		Early-Mid-1920s	1		Not Established
2-8-E		Mid-1920s-Early 1930s	1	$ 10.50 [1]	$ 35-75
2-8-E	Stars & Hearts	Mid-1920s-Early 1930s	1	10.00 [1]-10.50 [2]	Not Established
3-8-E		Mid-1920s-Early 1930s	1	5.95 [2]-7.20 [3]	50-100
I-3-8-E	Heat Indicator	Mid-1920s-Early 1930s	1	8.00 [3]	50-125
4-8-E		Mid-1920s-Early 1930s	1	6.95 [2]-7.50 [1]	Not Established

[1] List price, February, 1931, *Gage Electrical Encyclopedia.*
[2] Suggested retail price, 1930, Griswold company catalog.
[3] Retail Price, 1931, Miller Brothers Hardware Co., Richmond, Indiana; *Catalog #10.*

Griswold continued:

The following are commercial models listed in the company's catalog # E39 from the late 1930s.

1108E	16012E	360A12	6608E
11012E	310A8	6108E	66012E
1508E	310A12	61012E	1052 [1]
15012E	350A8	6508E	1066 [1]
1608E	360A8	65012E	

[1] Ice Cream Cone Waffle Baker

The company's 1946 catalog lists the following two commercial units:

Model 3112	A rectangular double unit
Model 3208	A round double unit

Gold Seal Electric Company

Model #		Approximate Years of Manufacture	Scarcity	Value Range
No #	Black handles	Early-Mid-1920s	2	Not Established
	Red handles	Early-Mid-1920s	1	Not Established
H-1084		Mid-1920s	2	$ 25-40

Hibbard, Spencer, Bartlett & Company *"Lady Hibbard"*
See: *"Dominion Electric Mfg. Co,." "Electrahot"*.

Hecla (Australian)

Model #		Approximate Years of Manufacture	Scarcity	Value Range
No #	Cast iron base	Mid-Late 1920s (?)	1	$ 50-75

Jacks Evans Manufacturing Co. *"Another Aunt Sarah's Product"*

Model #		Approximate Years of Manufacture	Scarcity	Value Range
No #	Suit of cards grill (?)	Late 1920s	2	$ 10-25

J.B. Zumwalt
See: *"Serva-Matic Corporation"*

J.C Penney *"Penncrest"*
See: *"McGraw-Electric"*

Jim Le Mondain (French)

Model #		Approximate Years of Manufacture	Scarcity	Value Range
No #	"J. Manil Vivier Au Court Serie 5 110A 130 Chrome") or ("J. Manil Vivier Au Court B.8.6.0.6 10A 150N 45"			
	1920s		1	Over-$ 50

J.K. MacLeod & Company Limited (Canadian) *"Reliance"*

This was a retail firm based in Toronto with a chain of outlets called MacCloud Mercantile Stores that were found in small towns throughout Canada from the 1920s to the 1950s. Its appliances were made by various manufacturers and labeled with the "Reliance" brand.

Model #		Approximate Years of Manufacture	Scarcity	Value Range
160	probably Arvin made	Late 1940s-Early 1950s	1	$ 10-35
850	possibly Superior made	Mid-1930s (?)	2	10-35

Justrite Electric Manufacturing Co. *"Colonial Tourist"*

Purchased by Dominion late 1920s

Model #		Approximate Years of Manufacture	Scarcity	Value Range
700	"Colonial Tourist"	Mid-Late 1920s (?)	3	$ 5-20
700	Black Painted Base	Mid-Late 1920s (?)	1	5-20
701	"Colonial Tourist"	Mid-Late 1920s (?)	3	5-20
JW-111		Mid-Late 1920s	2	10-25
No #	Full sized, plain pedestal, domed lid, black wood handles, large dial type temp gauge			
		Late 1920s	1	10-25

Kenmore (Sears Roebuck & Co.)

See: *"Dominion Electric Manufacturing Company"*

Knapp-Monarch Company *"Lady Dover" "Armaid" "Vogue"*

Model #		Approximate Years of Manufacture	Scarcity	Price New	Value Range
CM-342	or possibly GM-342				
		1940s-Early 1950s (?)	1		$ 10-35
E-1607-4	Modern Home Appliance Co	Late 1930s-Early 1940s (?)	1		5-25
JC-1168	Western Auto Supply Co.-"Wizard"	Late 1940s-Early 1950s (?)	1		5-25
K-89W	"Vogue"	Late 1930s (?)	1		5-25
OM-343	"Faultless Mfg. Co."	Late 1930s-Early 1940s	1		5-25
248	Same as Model 29-515				
249		Late 1930s	1		10-35
549-9WG	Series A	Late 1930s-Early 1940s	1	$ 7.95 [1]	5-25
710-R		Late 1930s-1940s	2		10-35
718-9		Late 1930s-1940s	2		5-25
718-R	"Armaid" Cat # 16-1501"	Late 1930s-1940s	2		5-25
960	Small party size	Early 1930s	2	6.00 [2]	10-35
961		Early 1930s	2	6.50 [2]	10-35
965	Pedestal type	Early 1930s	2	7.50 [2]	10-35
965	Tray mounted	Late 1930s-Early 1940s	3	7.95 [1]	5-20
967	Pedestal type	Early 1930s	2		5-35
967(-0)		Late 1930s-Early 1940s	2		10-35
968	Plastic handles-two versions	Early-Mid-1930s	2	4.50 [5]	10-35
968	Walnut handles	Late 1930s-Early 1940s	3		5-25
969		Early 1930s	1	6.75 [5]	5-25
969-0	Natural wood handles	Late 1930-Early 1940s	1		10-25
975	Black or red handles	Late 1920s-Early 1930s	2		10-35
980-0	Double Twin	Late 1930s-Early 1940s	2		15-60
989		Early 1930s	1		25-50
1313	Regal model	Late 1940s	1	16.95 [3]	10-35
16-1501	"Armaid" for "Affiliated Retailers NY,NY"	Late 1930s-Early 1940s	1	10-25	
24A-500		Late 1930s-Early 1940s	1		10-25
28A-500		Late 1930s-1940s	4		5-25
28A-550		Late 1930s-1940s	4		5-25
28-901	"Lady Dover"	Late 1930s-Early 1940s	3		5-25
29-500	"Armaid" Cat# 16-1501	Late 1930s-Early 1940s	2		5-25
29-501	Tel-a-Matic model	1940s-Early 1950s	3	15.95 [4]	10-25
29-510		1940s-Early 1950s	3	24.95 [4]	10-35

209

Knapp-Monarch continued:

Model #		Approximate Years of Manufacture	Scarcity	Price New	Value Range
29-511	Sandwich grids for 29-510		1	3.00 [4]	Not Established
29-515		1940s-Early 1950s	2	$ 18.95 [4]	$ 10-25
29-516	Sandwich grids for 29-515		1	2.50 [4]	Not Established
29-520		Late 1940s-Mid-1950s	4		5-25
29-525		Early 1950s	2		5-35

[1] List price, December, 1937, unidentified magazine advertisement.
[2] List price, February, 1931, *Gage Electrical Encyclopedia*.
[3] Catalog price, 1949, W. Bingham Company, Cleveland, Ohio; Retail catalog.
[4] Catalog Price, November, 1948, Salt Lake Hardware Company, Salt lake City, Utah; 1948-49 catalog.
[5] Retail price, early 1930s unidentified retail store catalog.

Kwikway Products Inc. (St. Louis, MO. distributor)

Model #		Approximate Years of Manufacture	Scarcity	Price New	Value Range
K-85		Late 1930s	1	$ 1.95 [1]	$ 5-15
K-88-0	Knapp Monarch made	Late 1930s-Early 1940s	1		5-20
K-88-9	Possibly Superior made	Late 1930s-Early 1940s	2		5-20
No #	Possibly Dominion made	Mid-1930s	2		5-15
28402	Possibly Knapp-Monarch	Late 1930s	2		5-20

[1] List price, 1937, Brown-Camp Hardware Company, Des Moines, Iowa; catalog.

Landers, Frary & Clark *"Universal"*

Model #		Approximate Years of Manufacture	Scarcity	Price New	Value Range
1313		1940s except war yrs	2		$ 10-25
B 3705		Late 1940s-Early 1950s	3		5-20
BI 1224		Late 1930s	2		20-35
EC 76	Commercial twin unit	1930s	1		Not Established
E 533	"Reliance Electric"	Late 1920s-Early 1930s	2		15-35
E 700	"Federal Electric" or "Federal Electric Merchandise Co. Chicago"				
		Late 1920s-Early 1930s	2		15-35
E 704		Late 1920s-Early 1930s	4		20-40
E 814		Late 1930s-Early 1940s	2	$ 5.50 [24]	5-25
E 930		Late teens-Early 1920s	2	16.00 [19]	30-50
E 931	Sold with separate oval aluminum tray Late teens		2		(Without tray) 30-50
E 1204		Late 1930s-Early 1940s	2		10-25
E 1224		Late 1930s-Early 1940s	2		15-35
E 1324	(A or B)	Mid-1930s	4		30-45
E 1360		Mid-1930s	2		10-25
E 1364		Mid-1930s	3		5-20
E 1370	Sandwich grill	Mid-1930s	3		15-25
E 1860		Early -Mid-1930s	2		5-25
E 1904		Mid-Late 1920s	4		5-20
E 2024	(E)	Mid-Late 1930s	3	10.95 [24]	25-75
E 2104	(D)	Late 1920s-Early 1930s	4		10-30
E 2860	(E)	Mid-Late1930s	2	11.95 [24]	10-25
E 3000		Mid-Late 1930s	4		15-35
EA 3001	Coronet pattern	Mid-Late 1940s	4	9.95 [20]-13.96 [6]-19.95 [11]	20-35
EA 3002	Coronet pattern	Early 1950s	3	13.25 [16]	20-35
EA 3201		Mid-1930s-Late 1940s	4	17.95 [6]	30-45
E 3274		Mid-1930s-Early 1940s	5		15-35
EA 3274		Late 1940s-Early 1950s	3	15.95 [11]-21.25 [16]	15-35
E 3601		Mid-Late 1930s	3		10-25
EA 3601	Coronet pattern	Mid-Late 1930s	5	12.95 [15]-15.95 [11]	10-25
EA 3602		Mid-1930s-Early 1950s	5	19.95 [16]	10-25
EA 3705		Early-Mid-1950s	2	21.50 [22]	5-25
EA 3801		Late 1940s-Early 1950s	3	29.95 [20]-39.95 [16]	5-25
E 3702		Early 1950s	2	25.30	5-25
E 3705		1950s	1	22.96 [17]	5-25
E 3710		1950s	3		10-25
E 3801		Late 1940s-Early 1950s	4	29.95 [1, 11]-29.50 [9]	5-20

Model #		Approximate Years of Manufacture	Scarcity	Price New	Value Range
E 3805		1950s	1		$ 5-25
E 3904		Early-Mid-1920s	2		40-60
E 3914		Mid-1920s	4		5-25
E 3931	Sold with separate oval aluminum tray Late teens-Mid-1920s		5	$ 10.00 [14]	20-50
E 4804	Streamlined pattern	Late 1930s-Early 1940s	2	6.00 [24]	10-35
(E)5304	Roman pattern	Late 1920s-Early 1930s	1	13.95 [23]	5-25
E 5314	Reliance model	Late 1920s	2		10-35
(E)5770	Empire pattern grill	Late 1920s-Early 1930s	2	24.60 [23]	5-25
E 6304	Ceramic lid	Late 1920s	2		35-100
E 6360		Late 1920s	2		10-30
E 6470	"Challenge"	Late 1920s-Early 1930s	2		10-35
(E)6824 (A,B)	Ceramic	Late 1920s-Early 1930s	2		40-100
(E)6904 (B)	Ceramic	Late 1920s-Early 1930s	2		35-100
E 6924	Ceramic lid	Late 1920s-Early 1930s	2		35-100
E 7104	Low Boy pattern	Mid-Late 1930s	4	6.30 [10]	5-25
E 7124	Low Boy pattern	Mid-Late 1930s	2	9.50 [10]	10-35
E 7133 (A)	"Corona"	Late 1920s-Early 1930s	2		10-35
E 7204 (B)		Late 1920s-Early 1930s	2		10-35
E 7234 (B)	Colonial pattern	Late 1920s-Early 1930s	2	13.75-17.80 [18] -29.70 [23]	40-75
E 7304 (N)		Mid-Late 1920s	2		20-40
E 7324 (H)		Late 1920s-Early 1930s	3		25-50
E 7334 (H)	Hamilton pattern	Late 1920s-Early 1930s	2	9.95-12.75 [18]	15-35
E 7344 (H)		Late 1920s-Early 1930s	4		25-50
E 7355 (H)		Late 1920s-Early 1930s	2		15-35
E 7360 (B)	Grill	Late-20's-Early 30's	2	17.50 [13]	10-35
E 7384		Mid-Late 1920s	3		15-35
(E)7404 (B)		Late 1920s-Early 1930s	5		15-35
(E)7424 (B)(C)(O)		Late 1920s-Early 1930s	3		25-45
E 7533 (A)		Late 1920s-Early 1930s	3		10-35
E 7534		Early 1930s	2		25-50
E 7704 (D)		Mid-Late 1930s	3	7.75 [24] -7.95 [5]	40-60
E 7707		Mid-1930s	3		10-35
E 7724 (A)(E)		Late 1930s-Early 1950s	4		15-40
E 7760		Mid-Late 1930s	2		15-40
E 7935 (A)		Late 1920s-Early 1930s	4		15-35
E 8104 (D)		Late 1930s	2		10-25
E 8124 (A)		Late 1930s	2		10-25
E 8204	Walnut Hill pattern-Twin non-auto units on single base Late 1930s-Early 1940s		3	9.95 [24] -10.30 [8]	10-30
E 8260	Walnut Hill pattern-Grill; Combination unit with flat and waffle plates is 18260 Late 1930s-Early 1940s		2	6.50 & 8.75 [24]	10-35
E 8360	Chevalier pattern	Late 1930s	2	10.60 [10] -13.20 [7]	5-25
E 8524 (E)		Late 1930s	3		20-40
E 8560		Late 1930s-Early 1940s	2		5-25
E 8564 (E)		Late 1930s	2		10-35
E 9300 (1)		Late teens-Mid-1920s	5	16.50 [14]	25-40
E 9305 (A)		Late teens-Early 1930s	5	6.95 [12] -12.00 [2] -18.30 [23]	25-50
E 9311		Early-Mid-1920s	1		25-40
E 9314 (A)(H)(N)		Mid-Late 1920s	4	8.00 [2] -10.12 [12] 15.00 [21]	20-50
E 9324 (A)	Old English pattern Mid-Late 1920s		3	17.50 [3]	20-45
E 9334		Mid-Late 1920s	3		10-25
E 9350		Early 1930s	1		50-100
E 9354	Empire pattern	Late 1920s-Early 1930s	1	20.40 [23]	5-25
E 9364	Marie Antoinette pattern	Late 1920s-Early 1930s	3		20-40
E 9384		Mid-Late 1920s	4		10-30
E 9510	Griddle	Mid-Late 1920s	1	15.00 [21]	Not Established
E 9511	Same as E 9510, sold without lid				
E 9533 (A)		Mid-Late 1920s	2		25-50
E 9533	"Winchester-W36" Mid-Late 1920s		2		75 to over 300
E 9574	Marie Antoinette pattern	Late 1920s-Early 1930s	2	14.75 [4] -22.00 [2]	35-50

Landers, Frary & Clark continued:

Model #			Approximate Years of Manufacture	Scarcity	Price New	Value Range
E 9674	(H)	Green handles	Late 1920s-Early 1930s	2		$ 10-45
E 9914	(H)		Mid-Late 1920s	5	$ 9.95 [2]	20-45
E 18960	(D)	or W 18960	Early-Mid-1930s	2		10-35
E 3690		"Thermax"	Mid-Late 1920s	2		10-35
E 75324		Empire pattern	Late 1920s-Early 1930s	2	7.95-9.00 [18]-16.50 [23]	10-35
E 7533		"Reliance"	Mid-Late 1920s	2		40-55
E 79354		Empire pattern	Late 1920s-Early 1930s	2	13.00 [13]	5-35
E 79384			Late 1920s-Early 1930s	2		10-35
E 79770		Grill/waffler	Late 1920s-Early 1930s	2		10-35
E 88360		Hostess set including E 8360 grill/waffle iron, five compartment glass dish, walnut cutting block, cutting knife, 15 ½ X 24 ½ Walnut tray				
			Late 1930s	1	24.00 [7]	Not Established
E 93011			Late teens-Early 1920s	4		20-50
E 96334		Green handles	Mid-Late 1920s	2		10-35
W 804			Late 1930s-Early 1940s	1		5-25
W 814			Late 1930s-Early 1940s	1		5-25
W18960	or E 18960		Early-Mid-1930s	2		10-35
15 UG-1		McGraw made	1960s	2		5-25

Accessory Pieces:

		Approximate Years	Scarcity	Value Range
Syrup Pitcher	Nickel	Mid-Late 1920s	1	Not Established
Batter Pitcher	Nickel	Mid-Late 1920s	1	Not Established
Muffineer	Nickel	Mid-Late 1920s	1	Not Established

[1] Retail price, 1950, advertisement *Holiday Magazine*.
[2] Retail price, 1928, unidentified department store catalog.
[3] Advertised price, 1931 *Good Housekeeping Magazine*.
[4] Advertised price, 1929, *Saturday Evening Post*.
[5] Advertised price, 1935, *Saturday Evening Post*.
[6] List price, January 1949, *Consumer Reports Magazine*.
[7] List price, 1938, Landers Frary & Clark Company; dealer's catalog.
[8] List price, 1939, Landers Frary & Clark Company; dealer's catalog.
[9] List price, August 8, 1954, Janney, Semple, Hill & Co.; dealer's catalog.
[10] Wholesale price, 1938 Vonnegut Hardware Company catalog.
[11] List price, late 1940s Raybro Electric Supplies Inc.; dealer's catalog.
[12] Wholesale price, mid-winter 1927, Butler Brothers Wholesaler's Catalog 495 Broadway, NY, NY.
[13] Retail price, 1931, Miller Brothers Hardware Co., Richmond, Indiana; *Catalog #10*.
[14] Wholesale price, 1924, Buhl Sons Co. Wholesale Hardware Iron & Steel, Detroit, MI.
[15] List price, 1949, Baker & Hamilton Wholesale Hardware Co. catalog.
[16] Wholesale price, 1951, Jensen-Byrd Co. Wholesale distributors of General Hardware, Spokane, WA; *Catalog #51*.
[17] Wholesale price, 1951, Moreley-Murphy Co. Distributors of Hardware & related fines, Green Bay WI; *Catalog #1951*.
[18] Wholesale/retail prices, 1929-30(?) Van Camp Hardware & Iron Co. Mfg'rs & Wholesalers, Indianapolis, IN; *Catalog #933*.
[19] List price, January, 1922, Belknap Hardware & Mfg. Co., Louisville, KY; *Catalog # 68*.
[20] Catalog price 1949, W.Bingham Company, Cleveland, Ohio; Retail catalog.
[21] Wholesale price, 1925, Belknap Hardware & Mfg. Co., Louisville,KY; *Catalog # 78*.
[22] Catalog price, 1955, Belknap Hardware & Mfg. Company, Louisville, KY; dealer's catalog.
[23] Retail prices, 1932, Belknap Hardware & Mfg. Co., Louisville, KY; *Catalog # 86*.
[24] Catalog price, 1939, Logan-Gregg Hdwr. Co. Pittsburgh, Pa; *Catalog #1831 Fall /winter 1939*.

Lehman Brothers Silver-ware Corporation "Kromaster Products"

See: *"Superior Electric Products Corporation"*

Liberty Gauge & Instrument Company

Model #	Approximate Years of Manufacture	Scarcity	Value Range
No #	"Royal-Made for Montgomery Ward & Co.-Automatic Signal Waffler" or "Liberty Automatic Adjustable Waffle Iron" 1926-1928	1	$ 25-60

Lion Electric Appliance Corporation

Model #	Approximate Years of Manufacture	Scarcity	Value Range
No #	Late 1920s-Early 1930s	1	$ 15-35

Lindemann & Hoverson Company *"L & H Electrics"*

Model #		Approximate Years of Manufacture	Scarcity	Value Range
315	Two versions	Late 1920s-Early 1930s	2	$ 20-40
317		Late 1920s-Early 1930s	2	25-45

Made-Rite Corporation *"Made-Rite"*

See: *"Dominion Electric Manufacturing Company"*

Majestic Electric Appliance Company *"Grideliere"*

(Initially called "Majestic Electric Development Company")

Model #		Approximate Years of Manufacture	Scarcity	Price New	Value Range
No #	Leg mounted grill/waffle iron-later redesigned as pedestal Model 151"Grideliere"				
		Early-Mid-1920s	1		$ 20-50
No #	Conventional iron	Late 1920s-Early 1930s	2		10-25
150		Early 1920s	1	$ 16.00 [2]	50-75
151	"Grideliere"	Mid-1920s	2		20-50
154	"Grideliere"	Late 1920s-Early 1930s	2	18.00 [1]	20-50
402	Dominion made	Early-Mid-1930s	1		15-50
W8406	"Grideliere"	Late 1920s-Early 1930s	2		20-50
W9549		Late 1920s-Early 1930s	2		20-40
W11508	"Grideliere"	Late 1920s-Early 1930s	2		20-40

[1] List price, February, 1931, *Gage Electrical Encyclopedia.*
[2] List price, May, 1922, Original owner's manual: *form #41*, 5-22.

Manning-Bowman Company *"M B Means Best"*

Model #		Approximate Years of Manufacture	Scarcity	Price New	Value Range
J-3	"Homelectrics"	Early 1930s	2		$ 5-25
J-33		Mid-1930s	3		15-25
K-4G		Late 1920s-Early 1930s	2		10-25
K-42		Early 1930s	2		10-25
K-44		Early 1930s	3		20-40
K-45		Early 1930s	2		5-20
K-50		Early 1930s	1		10-35
K-516		Early-Mid-1930s	1		10-40
K-1038		Early-Mid-1930s	2		25-50
K-1626	"Bamberger's"	Early 1930s	1		10-40
K-1633		Early 1930s	2		15-35
K-1635	Green Bakelite	Early 1930s	1		35-50
K-1636	Green Bakelite	Early 1930s	1		35-50
01		Early 1940s	4		5-25
04KW	Montgomery Ward prefix-See 86-XXXX numbers listed below				
04MW	Montgomery Ward prefix-See 86-XXXX numbers listed below				
40	"Homelectrics"-A few were labeled "Avona-Jordan Marsh Co."				
		Mid-Late 1920s	3	$ 10.00 [3]	5-25
62 G1		Late-1950s-Early 1960s (?)	3		10-25
84MW	Montgomery Ward prefix-See numbers following 86- in model number that are listed below				
85-495	Wards	Late 1930s	2		5-25
93-KW	Montgomery Ward prefix-See numbers following 86- in model number that are listed below				
398		Late 1920s-Early 1930s	3		10-25
400	Pancake cooker	Late 1920s	1	12.50 [3]	Not Established
400	Table cooker	Mid-Late 1930s	1		Not Established
400(1)	Table cooker set including 400 cooker, two double compartment crystal relish dishes, walnut cutting board, pick up server, utility knife, salt and pepper shakers, walnut tray				
		Late 1930s	1		Not Established
402		Late 1930s-Late 1940s	4		10-35
404		Early 1940s	2		10-25

213

Model #		Approximate Years of Manufacture	Scarcity	Price New	Value Range
410		Mid-Late 1930s	2		$ 15-35
412	Jubilee model	1940s-Early 50's (except war yrs.)	5	18.95 [1]	10-35
414		Late 1940s	3		20-30
423	Regent model	Late 1940s-Early 1950s	2		10-25
451	Waldorfer model	Early-Mid-1950s	2		10-25
475		Late 1930s-Early 1940s	2		10-25
515		Late 1920s-Early 1930s	1		50-75
516	Cook-All grill or				
516 [8]	Cook-All grill with waffle grids or				
516[89]	Cook-All grill with muffin pan, donut pan, meat loaf pan, oven attachment				
		1930s	1		Not Established
60	"Meteor"	Mid-Late 1920s	3		10-30
650X	Exterior identical to 1600				
		Mid-Late 1920s	3		5-20
663		1940s	2		10-35
725	Black handles	Mid-1930s	3		25-50
	Red handles	Mid-1930s	2		35-75
726	Orange & black handles				
		Mid-1930s	1		35-75
1028	Green handles	Late 1920s	2		10-35
1600	Jordan Marsh Co. "Avona"	Mid-Late 1920s	1		10-50
1601K	Black handles	Late 1920s	4	$ 15.00 [3]	10-35
	Green handles	Late 1920s	2	13.00 [3]	20-40
	Red handles	Late 1920s	2	13.00 [3]	20-40
	Yellow handles	Late 1920s	1	13.00 [3]	20-50
	Blue handles	Late 1920s	1	13.00 [3]	25-60
1602		Late 1920s	2		10-35
1605		Early-Mid-1920s	4	15.00 [5]-20.00 [4]	20-40
1606		Mid-Late 1920s	5		10-25
1611	"Meteor"	Late 1920s	2		10-25
1613		Mid-Late 1920s	3		10-25
1615		Mid-Late 1920s	5	15.00 [3]	10-25
1616		Mid-Late 1920s	4	15.00 [3]	15-40
1617		Late-20'-Early 30's	3	18.00 [3]	15-35
1618(21K)		Late 1920s	3	15.00 [3]	20-50
1620		Late 1920s	3		15-40
1621		Late 1920s-Early 1930s	4		20-40
1621K		Late 1920s-Early 1930s	3		25-50
1622		Late 1920s-Early 1930s	2		20-40
(K) 1626	"Bamberger's"	Late 20's Early 30's	1		25-40
1637		Early-Mid-1930s	4		15-40
1639		Mid-1930s	2		35-70
1640		Mid-1930s	1		35-70
1642		Mid-1930s	3		20-40
1643		Mid-Late 1930s	4		10-35
1644		Mid-Late 1930s	2		10-35
1646		Mid-Late 1930s	4		20-45
1648	Harmony model	Late 1930s	4		15-35
1649	Puritan model	Mid-Late 1930s	3		25-50
1650		Late 1920s	4		10-25
	Wood handle version	Late 1930s-Early 1940s	3		10-35
1652	Pioneer model	Late30's-Early 40's	3		15-35
1653	Pioneer model	Late 1930s-Early 1940s	3		10-35
1654		Late 1930s	3		10-25
1655		Late 1930s-Early 1940s	3		25-50
1656		Late 1930s-Early 1940s	4		15-35
1657		Late 1930s-Early 1940s	4		20-45
1659		Early 1940s	3		10-25
1660/4		Early 1940s	2		25-40
1662	Subdeb model	1940s-Early 1950s except war yrs	4	12.95 [1]	15-35
1663	Subdeb model	1940s-Early 1950s except war yrs	4	16.95 [1]	15-35
1664	Waldorph model	Late 1940s-Early 1950s	4	9.95 [4]	10-35
1665		Late 1940s-Eraly 1950s	2		15-35
1700 (X or P)		Mid-Late 1920s	4		10-35
1701		Late 1920s-Early 1930s	5		5-30

Manning-Bowman continued:

Model #		Approximate Years of Manufacture	Scarcity	Price New	Value Range
1702		Late 1920s-Early 1930s	4		$ 10-30
1703		Late 1920s-Early 1930s	3		15-50
1704	Homelectrics	Late 1920s-Early 1930s	2		10-35
1813		Late 1920s-Early 1930s	1		10-40
2105A	Wards	Entire 1940s except war years	3		5-25
2182A	Wards	Entire 1940s except war years	4		10-30
2521		Late 1940s-Early 1950s	2		10-30
2525	Twin	Late 1930s-Early 1950s	4	$ 16.95 [1]	15-40
2527	Oblong twin	Late 1940s	2		20-35
2625	Auto twin	1940s-Early 1950s	3		10-35
2626		1940s-Early 1950s except war yrs	4	19.95 [1]	25-40
4814	Wards	Late 1930s	2		5-25
4815	Wards	Late 1930s	2		5-25
4860	Wards	Early 1940s	2		5-25
4861	Wards	Late 1930s	2		5-25
4862	Wards	Late 1930s-Early 1940s	2		10-35
4863	Wards	Late 1930s-Early 1940s	2		10-35
4960	Wards	Late 1930s-Early 1940s	2	$ 6.95 [6]	10-35
4961	Wards	Late 1930s	2		10-35
5050	Twin-Over model	Late 30's-Early 50's except war yrs	3	12.95 [2]	25-75
5314	Wards	Late 1930s	2		5-25
6060		Twin-O-Matic model			5
16.00 [2]- 24.95 [1]		35-100			
6464	Kenmore	Late 1930s-Early 1950s 1940s	2	14.50 [1]	10-25
7649		Late 1930s	2		10-25
16520 (Set)	Pioneer Waffle Service -included #1653 iron, sugar duster, syrup pitcher, batter pitcher and walnut serving tray				
		Late 1930s-Early 1940s	1		Not Establihed
37500	McGraw Electric	Late 1950s	2		10-25
37501		Late 1940s-Early 1950s	2		5-25
37502		Late 1940s-Early 1950s	4		5-25
37502	McGraw Electric	Late 1950s	3		10-35
37505		Late 1940s-Early 1950s	3		5-25
37505	McGraw Electric	Late 1950s-Early 1960s	3		10-35
37507	McGraw Electric	1960s	2		10-35

[1] List price, January, 1949, *Consumer Reports Magazine*.
[2] List price, 1939 advertisement *Life Magazine* & 1947 Manning-Bowman magazine advertisement.
[3] List price, October, 1928, *Manning-Bowman Product Catalog*.
[4] List price, 1928, unidentified department store catalog.
[5] Advertised price, April, 1923, *Good Housekeeping Magazine*.
[6] Catalog price, 1938, Montgomery Ward, retail catalog.

McGraw-Electric *"Fostoria" "Everhot" "Toastmaster"*

(Name changed to McGraw-Edison in 1957)

Model #		Approximate Years of Manufacture	Scarcity	Value Range
No #	"Danby"-Canadian oblong grill/waffle iron			
		1950s	2	Not Established
B222	Commercial Toastmaster	1960s-1970s (?)	1	$ 100-150
2E2	Commercial Toastmaster	1930s	1	25-50
6A	"Fostoria" or "Twin Star"	Mid-Late 1950s	3	10-35
260	"Fostoria"	Late 1940s-Early 1950s	2	5-35
261		Late 1940s-Early 1950s	2	5-35
265		1960s	2	5-25
363	"Fostoria"	Late 1950s-Early 1960s	2	10-35
451	"Waldorfer"	Late 1940s-Early 1950s	3	5-25
3610	"Fostoria"	Late 1950s-Early 1960s	2	5-25
4888	Penney-"Penncrest"	1950s	2	10-35
4894	Penney-"Penncrest"	1950s	2	10-35
36101	"Fostoria"	1960s	2	5-25
36104	"Fostoria"	Late 1950s-Early 1960s	3	5-25

McGraw-Electric continued:

Model #		Approximate Years of Manufacture	Scarcity	Value Range
37100	"Fostoria"	Late 1950s-Early 1960s	3	$ 10-35
37100(1)	"Everhot"	Late 1950s-Early 1960s	2	5-25
37100(2)	"Everhot"	1960s	2	5-25
37105	"Fostoria"	Late 1950s-Early 1960s	3	10-35
37502	See Manning-Bowman 37502			
37505	See Manning-Bowman 37505			
37507(0)	See Manning-Bowman 37507			

Metal Ware Corporation *"Empire" "Empco"*

Model #		Approximate Years of Manufacture	Scarcity	Price New	Value Range
S-75	Rectangular	Early 1930s	1	$ 10.00 [1]	Not Established
S-76	Round pedestal	Early 1930s	1	10.00 [1]	Not Established
718	Painted base	1940s (?)	1		$ 25-60

[1] List price, February, 1931, *Gage Electrical Encyclopedia*.

Metelec (Australian)

Model #	Approximate Years of Manufacture	Scarcity	Value Range
N/18/WI-1	1940s-1950s (?)	1	Not Established
N/18/WI-3	1950s	1	Not Established

Mid-City Manufacturing Company *"Jiffy"* ·

Model #		Approximate Years of Manufacture	Scarcity	Value Range
No #	Bail handle	Late 1920s-Early 1930s	2	$ 5-25
No #	Knob handle	Early 1930s	4	5-20
No #	Knob handle, detachable cord	Early 1930s	1	5-25
No #	Bail handle, rectangular double unit			
		Late 1920s-Early 1930s	1	5-25
No #	Double handled rectangular double sandwich grill			
		Early 1930s	1	5-25

Mirro

See: *"Aluminum Goods Manufacturing Company"*.

Modern Home Appliance Company (Saint Louis, MO)

This was a retail distributor. See: *"Knapp-Monarch Company"* (Model E1607-4)

Monarch Aluminum Ware Company (Cleveland, OH)

Model		Approximate Years of Manufacture	Scarcity	Value Range
No #	Leg or skirt mounted grills	Mid 1920s-Early 1930s	1	$ 5-20

Monarch Company *"Therm-A-Hot"* *"Therm-A-Jug"*

Model #		Approximate Years of Manufacture	Scarcity	Price New	Value Range
950	"Therm-A-Hot"	Mid-1920s	1		$ 25-50
965		Late 1920s	1	$ 4.00-5.75 [1]	15-35

[1] Wholesale/retail prices 1929-30(?) Van Camp General Hardware & Iron Co. Mfgr's & wholesalers, Indianapolis, IN. *Catalog # 933*

Montgomery Ward *"Blue Line"* *"Signature"*

See: *Dominion Electric Mfg. Co., Electrahot, Liberty Gauge & Instrument Co., Manning-Bowman Co., Porcelier.*

National Everbrite Company Inc. *"Everbrite"*

This was a housewares retailing organization in New York state. Its waffle irons were made by Superior Electric.

National Stamping & Electric Works *"White Cross"*

Model #		Approximate Years of Manufacture	Scarcity	Price New	Value Range
154		Mid-Late 1920s	1		$ 10-35
156		Mid-1920s-Early 1930s	2	$ 7.50 [1] -9.00 [2]	10-35
228	Sandwich grill	Mid-Late 1930s	1	6.50 [4]	10-35
229	Sandwich grill	Mid-Late 1930s	1	4.45 [4]	5-25
250		Early 1930s	1		20-40
254		Early 1930s	2	6.00 [1]	15-35
254 T.S.	Set including Model 254 iron, batter pitcher, 16 in. oval polished aluminum tray.				
		Early 1930s	1		Not Established
255	Black or green handles	Early 1930s	2	8.00 [1]	20-35
255 T.S.	Set including model 255 iron, batter pitcher, 16" rectangular nickel plated tray.				
		Early 1930s	1		Not Established
257	Black or green handles	Early 1930s	2	8.80 [1]	15-35
258		Early 1930s	2	9.80 [1]	25-40
259		Early 1930s	2	8.50 [1]	20-35
262		Early-Mid-1930s	1		10-35
263		Early-Mid-1930s	2		20-35
363		Mid-1930s-Early 1940s	1	4.75 [4]	5-25
365		Late 1930s-Early 1940s	1	9.95 [4]	10-35
368		Late 1930s-Early 1940s	1	6.45 [4]	5-25
563		Late 1930s-Early 1940s	2		10-30
565		Late 1930s-Early 1940s	2		10-35
568		Late 1930s-Early 1940s	2		10-30
569		Late 1930s-Early 1940s	2		10-35
628	(B)	Late 1930s-Early 1940s	3		10-25
666	(A)	Late 1930s-Late 1940s	2	14.95 [3]	10-35
668		Late 1930s-Early 1940s	3		10-25
669	(B)(D)	Late 1930s-Late 1940s	3	14.95 [3]	10-35
1263	(N)	Early 1930s	2		10-25
1268		Early 1930s	1		10-25
N28X		Late 1930s-Early 1940s	1		25-50

[1] List price, February, 1931, *Gage Electrical Encyclopedia.*
[2] Advertised price, December, 1926, *Liberty Magazine.*
[3] List price, January, 1949, *Consumer Reports Magazine.*
[4] Catalog price, 1939, Logan-Gregg Hardware Company, Pittsburgh, Pa.; *Catalog #1831, Fall /winter 1939.*

Nelson Machine & Manufacturing Co. *"Mastercraft"*

Model #		Approximate Years of Manufacture	Scarcity	Price New	Value Range
200	Sandwich grill	Late 1930s-1940s	2		$ 5-20
201	Sandwich grill	Late 1940s-Early 1950s	2		5-20
211		Late 1930s-Early 1940s	1		10-35
250		Late 1940s-Early 1950s	3	$ 4.95 [1]	5-20
350		Late 1940s-Early 1950s	3		5-20
420		Late 1930s-Early 1940s*	3		5-25
440	"Mastercraft"	Late 1930s-Early 1940s*	3		10-20
450		Late 1930s-Early 1940s*	4		5-25
451 (C)	Plaskon handles	Late 1930s-Mid-1950s	3	8.60 [2]	10-35
511	Plastic handles	Late 1930s-Early 1940s*	3		5-25
	Wood handles	Late 1930s-Early 1940s*	2		10-25
550		Late 1930s-Early 1940s*	4		10-25

* May have been manufactured again after 1945.
[1] List price, January, 1949, *Consumer Reports Magazine*.
[2] List price, August 8, 1954, Janney, Semple, Hill & Co.; dealer's catalog.

Newark Appliance Inc. (Newark, New Jersey)

See: *"Dominion Electrical Manufacturing Company"* (Model P-104.)

Noblitt-Sparks Industries

See: *"Arvin Industries Inc."*

Nova (Belgium)

Model #	Approximate Years of Manufacture	Scarcity	Value Range
No #	Small rectangular, leg mounted, split cord, interchangeable grids, 220 volts Mid-1920s-Early 1930s	1	Over-$ 100

Perfection Electric Products Company *"Excelsior" "PEPCO"*

Model #		Approximate Years of Manufacture	Scarcity	Value Range
No #	"Excelsior"	Early 1920s	1	Not Established

Porcelier

Porcelier waffle irons were manufactured in relatively small numbers from 1934 to approximately 1940 making all models either scarce or rare. Active trading in them is very limited and prices vary greatly, depending on model, pattern, and condition. Many examples are found with chips, heat stress cracks, metal corrosion, or wear to the decal transfers. Undamaged examples command much higher prices than those in deteriorated condition. At the time of this writing, the Scalloped Wildflower pattern commands the highest prices, followed in order by Colonial Silhouette, Basketweave with Wildflowers, and Barock Colonial. Serv-All models, though more scarce than certain other models, seem to be in least demand. Models stamped with "Hankscraft" (Montgomery Ward) or "Heatmaster" (Sears Roebuck) labels [1] are less desirable to many Porcelier collectors than the same models with Porcelier labels. Overall, prices range from about $100 to $350. For details about each model see "Porcelier" in Company Biography Section.

[1] A Porcelier non-automatic in the Colonial Silhouette pattern appears in the Sears Roebuck 1934 Catalog for $5.25.

Precision Manufacturing Company *"Rainbow"*

Model #	Approximate Years of Manufacture	Scarcity	Value Range
70-A	1940s	3	$ 5-20
75-C	1940s	2	5-20
80W	1940s	3	5-25

Precision Mold & Foundry Company Incorporated

Model #	Approximate Years of Manufacture	Scarcity	Value Range
101	1920s	2	Not Established

Proctor & Schwartz Company

Model #		Approximate Years of Manufacture	Scarcity	Price New	Value Range
634	Sears 20E634	Early-Mid-1930s	1	$ 4.95 [1]	$ 5-25
698	Sears 20E698	Early-Mid-1930s	2	7.75 [1]	10-35
1510 (1)		Early 1930s	2		5-30
1510 (2)		Early 1930s	2		5-30
1510 (D)		Early 1930s	1		5-30
1515		Mid-Late 1930s	1		10-35
1516	Black painted or natural wood handles				
		Mid-1930s-Late 1940s	3		10-35
1517		Late 1940s	2		10-35

[1] Retail price, 1934, Sears Roebuck *General Catalog.*

Red Seal Appliance Company

See: *"Samson United Corporation."*

Reynolds Aluminum Company *"RACO" Ware*

Model #	Approximate Years of Manufacture	Scarcity	Value Range
No #	Early 1920s	1	Not Established

Robeson Rochester Corporation *"Royal Rochester"*

Model #	Approximate Years of Manufacture	Description	Price New	Value Range
E 6468	Late 1920s-Early 1930s	"Dictator," nickel	$ 8.95 [1]	$ 30-45
E 6469	Late 1920s-Early 1930s	"Berkley," nickel	7.25 [1]	40-55
E 6472	Late 1920s-Early 1930s	"Louis XIV," nickel	9.25 [1]	50-75
E 6473	Late 1920s-Early 1930s	"Golden Pheasant," nickel	16.75 [1]	60-90
E 6473 (Set)	Late 1920s-Early 1930s	"Golden Pheasant" with batter bowl, ladle		280
E 6474	Late 1920s-Early 1930s	"Royal Bouquet," nickel	10.95 [1]	60
E 6474 (Set)	Late 1920s-Early 1930s	"Royal Bouquet" with syrup pitcher & percolator		235
E 7468	Early 1930s	"Dictator," chrome		30-45
E 7473	Early 1930s	"Golden Pheasant," chrome	18.75 [1]	35-90
E 7474	Early 1930s	"Royal Bouquet," chrome		Not Established
E 7475	Early 1930s	"Modernistic," chrome		230-960
E 7477	Early 1930s	"Plain" or "Avalon," chrome	11.95 [1]	Not Established
230	Mid-Late 1930s	Grill/waffle iron, chrome		Not Established
250	Late 1930s	Grill/waffle iron, chrome	8.95 [3]	Not Established
11620	Late 1920s-Early 1930s	"Black Leaf & Myrtle," nickel		35-50
12000	same as E-6468			30-45
12010	same as E-6469			40-55
12020	same as E-6472			50-75
12110	same as E-6469 but with heat indicator		7.95 [1]	40-55
12120	same as E-6472 but with heat indicator		10.00 [1]	50-75
12260-A	Early-Mid-1930s	Low profile, automatic, oval tray base, chrome.		35-50
12270 (C33)	Early-Mid-1930s	Low profile, automatic, chrome.		$ 35-60
12290	Early-Mid-1930s	Low profile, automatic metal lid chrome with painted concentric rings.		35-50
12300	Early 1930s	"Kenwood," chrome.	10.95 [1]	Not Established

Robeson Rochester continued:

Model #		Description	Price New	Value Range
12310	Early-Mid-1930s	"Ambassador," metal lid, chrome, chevron handles.		$40-65
12320	same as E-7477		10.00 [2]	Not Established
12340	1930s	"Ambassador," metal lid, chrome	6.00 [3]	35-50
12360	1930s	Low profile, metal lid, chrome		20-35
12370	1930s	Low profile, metal lid, chrome		20-35
12390 (C38)	Late 1930s	"Queen Mary," chrome, walnut handles, non-auto, low profile	8.00 [3]	35-50
12530	same as E-6473			60-90
12540	same as E-6474			60
12770	same as E-7475			Over 200
12800	Early 1930s	"Black Leaf & Myrtle," chrome	14.75 [1]	80
		"Red Poppy," chrome		35-60
12820	same as E-7473			35-90
12840	Early-Mid-1930s	"Red Poppy," chrome	12.95 [1]	65
12870	Mid-Late 1930s	"Orange Luster," chrome		60-75
12870 (Set)	Mid-Late 1930s	"Orange Luster," batter bowl, syrup pitcher, walnut tray.		275
12900	Early-Mid-1930s	"Red Poppy," chrome		50-135
12900 (Set)	Early-Mid-1930s	"Red Poppy," batter bowl, syrup pitcher, ladle.		225
12920 (D33)	Early-Mid-1930s	"Red Poppy," chrome.		50-135
12910	Early-Mid-1930s	"Black Leaf & Myrtle," chrome.		60-75
12920 (A) (D35)	Early-Mid-1930s	"Golden Pheasant," automatic, chrome		55

Accessory Pieces:

Model #		Description	Price New	Value Range
?		Waffle Keeper (shallow chafing dish)"Golden Pheasant"		60-75
?		Syrup Pitcher "Cobalt & Pearl"		50
?		Syrup Pitcher "Golden Pheasant"		Not Established
?		Syrup Pitcher "Red Poppy" (two handle styles)		35-50
27000	(old # is 1370)	Batter Bowl "Golden Pheasant"	$ 6.25 [2]	45
27030		Batter Bowl "Red Poppy"	6.00 [2]	35
27040		Batter Bowl "Black Leaf & Myrtle"	6.00 [2]	30
27050 (?)		Batter Bowl "Orange Luster"		45
?		Ladle "Orange Luster" w/ walnut handle		Not Established
?		Walnut Tray "Orange Luster"		Not Established

[1] Suggested retail price, August, 1930, Company issued dealer's price list # 16 E.
[2] Suggested retail price, March , 1931, Company issued dealer's price list # 17 D.E.
[3] Wholesale price, 1938, Vonnegut Hardware Company catalog.

Rock Island Manufacturing Company

Model #	Approximate Years of Manufacture	Scarcity	Value Range
M-11	Late 1920s	1	Not Established
88-A	Early-Mid-1920s	1	Not Established

Rogers Electric Laboratories

Model #	Approximate Years of Manufacture	Scarcity	Price New	Value Range
No #	Early-Mid-1920s	1		$ 35-75
100	Late 1920s-Early 1930s	1	$ 6.00 [1]	25-50
103	Late 1920s-Early 1930s	1	7.75 [1]	25-50

[1] List price, February, 1931, *Gage Electrical Encyclopedia*.

R.Rønning (European)

Model #	Approximate Years of Manufacture	Scarcity	Value Range
2	1950s (?)	1	$ 30-50

Russell Electric Company *"Hold Heet"*

Model #		Approximate Years of Manufacture	Scarcity	Value Range
No #	Leg mounted flat top	Early 1920s	1	$ 35-65
14		Mid-Late 1920s	2	35-50
No #	"Cast-Rite Cookware, Chicago". Very similar to Model 14 above	Mid-Late 1920s	1	20-50
No #	Ivory Handles, parrot on swing ceramic lid insert	Mid-Late 1920s	1	35-75

Rutenber Electric Company *"Marion" "Flip-Flop" "Reco"*

Model #		Approximate Years of Manufacture	Scarcity	Price New	Value Range
77 (AC)		Late 1920s-Early 1930s	2	$ 10.25 [1]	$ 25-40
111	"Everyday Electric Co.- Marion, Ind."	Early 1930s	1		35-50
777		Mid-1930s	2		25-60

[1] List price, February, 1931, *Gage Electrical Encyclopedia.*

Samson United Corporation

Model #		Approximate Years of Manufacture	Scarcity	Price New	Value Range
60-A	"Seneca" ceramic	Early 1930s	2		$ 35-75
E 127		Late 1920s-Early 1930s	2		15-35
E 128	Poppy ceramic insert [1]	Late 1920s-Early 1930s	2		35-60
	Green ceramic insert		1		25-50
E 129		Early 1930s	2		25-50
E 130		Early 1930s	2		25-50
E 131 (V)		Early-Mid-1930s	3	$ 8.95 [2] -3.95 [3]	15-35
E 132		Late 1920s-Early 1930s	3	9.50 [2]	20-40
E 132-1	Auto version	Early-Mid-1930s	1	5.95 [3]	25-50
E 134	Grill	Mid-Late 1930s	1		20-45
E 178	Wild Flower lid	Early 1930s	1		35-60
E 232		Late 1930s	2		35-50
E 233		Mid-Late 1930s	1		25-60
E 234	Grill	Mid-Late 1930s	1		25-60
E 279	"Heatmaster"	Early 1930s	2		15-40
E 330		Mid-Late 1930s	2		15-35
E 331	This model has deco flower embossed in lid and was made for various retail chains including Firestone, Macys, Red Seal Appliance	Early-Mid-1930s	4		15-35
E 333		Mid-Late 1930s	2		15-40
E 379	Automatic w/swirl lid and handles Mid-Late 1930s		2		35-50
E 433		Mid-Late 1930s	2		10-35
E 435	Grill	Mid-Late 1930s	2		10-25
E 1127	"Senica"	Late 1920s-Early 1930s	2		20-50
E 1128	"Seneca" ceramic	Late 1920s-Early 1930s	1		35-75
E 1129	"R.H.Macy Co."	Mid-Late 1930s	1		15-35
E 1130	"R.H.Macy Co."	Mid-Late 1930s	1		15-35
E 1131	"Seneca"	Early-Mid-1930s	3		25-50
E 1132	"St. Regis-Brighten Sales Co. Brighten,NY" Early-Mid-1930s		1		15-35
E 1133	"Seneca"grill/waffle	Early-Mid-1930s	1		10-25
E 1606	"Monroe Service Co.- Firestone"-See E 331		2		15-35
2023	Sears Heatmaster 281-102-7592 Late 1930s-Early 1940s		1		10-35
2131	"Red Seal Appliance Co."- See E 331		2		15-35
5060		Late 1930s	2		10-35
5070	Model E 331 with modified chevron handles		2		15-35
5071		Late 1930s	2		10-35
5081	Model E 331 with swirl type handles		2		15-40
5082		Late 1930s-Early 1940s	3		10-25
5213	Wards	Late 1930s-Early 1940s	2	4.95 [4]	10-35

Samson United continued:

Model #		Approximate Years of Manufacture	Scarcity	Price New	Value Range
5214	Wards	Late 1930s-Early 1940s	1	4.95 [4]	$10-35
5215	Wards	Late 1930s-Early 1940s	2	3.69 [4]	10-35
5226	Wards	Late 1930s-Early 1940s	1	2.69 [4]	10-25
5360		Late 1930s-Early 1940s	2		10-25
5382		Early 1940s	2		10-25
5384		Early 1940s	3		10-35
5386		Early 1940s	3		10-25

[1] Samson offered matching pieces with this decal including a percolator, creamer and sugar bowl. These are often confused with similar pieces produced by Hall China who used a very similar decal. An octagonal body design was also used with this insert but has no model number.

[2] List price, February, 1931, *Gage Electrical Encyclopedia*.

[3] Retail price, 1934, J. Norman Pussy Hardware Co. Avondale, Pa.; home accessories catalog

[4] Catalog price, 1938, Montgomery Ward; retail catalog.

Sears Roebuck & Company *"Heatmaster" "Kenmore" "Challenge" "Energex"*

Sears did not manufacture its own waffle irons.

See: *"Arvin Industries, Bersted, Chicago Electric Mfg., Dominion Electric Mfg. Co., Electrahot, Manning-Bowman Samson United."*

Seneca

See: *"Samson United Corporation."*

Serva-Matic Corporation

Model #	Approximate Years of Manufacture	Scarcity	Value Range
AW-48	Late 1930s-Early 1940s	1	$ 10-50
DW-46	Late 1930s-Early 1940s	1	25-50
LE-58	Identical to DW-46 but labeled "Lady Evelyn- Mfg. for J.B. Zumwalt-Boston"		

Simpas (Lyon, France)

A small rectangular unit finished in white or light blue enamel, hinge mounted on a small rectangular enameled tray, able to be flip-flopped open. The entire unit is designed to be hung for storage. It appears to date from the 1920s and is marked "Simpas-Lyon, 600W/115V". This is a rare artifact and due to limited trading, a value cannot be assigned at this time. See photo in *"Miscellaneous & Odd"* section of company histories.

Son-Chief Electrics Inc. *"Magic Maid" "Speed Master" "Armaid"*

Model #		Approximate Years of Manufacture	Scarcity	Price New	Value Range
950	Black Angus, Duracrest, Penncrest 4888				
		1950s (?)	4		$ 5-35
960		1950s (?)	2		5-20
975		1930s-1940s	3		5-20
9132	(R)	Late 1930s-1940s	2	$ 19.95 [1]	5-25
9150	(A)	1950s (?)	2		5-35
9170		1960s (?)	2		5-20
9180-1		Late 1930s-1940s	4		5-25
9190	(R)	1940s-Mid-1950s	3	11.65 [2]-24.95 [1]-29.95 [1]	5-25

[1] Price sticker attached to New Old Stock unit. Dates unknown.

[2] List price, August 8, 1954 , Janney, Semple, Hill & Co. dealers catalog.

Standard Appliance Manufacturing Company (Toronto, Canada)

Model #		Approximate Years of Manufacture	Scarcity	Value Range
S 108	Grill	Late 1930s-Early 1940s	2	$ 10-25
T 92	Combination model	Late 1930s-Early 1940s	2	10-35

Sterling Electric Company See: *"Chicago Electric Mfg. Co."*

Stern-Brown Incorporated *"Super Star"*

Model #		Approximate Years of Manufacture	Scarcity	Value Range
No #		"Master Grill" with "M" design on lid -Two different handle variations		
		Mid-Late 1930s	4	$ 5-25
No #		"Thermo-Waffle" with Laurel branch lid design and temperature gauge		
		Late 1930s-1940s	1	10-35
No #		"Twin Snackette" Makes sealed "Puffies" sandwiches with special removable grill plate		
		1940s (?)	1	5-35
No #		"Lady Winsted, Thermo-Matic, Capital Products Co."		
		Late 1940s-Early 1950s (?)	1	10-35
No #		"Goodyear Associates"-Natural wood handles, square base		
		Late 1930s-Early 1940s	1	10-35
18		Late 1930s-Early 1940s	3	5-35
24		Late 1930s-Early 1940s	3	5-25
25		"Thermo-Waffle", Bakelite or wood handles		
		Late 1930s-Early 1940s	4	5-25
40	Twin	1930s- Early 40's (?)	1	5-20
60	Twin	Late 1930s-Early 1940s	1	10-25
720CW	Twin	Late 1930s	2	5-20

Sunbeam Corporation

See: *"Chicago Flexible Shaft Company"*

Super Maid Cookware Corp. *"Super Maid"*

Model #		Approximate Years of Manufacture	Scarcity	Value Range
No #	Plain black handled pedestal model	Mid-Late 1920s	1	$25-50
No #	Large pedestal with green marbleized handles	Mid-Late 1920s	1	40-75

Superior Electric Products Corp. *"Superlectric"*

Model #		Approximate Years of Manufacture	Scarcity	Price New	Value Range
5P		Early-Mid-1920s	2		$ 10-35
11-A	Waffle iron/Grill	Late 1940s-Early 1950s (?)	2		5-25
58	Grill	Early-Mid-1930s	2		10-35
105	Waffle iron/Grill	Early 1940s	4	$ 3.50 [4]	5-25
136-T1	Teflon	1960s	2		5-25
155	Waffle iron/Grill	Early 1940s	1	5.50 [4]	5-25
188		Late 1940s-Early 1950s	1		5-20
119-T	Teflon	Late 1960s	1		5-20
192-T	Teflon	1970s	2		5-10
55	"Lehman Brothers" or "Triplet" 1930s		2	4.69 [1]	20-35
370	Superior Electric-Canada Late 1920s-Eraly 1930s		1		10-35
557	Grill/Waffler	Late 1930s-Early 1940s	1		5-20
601	Nickel	Late 1920s-Early 1930s	2	6.25 [3]	10-35
	Chrome	Early 1930s	1	7.25 [2]	10-35
606	Early version- Flowers, ribbons & hearts ceramic lid insert.				
	Later version- Flowers only ceramic lid insert.				
		Late 1920s-Mid-1930s	2		35-75
632U	Ceramic insert with three hearts and love birds				
	Nickel	Late 1920s-Early 1930s	3	6.75 [1]	20-35
	Chrome	Late 1920s-Early 1930s	2	7.25 [2]	20-35
651	Nickel	Late 1920s-Early 1930s	2	9.50 [2]	25-40
	Chrome	Early 1930s	2	10.50 [2]	25-40
670U	Ceramic insert-three hearts & love birds Late 1920s-Early 1930s		3		25-50
686		Late 1920s-Early 1930s	3		10-40

Superior Electric continued:

Model #		Approximate Years of Manufacture	Scarcity	Price New	Value Range
695		Early 1930s	2		$ 10-35
700		Late 1930s	3		10-35
702	Wood ball handles	Early 1940s	2	$ 4.25 [4]	10-25
	Cylindrical wood handles		2		
5-25					
706	Twin unit	Late 1930s-Early 1940s	2		100-300
707	Metal lid- Sometimes marked "National Everbrite Co. Inc. NY"				
		Early-Mid-1930s	3		20-50
	Flowers ceramic lid insert	Late 1930s	2		25-50
707-X		Late 1930s-Early 1940s	2		5-25
708	"Buck Rogers" disc handles	Late 1930s-Early 1940s	1		200-400
	Octagonal lid-tray mounted	Late 1930s-Early 1940s	1		20-35
722		Late 1930s-Early 1940s	2		10-25
732-U		Late 1920s-Early 1930s	1		10-25
740	Gravy boat shaped	Early-Mid-1930s	1		5-75
750	Twin unit	Early 1930s	1	12.00 [3]	45-75
755	Grill/waffler	Late 1930s-Early 1940s	1		Not Established
766		Early-Mid-1930s	1		10-35
771	"Lehman Brothers Silver-ware Corp."	Early-Mid-1930s	1		20-35
777		Early-Mid-1930s	3		20-35

[1] Catalog price, 1938, Cussins & Fearn Co. catalog (Ohio department store chain)
[2] List price, 1939, company sales brochure.
[3] List price, February, 1931, *Gage Electrical Encyclopedia.*
[4] List price, January, 1940, company sales letter & flier.

Swartzbaugh Manufacturing Company *"Everhot"*

Model #		Approximate Years of Manufacture	Scarcity	Value Range
4	"Waf-Fil Baker"	Early-Mid-1930s	1	Over-$ 50

Thomas A. Edison Incorporated *"Edicraft"*

Model #		Approximate Years of Manufacture	Scarcity	Value Range
103000	waffle iron/grill	1929-1934	1	Over-$ 200
104000	waffle iron	1929-1934	1	250-1000

Toastess Corp. (Canadian)

Model #		Approximate Years of Manufacture	Scarcity	Value Range
51 or (7490)		Late 1940s	2	$10-25
551		Late 1940s-Early 1950s	4	10-25
562		1950s (?)	1	10-35
575-A	Teflon & yellow	1960s (?)	1	10-35

Toastwell Company See: *"Utility Electric Company."*

United Drug Company *"Electrex"*

Model #		Approximate Years of Manufacture	Scarcity	Value Range
X 233	Blue gray wood handles	Late 1920s	1	$ 25-50
	Black wood lid handle and steel carrying handles			
		Late 1920s-Early 1930s	3	10-35
X532	Burgundy wood lid handle and steel carrying handles			
		Late 1920s-Early 1930s	3	10-35

United Drug continued:

Model #	Approximate Years of Manufacture	Description	Price New	Value Range
X534	Green wood lid handle and steel carrying handles Late 1920s-Early 1930s		2	$10-35
X544	See Beardsley & Wolcott Model WY010			
X550	See Beardsley & Wolcott Model W2014			

Utility Electric Company *"Toastswell"*

Model #		Approximate Years of Manufacture	Description	Price New	Value Range
No #		Early 1930s	Green Handled Pedestal Model		$25-40
CWB		1950s-60's (?)	Commercial Waffle Baker		Not Established
CWBBT	"Toastwell Co."	1950s-60's (?)	Dual Commercial Waffle Baker Bread Toaster		Not Established
NBWB-L	"Toastwell Co."	1960s (?)	Single Commercial Waffle Baker		25-75
N-510	"Toastwell Co."	1940s-1950s (?)	Commercial Unit		25-100
830		1940s	Automatic Waffle Iron	$ 9.95 [1]	25-35
830-S		1940s	Model 830 with walnut tray & 12 oz Dripcut syrup pitcher & 48 oz Dripcut batter pitcher.	16.95 [1]	Not Established
907		1940s	Walnut tray, 2 condiment dishes, walnut cutting board.	5.00 [1]	Not Established
910		1940s	Non-Auto Sandwich Grill	5.95 [1]	5-25
910-W		1940s	Model 910 with 907 tray set	10.95 [1]	Not Established
911		1940s	Non-Auto Sandwich Grill	6.95 [1]	Not Established
911-W		1940s	Model 911 with 907 tray set	11.95 [1]	Not Established
915		1940s	Sandwich grids for 930, 970	$ 2.00 [1]	Not Established
916		1940s	Sandwich grids for 931, 971	2.00 [1]	Not Established
920		1940s	Non-Automatic Waffle Iron	5.95 [1]	$ 10-35
920-W		1940s	Model 920 with 907 tray set	10.95 [1]	Not Established
925		1940s	Waffle grids for 930, 970	2.00 [1]	Not Established
926		1940s	Waffle grids for 931, 971	2.00 [1]	Not Established
930		1940s	Non-Auto Grill/Waffle Iron	7.95 [1]	10-35
930-W		1940s	Model 930 with 907 tray set	12.95 [1]	Not Established
931		1940s	Automatic Grill/Waffle Iron	8.95 [1]	10-40
931-W		1940s	Model 931 with 907 tray set	13.95 [1]	Not Established
960		1940s	Automatic Waffle Iron	6.95 [1]	20-35
960-W		1940s	Model 960 with 907 tray set	11.95 [1]	Not Established
961		1940s	Automatic Sandwich Grill	7.95 [1]	5-35
961-W		1940s	Model 961 with 907 tray set	12.95 [1]	Not Established
965		1940s	Automatic Sandwich Grill	6.95 [1]	5-30
965-W		1940s	Model 965 with 907 tray set	11.95 [1]	Not Established
970		1940s	Automatic Grill/Waffle Iron	8.95 [1]	10-40
970-W		1940s	Model 970 with 907 tray set	13.95 [1]	Not Established
971		1940s	Automatic Grill/Waffle Iron	9.95 [1]	10-40
971-W		1940s	Model 971 with 907 tray set	14.95 [1]	Not Established

[1] List price, October, 1940, company issued price list.

Vornado Inc. (Garfield, New Jersey)

Model #		Approximate Years of Manufacture	Scarcity	Value Range
400	Probably McGraw-Edison	1950s (?)	1	$ 10-35
401	Probably McGraw-Edison	1950s (?)	1	10-35

Waage Electric Inc. (Kenilworth, NJ and Chicago)

Model #		Approximate Years of Manufacture	Scarcity	Value Range
No #	Low profile pedestal	Late 1920s-Early 1930s	1	Not Established
No #	Skirt legs grill	Late 1920s-Early 1930s	1	Not Established
187-DW8	Commercial Double Waffle dog baker-makes 8 at a time	Late 1920s-Early 1930s (?)	1	Not Established

Waters-Genter Company *"Toastmaster"*
(Name changed to Toastmaster Division of McGraw-Electric in 1937)

Model #		Approximate Years of Manufacture	Scarcity	Price New	Value Range
2A1	Commercial twin	Late 1920s- Mid- 1930s	1		$ 35-75
2B1	Commercial single	1928-1935	1	about $55.00	Not Established
2C1		1929-1935 [1]	3	$ 14.50-22.35 [6]	20-50
2D1		1935-1939 [1]	3	12.50 [2, 3]	20-50
2D2		1939-59 Except war years [1]	4	12.95 [7]- 21.95 [4]-27.15 [5]	10-35
2D3		1953-1962 [1]	3	32.50 [4]	10-25
2E1	Commercial twin	1950s-1960s (?)	1		50-150
2E2	Commercial twin	1930s-1940s (?)	1		75-150
6WBI	Waffle hospitality set including 2D2 iron, walnut veneer tray with inlayed leather, 9" Sprout Green Franciscan Ware bowl, 9 oz. Sprout Green Franciscan Ware pitcher, 10" Chrome ladle. Also referenced as 6F-1		1	16.95 [7]-40.15 [5]	Not Established
201		Late 1940s-Early 1950s	3		20-40
202		Mid-1950s	4		10-35
250		1960s	2		5-25
252 (A thru H)		1971-1997 [1]	5		5-25
254		Mid-Late 1950s	3		5-25
259 (A)		1960s	3		5-25
263		1970s	2		25-25
269 (A or C)		1970s	3		5-20
285		Late 1940s-Early 1950s	2		5-20
442A	Waffle cone maker	1970s	2		10-25
8211D	Commercial single	1950s (?)	1		25-75

[1] Dates courtesy Toastmaster Division, McGraw Electric Corporation.
[2] List price, 1937 & 1938 advertisements , unidentified magazines.
[3] List price, 1937, Brown-Camp Hardware Company, Des Moines Iowa, catalog.
[4] Catalog price, 1953(?), Morely-Murphy Co. Distributors of Hardware & related fines, Green bay WI. *Catalog # 1951.*
[5] Catalog price, 1951, Jensen-Byrd Co. Wholesaler distributors of General Hardware, Spokane, WA. *Catalog # 51.*
[6] Wholesale/retail price, 1929-30(?), Van Camp Hardware & Iron Co., Mfgr's & Wholesalers, Indianapolis, IN. *Catalog # 933.*
[7] Catalog price, 1939, Logan-Gregg Hardware Company, Pittsburgh,Pa. *Catalog # 1831, Fall/winter 1939.*

Wear-Ever

Model #	Approximate Years of Manufacture	Scarcity	Value Range
909	Late 1920s-Early 1930s	1	Not Established

Wells Manufacturing Company

Model #		Approximate Years of Manufacture	Scarcity	Value Range
D-230	Commercial-twin	1960s (?)	1	$ 50-150
L-12	Commercial-twin	1960s-1970s (?)	3	75-150
WB-2	Commercial-twin	1990s	3	50-150
No #	Pedestal unit	Late 1920s	1	20-50

Westinghouse Electric & Mfg. Company *"Every house needs Westinghouse"*

Model #		Approximate Years of Manufacture	Scarcity	Price New	Value Range
CBCA		Early 1930s	3		$ 50-100
CBC-4	Ceramic base	Early 1930s	3	$ 9.95 [3]	50-100
CB-24		Late 1920s	2		15-35
CDC-54		Late 1920s-Early 1930s	2		10-35
CDC-64		Late 1920s-Early 1930s	2		25-50
CD-2		Mid-1920s	2		10-25
CD-4		Mid-1920s	2		10-25

Westinghouse continued:

Model #		Approximate Years of Manufacture	Scarcity	Price New	Value Range
CD-12		Late 1920s	3		$ 10-35
CD-14		Late 1920s-Early 1930s	4		10-35
CD-22		Late 1920s	3		10-35
CD-24		Late 1920s-Early 1930s	3		15-35
CK-4		Mid-Late 1920s	3		20-35
CNC-4		Late 1920s-Early 1930s	3		25-45
CPC-4		Late 1920s-Early 1930s	2		35-50
CR-24		Late 1920s-Early 1930s	3		25-40
CTC-14		Late 1920s-Early 1930s	3		10-35
CT-4		Late 1920s-Early 1930s	3		10-35
G-501		1940s except war yrs	3		15-30
H27781	Canadian	Early 1930s	2		15-35
H32640	Canadian	1930s	2		10-35
H45815	Canadian version of WSA-24-Also marked WFD-2S				
HW-40-2		1960s	2		10-35
SGW-521	Waffle grid set for Model SGWB-521		-		Not Established
SGWB-521		Late1940s-Mid-1950s	3	$ 29.25 [5]-29.95 [4]	20-35
SG-50		1940s except war yrs	3		10-25
SG-501		1940s except war yrs	2		10-25
STC-14		1940s-Early 1950s except war yrs	3		10-25
STC-54		Late 1940s-Early 1950s	3	$ 17.75 [2]	10-25
STW-2	Waffle grids for Model STC-54			2.95 [2]	Not Established
Type "A"		Teens-Early 20's	4		(Without tray) 35-65
WA-2		Early 1920s	4		(Without tray) 35-65
WA-4		Early 1920s	4		40-75
WB-501		Late 1940s-Mid-1950s	3	26.85-35.76 [4]	5-35
WB-503		Late 1940s-Mid-1950s	3	18.25-24.30 [4]	5-25
WB-505		1940s- Mid-50's except war yrs	4		5-25
WB-521		Mid-1950s	3		5-35
WD-4		Mid-Late 1920s	3		15-40
WD-414		Late 1940s	4		15-35
WF(A)-4		Early-Mid-1930s	2		15-35
WF-14 (A)		Mid-Late 1930s	3		10-40
WF-24		Late 1930s-Early 1940s	5		5-35
WF-34	Restyled CBC-64	Late 1930s	2		10-35
WFA-4		Early 1930s	2		15-35
WFD-2S	Canadian Version of WSA-24				
WFT-4		Late 1930s-Early-1940s	2		5-25
WFT-14		Late 1930s-Early 1940s	4		5-25
WK-4(A)	With serving tray	Late 1930s-Early 1940s	2		5-25
WL-414		Late 1930s-Early 1940s	5		5-35
WS-4		Late 1930s-Early 1940s	3		15-35
WS(A)-14		Late 1930s	3		15-35
WSA-4		Late 1930s	3		15-35
WSA-24	Adjust-o-Matic model	Late 1930s-Late 1940s	4	17.95 [1,2]	15-40

[1] List price, January, 1949, *Consumer Reports Magazine*.
[2] Wholesale price, December 27, 1948, Salt Lake Hardware Company Catalog.
[3] Advertised price, December, 1932, *Good Housekeeping Magazine*.
[4] "Fair Trade List" and price "Each", Late 1940s, Moore-Handley Hardware Co. Birmingham, AL; *Catalog S3-6-M*.
[5] Catalog price, 1955, Belknap Hardware & Mfg. Company, Louisville, KY; dealer's catalog.

Winchester Arms Company

Winchester operated retail stores in the 1920s that sold everything from pocket knives to household goods (See "*Winchester Arms Company*" in company histories). Winchester divisions made some of the goods while original equipment manufacturers were contracted to make others. In the 1920s Landers, Frary and Clarke riveted a "Winchester" name plate to the front of its very inexpensive Model E-9533 pedestal waffle iron and designated it "W36" for Winchester. The Landers E-9533 is currently valued at $25-50. Even though the Winchester version is fairly plentiful, Winchester collectors seem to defy all logic and are willing to pay $75-400 for an unexciting waffle iron with a Winchester tag stuck on it. Although none have been detected to date, I would not be surprised to find counterfeits in the future.

Waffle Iron-Toaster Matches

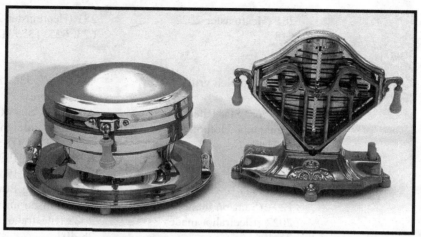

Landers Frary & Clark waffle iron **Model E-7334** with a companion piece, the **Model E-9410** toaster. Each shares identical ivory-colored Catalin handles. The waffle iron is one of several models that match this much sought after toaster. See accompanying list for others.
(Photo courtesy Michael Sheafe www.ToasterCentral.com)

The following is a compilation of toasters which have waffle irons and or grills that were either advertised together by the manufacturer, intended for sale as complimentary pieces, or have certain styling features or body parts such as handles, knobs, or other hardware items in common. This list is not complete and in certain instances may not be entirely accurate since the intent of the manufacturer cannot always be ascertained by examination of the artifacts, advertising, or catalogs.

Manufacturer	Toaster Model(s)	Matching Grill(s) or Waffle Iron(s)
Arvin	4200	3550, 3640
Bersted	60	217, 250, 251, 255, 350, 351
	72	260, 261, 361, 363
Beardsley & Wolcott	"Torrid" (with wood knob handles)	WY010 ("Torrid" York)
Chicago Electric	AEUS	5701
Chicago Flexible Shaft (Sunbeam)	B-5 (Toastwich)	F-3 (Wafflewich)
	T-1 series	D-33
	T-9	W-1
	T-20	W-2
	VT-40	W-2, CG series
Coleman	1	16, 17, 17A
	1C, 2	16, 16C, 17, 17A, 17C, 19A, 19C
Dominion	48 (Hexagonal handles)	67H (version 1)
	48 (round spindle handles)	67H (version 2), 73, 74
	50	64, 65
	364	589, 590
	1105	135, 583, 1301, 1302,
	1115 ("Pop-O-Matic")	1204, 1218, 1311, 1315
Edison Electric	"El Tosto"	"El Grillo"
	119T17	116Y53, 126Y53
	126T33	126Y53, 146Y53
	127T23	116Y53
	129T31	119Y155, 129Y175
	159T33 (Radio Toggle)	119Y155, 129Y175

Manufacturer	Toaster Model(s)	Matching Grill(s) or Waffle Iron(s)
Electrahot	281 (Heatmaster 2022)	281 (Heatmaster 2023)
	618	623, 625, 1355 (Dominion)
Electrex (See United Drug)		
Estate Stove	177	75
Fitzgerald	528 (Sandwich grill)	"Star Rite", 538 "Empress"
	529	538 "Empress"
	"Star" or "Star-Rite" 75000	All "Star""Star-Rite" irons
General Electric	"Centennial Hotpointer"	129Y23 "Raleigh"
	119T48	119Y192, 129Y193
	149T81	129W9, 129Y199, 149Y199
	159T77	119W4, 149Y194, 119WYDES
General Mills	5A	6A (Manning Bowman made)
Heatmaster	1291 (Samson made)	331 (Samson made)
	2022 (Electrahot made)	2023 (Electrahot made)
Kwikway	21-404	28-402
	K-55	K-85
Landers	E 945	E 931
	E 946	E 930, E 3931
	E 947	E 930, E 9305, E 93011
	E 1321 (Coronet)	EA3001, EA3201, EA 3601
	E 3342 (Thermax)	E 3904 (Thermax)
	E 3936	E 930, E 9305, E 93011
	E 3941	E 3914, E 3931
	E 7211	E 7234
	E 7212	E 7935
	E 7542	E 7533, E 7534
	E 7812 (Old English)	E 9314, E 9324, E 9914
	E 7822 (Moderne)	E 7704, E 7707
	E 7912	E 7935
	E 8612 (Chevalier)	E 8360
	E 9410	E 7224, E 7234, E 7344, E 7812
	E 9411	E 7224, E 7234, E 7344, E 7812
	E 95412	E 9914
	E 9574	E 7542
Lindeman & Hoverson	205	317
Majestic Electric	T-6974 (Type 66)	W-11508
Manning-Bowman	K639	1700X
	K1228	K1617
	K1232	K1601
	60	40
	82, 83	1656, 2182-A
	108	1646
	116	423, 451, 2521
	1225	1605
National Stamping & Electric	230	156
Nelson	94	250
Pacific Electric (See Edison Electric)		
Perfection Electric	4-7-A (Excelsior)	No # (Excelsior)
Porcelier	All toaster models have matching grills and waffle irons	

Manufacturer	Toaster Model(s)	Matching Grill(s) or Waffle Iron(s)
Precision Mfg.	No # "Rainbow"	80W "Rainbow"
Proctor & Swartz	1444,	1516
	1471	1516
Robeson Rochester	13250	12390, 250R
	13300, 13340	12270, 12310
	E 6410	12210, 12270
Rock Island	17-A	88-A
Russell Electric	No # "Hold Heet"	No # "Hold Heet"
Ruttenber	67	77
Samson	297	233, 234, 379
	5052 (or 25)	331
	5219 (Ward)	4960, 4961 (Both Ward)
	5217 (Ward)	5214, 5215, 5226 (All Ward)
	5353	5382 (or 40)
Son-Chief	Speedmaster Series 680	975
	622	9180, 9190
Stern-Brown (Superstar)	45 ("M" in doors)	Same motif on two unnumbered waffle irons, 210 combo unit
Sunbeam (See Chicago Flexible Shaft)		
Superior Electric	66, 66-4	706, 708, 755
	77	777
	333	606, 707
	444	105, 702
Toastwell (See also Utility Electric)	740	910, 920, 930, 960, 965, 970
	791, 794, 795	830, 911, 931, 961, 971
Toastmaster (See Waters-Genter)		
Thomas A. Edison	"Edicraft" 2 slice	"Edicraft" Grill, Waffle iron
Waters-Genter	1A2, 1A3, 1A4, 1B2, 1B3, 1B5	2C1
	1A4, 1B5, 1B6, 1B7, 1B8, 1B9	2D1
	1A5, 1B10,1B11, 1B12, 1B14	2D2
	1A6, 1B16, 1C4	2D3, 250, 259
	104	250, 254, 259
Westinghouse	WEP	"Type A"
	TDC-4	CBC-4
	TTC-74	CDC-64
	TT-3	WA-2
United Drug (made by Beardsley & Walcott)	X775	X233, X534
Utility Electric	754, 791, 795, 3359	830

232

Working with Waffle Irons

Many people have the misconception that making waffles is a lot of work and as much fun and mess as changing the oil in the family car. The folks that make those little frozen waffles sure hope you keep thinking that way, but let me try to convince you otherwise. In researching for this book my wife and I "test drove" more than 280 different waffle irons, and in the process baked at least 1500 waffles. No we didn't eat them all. The neighbors and back yard wildlife helped. After all of that baking, believe it or not, we both still enjoy making waffles. If it was hard work, we would have quit 1495 waffles ago. Like any skill however, waffle making takes a little experience, and there are a few tricks and techniques we've learned and would like to share, that makes cooking them easy, fun, and nearly fool-proof.

The Tricks of the Trade

Selecting a Waffle Iron or...
How to buy a pre-owned waffle iron without getting burned.

Making good waffles with the least amount of effort requires a decent waffle iron but not necessarily a new one. To me, the new models are not only plain looking but just down right boring. Compared to a nice pre-owned vintage model most are also expensive. Don't be fooled by the non-stick Teflon myth. Teflon isn't all it's cracked up to be. Waffles can and do stick to it. On the other hand, many vintage pre-Teflon era waffle irons are not only attractive but work as well as, or better than, their newer counterparts. Made during a time when new appliances were an expensive luxury, most were built to last for generations, and many have. Often they're available at very reasonable prices in secondhand stores, flea markets, antique stores, and from Internet auction sites. However, not all waffle irons were created equal. In fact, my wife and I encountered a few models that wouldn't allow us to make a good waffle, no matter how hard we tried. Fortunately, they're the rare exception. Most irons, new or antique, work quite well. You can find a general evaluation of a company's products at the end of most of the company biographies. The following is a list of considerations to ponder before searching for that "perfect," usable, "old fashioned" waffle iron.

1. Avoid purchasing any iron that is excessively greasy. There are plenty of clean examples available. Darkened well-seasoned grids are fine, but an iron covered with burned-on grease is a sure sign that the iron has been abused and will need to be rewired.

The lard witch strikes again!

2. Be certain both grids heat before making any purchase and check for missing or damaged handles and feet. Ask for a significant discount if testing isn't possible. Repairing a non-functioning iron requires special materials and expertise and can be costly. The author has found that the vast majority of clean irons will be in good working order.

3. Purchase an iron missing its cord only if it's equipped with round power cord prongs. Replacement cords are readily available for these in most hardware stores, but cords for those with odd-shaped prongs are nearly impossible to find.

Oddball Armstrong connector

4. Models made between the mid-1920s and the early 1950s are generally of better quality, more substantial, and more stylish than "modern" ones. Pedestal model bases stay cooler and usually catch overflows better than many low-profile types.

Stay cool base pedestal model

5. Combination models intended as grills and waffle irons often don't work as well as models designed for a single purpose. Unless you're collecting irons for the sake of collecting, avoid the rare, odd, or so called "off" brands.

6. Try to select an iron with a large easy-to-grip stay-cool lid handle. Those that stick out from the lid are usually best. Avoid very early Westinghouse models with pull-down-to-open handles. It was a design nice to look at but terrible to use.

Hot base low profile model

7. Models that make round waffles are easier to fill with batter than square or rectangular models and usually, but not always, cook more evenly.

8. "Twin" models that make smaller party or desert-size waffles, require more manipulating per amount of waffle produced and with more nooks and crannies, are harder to keep clean. However, some make nice freezable waffles that will fit in a toaster for re-heating.

Automatic twin model

9. Choose an automatic model only if it appears to be lightly used or has been professionally rebuilt and recalibrated. Heavily-used vintage thermostats may be unreliable and are often unserviceable.

10. Non-automatic models that make a standard 7 inch round waffle, should have heating elements rated at 600 watts or greater. Automatic models should be rated for at least 700 watts. Ratings are usually stamped on the bottom plate.

Preparing The Iron

After procuring an iron in good working condition, it must be "seasoned" only once, before using it. To do this, you need the following items…

No-stick cooking spray or unsalted cooking oil. **Do not use butter or margarine!**
A small basting brush. (An inexpensive 1 inch natural bristle paint brush works great.)
A small bowl.

Spray or pour about two tablespoons of cooking oil into the bowl. While the iron is cold, brush a small amount of oil from the bowl sparingly onto all areas of the cooking grids. **NEVER SPRAY THE OIL DIRECTLY ON THE IRON!** Doing so creates a mess. Unless a sticking problem occurs at some point, **THERE IS NO NEED TO REGREASE (SEASON) THE IRON EVER AGAIN.** Let the iron heat to operating temperature, which occurs when the grease begins to smoke.

Cooking

Prepare a waffle recipe of your choice. There are a number of tried and proven recipes listed elsewhere. I suggest for your first venture the *Quick and Easy Waffles* recipe. Shortly before you're ready to cook, turn on the waffle iron. If yours is a non-automatic model, time the following procedure for future reference. If it's an automatic model, set the temperature control at the mid-point. Allow the iron to heat for about five minutes, watching closely for the oil on the grids to begin smoking. It's wise to lift the lid briefly from time to time to best observe this. **No matter what any indicators, meters, lights or dials on the iron may show, a modest amount of smoke indicates that the iron has reached the correct baking temperature.** If you're working with an automatic model, when smoke is first noted, slowly adjust the temperature control downward until the heating elements just shut off. A jeweled viewing window in the lid or indicator light in the base can be used to monitor this. Note the position of the control for future reference. This setting will give a medium dark waffle with most recipes. If the iron shuts off before smoke appears, move the temperature control to a darker setting. Once you have the control set for the desired operating temperature you're ready to cook your first waffle.

Pour enough batter to cover about 3/4th of the bottom grid. Close the lid immediately and don't disturb it until you see little or no steam emanating from the iron. This normally takes from two to three minutes, but depends on the recipe and the iron. When you believe cooking is complete, carefully lift the lid and remove the waffle. If the lid doesn't open easily, the waffle may not be cooked sufficiently, in which case, allow a little more cooking time. You may wish to note how long it takes to bake to the degree of doneness desired.

Immediately pour more batter onto the grid and close the lid. **Any waffle iron, automatic or not, when hot, should be kept full.** Most non-automatic irons are self-regulating but should be monitored closely to avoid overheating which will destroy the seasoning. A short cooking cycle of less than about two minutes is an indication that the grids have become too hot. Unplug the cord from the wall outlet for a short time to allow the iron to cool slightly. With automatic models, simply adjust the temperature control to a lighter setting.

Clean Up and Storage

Unplug the iron when finished and let it cool with the lid open to preserve the seasoning. After it has cooled, wipe any spills with a damp cloth. Do not wash the grids. A brown stain to the grids is normal and desirable. A light wipe down or brushing with a stiff plastic or wire brush will suffice. Never immerse a waffle iron in water. Store your iron in a dry place with a few sheets of paper towel placed between the grids to absorb any greasy residue left from the cooking process.

Oooops. A Sunday morning Mt. Vesuvius. It happens. Don't panic. Just keep baking. By the end of the baking session much of the spillover will have baked firmly and will be easy to remove (and nibble on). After the iron cools use a damp cloth or paper towels to clean off the rest.

Waffle Recipes

Waffles have been baked for at least several hundred years, and because of their longevity, a great number of recipes have been developed for them. Below is a sampling of some interesting variations taken from antique recipe books. All work well and taste great. Before you begin, you may wish to read the following few tips for working with waffle recipes.

> Most pre-made baking mixes are no more than flour, baking soda, powdered milk and salt with a little hydrogenated soybean oil thrown in for good measure. Working from scratch is much less expensive and allows a great deal more control over the proportions of key ingredients.

> With only a few exceptions, waffle batters should be of a medium-thick pouring consistency with a certain amount of body. Too thick produces a tough doughy waffle, too runny and the waffle will be imperfect in shape. To thicken a batter, add flower; to thin, add milk.

> Waffles are not intended to be a health food. Tinkering too much with certain ingredients will create cooking disappointments. Reducing the oil for example may cause sticking problems. Reducing sugar or using very low fat milk or egg substitutes, will create less browning and a bland tasting waffle. However, some old recipes have a great deal of room for improvement in the health department. Experiment away!

> Adding extracts such as Vanilla, Maple, Orange, Cherry, Pecan, Walnut, etc. can make some very interesting and tasty variations. Start with ½ teaspoon.

> Adding crushed nuts to a recipe is an excellent variation, but be cautious when adding certain fruits. Sticking problems may occur. Sprinkling blueberries or bananas over finished waffles is much less messy and just as tasty.

> A recurring sticking problem with a particular recipe may indicate that there is not enough shortening in the recipe. Also be certain the iron is hot enough.

> If waffles from a certain recipe come out overcooked on the surface and underdone inside, reduce the heat of the iron and cook each waffle longer. It should take 2-3 minutes per waffle.

> If the batter of a certain recipe tends to overflow the iron consistently, reduce the baking soda. If the batter doesn't fill the grids consistently add more soda.

> If batter overflows from the iron, wait until you're finished baking and the iron is cool before cleaning up. You won't burn yourself and chances are the spilled batter will bake solid and fall right off the iron rather than being smeared around.

> To make a more crispy brown waffle add more sugar to the recipe, but be careful. Too much sugar will sticking or burning.

Now, heat up your "*Chrome on the Range*," pick a recipe, watch out for the steam and the hot parts, and go at it with gusto!! Have fun and happy eating!

Quick and Easy Waffles

(From *The Practical Cook Book* by Florence Austin Chase-1915)

1¾ cups all-purpose flour
1 teaspoons baking powder
1 teaspoon baking soda
2 teaspoons sugar
½ teaspoon salt

2 cups milk
2 eggs well beaten
1/3 cup vegetable oil

In medium bowl with wire whisk mix dry ingredients. In large bowl mix all wet ingredients. Gradually add dry mixture, beating until well blended. Batter should be about the same consistency as a medium-thick pancake batter. Add more flower to thicken or more milk to thin.

Modifying the quick and easy recipe...

Pecan: Prepare as above but also add 1 cup coarsely chopped pecans. Stir batter each time before pouring to distribute pecans

Buttermilk: Prepare as above but use 2 cups buttermilk instead of whole milk.

Jazzy Waffles: Add 1 teaspoon of vanilla and or orange, pecan, walnut, cherry, or maple extract to any of the above recipes

Wheat Germ: Sprinkle 1 or 2 teaspoons wheat germ over the batter immediately after pouring it onto the iron.

Berry: As soon as the basic mix is poured, sprinkle 2 tablespoons blueberries over batter, then bake (make certain iron is well seasoned since fresh fruit can stick and burn).

Cheese: Stir ½ cup shredded cheddar cheese into batter (make certain the iron is well seasoned). Bake and serve topped with creamed vegetables, meat, poultry, or seafood.

Corn: Stir 1 cup of drained canned whole-kernel corn into the batter. Serve topped with creamed ham or chicken or syrup.

Curry: Stir ½ teaspoon curry powder into the batter. Bake and serve topped with creamed poultry or shrimp.

Coconut: Stir 1 cup of chopped, flaked coconut into batter.

Healthy Waffles: Substitute unbleached flour, 2% milk, egg substitute, safflower oil but don't expect the rich flavor of the original recipe.

1884 Rice Waffles   (From *Practical Housekeeping* by Mrs. S.C. Lee, Baltimore, MD-1884.)

4 cups flour	1 quart of milk (2% also works)
3 cups cooked rice (cold)	5 eggs (can use egg substitute)
½ teaspoon salt	¼ pound butter or margarine

Melt butter or margarine and mix with cold rice. Add flour and salt to the rice. Separate eggs. Stir egg yolks into the milk . Add the egg/milk mixture to the dry ingredients. Beat egg whites until stiff. Add egg whites to batter and beat in vigorously. Bake waffles immediately.
These waffles are dense, chewy and taste rich. They also freeze very nicely. If you don't want so many at once, half the recipe works well.

"Superior Rice Waffles"   (From *Housekeeping in Old Virginia* by Marion Tyree-1879.)

1 quart flour	3 eggs
1 cup boiled rice beaten into the flour	Buttermilk (enough to make thick batter)
1 teaspoon baking soda	

"Make into a batter with buttermilk. Bake quickly in waffle irons. Batter made as above and baked on griddle makes excellent breakfast cakes."

238

Yeast Waffles

(From *Housekeeping in Old Virginia* by Marion Tyree-1879)

1 quart flour
3 tablespoons yeast
2 teaspoons salt

1½ pints "new" (whole) milk
6 eggs beaten lightly

"Set to rise at night, and stir with a spoon, in the morning, just before baking. When you want them for tea, make them up in the morning, in winter, or directly after dinner, in summer."

Sour Milk Waffles

(From *Housekeeping in Old Virginia* by Marion Tynee-1879)

1 cups (?) flour
½ teaspoon salt
1 teaspoon sugar
½ teaspoon baking soda

1 cup sour milk
2 eggs, separated
¼ cup melted shortening

"Sift flour, measure and sift with salt and baking soda. Beat egg yolks until light and foamy. Add sugar and shortening. Mix well. Add milk alternately with sifted dry ingredients to egg mixture. Fold in stiffly beaten egg whites. Bake in hot waffle iron."

Pound Cake Waffles

(A wonderful desert with powdered sugar)

1¼ cups flour
1 cup, fine granulated sugar
1 teaspoon baking powder
½ teaspoon salt

5 eggs separated
¾ cup butter
1 teaspoon vanilla and/or lemon flavoring

Beat the butter and sugar to a cream; add the well-beaten yolks of the eggs. Sift the flour, salt, and baking powder together and add to egg sugar butter mixture. Put in the flavoring and beat the batter thoroughly. At the last moment fold in the whites of the eggs beaten to a stiff froth, and cook as ordinary waffles.
A word of warning This batter will be stiff, will bake fast and overflow the iron if even a little too much is used. However, the taste is worth the potential mess.

Raised Waffles

(A recipe for someone with lots of spare time)

2 cups, sifted flour
2 tablespoons sugar
1 teaspoon salt
1 package active dry yeast

1¾ cup lukewarm milk (scald then cool)
¼ cup warm water (110-115 degrees)
3 eggs
¼ cup soft butter

In mixing bowl, dissolve yeast in warm water. Add milk, sugar, and salt. Beat in rest of ingredients with rotary beater. Cover with damp cloth. Let rise in warm place (85 degrees) until double, about 1½ hours. (if kitchen is cool, place dough on a rack over a bowl of hot water and cover completely with a towel.) Stir down. Cover and set in refrigerator. overnight or until ready to use. Stir down again when ready to use. Pour into hot waffle iron. Bake until brown and crisp.

Cereal Waffles   (From *Searchlight Recipe Book* by Ida Miglianio-1931)

1 cup flour	1 egg, well beaten
1 tablespoon sugar	4 tablespoons melted shortening (or oil)
1 teaspoon salt	1 cup milk
2 teaspoons baking powder	½ cup chopped raisins
1 cup uncooked granular cereal	

Sift flour, measure and sift with sugar, salt and baking powder. Add cereal and combine with egg, shortening, milk and raisins.

Chocolate Waffles   (From *Searchlight Recipe Book* by Ida Miglianio-1931)

1½ cups cake flour	½ cup milk
1 cup sugar	2 eggs, separated
2 teaspoons baking powder	½ cup shortening
¼ teaspoon salt	2 squares chocolate
½ teaspoon vanilla flavoring (coconut extract is good as well)	

Cream shortening and sugar. Add well-beaten egg yolks. Melt chocolate over hot water and add to creamed shortening and sugar mixture. Mix thoroughly. Measure flour, and sift with baking powder and salt; add alternately with milk to chocolate mixture. Add vanilla. Fold in stiffly-beaten egg whites. Bake in hot waffle iron. Serve with syrup, whipped cream, ice cream, or powdered sugar.   (Courtesy of Mrs. Lula Larson, Washburn, North Dakota)

Shaker Blueberry Waffles   (From *Searchlight Recipe Book* by Ida Migliano-1931)

1 cup flour	1 cup plain yogurt
1 cup rolled oats	2 eggs, well beaten
½ cup cornmeal	¾ cup vegetable oil
4½ teaspoons baking powder	1½ cups buttermilk
¼ teaspoon salt	
1 cup fresh blueberries (or well-drained frozen blueberries, thawed)	

Combine flour, oats, cornmeal, baking powder, and salt. In separate bowl combine yogurt, eggs, vegetable oil, and buttermilk. Stir flour mixture gradually into liquid mixture. Beat until thoroughly mixed. Fold in blueberries.

The following are from *All About Home Baking* courtesy the General Foods Corporation, 1933.

Every Day Waffles

2 cups sifted Swans Down Cake flour	1 cup milk
2 teaspoons Calumet Baking Powder	3 egg yolks, well beaten
½ teaspoon salt	3 egg whites, stiffly beaten
	4 tablespoons melted butter

Sift flour; measure, add baking powder and salt and sift again. Combine egg yolks and milk. Add to flour, beating until smooth. Add butter. Fold in egg whites. Bake in a hot waffle iron. Serve with Log Cabin Syrup or creamed chicken or mushrooms.

Bacon Waffles

Use prior "Every Day Waffles" recipe. Sprinkle batter for each waffle with diced uncooked bacon before closing the iron. Serve hot with scrambled eggs or cut into strips as accompaniment for salad.

Cornmeal and Blueberry Waffles

2/3 cup flour
1/3 cup cornmeal
2 teaspoons baking powder
1 teaspoon sugar
1/3 teaspoon salt

2/3 cup milk
2 egg yolks beaten until light
2 egg whites beaten stiff
2 tablespoons melted shortening
1 cup blueberries

Sift flour, cornmeal, baking powder, salt, and sugar together. Add milk, beaten egg yokes, shortening, and blueberries. Fold in the egg whites.

Sausage Waffles

1 cup flour
2 teaspoons baking powder
1 teaspoon sugar
1/3 teaspoon salt
½ cup sausage meat cut into small pieces

2/3 cup milk
2 egg yokes beaten light
2 egg whites beaten stiff
2 tablespoons melted shortening

Sift flour, baking powder, sugar, and salt together. Add milk and egg yokes. Add sausage meat separated into small pieces or sprinkle on each waffle when it is poured into the waffle iron. Fold in egg whites.

Santa Fe Waffles

1 cup flour
1 cup Quaker Oat Bran hot cereal
2 tablespoons sugar
½ teaspoon baking soda
½ teaspoon baking powder
½ teaspoon salt

1¼ cup skim milk
2/3 cup salsa
3 tablespoons vegetable oil
2 egg whites beaten to soft peaks

Beat egg whites until soft peaks form. Combine dry ingredients and mix well. Whisk milk, oil, and salsa until well blended. Add to dry ingredients mixing *just until moistened*. Do not over-mix. Fold egg whites into batter.

Potato Waffles   (From 1910 Wagner cast iron waffle iron instruction booklet.)

1 cup flour
2 teaspoons baking powder
1 teaspoon salt

1 cup milk
1 tablespoon melted butter
2 cups grated boiled potatoes

The recipe does not instruct as to how to combine ingredients. Good luck on this one.

Trivia

While researching this book I accumulated a considerable amount of little-known facts and information, i.e. trivia. I just couldn't throw it away. I thought instead that I'd share it with the reader. Now's your chance to amaze and astound friends and relatives with facts about appliances totally irrelevant to life as we know it. Quote a few of these out of context very earnestly to confuse an annoying boss or co-worker. After a few occurrences, they'll begin to question your sanity and leave you alone. This may work equally well at dinner parties with obnoxious blowhards or drunks.

> The term 'Art Deco' refers to a mix of styles from the 1920s and 1930s and was derived from *"Exposition Internationale des **Arts Decoratifs** Industrielset Modernes."* a decorative arts exhibit held in Paris in 1925. It was initially an architectural style used in building designs, but was later carried over into building fixtures and furnishings, and finally appearing on nearly every conceivable object. The use of the term 'art deco' did not originate in the 1920s however, but came into being in the 1960s, when the style made a revival. During its heyday it was referred to as the *Style Moderne*.

> Gadrooning, a French term, is the correct one for the fancy designs pressed into the edges of lids and bases of certain waffle iron models.

> Fretwork is the punched-out designs found on certain early waffle iron pedestals. These cutouts served not only as decoration but acted as cooling vents for the base.

> In the early 1940s, Jean Otis Reinecke, an Illinois farmer-turned-artist, designed those toasters with the three-loop pattern stamped on their sides. The purpose of the design was both decorative and to take attention away from scratches or dings often sustained later by the chrome surface.

> In 1905 William Hoskins, a high school drop out, was co-inventor of the Nichrome heat producing wire that is still used in most modern heat generating appliances. He is also credited by some with inventing the first electric bread toaster in 1907. Few people realize however that Hoskins also formulated the ingredients for Billiard chalk used by pool players all over the world on the tips of cue sticks.

> Before 1930, electric kitchen appliances nearly always came with six to eight foot power cords, a length necessary in those days due to the lack of convenient power outlets in many kitchens. Today a three-foot cord is the norm.

> In the teens and 1920s, many older homes retrofitted for electricity, often ended up with only one or two light sockets per room but no wall outlets. As a consequence, the earliest small electric appliances came with an adapter that allowed the power cord to be screwed into a light socket. In the housewares trade these were referred to as "lamp socket" appliances.

> Standards for appliance plugs and sockets were proposed in 1917, but it took until 1931 before all manufacturers adopted these standards to their electrical products.

> Until the 1930s, some power companies offered two electric rates depending on the purpose for which the electricity was used. Power consumed for cooking was metered separately and at a lower rate than that used for lighting. Some early electric ranges were advertised as having extra outlets from which the frugal homemaker could power her vacuum cleaner, hair curler, iron, fan, or sewing machine using the cheaper electricity.

> Until the 1950s most power cords were covered with cotton, rayon, or silk. The paired conductors in cords intended for heat generating appliances like toasters, waffle irons, laundry irons, hot plates, hair curlers, and space heaters were insulated with asbestos and cotton-wrapped rubber. Modern cords contain fiberglass or Teflon in place of the asbestos.

> By the early 1930s, waffle irons were one of the hottest selling small appliances (pun intended). In 1931, the household goods maker Landers, Frary and Clark alone offered 18 different waffle iron models.

> Old-fashioned non-electric stovetop waffle irons of the cast iron variety were still being produced in significant numbers well into the late 1930s, even though electric powered models had been around for almost two decades. Farm and ranch families liked waffles as much as city dwellers, but in 1935, only 10% of the 5 million U.S. farms had electricity. Roosevelt's Rural Electrification Administration (REA) was organized in 1936, and by 1941, had electrified 2,250,000 farms. However, it took until 1950 to reach the 90% mark and surprisingly, the country wasn't considered fully electrified until 1955.

> In older waffle irons a small depression is often molded into the top surface of each dimple. Although decorative, these depressions were put there to compensate for metal shrinkage common in the early gravity-fed die casting process. Without the depressions the sides of each dimple tended to become concave as the metal cooled. Modern die casting techniques inject molten metal into molds under pressure, creating a more dense, uniform casting and reducing the shrinkage problem.

> Approximately 25% of pre-1940 waffle irons found by the author had white paint splatters on their handles. "Sanitary" white enamel was the preferred color for kitchens from the teens through the 1930s. Apparently homeowners, while repainting their kitchens, often failed to move their appliances out of range of their splatter generating painting implements.

> Modern automatic waffle irons operate at a temperature of approximately 400 degrees at the medium setting. The typical adjustment range of the thermostat is about plus or minus 50 degrees from the medium setting.

> Henry F. Phillips received patents in 1936 for his new kind of screw and screwdriver. However, Phillips' screw didn't catch on for consumer goods until after World War II. So if you find anything held together with factory installed Phillips screws you can be fairly certain it was made after 1945.

> Harry Brearley, a British metallurgist working in 1913 in a research laboratory in Sheffield, England, was looking for wear-resistant steel for gun barrels. By mixing chromium with iron, he created a steel that didn't work well for gun barrels but was ideal for making knife blades that didn't rust, tarnish or stain. Brearley called his new alloy "Rustless" steel. An American company later copyrighted the term "Stainless" steel for it.

> Most early small appliances such as waffle irons had body shells formed from sheet brass. Before the 1920s, metal stamping technology had not advanced sufficiently for manufacturers to make complex or deep draw stampings using much less ductile steels. Henry Ford pioneered modern steel stamping technology and perfected the deep drawing of tough stainless steels in the late 1920s. The radiator shell of the 1930 Model A Ford was his first major success with deep drawn stainless steel.

> "Stainless" steel was always too expensive, too difficult to form and a bit too much overkill in the rust prevention department to be used in small household appliances. Plated steel was inexpensive and durable enough for most housewares. Only appliances intended for restaurant or other commercial applications were made of "Stainless" steel.

> Chrome plating on appliances was first offered by manufacturers in the mid 1920s, as a maintenance-free alternative to the standard nickel plating, which scratched easily and had a tendency to tarnish. Chrome generally added 10% or more to the price of the article. Unfortunately for the purchaser, early chrome plating was prone to peeling, blistering, and corrosion. Chrome plating technology was not perfected until the mid-1930s.

> Before steel can be chrome plated it must be nickel-plated and before it's nickel-plated it's usually copper plated. In other words all things steel that are chrome plated are nickel plated, but everything nickel plated isn't necessarily chrome plated.

> The number one cause for waffles to stick in a waffle iron is an iron that hasn't been allowed to reach the correct operating temperature. The second most likely cause of sticking is a recipe lacking sufficient shortening. The third cause is an impatient cook who can't resist peeking before the waffle is sufficiently cooked.

> The average cost of a waffle iron in 1950 was $17.00 (a whopping $115.00 in today's currency). Even at these prices, by 1956, one third of all electrified households had a waffle iron.

> In the 1930s and 1940s, waffle irons were considered the wedding gift of choice, but by the 1950s, more waffle irons were purchased in December for Christmas presents than any other month. For some reason, April was the worst month for waffle iron sales.

> Al Bersted, a pioneer in the appliance industry estimated that at one time or another, over 250 companies in the US produced appliances. Today they number less than two dozen.

> The peak year for waffle iron production in the US, was 1946. An incredible 3½ million units were manufactured that year to meet pent up demand created by the lack of production during the war years of 1942 through 1945. Yearly production after 1946 dropped steadily to current levels, which are currently below 250,000 units annually.

And finally, the ultimate trivia fact...

> According to an Edison Electric Appliance Company advertisement, which appeared in the February 1930 issue of *Ladies Home Journal*, **FEBRUARY IS NATIONAL WAFFLE MONTH. LET'S CELEBRATE!**

Bibliography

A History of Cleveland Ohio, Volume III, Chicago-Cleveland, The S.J. Clarke Publishing Company, 1910.

Adams, Jeannette T. *Electricity & Electrical Appliances Handbook*, New York, NY: Arco Publishing Company, 1976.

Artman, E. Townsend, *Toasters 1909-1960*, Atglen, PA: Schiffer Publishing Company, 1996.

Anzovin, Steven, Joseph Nathan Kane, Janet Podell, *Famous First Facts*, 5th Edition. New York, NY: H.W. Wilson Company, 1997.

Celehar, Jane H. *Kitchens and Gadgets 1920-1950*, Radnor, PA: Wallace-Homestead Book Company, 1985.

Cullen, John, Alexandra Villard de Borchgrave, *Villard, The Life and Times of an American Titan*, Doubleday Publishing Company, 2001.

Cunningham, Jo, *The Collector's Encyclopedia of American Dinnerware*, Paducah, KY: Schroeder Publishing Company, 1982.

Dummer, G.A.W. editor, *Timetable of Technology*, Hearst Books, 1982

Du Vall, Nell, *Domestic Technology*, Boston: G.K. Hall & Company,1988.

Everyday Inventions, New York, NY: Hooper & Merideth, 1976.

Franklin, Linda Campbell, *300 Years of Housekeeping Collectibles*, Florence, AL: Books Americana, 1992.

Fredgant, Don, *Electrical Collectibles*, San Luis Obispo, CA: Padre Productions,1981; Iola, WI: Krause Publications, 1999.

Friday, Franklin, Ronald F.White, Ph.D., *A Walk Through The Park*, Louisville, KY: Elfun Historical Society,1987.

Gorowitz, Bernard, ed. *The General Electric Story,1876-1986*, Schenectady, NY: Hall of History Foundation, 1986.

Greguire, Helen, *Collector's Guide to Toasters & Accessories*, Paducah, KY: Schroeder Publishing Company, 1997.

Grindberg, Susan E. *Collector's Guide To Porcelier China*, Paducah, KY: Schroeder Publishing Company, 1996.

Lehner, Lois, *Complete Book of American Kitchen and Dinner Wares*, Des Moines, IO: Wallace-Homestead Book Company, 1980.

Katz, Sylvia, *Plastics, Common Objects, Classic Designs*, New York, NY: Harry N. Abrams Inc. 1984.

Kelley, Fred C. *Seventy-Five Years of Hibbard Hardware: The Story of Hibbard, Spencer, Bartlett & Co.*, Chicago, IL: Hibbard, Spencer, Bartlett & Company, 1930.

Lehner, Lois, *Lehner's Encyclopedia of U.S. Marks on Pottery, Porcelain & Clay*, Paducah, KY: Collector Books, 1988.

Lifshey, Earl, *The Housewares Story*, Chicago: The National Housewares Manufacturers Association, 1973.

Lincoln, E.S.,Paul C.Smith, *The Electric Home: A Standard Ready Reference Book*, New York, NY: The Electric Home Publishing Company, 1936.

Long, Jennifer Harvey, *Larouse Gastronomique, World's Greatest Culinary Encyclopedia*, New York, NY: Crown Publishing Company, 1990.

Mariani, John F. *The Dictionary of American Food & Drink*, New York, NY: Hearst Books, 1994.

Matranga, Victoria Kasuba, *America At Home: A Celebration of Twentieth Century Housewares*, Rosemont, IL: National Housewares Manufacturers Association, 1997.

Meikle, Jeffrey L. *Twentieth Century Limited: Industrial Design in America 1925-1939*, Philadelphia: Temple University Press, 1979.

Miller, C. L. *Jewel Tea Company, Its history and Products*, Atglen, PA: Schiffer Publishing Company, 1995.

Morris, Robinson, Kroll, *American Dreams- One Hundred Years of Business Ideas and Innovation from The Wall Street Journal*, New York, NY: Lightbulb Press Inc., 1990.

Plante, Ellen M. *Kitchen Collectibles: An Illustrated Price Guide*, New York, NY: 1991.

Plante, Ellen M. *The American Kitchen, -1700 To The Present*, New York, NY: Facts On File Inc. 1995.

Rubin, Susan Goldman, *Toasters Toilets and Telephones: The How and Why of Everyday Objects*, Orlando, FL: Browndeer Press, Harcourt Brace and Company, 1998.

Smith, David G. *The Book of Griswold & Wagner*, Atglen, PA: Schiffer Publishing Company, 1999.

Stone, Orra L. *History of Massachusetts Industries: Their Inception, Growth and Success*, Boston, MA: The S.J. Clarke Publishing Company, 1930.

Thompson, Frances, *Antiques From The Country Kitchen*, Lombard, IL: Wallace-Homestead Book Company, 1985.

Toasters and Small Kitchen Appliances, A Price Guide, Gas City, IN: L-W Book Sales, 1995.

Travers, Bridget, editor, *World of Invention*, Detroit: Gale Research Inc.,1994.

Weber, Eva, *American Art Deco*, Greenwich, CT: Dorset Press, Brompton Books Corporation, 1985.

Whytmyer, Kenn, Margaret Whytmyer, *The Collector's Encyclopedia of Hall China*, Second Edition. Paducah, KY: Schroeder Publishing Company, 1994.

World Almanac Book of Inventions, New York, NY: New York World Almanac, 1998.

Bibliography continued:

Catalogs, Directories, Magazines, Newspapers, Pamphlets, Periodicals

American Cookery, Volume 21, No. 1 June-July, 1926,
The Boston Cooking School Magazine Company, Boston, MA.

American Heritage of Invention & Technology, Volume 17, No. 2, Fall 2001,
Forbes Inc. NYC, NY.

Better Homes & Gardens, Volume 26, No.10, (June 1948),
Meredith Publishing Company
1714 Locust Street
Des Moines 3, Iowa

Chicago Tribune, "WPB Permits Iron Output by Flexible Shaft," June 16, 1944

Cleveland Ohio City Directory, Years 1912-13, 1920-21, 1930, 1935,
The Cleveland Directory Company
Cleveland, Ohio.

Electrical Merchandising   Volume 84, No.1, (January 1952)
Volume 85, No.1, (January 1953)
Volume 88, No.1, (January 1956)
Volume 92, No.1, (January 1960)

Gage Electrical Encyclopedia, Number 10, (February 1931),
The Gage Publishing Company Inc.
461 Eighth Avenue, New York, NY

Gage Encyclopedia of Oil Burners, Electric Irons, Electric Ranges, Cloths Washers, Vacuum Cleaners, Electric Refrigerators, Radio Receiving Sets,
The Gage Publishing Company Inc. (1927),
461 Eighth Avenue New York, NY

Good Housekeeping Magazine, (March 1948),
Hearst Magazines Inc.
57th St. & 8th Avenue
New York 19, NY

Holiday Catalog, 1940-41,
Pittsburgh Electric Supply Company
6375 Penn Avenue
Pittsburgh PA

Industrial Education Magazine, Volume 34, No.12 , (June 1933),
Editors, William T. Bawden, Charles A. Bennett

Manning-Bowmann Electric Appliances Catalog No. C737, 1937,
Manning-Bowmann and Company
Meriden, Connecticut

Official Programme of Philadelphia's Second Electrical Exhibit
February 13th-25th, 1911 First Regiment Armory
Broad & Callowhill Streets, Philadelphia
Electrical Exhibits Company Ltd.
Baker Building, Philadelphia

Representative Clevelanders, 1927,
The Cleveland Topics Company
Cleveland, Ohio

Sanborn Fire Insurance Map, 1922, Vol. 11, Sheet 86,
Chicago, Ill.

Studies of Equipment for Electrical Cooking,
Lucile Harris, Master of Science Thesis, 1928,
Iowa State College, Ames, Iowa

The Saturday Evening Toast, Summer & Fall 2002 Issues,
Newsletter of The Toaster Collector Association,
3929 Kenmore Road
Berkley, Michigan 48072

Technology and Culture Magazine, January 1976, April 1983, July 1986

Welcome to the Coleman Museum (Museum booklet), 1980,
The Coleman Company Inc.
PO Box 1762
Wichita, Kansas 67201

Who's Who in Chicago and Vicinity, 1931 & 1936,
The A.N. Marquis Company
Chicago, Ill.

Westcenter Chicagoan, October 22, 1921,
Westcenter Commercial Association of Chicago
3131 Madison Street
Chicago, Ill.

Woman's Home Companion, Volume LVII, No.10, (October 1930),
The Crowell Publishing Company
250 Park Avenue
New York, NY

Index

Printed in the United States
By Bookmasters